Suicide

An Essential Guide for Helping Professionals and Educators

Darcy Haag Granello

The Ohio State University

Paul F. Granello

The Ohio State University

Boston • New York • San Francisco
Mexico City • Montreal • Toronto • London • Madrid • Munich • Paris
Hong Kong • Singapore • Tokyo • Cape Town • Sydney

Executive Editor: *Virginia Lanigan*
Series Editorial Assistant: *Matthew Buchholz*
Marketing Manager: *Kris Ellis-Levy*
Composition and Prepress Buyer: *Linda Cox*
Manufacturing Buyer: *Linda Morris*
Manufacturing Manager: *Megan Cochran*
Cover Coordinator: *Kristina Mose-Libon*
Editorial-Production Coordinator: *Mary Beth Finch*
Editorial-Production Service: *Stratford Publishing Services*
Electronic Composition: *Stratford Publishing Services*

For related titles and support materials, visit our online catalog at www.ablongman.com

Between the time Website information is gathered and then published, it is not unusual for some sites to have closed. Also, the transcription of URLs can result in unintended typographical errors. The publisher would appreciate notification where these errors occur so that they may be corrected in subsequent editions.

Library of Congress Cataloging-in-Publication Data

Granello, Darcy Haag
    Suicide: An Essential Guide for Helping Professionals and Educators/Darcy Haag Granello, Paul F. Granello.
       p. cm.
Includes bibliographical references.
ISBN 0-205-38673-3
1. Suicide—United States. 2.Suicide—United States—Prevention. I. Granello, Paul F. II. Title.

HV6548.U5G73 2007
362.280973—dc22

                                     2006046585

Printed in the United States of America

10 9 8 7 6 5 4 3 2 1   11 10 09 08 07 06

This book is dedicated to
Leon Joseph Granello
1960–1999

Contents

Preface

Suicide is the act of intentionally killing oneself. The definition of the word is not complicated. Yet as we have been working on this book, traveling around the country giving suicide trainings, talking with clinicians, and struggling with our own personal losses, the emotional and intellectual complexities of suicide have become more and more apparent. When we started this project, we thought that this book was one that was needed by both our students and our professional colleagues. We can only say that now, after interacting with many individuals—both professionals in the field of mental health and with the general public, we have become even more convinced that this book is very much needed. Many clinicians from around the country have shared with us their concerns about being inadequately prepared to work with suicidal clients. Most say they received, at best, an hour or two-hour lecture on suicide risk assessment during their graduate preparation. Many of these clinicians were told to "learn about suicide on the job." We believe that although there is no replacement for clinical experience, training programs do a disservice to their students—and ultimately to clients — by placing students in practica or internship experiences, or even graduating them, without adequate training on suicide risk factors, prevention, assessment, and managing a suicidal crisis.

Over the last three years we have given dozens of presentations on suicide—but we have yet to give even one presentation where people have not stayed after to share with us their stories of personal or professional frustration and loss by suicide of a loved one or client. So, we have very deliberately written a book that although cannot possibly be the definitive source of information about suicide, is intended to be a highly useable text. We hope it is one that is adopted by professors and actually read by their students. We hope clinicians and educators in a variety of settings will come to realize the utility of a book that uses the current research and clinical knowledge to ground the writing without getting bogged down in technicalities that make the book difficult to read and do little to assist with actual practice. Ultimately, we have tried to write a book that is useful for practitioners across all fields where professionals come into contact with suicidal individuals. After all, it is up to professionals in the human service fields to be the gatekeepers for detecting and interacting with potentially suicidal adults, adolescents, and children. *Suicide: An Essential Guide for Helping Professionals and Educators* is, therefore, intended first and foremost to be a useful and practical book. We hope that the book is useful for those who wish to increase their awareness, improve their skills, and take action to prevent suicides.

We would like to thank many people who have contributed to our work along the way. We have an amazing support system, filled with wonderful people who have assisted us in both direct and indirect ways. We would like to thank our parents, Meryl & Douglas Haag and Alanna & Leon Granello, who created an environment for us to grow up in that was supportive of learning and encouraged education. We know that the lifelong love and support you have shown us is the greatest gift anyone can give. Thank you. We also would like to recognize our gifted colleagues and professional mentors Dr. Mark Young, Dr. Mel Witmer, Dr. Richard Hazler, and Dr. Patricia Beamish. As we walk in your footsteps, we continue to recognize how lucky we have been—and continue to be—to work with each of you. You are each dear friends as well as brilliant mentors. Other friends, loved ones, and colleagues also have gone above and beyond in their support and love. We know that for the past three years, we have been the friends who talk about suicide at every dinner party! Thanks for not giving up on us and for coming to believe, as we do, in the power of suicide prevention. Kathryn Plank—you and Odin know what you mean to us. Dan, Dana, & Sophia Levitt, Joe Wheaton and Paula Nees, Jora DeFalco Young, Jean Underfer-Babalis, Jerry Juhnke, Terri Haag, and so many others. Thank you.

We are grateful for the helpful comments of the reviewers: Frieda Brown, Gardner Webb University; John H. Harvey, University of Iowa; Eugenie Joan Looby, Mississippi State University; Diane Mirabito, New York University; Eric Ornstein, University of Illinois at Chicago-Jane Addams College of Social Work; Barry W. Shreve, Greenville Technical College; and Jackie K. Titus, Columbus State University.

A great deal of thanks also goes to our editor at Allyn & Bacon, Virginia Lanigan. Virginia never gave up on us, even after we experienced a personal set-back that delayed our work on the book. Virginia patiently and steadfastly encouraged us and supported us throughout this project. Finally, we would like to thank our wonderful students from whom we continuously learn. You challenge us and help us to stay engaged and excited about the profession of counseling, and you remind us that a few committed and passionate individuals can change the world.

1

Introduction

Every day in America, about 85 people die by their own hand. Imagine that for a moment. Think about what we would do if a jetliner fell from the sky each and every day, killing 85 people on board—every day, 365 days a year, year after year. There would be national outrage. The government would step in and try to find ways to make flying safer. People would be talking about it. We would *do something*. But each day, 85 Americans die through suicide, and there is very little national dialogue about what to do.

Suicide represents a bit of a paradox. On the one hand, it is a relatively rare event—on average, about 12 people per 100,000 kill themselves in any given year. On the other hand, that adds up to a significant number of people who decide to take their own lives: 32,000—more than ten times the number of people who died in the World Trade Center bombings, *every year*—about half the number who died in the *decade-long* Vietnam War, *every year*. And behind each statistic is a story, a life, a person. For every number in the statistics, there is a person so desperate, so full of emotional pain, that self-destruction seems like the best solution. Behind every number is a lifetime of lost potential. And for every person dead, there is a family left grieving, trying to understand, looking for answers, and facing their guilt as survivors.

For every person who completes suicide, there are an estimated 10 to 20 who have attempted suicide. No one knows the exact figures, but government statistics estimate that about five million living Americans have tried to kill themselves.

This is a book about how to help the people behind these statistics—how to prevent, assess, and intervene so that a suicide can be stopped and a life can be saved—and, when all attempts to prevent a death are unsuccessful, how to help the loved ones who are left behind.

Approximately one in four mental health professionals experiences a client suicide.

This is a book for people in the helping professions: counselors, social workers, psychologists, nurses, teachers—anyone who comes into contact with suicidal individuals. In our professional (and personal) lives, people in the helping professions need to be prepared to work with those who are contemplating the decision to end their lives. Client or student suicide is a frightening possibility that is difficult to consider. This book contains practical information. It is a hands-on guide for practitioners that is intended to replace some of the fear and uncertainty with useful information. It uses existing research and the most up-to-date clinical knowledge to provide details on risk factors, comorbid mental and physical health issues for suicidal people, assessment tools, legal responsibilities, and intervention guidelines. It has resources, checklists, and prevention program models. It is a book that can be read through, cover to cover, or picked up as a reference guide when the need arises. However it is used, the main focus of the book is to help clinicians face what might be their most salient fear: how to work with suicidal clients.

This book may be grounded in practicality and research, but the cornerstone of the book is hope. Mental health professionals can and do make a difference in the lives of suicidal people and their families. Armed with information and training, clinicians can help people to find more hopeful solutions. They can identify risk factors that put individual clients in danger and can use appropriate interventions to safeguard high-risk clients or develop prevention programs for schools and communities. They can help surviving family members and friends overcome feelings of shame and guilt, and they can give hope where there once was none. Finally, clinicians can be reminded that they, too, need hope when they face the death of a client.

An Overview of Suicide

Suicide is the eleventh leading cause of death in the United States and the second leading cause of death among people between the ages of 15 and 24 years. Suicide accounts for 1.4% of the total deaths each year, or almost 32,000 Americans. Few people realize that in the United States, a person is more likely to kill himself or herself than to be killed by someone else. Suicide rates overall are 50% higher than homicide rates. That means that *for every two murders in the United States, there are three suicides.*

Suicide rates differ by age, gender, race, and geography. For example, in the United States:

- Male suicide rates are four times higher than female suicide rates.
- Suicide rates increase with age and are highest among males over age 75 years.
- Suicide *attempt* rates are three to six times higher for females than for males.
- Guns are used in more than half of all suicides.
- Men typically use guns and hanging; women typically use pills and gas.
- Suicide rates are more than twice as high for Caucasians as for African Americans.
- Suicide rates are lowest among African American females.
- Over 70% of all suicides are completed by white males.
- Suicide rates for African American male adolescents more than doubled in the period from 1980 to 1996.
- Suicide is the third leading cause of years of Potential Life lost.

- The state with the highest suicide rate is Nevada (22.7 deaths per 100,000).
- The state with the lowest suicide rate is New Jersey (7.2 deaths per 100,000).

The remainder of this book will discuss these rates and risk factors in greater detail. For now, consider the case of Sean:

Sean was a 24-year-old Caucasian male. He attended college for a few years to get a degree in computer science but dropped out because of poor grades and a recognition that he wasn't enjoying college. He drifted a bit, took part-time jobs, and lived with his parents. He used recreational drugs and drank with his friends, primarily on weekends. He had several girlfriends but had never been in a serious relationship.

Sean seemed to lack direction or meaning in life. His parents were frustrated that their son was not using his talents, but their talks with him seemed to make no headway. Sean would listen but not respond, and he did not seem to change. In retrospect, his parents said that Sean was probably depressed, but they did not recognize it as such at the time. They thought he was simply lazy and unmotivated.

During about a three-week period in early July, Sean became more withdrawn than usual. He stayed in his room, worked on his computer, and said little to his parents. His hygiene became worse, and he wore the same clothes for days on end. One night, Sean hanged himself in his room. His parents found him the next day when he did not come down for breakfast or lunch.

A suicide note left on his computer told his parents that he was sorry. He knew he had been a disappointment to them, and he did not understand why he could not be a better son. He had tried, he wrote, but he just did not have the energy or interest to make something of his life.

Sean's case is particularly tragic because there is a very real possibility that with the right kind of intervention, he did not have to die. Many times, warning signs are overlooked by family and loved ones. Maybe they do not want to believe that suicide is a possibility, or maybe they just do not know what to look for. But in this case and countless others each year, intervention by a mental health professional might have made a difference. We will never know. Sean and thousands like him are the reason for this book. If we can recognize the warning signs and know what to do, then we have a chance to save a life.

Problems with Classification

As large as the numbers of completed suicide are, they represent only the number of deaths that have been officially classified as suicides. In the United States, national mortality data are based on information on death certificates that are filled out by individuals with no standardized training. In some jurisdictions, coroners are elected officials with no medical training. In these jurisdictions, the determination of suicide often is made only when there is very clear evidence (e.g., a suicide note). Even in jurisdictions where the coroner is a medical practitioner, the objective determination of suicide can be influenced by the emotional trauma of suicide and the social stigma that affects the family and the entire community (Mościcki, 1995) and by ambiguities surrounding the death. Families, already overwhelmed with the loss, might be extremely reluctant to believe that the death of a loved one was truly a suicide and might adamantly resist such a classification on the death certificate. Consider the following examples, which, like most of the cases in this book, are based on actual cases.

David, a 63-year-old Caucasian male, had recently retired from a successful small business that he had started 35 years earlier. He was well known in the community as a self-made man, a philanthropist, and a role model. He initially expressed some reservations about retiring but reluctantly agreed to do so when his oldest son assured him that he could handle the business on his own. David appeared to be adjusting well to his retirement, although at times, he expressed irritation when his son was invited to important community and social events to represent the business that David had started. On the night he died, David's son was attending a community-wide gala. David had originally planned to attend, but his son asked David whether he would be willing to stay home so that the community would start to recognize the son, rather than his father, as the head of the business. David said that he understood his son's motivations completely and that he would gladly stay home. David was an avid hunter, and with hunting season approaching, he told his wife that he would spend the evening downstairs, getting out his guns, cleaning and oiling them, and preparing for the start of the season. At 10:00 that night, David's wife heard the shot that killed David. The coroner ruled the death accidental.

Was the death accidental? It is certainly possible that one of the guns misfired or that David was unaware that it was loaded. David had not given his family cause to believe he was suicidal. Yet he was an avid hunter who had been around guns all his life and was certainly aware of gun safety. When his family looked back at the months before the death, they identified some warning signs that they had missed (most notably, they started talking about David's depression and feelings of worthlessness that had emerged, although they had never been discussed in the family). Nevertheless, the standing of the family in the community, the emotional trauma of the family and the community, the lack of a suicide note, and the reported "good-natured way" David had behaved earlier in the evening all undoubtedly contributed to the coroner's decision to rule the death accidental. Years later, the family still does not know what really happened.

Carlos was a 19-year-old Cuban American living in Miami. His father and mother were first-generation immigrants, and Carlos had been raised in a family that considered the United States a golden land of opportunity. Carlos's mother and father reminded their children on a daily basis that they were to take advantage of all that their new country had to offer. Carlos's older sister had recently completed her bachelor's degree and had been accepted into medical school. Carlos's younger brother had just taken a job in a high-technology field, and the company had agreed to pay his college tuition. Meanwhile, Carlos had struggled to find his career path. He did well in high school, graduating with honors, but he never found a subject that truly inspired him. His parents pressured him to enter college and continue his education, but he did not want to continue until he knew what he wanted to do with his life. Carlos had always been a bit reckless, driving fast, driving after drinking, and engaging in other high-risk behaviors. A week before his death, Carlos had finally decided to pursue his education and apply to college to major in medicine, like his sister. His family was relieved that he had finally "settled down," but Carlos seemed distant and resigned, not at all excited about his future plans. On the day he died, Carlos mailed his college application and then went out drinking with friends. On the way home, Carlos drove his car at high speed into a concrete barrier and was instantly killed. Blood alcohol levels taken after his death revealed that Carlos was not legally intoxicated. The coroner ruled the death accidental.

Was this death accidental? We will never know whether Carlos was in control of his vehicle when it slammed into the barrier or whether he had planned this method of his death. The family could not believe that Carlos had intentionally taken his own life. There were strict religious injunctions against suicide, and Carlos was an intelligent young man with his entire future ahead of him. His friends, however, said that Carlos was acting strange the night he died, and before they parted for the evening, Carlos handed one of them the gold chain from his neck and told him that he had always considered him his best friend and that he would miss him. The friend assumed that Carlos meant that he would miss him when he went away to college, but now he wonders whether Carlos meant to kill himself that night.

Eileen was a 78-year-old widow who lived alone. She had chronic health problems, including diabetes, high blood pressure, and arthritis. Her daughter came to visit her about twice a week, and often, she found Eileen sitting in her chair, staring into space. Eileen said that the hobbies she used to enjoy (knitting and crocheting) were too difficult for her now, given her poor eyesight and arthritis. Most of the day, she just sat, neither watching TV (she said she wasn't interested in that nonsense) nor listening to the radio (she said all the noise gave her a headache). Her daughter was concerned and wondered whether Eileen should continue to live alone. One day, she broached the subject of an assisted care facility with Eileen, and Eileen became extremely angry and agitated, stating that she would never enter a nursing home. About two weeks after this conversation, an emergency call was placed from Eileen's home to paramedics, using an emergency panic button that Eileen kept around her neck. When the paramedics arrived, they found Eileen on the floor, shaking and bent at the waist. When they took her to the hospital, they discovered that Eileen had massive amounts of medication in her system—an overdose of all her existing medication. Although they pumped her stomach and used all possible medical interventions to assist, Eileen died two days later.

Eileen's daughter insists that her mother simply became confused about her medication and took the overdose by accident. She points to the fact that Eileen used her medic alert system to notify the paramedics and seek help. It is impossible to know whether the death was accidental or intentional.

Many suicide deaths are masked to look like accidents, and in the absence of hard evidence to the contrary, suspicious deaths are far more likely to be classified as accidents than as suicides. Thus, the number of suicides in the United States is undoubtedly much higher than the numbers in the official classification. Some authors have suggested that only one in five suicides are recorded (Jobes, Berman, & Josselson, 1989), although others have suggested a far more modest difference between numbers of actual and reported suicides (Brent, Perper, & Allman, 1987). It is obviously difficult to assign numbers to this phenomenon. What is clear, however, is that many suicides go unreported.

Suicide and Suicidal Behavior

Understanding the rates of suicide completion is clearly a difficult proposition. Even more daunting, however, is the process of attempting to understand the prevalence of suicidal thoughts (suicidal ideation), attempts, and behaviors. No national data have been collected on suicide attempts, although common estimates state that there are between 10 and 20 attempts for every completion. Estimates of lifetime prevalence of attempts in adults range from 1% to 4% (Mościcki, 1989). Suicidal ideation is even more difficult to measure than suicide attempts. Furthermore, suicidal ideation clearly occurs on a continuum from lesser to greater severity, and it is difficult to determine at which point on the continuum a person self-identifies as "thinking suicidal thoughts." Rates of suicidal ideation are obviously higher than rates of attempts. One study found that almost 6% of adults had considered suicide in the 12 months preceding the survey (Crosby, Cheltenham, & Sacks, 1999).

Even with the limited information that is available, several patterns are clear. First, suicidal ideation and suicide attempts do not appear to differ on the basis of education, income, or socioeconomic status. That is, suicidal thoughts and attempts are not just the domain of the poor or the uneducated. Suicidal thoughts and behaviors are not based on status or wealth.

A second pattern is that although suicidal thoughts probably do not differ by gender, suicide attempts do. Females are far more likely to attempt suicide, and males are more likely to complete. In other words, males and females are equally likely to think about suicide, but when thoughts turn to actions, men and women respond differently. More than 80% of suicide completers are men, while the majority of attempters are women. In one psychiatric survey of adults in five communities, there were 18 attempts for every suicide completion. Notably, the estimated ratio by gender was 8 attempts for every completion for males and 59 attempts for every completion for females (Petronis, Samuels, Moscicki, & Anthony, 1990). Thus, females were more than seven times as likely to attempt suicide, but males were more than four times as likely to complete a suicide. (Suicide patterns by gender are discussed in Chapters 3–5.)

A third pattern of attempts relates to method. Guns consistently account for 60% of all suicide deaths and are the method of choice for completers, both male and female. Drug overdose, on the other hand, is the method that is used most often (70%) by those who attempt suicide but do not complete.

Finally, a fourth pattern of suicidal thoughts and attempts for adults is differences based on race. Members of all races are probably equally likely to have suicidal thoughts, but members of the Hispanic population are more likely to make attempts than are Caucasian/non-Hispanics or African Americans. Caucasians are more likely to complete a suicide. (Suicide patterns by race are discussed more fully in Chapter 6.)

Suicidal thoughts and attempts are remarkably frequent among adolescents. Adults who are no longer in high school are often amazed at the prevalence of depression and suicidal behaviors in school. A large-scale study by the Centers for Disease Control and Prevention (2001) (CDC) surveyed over 16,000 adolescents in 151 schools. They found high levels of suicidal ideation and suicide attempts. Specifically, in any given year:

- Depression:
  - 28% of students felt so sad or hopeless for more than two weeks that they stopped doing their usual activities.

- More female students (35%) than males (22%) felt sad or hopeless.
- Hispanic students (34%) were more likely than African American (29%) or Caucasian (27%) students to feel sad or hopeless.
- Hispanic females (42%) were more likely than Caucasian females (32%) to feel sad or hopeless.
- Suicidal ideation:
  - 21% of students had seriously considered attempting suicide during the 12 months preceding the survey.
  - Female students (27%) were more likely than male students (15%) to have considered attempting suicide.
  - Hispanic students (23%) were more likely than African American students (16%) to have considered attempting suicide.
- Suicide plan:
  - 16% of students had made a specific plan to attempt suicide during the 12 months preceding the survey.
  - Female students (20%) were more likely than male students (12%) to have made a suicide plan.
  - Hispanic students (20%) were more likely than Caucasian students (14%) and African American students (13%) to have made a suicide plan.
- Suicide attempts:
  - 8% of students had attempted suicide one or more times during the 12 months preceding the survey.
  - Female students (12%) were more likely than male students (5%) to have attempted suicide.
  - Hispanic students (11%) were more likely than Caucasian students (6%) to have attempted suicide.
  - Nearly 3% of students reported having made a suicide attempt during the 12 months preceding the survey that resulted in an injury, poisoning, or overdose that required medical attention.

These statistics mean that *in the past year*:

1 in 5 high school students had thought about suicide.
1 in 6 had a plan.
1 in 13 made a suicide attempt.

Put another way, in a typical high school of 1,000 students, *in the past year*, more than *280 students* met criteria for clinical depression, more than *200 students* thought about suicide, more than *150 students* made a suicide plan, 77 *students* attempted suicide, and *26 students* required medical attention for their suicide attempt.

As with adults, the patterns with adolescents indicate that females attempt suicide more often and that Hispanic adolescents make more attempts than their Caucasian or African American counterparts. Perhaps the most remarkable findings from this survey, however, is the widespread prevalence of suicidal thoughts and behaviors during adolescence. These numbers are astounding and suggest that suicidal thoughts and behaviors during adolescence are much more common than most adults suspect. Clearly, a large proportion of adolescents are receiving a message that suicide—or suicidal behavior—is a viable solution to life's problems.

Understanding Suicide

The Social Context

Talking or thinking about suicide and suicidal behavior makes most of us very uncomfortable. We work hard to convince ourselves that suicide is something that happens to "sick people"—people who have a mental illness or are otherwise disturbed, psychiatric patients, or people who are older and/or medically ill. We try to think of suicide as something that happens to "others," certainly not to my loved ones or me. By emotionally distancing ourselves from suicide, we try to protect ourselves from the very harsh reality. Even the media helps with our denial. Suicide is rarely discussed, and then only in dramatic terms when a celebrity or politician takes his or her own life. Consider media reports of the death of Marilyn Monroe, Kurt Cobain, or Vincent Foster. In these instances, the drama of the suicide is highlighted, not the tragedy of the painful life. Why do we focus on the celebrity suicide deaths with morbid fascination and ignore the everyday realities of nearly 32,000 lives lost a year? Why is it that a thoughtful and well-presented story about suicide so rarely makes the evening news?

Suicide is, of course, considered a depressing subject to discuss and one that is to be avoided if at all possible. At least one reason for our societal denial is the historical taboo of suicide as a "mortal sin" or unspeakable atrocity for which a family should be ashamed or even punished. (You will read more about the history of suicide in Chapter 2.) Perhaps, too, it is simply that talking about suicide is talking about death, and discussions about death make most of us feel somewhat anxious, uncomfortable, or morbid. Death, especially violent death and abnormally caused death, as suicide is, is not a subject that most of us like to dwell on. Yet pretending that some unpleasant behavioral phenomena do not exist (for example, drug dependence) because they are difficult for us to discuss does not make them go away. In fact, it might only lead to an exacerbation of the problem. As you have read, suicide has reached epidemic proportions in the United States; and as mental health professionals, we need to work to open the discussion about this often misunderstood and perhaps most personal of human behaviors, even if it makes us uncomfortable.

Myths about Suicide

Until very recently, suicide has not been a subject that has been openly discussed in public forums. In the absence of accurate information and education, people are left to struggle to make meaning out of complex behavior such as suicide. As a result, individual perceptions and misinformation can be passed from person to person. Sometimes, this information can be presented not as an opinion but as fact, and a myth is born.

Myths are traditional beliefs about a subject that might or might not have once been based in historical fact. Following are 12 myths about suicide, many of which have been shown to be inaccurate and potentially harmful.

Myth 1: People Who Talk about Suicide Do Not Commit Suicide. The fact is that approximately 80% of those who commit suicide spoke to someone before taking their own lives. Talking about suicide can be a plea for help. When someone threatens suicide, it is important to show concern, to get them to keep talking, and to conduct a thorough suicide assessment.

Myth 2: Suicide Happens without Warning. People who commit suicide often give some warning of their intent to harm themselves. Sometimes these are verbal statements (perhaps a preoccupation with talking about death or dying), and sometimes they can be behaviors, such as giving possessions away, putting finances in order, making extreme changes in eating habits, increasing use of alcohol or other drugs, or withdrawing from social support.

Myth 3: Suicidal People Want to Die. If a Suicidal Person Is Determined to Kill Himself or Herself, Nothing Can Stop the Person. Even the most depressed person has ambivalent feelings about suicide. Most people who feel suicidal do not want to die, but they do want their pain to end. In the moment, they cannot see alternatives to suicide that will bring their suffering to an end. Most suicidal crises are short lived and can be managed. Immediate practical help, such as staying with the person, encouraging them to talk to loved ones, or helping them to see positive alternatives for the future, is often very helpful during the crisis. It is important that people get the proper counseling even after they are no longer in crisis.

Myth 4: Suicide Is Related to Socioeconomic Status. Both rich and poor people commit suicide. There is no consistent data to support the idea that suicide differs by wealth, income, or socioeconomic status.

Myth 5: People Who Commit Suicide Are Mentally Ill, Crazy, or Insane. Perhaps as many as 90% of adults who commit suicide *do* have a diagnosable mental illness or a substance abuse disorder. However, suicide is a complex phenomenon that cannot be explained as simply as "she was crazy" or "he was drunk." Moreover, the vast majority of people who have a mental illness never commit or attempt suicide, so explaining suicide away as a symptom of mental illness simply is not accurate. Our understanding of suicide leads us to believe that when people take their own lives, they are working from a variety of complex and intertwined motivations. Some of these may include mental illness, substance abuse, environmental stressors, and poor coping skills, but there are many others. It appears that both intrapsychic factors (psychological pain, rigidity in thinking and poor problem-solving ability, inability to cope) and interpersonal factors (interpersonal relationships, environmental stressors) are involved in suicidal decisions.

Myth 6: People Who Threaten Suicide Are Just Seeking Attention. All suicide attempts must be taken seriously. It is essential that clinicians never dismiss a suicide threat or attempt as simply an attention-gaining device. The fact that this individual feels that it is necessary to use threats of self-harm as a means to gain the attention of others is enough to warrant attention. When it comes to working with suicidal clients, it is always better to err on the side of being overprotective than to dismiss their attempts to communicate and regret the completion of a suicide later.

Myth 7: Most Suicides Occur around Holidays or in the Winter Months. Although holidays and the winter months can be rough times for many people, the data actually show that suicide occurs at about the same frequency throughout the year, with small elevations for adults during the spring and early summer months. Little is know about children's and adolescents' seasonal patterns, although the information that is available suggests that attempts are more common in the spring and less common during the summer months.

Myth 8: Suicidal Tendencies Run in Families and Are Genetically Inherited. There are currently no scientific data that support a genetic basis for suicide. It is important to note that a significant risk factor of suicidal behavior is the previous completion by a close family member or relation. The completion of a suicide in a family might encourage other family members to begin to see suicide as a viable option, but there is no evidence to suggest that this has a biological or genetic basis. Of course, there is a genetic link to mood disorders, and family patterns of depression or anxiety may be linked to increased risk. The very belief in this genetic inheritance myth may facilitate suicidal ideation in family members.

Myth 9: Talking about Suicide or Asking Someone if He or She Is Suicidal Will Encourage the Person to Attempt Suicide. Asking a client about suicide opens the door for the person to disclose his or her feelings. Fears and anxieties that are shared are more likely to be diminished and act as a deterrent to self-harming behavior. Research shows that talking about suicide actually decreases risk among depressed and suicidal adolescents if it is done in an appropriate way. The simple inquiry concerning a person's suicidal intent is the first step to a dialogue and processing of emotions that may save a life. It should be noted that suicide should never be discussed in a joking way, glorified, or made to seem like a reasonable alternative for anyone.

Myth 10: Once an Individual Is Past a Suicidal Crisis or Survives an Attempt, the Person Is Free from Danger. Approximately 10% of previous suicide attempters will go on to eventually take their lives. Thus, a previous suicide attempt is a significant risk factor for future attempts and completions. Many individuals who survive an initial suicidal crisis may show significant initial improvement but then be at risk later. Many suicide completions occur within the first 90 days after the initial suicidal crisis. One theory regarding this phenomenon is that as suicidal individuals begin to improve, they muster the energy to carry out their suicide plan.

Myth 11: Suicide Is Painless if Done "Correctly." Suicide is not painless. Many suicide methods are painful. Fictional presentations of suicide in books or movies often do not accurately present the extent of pain in suicide. Suicide is not "a neat and clean way to go," and it is often loved ones who discover the traumatic aftermath of the completed suicide. Furthermore, incompleted suicide attempts often lead to terribly cruel fates, such as severe traumatic brain injury.

Myth 12: "Nice" People Do Not Kill Themselves, and Suicides Do Not Occur in "Good" Families. This myth is particularly difficult for family members and friends of people who have committed suicide to overcome. The power in this myth is the shame it brings to families and how it colors and misrepresents the memories of lost loved ones. Of course, even good, nice, kind, and loving people kill themselves. The act of suicide is seldom based on a person's desire to hurt others; it is more often based on a desire to stop the hurt from within.

This list of myths is not intended to be exhaustive. Perhaps you have heard of others. This list is based on the work of N. L. Farberow and E. S. Shneidman and was first published in 1961. Different versions of it are commonly used in books and resources and on web pages on the Internet. These myths highlight the fact that the general public has many misunderstandings about suicide as a human behavioral phenomenon and perhaps even more about how to cope with suicidal people. It seems obvious that all human service providers need to be as well educated about suicide as our current scientific understanding will allow. Clinicians can then help to educate the public to be more helpful and can use their special training as professional helpers to work successfully with suicidal individuals and their families.

Understanding the Mind of the Suicidal Person

Shneidman (2005) reminds us of the extreme psychological pain of the suicidal person, using a concept he calls *psychache*. The psychological pain of fear, shame, anxiety, rejection, threat, guilt, unhappiness, and all the other negative emotions that overwhelm a person lead to a mind that is overcome with pain. He cautions clinicians to use research and study but never to lose sight of the human being and the unique human experience of the person sitting in front of us. Identifying, understanding, and helping to alleviate the individual psychache is at the core of all suicide work, and recognizing how a person's psychological needs are not being met can help clinicians to find a starting place for their work with suicidal clients. The point is that as we go through the book, it might be easy to focus on the research and statistics and lose sight of the people. The frequent use of case studies in this book are one way to help us all remember that there are very real people who need our help, not just research subjects and numbers. We recommend Shneidman's excellent book *The Suicidal Mind* (1996) as a great reminder of the human despair we are trying to help alleviate.

The Impact of Suicide on Survivors

It is difficult to measure the toll that suicide takes on friends, family members, the community, and the mental health profession. When a person decides to take his or her own life, there are enormous consequences for those left behind. Until the nineteenth century, family members were often punished for a suicide. Desecration of the corpse, confiscation of the survivors' property, fines, and loss of family reputation were all used to discredit both the person who committed suicide and the family. Today, the consequences of suicide are no longer dictated by law, but the emotional cost of suicide remains high. It is measured in the grief of loved ones; the hole left in a school, a church, a workplace, or a community; and the guilt of the survivors. And although they certainly pale in comparison to the emotional costs, there are financial costs as well. A suicide death results in the loss of potential earnings, the cost for a community if loved ones require financial assistance to replace the earnings, and the immediate and long-term financial burden that is placed on family members. In fact, the CDC report the financial cost of suicide in terms of years of potential life lost. By this indicator, suicide is the third leading cause of Years of Potential Life Lost in the United States.

Suicide survivor is the widely accepted term used to denote those who have experienced the death by suicide of someone whom they care about. The Surgeon General's *Call to Action to Prevent Suicide* (U.S. Department of Health and Human Services, 1999) estimates that for every person who commits suicide, there are approximately six suicide survivors, although that number obviously differs greatly for each individual. Using an average of six survivors for each suicide death means that the number of survivors grows by 186,000 people a year. By this definition, since 1971, 1 in every 59 Americans is a suicide survivor.

Suicide survivors go through a different grieving process than do those who have lost a loved one from other causes (Bailley, Kral, & Dunham, 1999). The social stigma of suicide often means that the death is accompanied by secrecy, silence, and even distortion. All of these impositions affect a person's ability to grieve. Suicide survivors are far more likely than those grieving other types of deaths to have grief reactions that meet diagnostic criteria for mental health disorders, such as depression and anxiety.

The two most common negative feelings that differentiate the bereavement of suicide from other kinds of death are *shame* and *guilt*. Shame occurs because the taboo against suicide often brands the family as well as the deceased. Guilt typically is based on the pervasive concern that one might have had a role in precipitating the suicide or could have prevented it.

Suicide survivors also are at high risk for suicide. The following risk factors have been identified as increasing the potential for survivor suicide (Mauk & Rodgers, 1994):

- Anyone who participated in any way with the completed suicide, helped to write the suicide note, provided means, was involved in the suicide pact, and so on
- Anyone who knew of the suicide plans and kept them a secret
- Siblings, other relatives, best friends
- Anyone who was the "self-appointed therapist" to the deceased person
- Anyone with a history of suicidal threats or attempts
- Anyone who identifies with the victim's situation
- Anyone who has reason to feel guilty about things that he or she said or did to the deceased prior to the death
- Anyone who is desperate and now sees suicide as a viable alternative

The stigma of suicide can add to the devastating loss felt by suicide survivors and can complicate the grieving process. Thus, clinicians need to be aware of the special needs of this population so that they can take actions to support suicide survivors, provide appropriate mental health care, and serve as a buffer between the survivor and society.

The Role of the Mental Health Professional

As mental health professionals, we cannot turn away from the reality of suicide. We cannot ignore this epidemic or assume that others will step in to meet the challenge of working with suicidal people. We cannot afford to let our own discomfort or denial get in the way. Our role in working with suicidal people is to be clinically competent and proactive. Studies indicate that the most promising way to prevent suicide and suicidal behavior is through the early recognition and treatment of mental health disorders (National Institute of Mental Health, 1999). Competent professionals who can diagnose, treat, or appropriately refer a person at the early stage of a mental health disorder, such as depression or a substance abuse disorder, can have a significant impact on the numbers of completed suicides.

For a mental health practitioner in any setting, being clinically competent means being informed about (1) suicide, suicidal behaviors, and suicidal ideations; (2) the general risk factors and specific populations at risk; (3) potential comorbid disorders; (4) methods of assessment, both formal and informal; (5) referral methods, for those individuals who will not work directly with clients in crisis; (6) treatment and crisis management; (7) generalized prevention programs and specific targeted prevention efforts; (8) legal and ethical considerations in suicide risk management; and (9) how to cope with the aftermath of a suicide completion. It is no coincidence, then, that these are the major topics discussed in this book. The goal of the book is to increase clinical competence in each of these areas.

Mental health professionals also can be preventive and proactive about suicide. Over half of people who attempt suicide never seek professional mental health help (Crosby, Cheltenham, & Sacks, 1999). Clinical professionals can advocate for discussion about mental health issues and suicide prevention in their respective practice or educational environments. Open discussion and encouragement of the importance of seeking help for mental health problems or suicidal thoughts or behaviors are essential to helping those who are afflicted. People who are having suicidal ideation need to know that help is available and that they need not be ashamed, afraid, or isolated with their thoughts.

The intent of this book is to help you to become a well-informed mental health professional who is both clinically competent when working with suicidal clients and proactive in the prevention of suicide. This is definitely a topic that requires advanced preparation; suicide counseling is not best learned on the job. Each of the sections in this book presents an important issue related to the topic of suicide. We hope that you will discuss this information with your colleagues, faculty, and fellow students (if you are in a preparation program) and, of course, with those you counsel.

We believe, and the research supports, that suicidal thoughts and behaviors seldom represent a true wish to die. Most of the time, suicidal individuals suffer from tremendous intrapsychic (internal) pain, and they just want the pain to end. Suicide becomes the method to end the pain, not a conscious decision to quit living. In fact, many suicidal people are quite ambivalent about death. This actually works to our benefit—it means that we can do something. We can intervene, get the person help, and generate other options for helping to make the pain lessen so that the person can go on living. Therefore, this book is written with a profound sense of optimism. In the face of the deepest of human despair, we can make a difference.

In addition to reading this book, you might wish to check out some of the resources offered in Appendices B–D. There are excellent resources on the World Wide Web, and many have useful resources for suicidal people, prevention programming, and tips for families. Finally, here is a tip for you to follow up on today: If you are not familiar with your school or agency policy on working with a suicidal individual, take the time to familiarize yourself with it now. Do not wait until you are faced with the situation to find and read the policy and procedures manual. If your agency or school does not have a written policy concerning suicidal clients, offer to write one and share it at your next staff or faculty meeting for feedback. This is one instance in which an ounce of prevention might save a life.

Summary

This chapter overviewed the magnitude of suicide, giving some indications of risk factors and differences in risk between segments of the population. All of the information

BOX 1.1 • *What Is Your Experience?*

Many people have had some personal connection to suicide in their lives. Family, friends, classmates, clients, or coworkers may have committed suicide, attempted suicide, or had people in their lives commit suicide. We all have had connections to suicide through the media—Marilyn Monroe, Kurt Cobain, Freddie Prinze—or someone in our local communities whose suicide was in the news. The point is that no one comes to the topic of suicide without some preexisting experiences, beliefs, and values.

Stop for a moment, and consider these questions:

1. What experiences have you had with suicide or suicidal behavior?
2. Have you experienced or heard about probable suicides that were ruled to be accidents? If so, why do you think suicides are classified that way? Why was it classified as an accident in the case(s) you know about?
3. What effects on family and loved ones have you seen or heard about from a person's suicide or suicidal behaviors?
4. What do you believe about suicide and suicidal behavior, on the basis of these experiences?
5. How could these experiences and beliefs affect your ability to work with suicidal people in your professional or personal life?

presented in Chapter 1 will be discussed in much greater detail throughout the book; this chapter is intended only to give a broad and brief overview.

There are difficulties in determining classification for suicide, and many suicides are undoubtedly misclassified as accidents. Suicide rates are probably much higher than what is reported. Although in general, risk increases with age, it is clear from the CDC report that there is a high risk for depression and suicidal thoughts and behaviors among adolescents. Suicide survivors, those left behind after a completed suicide, require special attention to assist with their grieving process. Finally, the chapter ends with the role of the mental health professional in preventing suicide and reminds us that suicide prevention is everyone's responsibility.

2

Historical and Theoretical Foundations

Historical Foundations of Suicide

The English word *suicide* is derived from two Latin words: *sui* meaning "self" and *caedere*, meaning "to kill" (Marcus, 1996). "Self-kill" is the simplest definition for the word *suicide*. Although, the word *suicide* is not that difficult to define, the act of committing suicide is a very complex phenomenon with biological, social, and psychological components. This chapter will first examine some of the historical views that have been taken of the act of suicide and then examine some of the theories that have tried to provide explanations for the many reasons that humans kill themselves.

One of the earliest references to suicide in recorded history was written in Egypt approximately 4,000 years ago and appears in *The Dispute Between a Man and His Ba*. In this writing it states that "a man who is tired of life and buffeted by ill fortune considers killing himself" (Colt, 1992). Evidence exists, therefore, that human beings have been killing themselves since our earliest recorded history and that suicide was a significant enough event to record. Throughout history, there has been concern, interest, or perhaps just a morbid curiosity about individuals who commit suicide, which has led many societies to grapple with the issue of suicide.

Historically, the act of committing suicide has been viewed from a wide variety of perspectives, including individual human rights, religious doctrine, social responsibility, economic phenomenon, psychological illness, and public health issues. Some of the historical perspectives of suicide might seem very congruent with modern views, while others seem very foreign or strange. The following sections are not intended to be an exhaustive review of suicide in cultural history; rather, they will give examples of the multiple ways in which the human phenomenon of suicide has been perceived around the world and throughout history.

Suicide as a Philosophical Issue

The ancient Greeks documented their public debate concerning the behavior of self-killing from several opposing philosophical viewpoints related to basic human rights. One of the earliest recorded and most famous of Greek suicides was that of Socrates in 399 B.C. Socrates, who chose to drink a poison tea brewed from hemlock rather than renounce his teachings, believed that man should have responsibility for and control of his own fate (Stillion & McDowell, 1996). Socrates gained honor and respect by holding to his philosophy rather than waiting to die at the hands of his enemies. Dying for one's beliefs is also evident in the events surrounding the mass suicide in A.D. 73 at Masada, where 960 Jews killed themselves rather than surrendering to the Romans and enslavement.

The Greek Stoics (300 B.C.–A.D. 300) viewed suicide as a rational act that allowed a human to have control over his death (Stillion & Stillion, 1999). Stoicism as a philosophy was strong in Greece and also became practiced in Roman aristocratic culture. Seneca, a teacher of the Roman emperor Nero, and a famous stoic, committed suicide in A.D. 65. Seneca taught that it was quality of life that mattered, not quantity, and when faced with a diminished quality of life (Nero had become mentally unstable and ordered Seneca's execution), he chose to take his own life, as did his wife Paulina shortly thereafter (Stillion & McDowell, 1996). Despite the widespread effects of Stoic thinking, the general public in ancient Rome did not regard suicide as heroic. In fact, the behavior was viewed with condemnation and disapproval, especially if it was committed selfishly without rational contemplation as an emotional act (Van Hoof, 2004).

Quite different from the beliefs of the Stoics, Aristotle, in approximately 350 B.C. declared that suicide was unlawful in all circumstances. He argued that taking one's own life was detrimental to the community as a whole. This was quite different from the Stoic belief of individual rights. Rather, Aristotle argued that the welfare of the community was paramount, and an individual did not have the right to deprive the community of his or her contributions. Therefore, the needs or desires of the individual should be secondary to the needs of the group (Stillion & McDowell, 1996). Aristotle's intent was to discourage suicide. However, the same philosophical stance that he espoused also has been used to justify suicide among some social groups. For example, the ancient Scythians, who led a nomadic lifestyle, considered it more honorable to take one's own life as a possible benefit to the community than to allow oneself to become a burden to younger members of the tribe with their care in old age (Alvarez, 1990). Other cultures, especially nomadic ones, such as the Norse, Eskimo, Samoan, and Crow Indian, also accepted the idea of self-sacrifice or altruistic suicides (Jamison, 1999).

Some Eastern cultures have linked the suicide of an individual to social purposes and meanings. Suicide traditionally has been viewed in Chinese culture as an honorable way to escape shame and humiliation. Ritual suicide has historically been relatively common, not only as a face-saving practice, but also as a form of political protest. During the communist Cultural Revolution in China (1966–1976), numerous intellectuals (writers, artists, and political figures) commited suicide, typically to escape persecution (Wikipedia contributors, 2005).

Suicide has been closely tied to gender in Chinese culture, both historically and today. Female suicides in premodern Chinese history were usually in reaction to oppression or misfortune, such as ostracism by family members. Today, using agricultural pesticides as a preferred method, rural females in China have what is commonly accepted to be the highest suicide rate in the world, as many as 100 per 100,000 women, making suicide the leading cause of death among young women in China.

Traditional Japanese culture also takes a view that has been relatively tolerant of suicide. Suicide is viewed as one method of maintaining one's honor. A thousand years ago in Japanese feudal society, suicide was approved of by the state for the military class known as samurai. The samurai followed an ethical code, called the Bushido, that allowed a soldier to honorably take his own life to avoid humiliation at the hands of his enemies (Colt, 1992). A ritual method of suicide by self-disemboweling known as seppuku was in common use among samurai families in feudal Japan. Although suicide is publically discouraged in modern-day Japan, beliefs derived from this cultural heritage remain among many Japanese people of today. Suicide remains an acceptable way for an individual to avoid bringing shame or dishonor on the family. Japan currently has some of the highest rates of suicide in the world, particularly among younger people. Today in Japan, Internet suicide clubs have begun to take hold. Young people meet on the Internet for the purpose of finding others who want to die. They meet at a designated time and commit suicide together, so no one has to die alone. The Japanese government has recently taken a more critical view of suicide, viewing the practice as a social problem.

Suicide as a Religious Issue

Religious beliefs have been related to the phenomenon of suicide since ancient times. For example, the Vikings believed that it was necessary to die a violent death to enter into Valhalla. After death in battle, suicide was seen as the next most viable method of dying and superior to dying of disease or other natural causes (Marcus, 1996). However, historically, most of the world's major religions (Judaism, Islam, Christianity, Hinduism, and Buddhism) have viewed suicide as a violation of the natural order of life and therefore as a sin or unholy practice. Jewish law specifically states that those who die by suicide should not be honored with the same funeral rites as those who die from other causes. In Islamic law, suicide is considered a crime, just as severe as homicide (Jamison, 1999). However, most religions also provide for exceptions to this doctrine, such as in cases of refusal to deny the faith, as in martyrdom, or by lessening the severity of moral condemnation by allowing for the role of mental illness in judging an individual's ability to control his or her behavior.

In Christianity, the Old Testament contains four instances of suicide (Samson, King Saul, King Saul's armor bearer, and Ahitophel) that are reported simply as matters of fact. The Old Testament does not provide insight into the prevailing social values of the time regarding the behavior (Stillion & McDowell, 1996). The New Testament relates the suicide of Judas Iscariot, the disciple who hanged himself after betraying Jesus to the temple priests. Again, the author, the apostle Matthew, does not provide information that describes the social view of this behavior. It should be noted, however, that all of the cases of suicide in the Bible follow tragic events, such as military failures, death of loved ones, death of those owed allegiance, or the betrayal of one's religious faith. Suicide might have been viewed as a method to atone for a significant breach of social conduct, an avowel of religious faith, or a reaction to grief.

Early Christians sought martyrdom, the act of dying willingly at the hands of others for one's faith, as they believed that this practice would guarantee them entry into heaven. Although not suicide in the sense of killing oneself, the practice of martyrdom became so widespread that early Christians were perceived as glorifying martyrdom, often seeking even flimsy reasons for which to give their lives in the faith (Alvarez, 1990). Martyrdom is one type of altruistic suicide, in which individuals kill themselves (or, in this case, allow themselves to be killed) for reasons that are intended to benefit others, in this case the faith. Martyrdom is important to include in any history of suicide because it had significant effects on both the religious and secular views of suicide throughout the rest of Western history.

In A.D. 400, in reaction to the popularity of martyrdom, St. Augustine proclaimed self-killing to be a sin. Augustine argued that self-killing was a violation of the Sixth Commandment ("Thou shalt not kill") and that by taking one's life, the individual avoids the divine will of the Creator, who alone should determine the time of an individual's death (Stillion & McDowell, 1996). The Catholic Church followed this doctrine, proclaiming for the next 600 years that suicide was a sin, with a series of church councils laying down increasingly more punitive penalties for people who committed suicide. These penalties included excommunication and denial of funeral rites (regardless of the reason for the suicide, social position, or method). Thomas Aquinas published his monumental work summarizing church doctrine, *Summa Theologica*, between A.D. 1265 and 1272. In it, he made strong arguments against "self-murder" and particularly promoted the idea of suicide as a serious or mortal sin (Stillion & McDowell, 1996). One of the most severe punishments for suicide, pronounced in A.D. 1284 at the Synod of Nimes, stated that the bodies of those who had committed suicide could not be given a Christian burial and would have to be buried in unhallowed ground. Policies also targeted the families of those who committed suicide. For example, families could not inherit the suicide victim's property. As a result of the church's condemnation of suicide as a mortal sin, the bodies of suicide victims were often dragged behind carts and buried at a crossroads with a stake through the heart (Farberow, 1975).

By the thirteenth century, under the strong influence of the Christian church, the Western societal view of suicide clearly had changed from one of self-sacrifice or honorable face-saving to one of abhorrence that sought to punish not only suicide victims, but their families as well (Stillion & Stillion, 1999).

Suicide as a Secular Social Issue

As the centralized power of established religion began to wane starting in the Renaissance and later in the Reformation, new secular ideas, including science and the humanities, emerged. Published in 1621, *Anatomy of Melancholy* by Robert Burton, a widely read book, argued for mercy for those who committed suicide. John Donne's book *Biathanatos* was the first major work that argued against the church's stance that suicide was a sin in all cases. John Donne was the dean of St. Paul's Cathedral in

London. Interestingly, the book was not published until 1647, after Donne's death, so that he could avoid ostracism from the church. In spite of these calls for clemency for some suicide victims, the first secular laws against suicide were passed in 1670 and were extremely punitive in nature. According to these laws, suicide was a triple crime of murder, treason, and heresy.

It was just 100 years later, in 1763, that Merian, a French physician, published a treatise that defined suicide as an emotional illness. This was a significant milestone and was followed by a number of important writings, such as Hume's *An Essay on Suicide* in 1783, which sought to view suicide as a behavior resulting from an illness or social cause rather than as a sin to be punished. The judicial verdict of *non compos mentis*—not in one's right mind or due to insanity—came about in the mid-seventh century, although only one in ten cases of suicide were adjudicated as being due to insanity. However, by the end of the eighteenth century in both English and U.S. courts, the majority of suicides were judged to be the result of non compos mentis (Jamison, 1999). These changes in public attitude regarding suicide were the result of many factors, including the rise of scientific inquiry, changes in the nature of personal property laws, and in general the ideas about the rights of the individual asserted over government in both the American and French revolutions.

It was in this climate of social change regarding suicide that one of the most influential books on suicide of all time was published. *Le Suicide* was written by Emile Durkheim in 1897 and espoused a sociological view of suicide. Durkheim introduced the first typology for classifying suicides and believed that an individual's integration into or isolation from social support was a significant factor that contributed to suicidal behavior. A great deal of the suicide literature in the decades that followed the publication of *Le Suicide* was written either in support or criticism of Durkheim's work. It might be fair to say that much of Durkheim's work serves as the foundation for sociological theory on suicide to the present day (Joiner, 2001).

Modern Views of Suicide

As the twentieth century progressed and the scientific method came to dominate much of Western culture's approach to understanding the world, more emphasis was put on studying suicide as a behavioral phenomenon with biological, psychological, and social causes. Just as many other scientific fields of study became formalized during the early twentieth century, so too did the fields of psychiatry and psychology. The work of Sigmund Freud placed emphasis on the psychological nature of suicide. In two of his works, *Mourning and Melancholia* (1917) and *The Ego and the Id* (1923), Freud theorized that suicide resulted from intrapsychic reasons and was the result of a mental illness. By the middle of the twentieth century, many theories were emerging concerning suicide that coincided with the great growth of American psychological theory. There were now behavioral, humanistic, and cognitive theories concerning mental illness and suicide. The study and research into the phenomena of suicide became a recognized discipline, called *suicidology*. A major milestone in the history of suicide prevention in the United States occurred in 1958, in Los Angeles, California, with the establishment of the first suicide prevention clinic by Dr. Edwin Shneidman and Dr. Norman Faberow. They were the first scientists to receive a public health grant to prevent suicide and pioneered the foundations of suicide prevention, such as the use of crises hotlines. Within a short time, every major city in the United States had established a suicide clinic not only to prevent suicides, but also to study their causes and consequences (Wallace, 2001).

Suicide, of course, is not just an esoteric subject for academic research but has continual effects on our society. In later decades of the twentieth century, the technical advances in medicine for prolonging life led to the evolution of the right to die movement and the field of medical ethics. Lawsuits both in support of and opposing an individual's right to die have found their way into the courts. The debates continue around the legal status of physician-assisted suicides, in which a doctor, at an individual's request, administers a lethal injection (Woodell & Kaplan, 1998). In 1990, the issue of physician-assisted suicide became news in the popular media. Dr. Jack Kevorkian will be remembered for his assistance in over 100 patient suicides, documented in widespread coverage in the media. During this same period, the voters of the state of Oregon passed the Death with Dignity Act in 1994, which was upheld in 1997. This was the first law allowing physician-assisted suicide. Professional and public debate regarding the ethics, rights, and responsibilities concerning these issues is still playing itself out in the popular media and in our federal and state court systems (van der Weide, Marijke, Onwuteaka-Philipsen, & van der Wal, 2005). As recently as 2005, a substantial and bitter legal battle was portrayed in the media. The Terri Schiavo case involved the courts, the legislature and governor of Florida, and even the U.S. Congress as various parties fought to stop the legal request of Michael Schiavo that his wife be removed from life support.

In contrast to the individual legal battles that have left people divided on the issue, there is more widespread support for the recognition of suicide as a public health problem. In 1999, the U.S. Surgeon General released a report identifying suicide as a significant public health problem and called for the implementation of a national suicide prevention strategy. The New Freedom Commission on Mental Health published its report entitled "Achieving the Promise: Transforming Mental Health Care in America" (2003), which featured suicide as a target for national public health. In response to the suicide death of the son of a U.S. Senator, Congress passed the Garrett Lee Smith Memorial Act in 2005, providing for the first federal funding directly for suicide prevention on college campuses.

Thus, suicide continues to be a difficult topic, from our ancient history right up through the present day. Research and public debate about suicide have continued into the twenty-first century and will probably continue as long as human beings struggle with questions about life and its meaning.

Theoretical Foundations of Suicide

When a person commits suicide, it leaves those who survive with many questions and emotional consequences. Why did they choose to kill themselves? What caused them to want to kill themselves? Am I to blame for not stopping them? Attempting to help answer questions like these has led researchers to the development of theories concerning the etiology of suicidal behavior. Perhaps it would be easier to answer these questions about suicide if a uniform cause or etiological understanding for suicide could be established. The complexity of suicide behavior has led to a diversity of theories including the sociological, psychological, and biological (Leenaars, 1996), each of which is discussed briefly in the following sections of this chapter.

Sociological Theories of Suicide

Sociological theories of suicide place the emphasis on social factors, such as social integration, regulation, economic status, and access to adequate health care, as important determining factors for suicidal behavior. The most influential sociological theory still remains that of Durkheim, first proposed in 1897 (Lester, 2000). Durkheim argued that suicides are caused by a lack of fit between the individual and the society in which they live. He presented two major variables as social principles of suicide:

- Social integration: the level to which people are enmeshed in social networks
- Social regulation: the degree to which people's desires and emotions are regulated by social norms and customs

On the basis of the relationship between these two principles, Durkheim suggested a typology of four different types of suicide:

1. *Egoistic suicide:* results from the individual's lack of connection to society; the individual becomes isolated and self-involved (lack of social integration).
2. *Altruistic suicide:* results when an individual overidentifies with rules and social mores; the individual commits suicide in an effort to conform or meet social expectations (too much social integration).
3. *Anomic suicide:* results when an individual does not feel that his or her behavior must correspond to social rules; the individual feels freedom to experiment with behavior outside of social norms (too little regulation).
4. *Fatalistic suicide:* results when an individual experiences oppressive conditions in the society in which he or she is living (e.g., slavery, poverty, prison, or concentration camp) (too much social regulation).

Durkheim's ideas have been widely researched and expanded over the more than 100 years since he first proposed them (Breault, 1986; Tartaro & Lester; 2005; Trovato, 1992). In recent years, however, the ideas have come under criticism. Critics argue that Durkheim's theory lacks clarity, has limited empirical support, has a cross-cultural lack of generalizability, and does not easily allow for classification of actual individual suicides (Joiner, 2001; Lester, 2000). Although modern investigators are questioning the theory's utility, Durkheim's work continues to be recognized for its foundational historical significance in the world of suicide research.

Psychological Theories of Suicide

Psychological theories of suicide place the emphasis on an individual's personality traits, cognitive processes, and developmental experiences as important and determining causes for suicidal behavior. All of the major schools of psychological theory (psychodynamic, cognitive, behavioral, humanistic, etc.) have advanced ideas concerning the nature of suicidal behavior. All of these theories assert that suicide is a deviation from the normal course of human behavior and is indicative of a psychological dysfunction. Each theory is differentiated by the unique causal explanation offered for suicide that is derived from its own school's approach for explaining human behavior. The following box briefly summarizes several of the major psychological schools' theoretical explanation for suicide.

In addition to these general psychological theories, more specific theories and models have emerged about suicide from within the more focused field of suicidology over the last 50 years. Suicidologist Dr. Anton Leenaars (Leenaars, 2004) has built on the pioneering work of Dr. Shneidman to advance a more specific theory for explaining

BOX 2.1 • *Summary of Theoretical Perspectives for Explaining Suicide*

Theoretical Orientation	*Explanation for Suicide*
Psychodynamic	Suicide is a failure of the intrapsychic system of ego, id, and superego to cope and remain in equilibrium. Failure may result from a collapse of ego defense mechanisms, overactive and dominating superego, fixation at a developmental stage, or extended intrapsychic conflict.
Developmental	Suicide results from a failure to satisfactorily achieve success in completing tasks associated with developmental stages. Individuals who do not positively complete developmental stages learn negative psychosocial lessons such as mistrust, shame, guilt, inferiority, role diffusion, isolation, stagnation, and despair. These negative lessons contribute to an inability to cope, which is then related to suicide.
Behavioral	Suicidal behavior is learned through imitation (modeling) or by experiencing unavoidable consequences that are perceived as painful or a loss. Unavoidable loss can lead to learned helplessness.
Cognitive	Hopelessness is a key variable in the cognition of individuals who are at risk for suicide. Beck's cognitive triad (negative thoughts about the self, the world, and the future) indicate risk for depression and potential suicide.
Humanistic-Existential	Suicide results from experiencing insufficient conditions for growth and maturation. Deficiency leads to an inability to meet needs. Individuals experience a lack of meaning and purpose in their lives, which may lead to suicide.

suicide behavior. Leenaars uses Shneidman's definition of suicide as a multidimensional malaise as a jumping-off point to exemplify his belief in the interpersonal and intrapsychic nature of suicide. Multidimensional malaise is explained by Leenaars as "biological, psychological, intrapsychic, logical, conscious and unconscious, interpersonal, sociological, cultural, and philosophical/existential elements" that contribute to the suicidal event (Leenaars, 1996, p. 222).

Leenaars indicates that the two concepts of lethality and perturbation are essential to understanding suicide behavior. *Lethality* can be defined as probability of a person's killing himself or herself, and *perturbation* can be defined as an individual's subjective distress. Leenars points out that one can be highly perturbed and still not suicidal. The essential factor in suicide is lethality (Leenaars, 2004). The theory advanced by Leenaars therefore has both intrapsychic and interpersonal causal factors to predict suicide behavior that are related to the concepts of perturbation and lethality. Following is a brief summary of these factors:

Intrapsychic Factors

1. Unbearable psychological pain: Suicidal people are in a great deal of psychological pain. Suicide might be less a wish to die than a wish to end suffering.
2. Cognitive constriction: Suicidal people create a restricted mental set of cognitions that impairs their problem-solving abilities. Functioning in this restricted way of thinking, they come to view suicide as their only option for action.
3. Indirect expressions: Suicidal people are conflicted. They may express love and hate for others, themselves, and life. The conflicted state leads to many different emotional states, from peaceful acceptance to anger to depression. An internal conflict between survival and pain leads to many contradictory verbal and emotional experiences and expressions.
4. Inability to adjust: Suicidal people have an inability to cope with life events. They may have internal skill deficits or be simply overwhelmed by events that they view as traumatic. They do not believe that they have the power to overcome traumatic events.
5. Ego: Suicidal people have a weakened ability to distinguish reality from fantasy or resist aggressive drives. They have a diminished ability to develop constructive or coping characteristics for their environment.

Interpersonal Factors

6. Interpersonal relations: Suicidal people often have significant interpersonal problems. They may have difficulty establishing or maintaining positive social relationships. Suicide is committed because of thwarted or unfulfilled needs, needs that are often frustrated interpersonally.
7. Rejection-aggression: Suicidal people have hate directed toward others and self-blame. These individuals are deeply ambivalent, and suicide may be the turning back on oneself of lethal impulses that had previously been directed against a traumatic event, most frequently someone who had rejected that individual. Suicide may be veiled aggression—it may be murder in the 180th degree (Shneidman, 1985).

8. Identification-egression: Suicidal people often have an intense identification with a lost or rejecting person or a lost ideal (e.g., health, youth, employment, freedom). The inability to recover this idealized person or situation causes the suicidal person to want to leave the world.

Leenaars's comprehensive theory of suicide explains both the internal psychological factors of pain, conflict, confusion, and diminished resources that a suicidal individual may experience and how these factors interact with external factors, such as life events, relationships, and social constraints on aggressive behavior.

In addition to Leenaars's theory, suicidologists have also developed other models to test specific aspects of suicidal behavior. Although these models are not as all-encompassing as the general psychological theories or as broad as Leenaars's theory, they have great utility in that they define and operationalize specific suicide variables so that researchers can study them in detail. The following box gives a few examples of models that have been researched in the suicidology literature (Westefeld et al., 2000).

BOX 2.2 • *Summaries of Specific Suicide Models*

Model Name	Key Points
Escape (Baumeitser, 1990; Dean & Range, 1999).	• Suicide is an attempt to escape aversive self-awareness. • Stressful life events are attributed to internal failure causing aversive self-awareness; this leads to negative affect and cognitive constriction, which in turn leads to hopelessness and depression.
Approval (Agnew, 1998)	• Individuals who are more approving of suicide as an acceptable behavioral choice are more likely to take their own lives. • Individuals who are more approving are likely to (1) have problems that have not been solved through conventional channels, (2) have been taught that suicide is an option, and (3) not feel part of any social networks or specific relationship.
Hopelessness (Abramson et al., 2000)	• The individual has the expectancy that highly desired outcomes will not occur or that highly aversive outcomes will occur. • The individual believes that one can do nothing about these outcomes, and this leads to hopelessness and depression.
Self-Discrepancy (Higgins, 1987)	• Individuals are motivated to achieve consistency between their self-concept and their self-evaluative standards. • Significant discrepancy between self-concept and ideal self leads to depression.

(continued)

BOX 2.2 • Continued

Model Name	Key Points

Overlap
(Blumenthal, 1988)
	• Consists of five areas or domains:
	  a. the psychosocial milieu (primarily viewed in the context of social support),
	  b. biological vulnerability (e.g., early biological development and later aging),
	  c. psychiatric disorders (specifically, affective and conduct disorders, schizophrenia, and organic mental disorders),
	  d. personality factors such as hostility, impulsivity, and depression,
	  e. family history and genetics.
	Interaction of the five domains represents a high risk for suicide.

Three Element (Jacobs, Brewer, & Klein-Benheim, 1999)	• Predisposing factors include affective disorders, alcoholism, and schizophrenia. • Potentiating factors include family history and the broad social milieu, personality disorders (especially borderline, antisocial, and narcissistic personality disorders), life stressors (including severe physical illnesses), and access to means of committing suicide (in particular, firearms). • Predisposing and potentiating factors combine, moving an individual across a suicidal threshold toward suicidal behavior.

The Cubic Model
(Shneidman, 1987)
	• Represented by a cube made up of 125 cubelets. The cube has three planes: press, pain, and perturbation.
	  • Press: events to which the individual reacts. Presses can be positive or negative, but it is the negative experience of press that moves one to suicide.
	  • Pain: intolerable psychological pain derived from unmet psychological needs. Needs for autonomy, achievement, recognition, succor, and an avoidance of shame, humiliation, and pain are relevant.
	  • Perturbation: a state of being emotionally aroused that is associated with cognitive and perceptual constriction.

What is clear from this box is that there have been many attempts to understand suicide and suicide risk from a psychological perspective. The existence of so many theories is a good indication that no single theory as yet has been sufficient to explain suicide risk. Nevertheless, they all contribute in meaningful ways to our understanding of suicide.

Biological Theories of Suicide

Biological theories of suicide place emphasis on genetic inheritance, gender differences, and neurotransmitter dysfunction as important and determining causes for suicidal behavior. Suicide researchers have noted familial patterns in suicide behavior and have sought to identify associated genetic traits (Battin, 1995). However, according to Lester (2000), all of the published twin studies to date have not studied separated twins but rather those who have been raised together. Therefore, although a concordance rate has been shown among these twins, it is not possible to separate out learned behavior or other environmental factors. It may also be more likely that there is not a "suicide gene" but rather a familial vulnerability to affective disorders that underlies the potential to commit suicide (Mościcki, 1995). However, in a review of twin and adoption studies, Blumenthal and Kupfer (1986) indicated higher rates of suicide for monozygotic as opposed to fraternal twin pairs and higher rates of suicide in adoptees with a history of suicide in biological relatives. They also noted that 50% of psychiatric inpatients who had a relative that committed suicide had attempted suicide themselves. Of course, there are genetic links to mood disorders (e.g., depression, bipolar disorders), and it is possible that these studies are simply finding genetic links to depression, a factor that increases vulnerability to suicide, rather than genetic links to suicide per se.

A second and promising area of biological research does not look for genetic links but rather looks for biological links between depression and suicide. Specifically, the research on the neurotransmitter serotonin and its metabolite 5-HIAA is of importance. Serotonin is the neurotransmitter that has been shown to be most involved in depression (Traskman, Asberg, Bertilsson, & Sjostrand, 1981). Depleted levels of serotonin have been found in the brain tissue of suicide completers, and depleted levels of serotonin have been found in the spinal fluid of suicide attempters (Asberg, Eriksson, Martensson, & Traskman-Bendz, 1986). Since a deficiency of serotonin has been linked to depression, emotional regulation, aggression, and impulsivity, researchers believe that it may be linked to impulsive suicides (van Praag, 2000). Further support for the serotonin-suicide link is research completed by Asberg et al., demonstrating that among those patients who had been admitted to a hospital in conjunction with a suicide attempt, the patients with the lowest levels of 5-HIAA were more likely to have died of suicide a year later than were those with high levels of the metabolite.

A third area supporting a biological basis for suicide is in the area of gender. Males complete suicide at higher rates than do females in all developed countries where suicide records are kept. Consistent sex differences for behaviors across cultures indicate the possibility of a biological substrate. Human males, who inherit their Y chromosome from their father, typically have higher rates of aggression than do females. If suicide is conceptualized as aggression turned on the self, then it would follow that males, being more aggressive than females, would also have higher rates of suicide. However, females have higher rates of attempts, and this does not fit with this biological theory.

Suicide and Specific Risk Factors

A very different approach from theoretical development to understanding suicide behavior is to take a strictly empirical or statistical approach. The epidemiological approach seeks to identify the risk factors that are associated with suicide. Rather than trying to understand suicide from a theoretical perspective, the goal of this approach is to develop prevention and treatment programs to reduce the incidence of suicide. A great number of studies on suicide have focused on attempting to identify risk factors associated with individuals who have attempted or completed suicides (mental illness, gender, age, race, employment status, marital or partnered status, poverty, past behavior, access to firearms, specificity of a plan, religion, quality of social network, degree of hopelessness, and many others) (Stack, 2001). What has emerged from these studies of risk factors is the ability to identify groups who are at risk for suicide attempts and completion. The most common specific factors that combine to increase risk include (Lester, 1993a):

Completers	*Attempters*
Gender = Male	Gender = Female
Age = Older	Age = Under 30
Race = White	Race = White
Mental health = Psychiatrically disturbed	Marital status = Married
Living situation = Lives alone	Method = Drug overdose
Stress = Life history and past few months	
Method = Firearm	

However, it is very clear that although these risk factors help us to identify *groups in the population* who are at highest risk for suicide attempts or completion, they do not assist us in identifying *individuals* who are at risk. Many psychological, social, cognitive, and environmental variables have been shown to have empirical significance in determining risk level. Because of this complexity, researchers to date have not been able to identify any variable or combination of variables that has been shown to represent a definitive etiology for all suicides (Lester, 1994a). It is, in fact, very difficult to predict suicidal behavior in *individuals*. Therefore, we must be extremely careful when using the research on risk factors to discuss suicide. First, no one risk factor has been shown to be able to absolutely predict or determine suicide. This means that risk factors must be examined with clinical judgment and in the context of an individual's entire life. Second, risk factor research, while it does explore relationships between demographic, psychological, and sociological variables, does not provide an overarching theory as to the causality of suicide and does not explain the complexity of suicidal behavior (Rogers, 2001). Although much of the rest of this book is dedicated to helping clinicians to understand both group and individual risk, it is always worth remembering that suicide prediction is a *very inexact science*. As a result, researching risk factors is important for practical reasons, but it does not provide us with all the answers we need. It is for this reason that *it is always important to ask individuals about their suicidal ideation even when they are not exhibiting any identifiable risk factors.*

Integrated Models Approach

In today's mental health practice environment, most clinicians would describe their theoretical orientation as eclectic (Young, 2004). Our therapeutic approaches to working with clients have become more sophisticated to include elements from a variety of theories as we have gained knowledge regarding the complexity of the biological, social, and psychological elements that make up many mental illnesses. Given the complex nature of suicidal behavior, suicide models likewise benefit from integration. Each of the theoretical perspectives or models illustrated in this chapter has something to offer, yet none can completely explain why a person chooses to commit suicide. The most recent theories of suicide behavior endeavor to take a biopsychosocial approach to understanding suicide and are often referred to as *integrative* theories or models.

Integrative theories propose that there are a number of different types of variables that influence suicide (e.g., sociocultural, psychological, and biological). These variables combine to determine patterns of suicide among populations and to predict whether an individual is at high risk of suicide. These integrative theories or models often employ complex statistical methods and models to describe direct, indirect, and complex interactions between the variables related to suicide (Maskill, Hodges, McClellan, & Collings, 2005). The following box gives a brief description of five of these models.

BOX 2.3 • *Examples of Integrative Suicide Models*

Model Name	*Key Points*
Suicide Trajectory (Stillion & McDowell, 1991)	• Focus on triggering or "final straw" events in the presence of specific thoughts about suicide. Biological, psychological, cognitive, and environmental risk factors interact to cause suicide behavior. • Biological: genetic predisposition to depression; male gender. • Psychological: depression, hopelessness, helplessness, low self-esteem, poor coping skills. • Cognitive: cognitive rigidity and distortions. • Environmental: negative family experiences, negative life events, loss, the presence of lethal methods. • Combinations of the risk factors, thoughts of suicide as a viable option, and the presence of a triggering event lead to suicide.
Integrative Social and Psychological (Giddens, 1971)	• Integrates Durkheim's social integration approach and Freud's psychological perspective concerning internal conflict and depression. • Emphasizes importance of society influencing the development of the individual but also acknowledges the ability of individuals to create their own social environment.

(continued)

BOX 2.3 • Continued

Model Name	Key Points
Multifactorial Model (Phillips, 1999)	• Stresses the interaction between socioeconomic factors and mental illness. • Asserts five factors crucial to understanding suicide behavior: (1) cultural beliefs about the after-life, (2) prevalence of social problems that create hardship, (3) psychosocial problems that limit the ability to the individual to cope, (4) availability of methods to commit suicide, and (5) availability of suicide prevention services.
Continuum Multifactor Model Beautrais (2000)	• Risk factors for both completed and attempted suicide are similar. • Individual factors: genetic/biological factors, social/demographic factors, family characteristics/childhood experiences, and personality traits/cognitive styles interact with environmental factors and psychiatric morbidity, which in turn influence suicidal behavior.
Suicide Career Model (Maris, 1997)	• Based on clinical interviews with the relatives of completed suicides, case-control studies, studies of population-level factors. • Individuals who committed suicide have "suicidal careers" spanning several decades and involving complex interdependent biological, social, and psychological factors. Social, individual, and biological traits and states thus interact over time to produce a suicidal individual. • The crucial proximate cause of a suicide could be a nonsocial trait or state such as a serotonin disturbance or neurotransmitter imbalance.

Clearly, each of these models is complex and would require entire books, or at least chapters, to fully explain them. The point is that suicide is multifaceted, and attempts to understand risk have led to a variety of models to help clinicians improve their prediction abilities. It appears that adopting a biopsychosocial approach to understanding suicide may provide a richer perspective for mental health practitioners than any one individual theoretical perspective. Completed suicides often include elements of biological, social, and psychological areas of human functioning. In their day-to-day practices with suicidal individuals, clinicians must attend to all areas to help them identify and prevent potentially suicidal individuals from completing suicide. Although in practice, it is improbable that any clinician would keep each of these models in their minds when completing a suicide risk assessment, the models do help to determine what should be included in risk assessments and prevention programming. This is their primary utility.

Summary

Suicide and societal reactions to it have a long and complicated history that underscores the difficulties that arise when we try to make sense of the larger, philosophical questions about the meaning in life. Throughout history, suicide has been viewed in extremes: a noble decision and a mortal sin. Today's debates about "death with dignity" and the sanctity of life continue to mimic these extreme positions. The reality is that talk of suicide brings up very core beliefs in each of us and is a topic fraught with emotionality.

For more than 100 years, since the publication of Durkheim's work, sociologists, psychologists, and, more recently, suicidologists have looked for theories and models to describe the phenomenon of suicide. Sociological, psychological, and biological models all have been proposed, with other models focusing on specific risk factors outside of attempts to develop general models or theories of suicide. More recently, integrated models have attempted to view suicide from a biopsychosocial perspective, which recognizes the complexity of risk in this area.

3

Suicide and Suicide Risk Factors in Children and Adolescents

To more fully understand suicide risk, Section II of this book takes the reader through selected populations and discusses the specific risk factors in each of these groups. Chapters 3–5 discuss suicide risk based on age, with attention to developmental risks. Chapters 6–9 discuss specific segments of the population, regardless of age, in which specific suicide risk factors have been identified. The goal of the seven chapters in Section II is to provide a fuller understanding of determining who is at risk. Regardless of setting, each of us will come into contact with people who have specific risk factors, and in both our professional and personal lives, an understanding of these risk factors will help us to save lives. Chapter 3 begins this section with a discussion of suicide risk in children and adolescents, up through age 19 years.

Suicide in children and adolescents represents both a personal tragedy and a national public health problem. Perhaps more so than in any other segment of the population, suicide in young people is difficult to understand and frightening to contemplate. Suicide in this population challenges widely held beliefs about childhood and adolescence as a time of security and hope and the protective shelter of parents and other caring adults. What makes suicide so tragic for this age group is that it represents a life that is cut terribly short before the person has even fully begun to live.

Yet suicide does occur among young people—and at higher rates than most people know. Suicide is the third leading cause of death for children ages 10–14 years and the second leading cause of death among those aged 15–19 years. In part, this is because children and adolescents do not have high rates of death from other causes; therefore, suicide rates are higher than for other age groups. The actual numbers for completed suicides among those aged 15–19 years is approximately 10 suicides per 100,000 people. Nevertheless, rates of suicide for young people continue to increase, and the rates of suicidal thoughts and attempts are alarmingly high.

This chapter gives an overview of suicide risk in children and adolescents, ages 5–19 years. Because it is so difficult and painful for most adults to consider suicide in this population, it is especially imperative for all mental health professionals to be acutely aware of the risk factors and warning signs. Parents and other adults might ignore the signals in a conscious or unconscious attempt to deny the reality of the risk. Therefore, it becomes incumbent on professionals to ask the difficult questions as well as to respond to the challenging answers.

Suicide Risk in Children

Very little is known about childhood suicide. There has been a recent spate of research and writing on adolescent suicide, but only a few empirical articles on suicide risk in preteens. Until recently, it was believed that children never committed suicide. Most adults want to believe that early childhood is an idyllic time of happiness and carefree living. Even among adults who recognized that childhood for some children can be fraught with stress and pain, most believed that children were not capable of making life-and-death decisions such as suicide. Recent research has dispelled that myth.

Suicide in children is on the rise. In a 20-year period between 1970 and 1990, suicide rates tripled among children ages 5–14 years. Suicide rates among this group are relatively low, accounting for about 1% of all completed suicides. Nevertheless, although children kill themselves at lower rates than the rest of the population, suicide is the third leading killer among children ages 10–14 years (behind accidents and cancer). And although completed suicide is relatively uncommon, suicidal behaviors are quite prevalent. Every year, about 12,000 children ages 5–14 years are admitted to psychiatric hospitals for suicidal behavior. One study found that 33% of a group of 39 outpatient psychiatric children (ages 6–12 years) had contemplated, attempted, or threatened suicide (Pfeffer, 1984). Even children with no psychiatric history appear to have suicidal thoughts; about 12% of elementary school children admit to suicidal ideas, threats, or attempts (Pfeffer, Zuckerman, Plutchik, & Mizruchi, 1984). Unlike in the adult population, both suicidal attempts and completed suicides are more common among boys than among girls.

It should be noted that although suicide is underreported among all age groups, this is particularly true for children. Children seldom leave suicide notes, and they typically have less access to suicidal methods (e.g., guns, pills). When child suicides do occur, they often are officially reported as accidents.

Bryan was a hyperactive 9-year-old with a learning disability. He was diagnosed with ADHD when he was 6, after his mother was hospitalized briefly because of "nerves." Bryan had extreme difficulty in school, was labeled a severe behavioral problem by his teachers, and had been through a series of medications designed to help him "slow down and focus." He got into everything, and his family went to extreme measures to limit his access to anything that he might get into trouble with, not only locking up guns and knives, but also locking the shed where power tools, the ladder, the lawnmower, and other items were stored. Last year, Bryan watched a neighbor using an electric hedge trimmer. When the neighbor went inside the house for a moment, Bryan picked up the trimmer and starting hacking away at trees. He received severe cuts on his forearm and leg and had to be rushed to the hospital, where he received over a hundred stitches.

The children in Bryan's class were extremely frustrated with him as well, and he was constantly teased and made fun of. After the hedge trimmer incident, his classmates teased him relentlessly, calling him names and running up behind him and making noises like the trimmer. Bryan responded to these attacks by lashing out at his classmates, both verbally and physically. He spent a lot of time in the principal's office, the counselor's office, and detention. He told his school counselor that he wished he could make friends, and in a rare moment of self-reflection, he became extremely tearful and agitated and stated that he believed that he would never have a friend or be loved by anyone—even his mother was sorry he had been born.

Two days later, Bryan's body was found by his sister with a gunshot wound to his head. He had picked the lock on his father's gun cabinet, found a pistol, and shot himself. His parents believe that he was being his natural inquisitive self—that he picked the lock because he was bored, and when he found the gun, he couldn't resist playing with it. His school counselor believes that Bryan's act was intentional but that he was incapable of understanding the finality of suicide. Therefore, the school has avoided using the term *suicide*, since that implies that Bryan meant to take his life and understood the finality of the decision.

It is impossible to know whether Bryan killed himself intentionally or whether he understood the finality of the decision. In cases like this one, the death is typically ruled accidental. Interviews conducted with coroners found that they are often reluctant to rule childhood deaths as suicide, even in cases of clearly self-inflicted injuries, because there is a general belief that children do not fully understand the implications of their actions and therefore are incapable of committing suicide (Mishara, 1999). The coroner's ruling of Bryan's death as accidental is consistent with this belief.

Developmental Considerations of Childhood Suicide Risk

As was noted in the case of Bryan, one of the most salient aspects of understanding suicide risk in children is determining whether children have an understanding of the permanence of suicide and death. This question was originally raised toward the end of World War II by researchers who interviewed children about what they thought happens when a person dies. Two researchers (Anthony, 1940; Nagy, 1948) developed a series of stages through which children progress in their acquisition of a mature understanding of death. Children with immature belief systems did not believe that death was permanent, inevitable, or universal. These early researchers attempted to delineate stages that were fixed to chronological age, with very little success.

Research during the 1970s found that beliefs about death were not necessarily related to chronological age. Both Koocher (1973) and Melear (1973) found that cognitive development, rather than chronological age, determined conceptualizations of death. Other research found that exposure to death increased the likelihood of mature understandings of the concept. Raimbault (1975) found that terminally ill children had advanced understandings of death, even at very young ages.

More recently, Normand and Mishara (1992) attempted to understand what children know about death and when they know it. They found that 87% of elementary

BOX 3.1 • *Myths About Childhood Suicide*

All of these myths (and more) have been uttered about childhood suicide. How many of them have you heard? Can you add any others to the list? Do you believe any of them?

- MYTH: Childhood is a relatively carefree time in a person's life.
  - FACT: Research tells us that children experience extreme stress and have symptoms similar to those of adults. However, unlike adults, children do not have the skills to manage their stress in appropriate ways.
- MYTH: Children do not get depressed.
  - FACT: All children "feel blue" from time to time or have a bad day. In some cases, however, children meet criteria for clinical depression. Approximately 1 in 33 children (and 1 in 5 adolescents) meet criteria for depression.
- MYTH: Children do not understand the finality of death.
  - FACT: It is hard to know what children understand and when they understand it. There is, however, growing evidence that children as young as elementary school age understand the finality of death.
- MYTH: Children are always resilient.
  - FACT: Although we want to raise resilient children and there are resources to help foster resiliency, not all children (or adults) have the ability to "bounce back" after stressors in their lives. Challenges such as poverty, divorce, illness, or trauma can seriously affect resiliency and can lessen children's ability to face additional stressors, in their lives.
- MYTH: Most children's stressors and problems are minor in comparison to adult problems and are not serious enough to place the child at risk for suicide.
  - FACT: All of the developmental literature agrees that problems and stressors are relative: that is, they may be very acute and severe to a young person, who does not have the life experiences and cognitive abilities to put them into perspective. Adults should never minimize or ridicule the stressors of a young person who feels suicidal and overwhelmed.
- MYTH: Children do not feel loss as acutely as adults do.
  - FACT: For children, loss and fear go hand in hand. Children often have very little control over the logistics of their lives, and adults control the context and the shape of children's relationships. When adults move, separate, divorce, or otherwise disrupt children's relationships, it is often done after adults have had time to adjust to the impending transition. When the children are informed, they often have less time—and fewer coping skills—to adjust. When losses occur, children may be afraid; they don't know what will happen to them, and this fear intensifies and complicates all of the other emotions that are typically associated with loss.
- MYTH: Children do not commit suicide. Most deaths that have been ruled as suicides are really just accidents.
  - FACT: The information in this chapter challenges this myth. It is difficult to know when children understand suicide and how they decide to take their own lives, but all available research leads us to believe that the opposite of this myth is true: that many deaths that are ruled to be accidents may actually be suicides.

school age children understood the concept of the universality of death, and 90% understood the finality. In their study, all children had a mature concept of death by the age of 10 years. When asked about suicide, only 10% of first graders knew what the word *suicide* meant, but when fifth graders were interviewed, 95% had an understanding of the word.

In 1999, Mishara extended the original study. He found that students in first grade had relatively immature concepts of death, although the majority understood the permanence of death. Students in fifth grade had a very mature understanding of death. There was strong evidence that as children matured, they grew in their understanding of death. They concluded that most of the children in this and the 1992 (Normand & Mishara) studies understood the permanence and finality of death, even at very young ages. Additionally, Mishara (1999) found that 100% of children in second grade and higher understood the concept of suicide or "killing oneself," including the permanence of the act. Therefore, it might be inappropriate to argue that self-injurious behaviors in children should not be called *suicides* or *suicide attempts* because of their immature belief systems. It appears that most children over the ages of 7 or 8 years—at least those in the studies reviewed here—do understand that self-injurious behaviors can lead to permanent death. However, it should be noted that in a 1994 study, suicidal hospitalized children ages 8–10 were less likely to understand the finality of death than were their nonsuicidal same-aged peers (Carlson, Asarnow, & Orbach, 1994). Thus, it appears that immature conceptualizations of death may be a risk factor for childhood suicide.

Specific Childhood Risk Factors

In their 1996 book *Suicide Across the Lifespan*, Stillion and McDowell list risk factors for childhood suicide. Their ideas represent a comprehensive look at the phenomenon of suicide in the very young, a population whose risk factors have received very little attention in the research and literature. Many of the ideas in this section are based on Stillion and McDowell's text.

Biological Risk Factors.   It appears that suicidal behavior can be attributed to impulsivity in children more than in any other age group. Therefore, the suicidal acts of children tend to be more impulse-based (e.g., running in front of a car, jumping from a building) than acts that require planning (e.g., hoarding and taking medication). Children who are at high suicide risk are those who are angry and impulsive and who use an assaultive approach to problem solving. These children are often labeled *ADHD, antisocial, behaviorally disordered,* or *brain damaged.* Children in this high-risk group are seen as impulsive, hyperactive, destructive, and hostile. These children may come from homes with parents who display similar behavioral patterns. Thus, it is difficult to determine whether these behaviors are biologically based or simply learned coping patterns.

Emotional Risk Factors.   Suicidal children often evidence a variety of mental health issues, depression being by far the most common. Depression is more common among suicidal children than among nonsuicidal children. Severely depressed children "think about suicide and . . . they think about it more often than nondepressed children or those who are suffering only mild depression" (Stillion & McDowell, 1996, p. 83). As is true for all age groups, the depressive symptom of hopelessness is a stronger predictor of suicide than is general depression alone. Thus, children who are unhappy, have low self-esteem, and are generally depressed may be at risk for suicide, but when hopelessness about the future is added to the clinical picture, the severity of the risk becomes much higher.

Another psychological risk factor for children is the *expendable child syndrome*, in which adults communicate to the child that he or she is expendable. In these instances, adults respond to the children with low personal regard and hostility, withdrawing love and affection. Children come to believe that their death will not matter to anyone, and committing suicide is a way to relieve others of the burden of their existence. This phenomenon was first identified by Sabbath in 1969, and since that time, case studies of childhood suicides have supported its existence, although no systematic research has been conducted to determine the prevalence of this syndrome, and it is difficult to determine the magnitude of this occurrence. Nevertheless, mental health practitioners should be aware of the possibility of increased suicide risk if a child feels that she or he is expendable.

Cognitive Risk Factors. As we discussed earlier, an immature view of death may be partially responsible for suicidal behaviors in the very young or in the cognitively disabled. Children who view death as not permanent might believe that suicide is a satisfactory option for a temporary problem. Orbach and Glaubman (1979) believed that even if children have a mature view of death, they may regress to a more immature view once they begin to contemplate suicide. Children who understand the abstract nature of the finality of death might succumb to more concrete thinking when they are suicidal that allows them to view their own death as pleasant and transient. Work with suicidal children has supported this regression to concrete thinking.

Concrete operational thinking, even outside of the context of beliefs about death and suicide, also has been linked to suicidal risk in children. Children who have a rigid cognitive structure in general are at higher risk for suicide and other destructive behaviors. These children cannot generate multiple solutions to problems and tend to think dichotomously (black/white, right/wrong, life/death). Support for this risk factor comes from research such as a 1984 study that found that suicidal children were more rigid in their thinking than were either nonpsychiatrically involved children or children with terminal illnesses (Orbach, 1984). In this study, suicidal children were significantly more likely to be rigid in their problem solving, and cognitive rigidity was found to be highly correlated with a measure of attraction to death among suicidal children. Orbach concluded that cognitive rigidity is an important intervening variable for childhood suicide risk. These children handle life stressors poorly, tend to overestimate the seriousness of their problems, consider very few solutions to their problems, and are overly attracted to suicide as a solution.

Another cognitive risk factor is what Stillion and McDowell labeled "attraction to and repulsion from life and death" (1996, p. 86). On the basis of the work of Orbach and others, they noted that positive and healthy children should be attracted to life and repulsed by death. Suicidal children hold the opposite views. Studies have shown that suicidal children showed more "repulsion from life, less attraction to life, more attraction to death, and less repulsion from death than nonsuicidal children" (Stillion and McDowell, 1996, p. 86). Children who are attracted to death talk about death, draw death-related pictures, and fantasize about death. Although not every child who draws skulls or wears black (popular in the Goth culture) is at risk for suicide, it is important that such children be approached in a nonconfrontational manner to ascertain whether they are at risk for suicide.

Environmental Risk Factors.   The most common environmental risk factor is early loss. Suicidal children, as a group, have experienced more frequent and earlier loss than their nonsuicidal peers. Parental death, separation, and divorce rates for suicidal children are higher than the national averages. Parental absence is identified as a major risk factor for suicidal thoughts and behaviors.

Family dysfunction is a second important environmental risk factor. Suicidal children are more likely to live in homes with significant dysfunction, including parental conflict, physical violence, parental substance abuse, family inflexibility, resistance to change, and unclear parent/child boundaries and role definitions. The families are often rigid in their belief systems and unwilling to consider new ways of handling problems.

Child abuse and neglect also are important risk factors in childhood suicide. Children who are abused have higher rates of depression and hopelessness than do nonabused children. A seminal study by Green in 1978 found that 50% of physically abused children and 17% of neglected children demonstrated suicidal behavior, compared with 7% of their peers. In 2001, Finzi and colleagues found that in their sample of physically abused children, more than half demonstrated suicidal thoughts and/or behaviors, compared with 6% of the nonabused control group. Risk-taking behaviors (e.g., running into the road without caution, climbing without thoughts of safety, ingesting nonedible substances) also was higher in children who had been physically abused (75%) compared with the nonabused control group (9%). These studies and others point to the increased risk of children of abuse and neglect.

Environmental factors outside of the family also can contribute to suicidal behaviors. In a 1999 study of bully-victim problems in schools, Rigby and Slee found that children who are more frequently victimized by their peers at school and feel generally unsupported by others when they have a problem are, in general, more likely to experience suicidal ideation. They also found that among boys, children who engage in bullying may be more likely to experience suicidal ideation than their peers.

Now that you have read about risk factors in children, you can see how many risk factors Bryan had that contributed to his death: impulsivity, hyperactivity, aggression, depression, and many more. Reread the case, and try to identify these specific risk factors.

Warning Signs for Childhood Suicide

Because childhood suicide tends to be a very impulsive act, it is often difficult to predict when children move from being generally at risk to being imminently in danger. One

BOX 3.2 • *Childhood Suicide Risk Factors*

- Biological risk factors
  - Impulsivity
  - Aggression
  - Hyperactivity
  - Brain damage
- Emotional risk factors
  - Depression (particularly hopelessness)
  - Expendable child syndrome
- Cognitive risk factors
  - Rigid cognitive structure
  - Limited problem-solving ability
  - Immature views of death and suicide
  - Attraction to death and repulsion from life
- Environmental risk factors
  - Early loss
  - Family dysfunction
  - Child abuse and/or neglect
  - Bullying (among boys) and victimization

general warning sign is poor school performance that is not linked to intelligence. Other general warning signs include anxiety (including refusing to attend school), sleep disturbances, aggression, impulsivity, and low tolerance for frustration. Suicidal behaviors in this age group can be triggered by small incidents, which might seem trivial by adult standards. In a child with suicidal tendencies and poor coping skills, a small event, such as being yelled at by a teacher or teased by other children, can trigger a suicide attempt.

Because suicidal behaviors are so linked to impulsivity, prevention methods must include a more proactive approach to teaching social skills and problem-solving skills. It is extremely difficult to intervene at the time of imminent suicidal risk as it appears that most children who commit suicide do so because of opportunity (e.g., they find a gun, they jump from a window or in front of a car) rather than through planning. Therefore, intervention must be focused on children who are at risk in general, either through emotional, cognitive, or environmental risk factors. You will read more about prevention and intervention for childhood suicide in Chapters 10 and 12.

Suicide Risk in Adolescents

Adolescents are the most highly studied and written about population for suicide risk. Adolescents have the highest ranking for suicide of all age groups: Suicide is the second leading cause of death for adolescents aged 15–19 years (after accidents). During the year 2000 alone, almost 4,000 adolescents (3,994) aged 15–24 years killed themselves. That works out to about 11 young people per day. What is even more alarming than the number of completed suicides is the amount of suicidal thoughts and behaviors in this age group. More than 60% of high school students report having had some degree of suicidal ideation during their lives, and approximately 9% report a suicide attempt during the past 12 months (Wetzler et al., 1996). The CDC noted that during the last half of the twentieth century, the adolescent suicide rate nearly tripled, from 4.5 per 100,000 in 1950 to 13.2 per 100,000 in 1995. Suicide rates for adolescents increased more rapidly than those for any other age group. What is even more alarming is the number of suicide attempts in this age group. Estimates range from 50 to 200 suicide attempts, of varying severity, for every completed suicide (McEvoy & McEvoy, 1994). In 1988, the state of Oregon became the only state to begin collecting data on suicide attempts for individuals 17 years old or younger who required medical attention. Between 1988 and 1993, suicide attempt rates were 326.4 per 100,000 for females and 73.4 per 100,000 for males. Completion rates were 6.4 per 100,000. Of those who completed suicide, 42% had a previous attempt. In spite of these numbers, only 36% of youths who are at risk for suicide receive mental health treatment or counseling (National Household Survey on Drug Abuse, 2002). Perhaps because the risk is so high and the potential loss so great, the adolescent population engenders much attention in the suicide literature and in the mental health profession at large.

As you read in Chapter 1, suicidal ideation (thinking about suicide), suicidal behaviors (self-injurious behaviors), and suicide attempts are surprisingly common among high school students. During a typical 12-month period, one in five high school students considers suicide, one in six develops a suicide plan, and one in 13 makes a suicide attempt. These high rates of suicidal ideations and behaviors mean that adolescents are, in general, at risk for completed suicide.

Adolescents use a variety of methods to attempt and commit suicide. Among males in the 15–19 age group, just over one half (55%) of completed suicides involve firearms. The remaining male suicides used hanging (34%), poisoning by solid or liquid substances (5%), and other (6%). Among female completers in this age group, handguns were used less often than among male completers (36%), and hanging (37%) was the most common method. Poisoning accounted for 19% of completions (CDC, 2004). In general, handguns are used less frequently by both males and females than they were in the previous decade, and hanging is increasing in frequency as the method of completion for both genders.

The following case demonstrates many of the risk factors for adolescent suicide.

Lucinda was a 17-year-old Hispanic female, the oldest of seven children. The family lived in a lower-middle-class suburb of Chicago. Lucinda's mother worked two jobs to try to keep a roof over the children's heads and food on the table. Many of the children in the family were from different fathers, and none of the fathers offered the family any financial or emotional support. As the oldest, Lucinda was responsible for taking care of her younger siblings while her mother was at work. She cooked and cleaned and kept an eye on the younger ones. Two of her younger brothers caused the family particular pain. Both were involved in gangs and lived lives of danger. Lucinda tried desperately to help her brothers, with little success. Much of the family energy and focus went into keeping her brothers alive and out of trouble with the law. Lucinda was an average student at her local high school, but she had few friends and did not participate in any extracurricular activities. Recently, her music teacher had tried to get Lucinda involved in a high school musical because during music class, Lucinda had demonstrated a real talent for singing. Lucinda refused to discuss the possibility, knowing that she had to go home after school to care for her siblings, but she did not tell her teacher the reason. She simply refused with the one word "no." This was typical of her interactions with others. She kept to herself and was socially isolated. Her classmates thought that she was odd and a loner. During middle school, they used to tease her, but by the time they all entered high school, her classmates had tired of teasing her because they got no reaction. For the most part, they simply left her alone.

By the beginning of Lucinda's senior year, most students in her class were making plans for their futures, applying for local colleges or trade schools or working part time. Lucinda was making no plans. She simply got up each morning, went to school, came home, took care of her siblings, went to bed, and arose to do it again the next day. She did not gain the attention of her teachers or her school counselor because she never exhibited any behavioral problems or got into trouble. In fact, after her suicide, many members of the high school student body and staff could not visualize what she looked like or who she was.

One night, after all of her siblings were in bed and her mother was at work, Lucinda curled up in her top bunk and took an entire bottle of sleeping pills, which had been prescribed to help her overworked and overwrought mother sleep at night. No one noticed that she was dead until the next morning, when she did not get up to help get the younger children ready for school.

Developmental Considerations for Adolescent Suicide Risk

Adolescence is a time of turmoil and transition. This stage of life is marked by identity development (Erikson, 1968), and young people struggle to determine both who they are and who they want to become. Adolescents turn to others to assist them in their struggle, including parents and other adults as well as same-aged peers and the media. Adolescents who do not navigate this developmental stage successfully may remain confused about their identity and struggle to meet the challenges of the next developmental stage: intimacy. Difficulties with identity and with intimacy have been linked to low self-esteem and depression, common risk factors for suicidal behaviors.

Adolescents live in a world where they are no longer children but are not yet fully adults. In his 1994 book about adolescent development, *In Over Our Heads*, Kegan discussed the contradictions of adolescence. He noted that adolescents are moving from a dualistic world of right and wrong to a more multiplistic way of thinking or of viewing the world in shades of gray. Adolescents are struggling to make meaning of this new world, which is no longer the absolutist world of parents and rules. Kegan argued that in today's highly complex and technological world, teens have more access to information and appear more sophisticated in their thinking than did teens of previous generations. Therefore, they are given more and more adult-level responsibilities and decisions by adults who give less direction and guidance with fewer rules. However, the appearance of sophistication is only sophistication of content, not of thought process. Thus, adolescents are no more prepared to handle complex decision making than their predecessors, yet they are more often confronted with adult-level, complex, and ambiguous situations. Today's teens even mature physically at younger ages than did their predecessors, but this physical maturity may belie a mental and emotional immaturity. Kegan's message reminds us that adolescents might appear outwardly able to handle today's complex world, but they still require direction and guidance.

BOX 3.3 • *Myths About Adolescent Suicide*

All of these myths (and more) have been uttered about adolescent suicide. How may of them have you heard? Can you add any others to the list? Do you believe any of them?

- MYTH: Talking about suicide to adolescents increases suicide risk.
  - FACT: When suicide education is taught in a sensitive, appropriate context, it does not lead to or cause suicide attempts or deaths. In fact, educating students about suicide is particularly important, as research shows that young people who are thinking about suicide are more likely to tell a peer than to tell an adult. Thus, peer assistance programs are an important component of adolescent suicide prevention.
- MYTH: Adolescents from wealthy or educated families do not commit suicide. Paradoxically, another myth that exists is: Adolescents who commit suicide are mostly from upper-class and educated families.
  - FACT: Suicide knows no socioeconomic boundaries. All people, from all walks of life, are at risk.
- MYTH: Adolescents use the word *suicide* only to attract attention. Those who talk about suicide never actually attempt suicide.
  - FACT: Talking about suicide is one of the most ominous warning signs and should be treated seriously. Adolescents who make threats of suicide should be provided help; nine out of ten adolescents who commit suicide give clues (verbal warning or other warning signs) before their suicide attempt.
- MYTH: All adolescents exhibit symptoms of depression, anxiety, and angst. Therefore, it is impossible to determine which ones are at the greatest risk for suicide.
  - FACT: Although many adolescents experience sadness, stress, or anxiety, about one in five exhibits symptoms of clinical depression. Depression is a serious problem that contributes to suicide risk, and adolescents who are depressed require prompt and appropriate treatment.
- MYTH: Every adolescent who commits suicide is depressed.
  - FACT: The majority of adolescents have thought about suicide at least once in their lives, and although mental illness may be a contributing factor in many suicides, not all adolescents who engage in suicidal behaviors suffer from a mental disorder.
- MYTH: Most adolescents who attempt suicide fully intend to die.
  - FACT: Most suicidal persons do not really want to die; they just want the pain to end. Thus, they find themselves ambivalent: They want to die to take away the psychological pain, and they want to live in a more hopeful environment. Luckily, this ambivalence becomes an effective place to intervene.

Specific Adolescent Risk Factors

Many specific risk factors have been identified for adolescent suicide. In fact, to name all of them would be almost as unhelpful as naming all adolescent thoughts, emotions, and behaviors. Therefore, what we list below are the demographic, psychological, cognitive, and environmental risk factors that are most supported through research and are most prevalent among adolescents at risk.

Demographic Risk Factors. Completed suicides in adolescence remain a primarily Caucasian male occurrence, with 73% of suicides in this age range committed by white males. However, rates are rising among African American males, doubling in the past 20 years, making them the population with the greatest increase in risk. (A more thorough discussion of the rise in rates for African American males is presented in Chapter 6.) Additionally, there is concern that suicide rates among young African American males may be masked by high homicide rates, with some research suggesting that many of the homicides may include elements of suicide (Lyon et al., 2000).

Although suicide completion in adolescence is primarily the purview of males (who complete suicide four to five times as often as females), suicidal ideation and attempts are much more common in females. Over one third of adolescent females rate themselves as significantly depressed or hopeless almost every day for more than two weeks during the past 12 months, compared with 22% of males. Female adolescents (24%) were significantly more likely than males (14%) to have considered suicide in the past year, and females were significantly more likely (18%) than males (12%) to have developed a plan (Centers for Disease Control and Prevention, 2004).

Emotional Risk Factors. Adolescent suicide attempters and completers have overall higher rates of psychological distress than their nonsuicidal peers. All major classifications of mental health disorders are represented in the at-risk population at higher rates than in the population of those not at risk (Wetzler et al., 1996), and approximately 90% of completers have at least one major psychiatric disorder. A review of autopsy studies (Brent et al., 1993) found the most prevalent mental health disorders among adolescent suicide completers were as follows:

- Affective disorders: Studies show that a range of 35–76% of adolescent suicide completers suffered from an affective disorder, most commonly depression followed by bipolar disorder and anxiety.
- Schizophrenia: Studies show that from 0–17% of adolescent completers have schizophrenia. However, most research demonstrates that individuals with schizophrenia are at the highest risk for suicide during their thirties and forties.
- Substance abuse: Typically between one third and two thirds of the sample in most studies of adolescent completers have a substance abuse disorder. Substance abuse is more likely to be a risk factor when it occurs in the presence of a coexisting affective disorder.

Other psychological risk factors include problems with identity (including sexual identity, which will be discussed in Chapter 9), fluctuating mood states, hopelessness, anger and impulsivity (Wetzler et al., 1996), and antisocial personality disorder/conduct disorder (Apter, Bleich, Plutchik, Mendelsohn, & Tyano, 1988; Brent et al., 1993). Anxiety (Sareen, Cox, Clara, & Asmundsen, 2005; Strauss et al., 2000) also has been linked to suicidal behaviors, particularly when a person has both anxiety and depression.

As with all age groups, the depressive factor of hopelessness appears to be the most salient in moving from a general depression to a high risk for suicide (Beautrais, Joyce, & Mulder, 1999). Adolescents who have no hope for the future or cannot envision a future, a more and more common occurrence among inner-city youths, appear to be at very high risk.

The psychological trait of impulsivity is particularly disturbing and has only recently received attention in the literature. A 2001 study found that among nearly lethal suicide attempts of young people (ages 13–34 years), almost one quarter (24%) of the attempts occurred with less than five minutes between the decision to attempt suicide and the actual attempt (Simon et al., 2001).

Substance abuse increases the suicide risk in adolescents. Youths who reported alcohol or illicit drug use over the past year are much more likely to be at risk for suicide. Those who use alcohol have more than double the risk, and those who use illicit drugs have nearly three times the risk of suicide than those who do not (National Household Survey on Drug Abuse, 2002).

Chemically dependent adolescents have been found to have higher rates of suicide attempts before treatment than chemically dependent adults (36% versus 26%) (Holland & Griffin, 1984). Further studies have shown that chemical abuse or dependence may be secondary to an affective disorder in determining suicide risk. That is, adolescents who are depressed and use substances appear to be more at risk than those with depression or substance abuse alone.

Cognitive Risk Factors.   A primary cognitive risk factor in adolescents, just as in children, is a rigid cognitive structure with poor coping skills. Adolescents who have an inability to generate solutions to problems may find themselves more likely to fixate on suicide as the only possible option. Adolescents have fewer life experiences to draw on

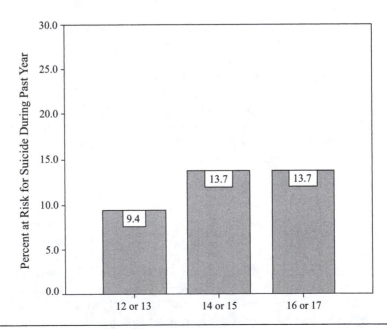

FIGURE 3.1   Percentages of Youths Aged 12–17 at Risk for Suicide During the Past Year, by Age: 2000.

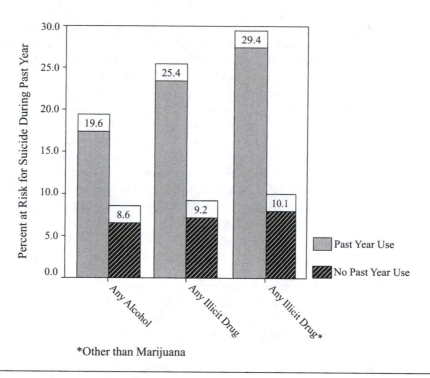

*Other than Marijuana

FIGURE 3.2 Percentages of Youths Ages 12 to 17 at Risk for Suicide During the Past Year, by Past Year Alcohol or Illicit Drug Use: 2000.

Source for both figures: NHSDA Report, 2002.

than adults do, and the ability to problem solve by generating options, rather than relying on past experiences to generate ideas, appears to be of particular importance. Cognitive distortions (e.g., overgeneralizations, preoccupation with a single thought or idea, all-or-nothing thinking) are often present. A study of suicide notes of adolescents found a high incidence of cognitive constriction (e.g., rigidity in thinking, narrowing of focus, tunnel vision, concreteness). They seem preoccupied with one trauma (e.g., rejection of a boyfriend or girlfriend, conflict with a parent), and their notes contain words such as *always, no-one, all,* and *never* (Leenaars, de Wilde, Wenckstern, & Kral, 2001, p. 53). They appear to choose suicide because of a lack of perceived options.

Another cognitive risk factor is the presence of a learning disability. Adolescents with learning disabilities have high rates of emotional and behavioral problems and generally perceive themselves as less socially competent than their peers (Svetaz, Ireland, & Blum, 2000). It is impossible to determine from the current research whether the learning disability is in and of itself a risk factor or is simply correlated with suicide because of the associated emotional, behavioral, social, and cognitive strains. Nevertheless, adolescents with learning disabilities, particularly those with accompanying psychological distress and poor coping skills, are at particular risk.

Other cognitive risk factors that have been identified are an external locus of control and an absence of future-time perspective (Beautrais, Joyce, & Mulder, 1999).

Individuals with an external locus of control believe that they have limited—or no—ability to determine their own outcomes in life. External events, people, and the environment dictate their actions, and they are simply reactive, rather than proactive, in their lives. Thus, people with an external locus of control might believe that that they are "led" to suicide and cannot live out other options.

A final cognitive risk factor is perfectionism. Ironically, there are some adolescents who are academically high-achieving, socially successful, and appear to be very future-oriented who are at risk for suicide if they are also perfectionistic. Perfectionism, which can be adaptive when used appropriately for goal orientation, also can be extremely maladaptive. Perfectionism is maladaptive "when one fails to meet personal expectations or standards are set too high" (Donaldson, Spirito, & Farnett, 2000, p. 100). Individuals with high levels of perfectionism may respond to failure—or anticipated failure—with depression or anxiety. These people typically fear disapproval from either "self" or from "others," and experience enormous amounts of inappropriate guilt. They use suicide or suicidal behaviors as coping mechanisms. Perfectionism that leads to suicidal behaviors is most prevalent in adolescence and does not appear to be a significant risk factor in adults. It appears that it is at this stage of development that early personality and cognitive traits of perfectionism become more locked in, leaving fewer alternative paths. Inability to adjust to change or to adapt is a hallmark of perfectionism, and this ties in with a rigid cognitive style that is also a risk factor for this age group. Adolescents who are striving for an identity seek identity as a perfect—or nearly perfect—person. Thus, some adolescents who appear to "have it all" may be at particular risk, yet they seldom receive mental health assistance. Parents, teachers, school counselors, and other adults perceive these students as models of success and happiness, and their mental health problems often slip under the radar.

Environmental Risk Factors.   Among suicidal adolescents, there is a higher incidence of family dysfunction of all types compared to their nonsuicidal peers. Common familial risk factors for adolescent suicide include coming from highly conflicted families that are unresponsive to the adolescent's needs, families with parental alcoholism or substance abuse, and families with physical or sexual abuse. Families of suicidal teens also have higher levels of medical and psychiatric problems (Garfinkel, Froese, & Hood, 1982). Finally, families who have had a suicide completion are at higher risk for another.

Social isolation and poor peer relationships are two additional environmental risk factors. Suicidal adolescents often feel alienated, both within the family and with their peers (Stillion & McDowell, 1996). They are more likely to have poor social skills, to have ineffective peer relationships, to be nonjoiners, and to be generally unpopular.

Now that you have read about risk factors in adolescents, you can see how many risk factors Lucinda had that contributed to her death: depression, inability to envision a future, family dysfunction, and many more. Reread the case, and try to identify these specific risk factors.

Warning Signs for Adolescent Suicide

When adolescents become suicidal, they often have a period of poorer school performance and truancy, although these also are signs of general emotional distress, which

BOX 3.4 • *Adolescent Suicide Risk Factors*

- Demographic risk factors
  - Caucasian males are at highest risk for completion
  - Fastest growing rates are among African American males
  - Females are much more likely to have suicidal ideation and attempts
- Emotional risk factors
  - All mental disorders, but most prevalent are:
    - Depression (particularly hopelessness) and other affective disorders (particularly bipolar disorder)
    - Schizophrenia
    - Substance abuse
  - Identity problems
  - Anger and impulsivity
  - Impulsivity
  - Antisocial personality disorder/conduct disorder
- Cognitive risk factors
  - Rigid cognitive structure
  - Poor coping skills
  - Limited problem-solving ability
  - Learning disability
  - External locus of control
  - Inability to envision a future
  - Perfectionism
- Environmental risk factors
  - Family dysfunction, including:
    - High levels of conflict
    - Parental alcoholism or substance abuse
    - Physical or sexual abuse
    - High levels of medical or psychiatric problems
    - Suicide within the family
  - Social isolation
  - Poor peer relationships
  - High school graduation with no ability to foresee or plan for a future

is correlated with suicide. Other warning signs include lack of interest in their own personal welfare, preoccupation with death and violent themes, difficulty concentrating, and altered eating and sleeping habits. Just as with adults, a sudden improvement after a long period of depression might signal an imminent suicide. In these cases, they are responding to the calm that they feel when they have made a decision to end their suffering and take their own lives.

Suicidal adolescents exhibit some warning signs that are specific to their age group. As a whole, they are more likely than suicidal adults to show dramatic changes in their behaviors (e.g., stopping a favorite activity, becoming impulsive or sexually promiscuous). They are also more likely to self-mutilate, including actions such as carving their initials into their forearms with pocket knives (Stillion & McDowell, 1996). Many suicidal people attempt to "put their affairs in order" before they die, and suicidal adolescents are no exception. They may organize their papers or journals or clean up their rooms. Suicidal adolescents also are more likely than suicidal people in other age groups to give away prized possessions before their death.

Suicidal adolescents sometimes engage in verbal cues that refer to their decision. They might say things such as "They won't have me to kick around anymore," "She'll be sorry," or "I'll show them how serious I am." Some adolescents might make direct threats, such as "I'm going to kill myself" or "I want to die," while others might use more abstract or individualized language. These messages—direct or indirect—may be cries for help and uttered with the hope that someone will intervene. You will learn more about ways to intervene with suicidal adolescents in Chapter 12.

Triggering Conditions

Adolescents who are at risk for suicide may respond to one or several situational or personal stressors. These have been outlined by McEvoy and McEvoy (1994) and are listed below.

Situational Conditions
- Death of a family member or close friend
- Anniversary dates of painful life events, such as the death of a parent or other loved one
- Tough transition times (e.g., parents' divorce, breakup with a dating partner, severe dread of the "real world" following graduation, loss of a valued peer relationship, transferring to a new school)
- Being socially isolated (lack of close personal relationships)
- Involvement in blended family relationships in which there is frequent and serious conflict with stepparent or siblings
- Chronic and intensifying conflicts with parents, employers, teachers, or peers
- Prolonged presence in a pathological family (e.g., parental substance abuse, incest, family violence)
- The onset of severe illness or disability in self or a family member with little hope of improvement
- For the disabled or seriously ill, the worsening of the disability or pain (or fear of progressive deterioration), especially when coupled with the discouragement of the medical personnel or the withdrawal of treatment or support services
- The experience (or anticipated experience) of significant failure or embarrass- ment (e.g., flunking, being bullied in front of others)
- The loss of a job or other valued role
- Incarceration or other significant trouble with the law
- Serious alcohol or other drug abuse (This may be a symptom of depression as well as a condition producing depression.)
- Confirmation of an unwanted pregnancy, especially before parents or peers find out
- Being forced to assume significant responsibilities while lacking the emotional resources and skills to do so

- Intense and relentless emphasis by others (e.g., parents) on one's achievement coupled with the fear of disapproval for failure to achieve
- Conflicts over one's emerging sexual identity or preferences
- Suicides by peers or famous people

Personal Conditions

- Marked changes in behavior, which may include changes in sleeping habits, the onset of eating disorders (including dramatic weight gain or loss), extreme promiscuity, dramatic emotional outbursts, uncharacteristic acts of rebellion, or dramatic decline in school performance
- Voluntary isolation from friends and withdrawal from normally sociable activities
- Significant increase in the use of alcohol or other drugs
- Neglect of personal appearance
- Senseless risk taking or clear lack of concern for personal welfare
- An exaggeration of health complaints or the emergence of psychosomatic illnesses
- A pronounced difficulty in being able to concentrate on tasks (often coupled with dramatic mood changes)
- Preoccupation with death, with morbid thoughts, or with themes of destruction
- Expressions of pervasive and enduring sadness, or expressions of inappropriate affect (bursts of laughter or crying that do not fit with the social context)
- Serious distortions in perceptions of reality
- Inability to make even the most minor decisions
- Very low self-esteem
- Preoccupation with escape fantasies
- Intense anger or desire for revenge against real or imagined enemies
- Behavior that is characterized by trying to put one's life in order (e.g., giving away possessions and settling accounts)
- Constant seeking of attention through inappropriate behaviors
- Suicide threats or attempts to commit suicide

Source: McEvoy, M. L., McEvoy, A. W. (1994). *Preventing youth suicide: A handbook for educators and human service professionals.* Holmes Beach, FL: Learning Publications, pp. 34, 36.

Two final triggering conditions are suicide contagion ("copycat" suicide) and entering into a suicide pact. Suicide contagion, or copycat suicide, is a phenomenon that appears to be unique to young people and occurs when adolescents are exposed to the suicidal behavior of others, either actual or fictional. Others then attempt to copy the suicide of the deceased person. The completed suicide of the other person (e.g., a well-known celebrity, someone in the media, or someone at a school) serves as a model. In the absence of protective factors, others who know of the suicide might be at risk. Sometimes these copycat suicides spread through a school system or a community, and their existence highlights the need for quick and thorough postvention activities after a completed suicide to minimize the risk of suicide contagion. (Postvention is discussed in greater detail in Chapter 10.) In some instances, it appears that the susceptibility and impulsiveness of some adolescents toward suicidal behavior increase when the adolescents are exposed to the suicide of others. It is for this reason that many mental health professionals have asked that the media downplay the suicides of famous people, in particular limiting the glamorizing of such events. The suicide death of grunge music star Kurt Cobain in April of 1994 at age 27 represents how relentless media coverage (including a cover story in *Newsweek* magazine when his diaries were released, more than eight years after his death) and Internet sites (a search for Cobain's name yields over 165,000 hits) can perpetuate and glamorize suicide. More than ten years after his death, Internet message boards dedicated to Cobain still receive hundreds of messages per day, many of them related to the suicidal thoughts and behaviors of the participants.

Suicide pacts among adolescents (between boyfriend and girlfriend or in peer friendship groups) are a dangerous and poorly understood phenomenon. Although relatively rare, they are often highly lethal endeavors with apparently high completion rates. Although suicide pacts exist in the adolescent world, they are typically more common among middle-aged or older spouses. The pacts often are instigated by a depressed person with a history of attempts. The other person or people are more passive-dependent. The main motivation in adolescent suicide pacts appears to be the threat of loss suffered by the passive-dependent member(s) due to the upcoming suicide of the dominant member (Santy, 1982). Family conflict and loss appear to be even more prevalent in suicide pact members than in suicidal adolescents as a whole. Adolescents who engage in suicide pacts are also, as a group, more likely to be socially isolated from others and dependent almost exclusively on other members of the pact for all their interactions and support (Granboulan, Zivi, & Basquin, 1997). Hemphill and Thornley (1969) called this an "encapsulated unit" (p. 1336) and suggested that the suicides may occur because the unit feels threatened by an external force (e.g., one of the families is moving away, one of the members is being sent to a juvenile detention facility). As a rule, the actual attempts are decided on rather impulsively, although the pact might have been in force for quite some time.

Summary

Suicide rates are increasing among children and adolescents. Although still relatively uncommon (rates are approximately 10 per 100,000), suicide is the second leading cause of death among adolescents, and in general, rates for the 10- to 19-year-old age group are increasing. Children are at risk for biological, emotional, cognitive, and environmental reasons, and there is still some uncertainty about the age at which children can make informed choices about suicide and understand the finality of death. Impulsivity is a particular problem for suicide prevention in children, and proactive work, including social skills and problem-solving training, might be the best method of prevention for this age group.

Adolescents are the most-studied group in regard to suicide, and it is clear that there are high rates of suicidal thoughts and behaviors among the 15- to 19-year-old age group. Adolescent females have many more thoughts and attempts, and adolescent males are more likely to complete. Although suicide completions remain a primarily Caucasian male phenomenon, suicide rates are in increasing in African American males. Handguns are the most common method for males, however, hanging is becoming a more common method of completion and has surpassed handguns as the most common method for females. Risk factors for adolescents are many and varied, and it is difficult to use wide-ranging risk factors to determine individual risk. Thus, warning signs and triggering conditions also can be used to help determine individual risk.

4

Suicide and Suicide Risk Factors in Young and Middle-Aged Adult Populations

Adulthood is a broad term that is used to describe people from age 20 to 64. With such a broad age range, it is important to consider developmental risk factors within each of the segments of this population, and this chapter is divided into broad age groups: young adults (20–34 years), middle-aged adults (35–54 years), and older middle-aged adults (55–64 years). People over age 64 years will be discussed in the next chapter (Chapter 5). This chapter outlines the risk factors for each of these age groups.

The adulthood years represent a period of significant risk of suicide for many individuals. As you read in Chapter 2, suicide is the second leading cause of death among adolescents, and this trend continues into young adulthood, in which suicide remains the second leading cause of death through age 34 years. Again, although older people commit suicide at higher rates than do people in young and middle adulthood, older people also are more likely to die from other causes as well. The period of adulthood through age 34 years does not have high death rates overall (much of the risky behaviors that are common in earlier age groups has subsided, and many of the other health risks have not yet become lethal). Suicide, then, ranks high for this population.

The period of young and middle adulthood has not been heavily studied in the suicide literature, and in comparison to younger and older populations, we know very little about suicide in this group. In general, this time period is one of settling down, getting married or partnered, deciding on a career, having children, and in general taking on more and more adult responsibilities. Although many of these developmental milestones represent times of joy, they also are full of additional stressors. People with poorly developed coping systems are ill prepared for adult-level responsibilities and may find themselves at particular risk.

Adult Developmental Characteristics and Suicide

Young Adults (Age 20–34 Years)

The suicide rate for young adults is approximately 13 per 100,000 each year. Young adult males commit suicide at a rate approximately five times that of young adult females. Within this age group, Caucasian males have the highest incidence, followed by African American males, and Caucasian females; African American females have the lowest incidence. Research indicates that only about 25% of young adults receive medical care following a suicide attempt (Crosby, Cheltenham, & Sacks, 1999). This lack of follow-up care is particularly significant given evidence that young adults have the most medically serious and potentially lethal suicide attempts (Swahn & Potter, 2001).

Developmentally, young adults (20–34 years), having achieved some sense of identity in their adolescence, are faced with a highly challenging and dynamic set of life tasks. Primary among these are the need to find intimacy and the need to find a life career or occupation. Havighurst (1972) specified several important tasks for young adults, including the following:

- Finding an intimate emotional, intellectual, and physical relationship with a suitable partner
- Learning to live happily with the partner
- Establishing economic self-sufficiency through work and career
- Grappling with issues concerning parenthood and child rearing
- Assuming home management responsibilities
- Participating in society by taking on civic responsibilities
- Beginning life goals and aspirations in areas of work and career

Given the great number of significant life tasks that must be accomplished by young adults, it is not surprising that many people encounter difficulties in mastering them all. They may experience significant stress, comparing themselves either to "more successful" peers or to their own internal expectations of where they "ought to be" at this stage of their lives.

Around age 30, young adults may begin to reevaluate their lives and determine that their earlier choices do not suit them. Perhaps this is because of the number of life tasks and transitions and the stress that accompanies them. They may divorce, return to school, or change careers. It may be for these reasons that the rate of young adult suicide is higher than that for adolescents and slightly higher than that for the general population. Marital difficulties, divorce, and the presence of children are significant factors influencing the suicides of both male and female young adults. Among white males, marriage has a negative effect on suicide risk, but divorce or separation significantly increases the risk (Kposowa, Breault, & Singh, 1995). Depression, a significant risk factor for all adults, is particularly prevalent in young adults. Young adult females have higher rates of depression than do females in any other age group.

Middle-Aged Adults (Age 35–54 Years)

It is difficult to sum up the developmental tasks of middle-aged adults, given the great diversity of people and practices that occur within this age range and the absolute neglect of the topic in developmental writings, most of which lump "adulthood" into a large range beginning in the twenties and lasting until death. Generally, however, adults in middle age struggle with finding meaning and, in the words of Erikson, being generative (through children, career, and service) versus becoming stagnant. In addition, as people age, they must adjust to the increasing disabilities of their own bodies. Decreases in self-esteem and increases in depression may be the result of the realization that they can no longer accomplish what they once could, and the new demands for flexibility (in physical, emotional, and mental activities) mean that people with rigid cognitive and emotional structures might be left unprepared for life's challenges.

Robert Peck (1956) noted four major tasks of people in middle adulthood:

- Moving from valuing physical prowess to valuing wisdom (acknowledging that one can no longer do all that one could)
- Shifting from sexualizing to socializing in human relationships
- Striving for cathetic (emotional investment) flexibility versus cathetic impoverishment
- Striving for mental flexibility versus mental rigidity (work to not get "stuck in our ways")

The age group of 35–54 years has the highest rate of suicide of any population with the exception of men over age 75. At more than 15 per year per 100,000 in the population, the suicide rate among this age group would dictate that more should be done to understand the phenomenon of suicide in this population, yet relatively little is known.

Older Middle-Aged Adults (Age 55–64 Years)

The aging of the "Baby Boom" population into older middle age has brought this group into the media limelight in recent years. Previous developmental research, which tried to label this time in terms of the broader "generativity versus stagnation," no longer can be universally applied. People in this age group may be looking after young children or grandchildren. They may be going back to school, dating, or starting a business. The Baby Boom generation has achieved more material success than those before it, but it also has higher rates of depression than the generations that preceded it. Some experts have noted that with high achievement comes high stress and that stress may be linked to depression. Others have noted that a decline in physical health or in perceived importance in the workplace has precipitated the depression. One final idea that has been put forth pertains only to those who are already at risk. This idea focuses on "off-time" role transitions, which is particularly relevant at a time when many of the social mores are changing for this age group. The crux of the idea is that when something occurs to people that is developmentally out of sequence (e.g., they get married late, their spouse dies young, they retire early, a child precedes them in death), they suffer from asychronization of the normal life course. When several of these off-time events occur during life, the person may have dislocation in several life roles, resulting in poor adjustment and low life morale, which become risk factors for suicide (Cohler & Jenuwine, 1996). It is unclear to what extent these off-time transitions affect the suicide rate in older middle-aged adults (or other age groups), but it has been hypothesized as a developmental risk factor that should be considered in working with adult populations.

Suicide Risk in Young and Middle Adulthood

During the year 2000, the following occurred:

- 2,373 people age 20–24 years killed themselves. This means that more 20- to 24-year-olds died of intentional self-harm than died of the next seven causes of death (cancer, heart disease, congenital deformations, HIV, cerebrovascular diseases, pneumonia, and diabetes) combined.
- 4,792 people age 25–34 years killed themselves, making this the second leading cause of death.
- 6,562 people age 35–44 years killed themselves, making this the highest-ranking age group in terms of sheer numbers of suicides.
- 5,437 people age 45–54 years killed themselves.
- 2,945 people age 55–64 years killed themselves.

Thus, the total number of adults, ages 20–64 years, who were officially reported as having completed suicide in the United States in the year 2000 was *22,109*, or approximately *two adults every hour* (Kochenek & Smith, 2004). Suicide rates for adults have been relatively consistent over the last decade after several decades of decline.

In 2000, a large-scale study with over 157,000 adults in a managed-case system was completed, and data were collected over a 15-year period on suicide attempts and completions (Iribaren, Sidney, Jacobs, & Weisner, 2000). Although the final numbers that were reported in the study were somewhat different from the data presented by government sources, in general the patterns that were uncovered were very consistent with our current understanding of adult suicide attempts and completions. For example, the study supported the idea that more adult women than men *attempt* suicide (111 female attempts serious enough to require hospitalization compared to 58 male attempts requiring hospitalization). The study also was consistent with governmental statistics when it found that more men than women *completed* suicide (218 male completions compared to 101 female completions). This paradoxical pattern of higher rates of attempts in females and higher rates of completions in males appears to be consistent across the research on adult suicides.

The same study also reported many other results that are revealing enough to be worth reporting in significant detail (Iribaren et al., 2000).

- *Age:* When suicide attempts and completions were compared across differing age groups, the following patterns emerged:
  - Attempt rates were highest among young women ages 15–24 years. For men, the highest attempt rates were among the 65- to 89-year age group. (Suicide in the elderly is discussed in greater detail in Chapter 5.)
  - For both sexes, the highest rates of completion occurred between ages 15 and 24 years, although men also had elevated rates of completion in the 65- to 89-year age group.
- *Race:* In comparing attempts and completions among the races, the following patterns emerged:
  - Attempts
    - Caucasian women had the highest rates of hospitalizations for suicide attempts when comparing all racial groups across both genders.
    - African American women had the lowest rates of attempts among females of all racial groups.
    - Caucasian men had the highest rates of hospitalizations for suicide attempts among males of all racial groups.
    - Asian men had the lowest rates of attempts across all racial groups and both genders.
  - Completions
    - Among women, Asian women had the highest rates of completed suicides, with Caucasian women next, and African American women last.
    - Among men, Caucasian men had almost twice the completion rate of African American and Asian American men.
    - Rates among African American men and Asian American men were nearly identical.
- *Marital status:* The sample was divided into the following categories: never married (25%), married (55%), separated/divorced (15%) and widowed (5%). Among these categories, the following patterns emerged:
  - Never married men had an increased risk of suicide attempts and completions compared to men in other marital status groups.
  - Never married women and divorced/separated women had higher rates of suicide completion than did women who were married.
- *Methods:*
  - Attempts
    - Both men and women who received hospital care for a suicide attempt were most likely to have used ingestion of drugs as their method of choice.
    - Ingesting of drugs or other medicinal substances accounted for 80% of male attempts and 84% of female attempts.
  - Completions
    - Overall, among those who completed suicide, women were more likely to use overdoses (40%) while men were more likely to use firearms (52%).
    - Top three methods for completions:
      - Women
        - Drugs or other medicinal substances (40%)

- Firearms (26%)
- Hanging (12%)
- Men
  - Firearms (52%)
  - Hanging (14%)
  - Poisoning by motor vehicle exhaust (7%)
- *Other sociodemographic variables:* The study compared other information (e.g., educational attainment, personal history of hospitalizations for suicide, and personal history of negative events, such as emotional problems, family problems, financial problems, and job problems). The following patterns emerged:
  - Prior hospitalization for a suicide attempt was the best predictor of a completed suicide. Women with prior attempts had 21 times the risk and men with prior attempts had 25 times the risk of suicide completion.
  - Low education attainment (less than 12 years) was a significant predictor of hospitalization for an attempt in both genders.
  - Medical (nonpsychiatric) illness was a significant predictor of attempts in men.
  - Job problems were a significant risk factor for attempts in men but not in women.

This large-scale study leaves us with some important understandings. First, it confirms that more women attempt suicide and more men complete suicide, a fact that holds steady across all ages and races and has been supported by much research. Second, it demonstrates that completed suicide remains a primarily Caucasian male phenomenon, a fact that fits with the government statistics (about 73% of all completed suicides are by Caucasian males), but suicide attempts are a primarily Caucasian female phenomenon. Third, it appears that people who are not partnered are at greater risk for both attempts and completions, a factor that fits with our understanding of the importance of social support in lowering suicide risk. Fourth, handguns, overdoses, and hangings are the most common methods for attempts and completions, although there is some variation by gender. Finally, people who have previous attempts and/or significant life stressors (loss of job, low education, illness) are at greater risk.

Mike was 45 years old and a computer systems administrator for a large telecommunications company. He worked an average of 65 hours each week, but he earned a very good salary. He had been married for 23 years to Jean and had three children who were 22, 19, and 17 years of age.

Mike believed that he was instrumental in building the success of the company. He had been employed by them for almost 20 years and showed significant loyalty by staying with the company during the 1990s, when he and others were frequently offered lucrative positions if they would "jump" to one competitor or another. Although Mike's skills were very much in demand during the 1990s while the telecommunications industry was booming, his employer had recently been laying off many long-term employees.

Mike told Jean that if he was laid off, he wasn't sure what he would do because he knew that many younger guys were having trouble finding jobs in this economy. Mike had been particularly worried because about five years ago, he and Jean had purchased a large "dream home" with significant mortgage bills and utility expenses. He and Jean had put a lot of work into decorating and landscaping the house. Mike also was sending his 22- and 19-year-old sons to college and his 17-year-old daughter to a private high school. Mike had lost a lot of his retirement savings because of the poor performance of the stock market and knew that he had to keep working to make ends meet.

Lately, Mike had been more and more depressed and anxious when he thought about his situation. He had been waking up at night in cold sweats and had been having difficulty concentrating at work. He had been reluctant to tell Jean about his emotional reactions to the stress, and he had been careful not to tell her how serious he thought the situation really was. More than anything, he had been trying to protect Jean and his children from losing the life he had created for them through his hard work with the company.

One Friday evening, Mike's boss called him at home to tell Mike that his services would no longer be needed by the company. Mike was told to come in to work on Monday and that he would be escorted by a security guard to clean out any personal effects that he might have at his desk. Mike's boss indicated that he was sorry and that he would write Mike a good letter of reference. Mike hung up the phone in shock. He told Jean that he wasn't sure what he was going to do because he knew there were no jobs in his line of work in the city where they lived.

The next morning, after Jean had gone out shopping with their daughter, Mike took his pistol and drove over to the parking lot of his employer. He fired three shots at the building where he worked and then shot himself in the temple. He was rushed to a nearby hospital after the weekend cleaning crew called 911, but he was dead soon thereafter.

Mike's death demonstrates the complexity of understanding midlife suicide risk. Although Mike appeared to have many protective factors, the loss of his job and the security it offered proved to be too much. As you read the next section, think about the case of Mike and what risk factors he presented.

Marvin was a 56-year-old Caucasian male who had worked on and off at a convenience store and other minimum-pay jobs throughout his adult life. He had a hard time holding a job and had been on welfare, but the welfare reforms of the 1990s left him without an income, and he had been trying to maintain a job ever since, with varying success.

Marvin was never a stellar student in school, but he was not one to be in trouble either. He smoke and drank with some regularity, habits that he continued into adulthood, but he did not have substance abuse or dependency and had had only minimal encounters with the law. He dropped out of school at age 16 and had drifted thoughout his adult life. He was married several times and had five children with different wives or girlfriends but had limited contact with his former partners or his children. Several of the mothers had attempted to collect child support from Marvin, but his inconsistent income made this difficult.

Marvin lived in a garage apartment in a rather dangerous part of town, worked at his convenience store job, and spent most of his evenings watching television. Once a week, he played poker with some buddies.

Marvin had had mental health problems for much of his adult life. He said he had problems with impulsivity and attention as a child and had difficulty learning in school. He had always thought he was dumb. (The mental health counselor determined that he might have had ADHD and possibly even a learning disorder.) He had suffered from depression for much of his adult life, and he had felt suicidal several times before. He made several suicide attempts when he was in his twenties and once in his forties, when his third wife left him.

Over the last month, Marvin was fired from his job for poor attendance and tardiness, his landlord informed him that he needed to move out of his garage apartment because his landlord's brother's son needed to move in there, and one of his daughters refused to let him see his grandson, stating that he was a bad influence on the child. When he came to his usual Wednesday night poker game, he learned that two of his friends would be unavailable to come to the game in the future; one had just taken a second-shift job, and one planned to move to another part of the state to be closer to his children. The third man said that he was not interested in finding other poker partners, and he needed to spend more time with his wife anyway.

When Marvin returned home, he felt utterly depressed and hopeless. Every aspect of his life seemed to be unraveling, and he could not imagine how he would make it better. He had no place to live, no job, no connections with his family, and now even his friends had deserted him. He pulled off his belt, looped it over a rafter, and hanged himself.

Marvin's case represents quite a different experience from the case of Mike. In the case of Mike, a well-crafted life came quickly apart. In the case of Marvin, a lifetime of risk factors eventually became too much to handle. Both men, however, were utterly hopeless about the future and unable to foresee any improvements. Neither man reached out, either to family or friends or to a mental health worker or hotline, and both men committed suicide without much planning or forethought.

Risk Factors in Adults

Suicide risk factors in adults have been identified in biological, cognitive, emotional, and environmental domains. All have been studied to help mental health professionals identify people who are at risk and target prevention and treatment resources effectively.

Many of the risk factors that have been identified for suicide in the adult population are related to specific psychiatric diagnoses. Having a diagnosable mental health disorder is one of the single greatest predictive risk factors for suicide in adults, and it is estimated that 90% of people who complete suicide have a diagnosable psychiatric disorder. Disorders such as schizophrenia, major depression, bipolar disorder, alcohol and drug addictions, and certain personality disorders have been linked to increased suicide risk (Swahn & Potter, 2001). In recognition of this powerful association between suicidality and psychiatric diagnoses, an entire chapter is devoted to reviewing the relationships between mental health disorders and suicide later in this book (Chapter 7). However, only a small percentage of those with a diagnosable disorder actually complete suicide, so the presence of a psychiatric disorder in and of itself is not a sufficient predictor of suicide (Conner, Duberstein, Conwell, Seidlitz, & Cain, 2001). In addition, there are a multitude of psychological vulnerabilities that may place a person at risk for suicide and may exist independently of a diagnosed disorder. Hopelessness is one such psychological vulnerability that has been identified as an important risk factor. Hopelessness may occur as a symptom of a major depression, but it may also be a cognitive-emotional state in individuals who do not meet the criteria for any diagnosable psychiatric disorder.

Although the list of suicide risk factors developed from biological, social, and psychological research is extensive, there is to date no definitive list that will always predict risk. Suicide in adults, just as in other segments of the population, is a complex behavior, likely involving constellations of variables from several domains (affective, cognitive, and environmental). More research is needed that will examine these constellations of suicide risk factors and determine not just new factors, but also how these factors interrelate and influence each other. Complex questions, such as "How does an individual's psychological characteristics interact with the person's biology and social context to lead the person to choose to kill himself or herself?" have yet to be researched.

So in this context, the risk factors discussed below are not intended to provide an exhaustive list of all of the factors that have been identified in the research but rather to present some of the major findings that characterize each of the larger research domains.

Biological Risk Factors

Young adults are generally at the peak of biological wellness. Adults at this age, when compared with other ages in the population, are typically free of diseases and illnesses. It is for this reason that suicide ranks number two in the leading causes of death among the young adult population. People in this age category simply are not at great biological risk for death. (The number one cause of death in this age category is accidental and unintentional injuries.) However, several biological risk factors have been identified among the adult population. Gender and health behaviors will be discussed here as two examples of biologically related risk factors.

Gender.   Throughout the first half of this book, there is frequent mention of the considerable differences between males and females concerning suicidal behavior. Males have significantly fewer suicide attempts than females do; however, males complete suicide at significantly higher rates than females. Females also commit deliberate self-harm (DSH) more often than males. Females are much more likely to report suicidal ideation and receive treatment from professionals than are males (Hawton, 2000; Sachs-Ericsson, 2000). DSH in females is thought to be used to communicate or alleviate distress or to modify or manipulate the behavior of others (see the discussion of motives below), whereas DSH in males is more closely linked to a failed suicide attempt.

Several different theories have been advanced to explain this male-female pattern. First, there is a difference in lethality of methods. Males use firearms more often than females do and thus have higher completion rates. Several authors have linked these differing methods to overall gender differences in aggression and violence, with females using less violent methods to end their lives. Second, the differing rates also have been linked to rates of depression and alcohol abuse. In general, females are treated for depression at greater rates, and males abuse substances more frequently. Whereas depression might be linked to suicide attempts, the impulsivity that occurs with substance abuse, along with the lethality of preferred method, might lead to the higher completion rates in males. A third reason for the differing rates is linked to recall bias. In general, women are better reporters of health behaviors than men. Therefore, the higher rates of reported suicidal ideation, feelings, and attempts could be the result of more accurate reporting by women of suicidal behaviors on self-report surveys. Finally, the differing rates have been linked to gender socialization. Social scripts define gender-appropriate behavior in all aspects of life, and behaviors around suicide and suicidal behavior are no different. Certain methods or behaviors might be seen as more feminine or masculine and therefore be carried out more frequently by one of the genders (Canetto & Sakinofsky, 1998).

The paradoxical gender pattern seems to be very consistent across most countries with the exception of China, which has high rates of young female rural suicides (Cantor et al., 2000). In fact, in general over the last ten years, suicide completion rates for females have remained stable or decreased while they have increased for males (Hawton, 2000).

Additional gender-related differences occur in the areas of menstruation and childbirth. Some experts have hypothesized that premenstrual syndrome, with its characteristic hormone imbalances and subsequent effects on mood, might make some already at-risk females more vulnerable to suicide and suicidal behaviors. One study found suicide attempts to be 1.7 times higher among women who were menstruating (Baca-Garcia et al., 2003). The presence of postpartum depression also might elevate risk in some females with a predisposed vulnerability to suicide. Others have found that being pregnant or having a small child can reduce rates of suicide. According to these findings, it is the presence of children, not marital status, that reduces risk in women. When the presence of children (or of pregnancy) among women is factored out, being married is not a protective factor for suicide. Thus, having children, rather than marital status, is likely a preventative factor for females, whereas for males, being married is in itself the protective factor (Appleby, 1996).

Health Behaviors.   Cigarette smoking has been linked to suicide risk in white males. The more cigarettes smoked, the higher the risk. In one study, the relative risk for suicide was 1.4 times higher for former smokers, 2.6 times higher for light smokers, and 4.5 times higher for heavy smokers when compared to the nonsmoking population. It is difficult to understand the reason for this increased risk or what factors occur in male smokers that increase their risk. The increased risk factors were determined after controlling for marital status, degree of sedentariness, alcohol consumption, and development of cancer (Miller, Hemenway, & Rimm, 2000).

Obesity for women and being underweight for men also have been linked to suicide risk. One study of over 40,000 people found that for women, a higher body mass index (BMI) was related to higher rates of depression and suicidal ideation. Conversely, for men, lower BMI was related to major depression, suicide attempts, and suicidal ideation. No racial differences were found (Carpenter, Hasin, Allison, & Faith, 2000). Others have attempted to make sense of the link between obesity or being very underweight and suicide risk and have concluded that the coexistence of depression and hopelessness in each of these groups is what increases risk, not the BMI itself.

Cognitive and Emotional Risk Factors

In 2001, several researchers conducted a comprehensive literature review of all the available research on suicide risk in adults that was published between 1966 to 2000 (Conner et al., 2001). Using strict selection criteria, such as including only those studies with more than eight suicides and that used standardized instruments, they found 46 studies for inclusion in the review. After careful analysis of each of these studies, the authors determined that five cognitive or emotional constructs were consistently associated with completed suicides:

1. Impulsivity/aggression
2. Hopelessness
3. Depression
4. Anxiety
5. Social disengagement

Impulsiveness and Aggression.   Just as with adolescents, impulsivity and aggression in adults increases suicide risk. Impulsivity involves swift action without forethought or conscious judgment. Researchers have identified three components of impulsivity: (1) acting on the spur of the moment (motor activation), (2) not focusing on the task at hand (inattention), and (3) not planning and thinking carefully (lack of planning) (Patton, Stanford, & Barratt, 1995). People whose judgment is impaired through impulsivity, either by the use of substances or because of an impulsive temperament, are more likely to attempt or complete suicide as an immediate reaction to an immediate stressor. Impulsivity is a key feature of several psychiatric disorders, including conduct disorders, some of the personality disorders, substance use disorders, and bipolar disorder. Impulsivity, whether occurring within the context of a diagnosable mental disorder or as a personality trait that does not meet the criteria for a mental health diagnosis, significantly increases suicide risk.

Several features of impulsivity have been linked to suicide risk. First, impulsivity increases suicide risk for individuals who have a *predisposition* to impulsivity. In other words, the impulsiveness is a pattern of behaviors, not a single act. Second, people are at increased risk when their impulsivity involves *rapid, unplanned action*. Impulsivity for these individuals is not just impaired judgment, but action *before judgment can occur*. Third, impulsivity increases risk when action occurs *without regard to the consequences* (Moeller, Barratt, Doughtery, Schmitz, & Swann, 2001). In these three instances, impulsivity can greatly increase suicide risk (Horesh et al., 1997).

Impulsivity may be a predictive factor in assessing suicide risk among people who are depressed. There is evidence that the personality trait of impulsivity occurs in depressed attempters and completers. In other words, the combination of a personality trait of impulsivity and the clinical diagnosis of depression may be particularly dangerous. People who are depressed and hopeless and who have a personality trait that encourages them to make quick, unplanned decisions without regard to the consequences may be at particular risk (Corruble, Damy, & Guelfi, 1999).

Aggression and violence also have been linked to suicide risk. Similar to impulsivity, aggression and violence have been associated with more lethal suicide attempts, and there is sound research that links self-reported aggression and hostility with completed suicide (Angst & Clayton, 1986; Romanov et al., 1994). Just as with impulsivity, high rates of aggression and violence are found in individuals with substance use disorders. Persons who are aggressive and/or violent and who have a substance use disorder are at particular risk for suicide. The combination of this aggressive temperament and substance use in males, for example, increases suicide risk by a factor of seven in comparison to males who are not violent or aggressive and have no substance abuse history. In females, the combination of aggression/violence and substance abuse results in a suicide risk eight times that of women who are not aggressive/violent and have no history of substance abuse. Even without a history of substance abuse, however, violence and aggression have been linked to suicide risk. For people with aggressive or violent temperaments and no history of substance abuse, the increased risk for suicide is 4.6 times that of their nonviolent peers.

Hopelessness. *Hopelessness* can be defined as "causing despair, impossible to solve, deal with . . ." (Merriam-Webster, 1994). Hopelessness has been linked to completed suicides. In one study, the Beck Hopelessness Scale had a specificity rate of 41% for the prediction of eventual suicide (Beck, Brown, Berchick, Stewart, & Steer, 1990). In other words, 41% of those who completed suicide had previously indicated high levels of hopelessness. Hopelessness also has been linked to medically serious suicide attempts (Swahn & Potter, 2001) and to increases in the severity of suicide ideation (Beck, Brown, Steer, Dahlsgaard, & Grisham, 1999). Hopelessness appears to be more related to a lack of positive affect than to high levels of negative affect (Duberstein, Conner, Conwell, & Cox, 2001). In other words, people who are hopeless are unable to generate images of positive outcomes for the future more than they have specific negative images of or beliefs about the future. Hopelessness has been identified as a key psychological factor in suicide ideation, attempts, and completion. Assessing whether a person believes that there is any hope for a solution to his or her problems is an extremely important aspect of suicide assessment. Likewise, helping people to find hope is an essential component of suicide prevention. Even a small glimmer of hope for a temporary respite from psychological pain may be sufficient to get someone through an immediate suicidal crisis. Hopeless people engage in desperate acts, such as suicide, because they do not see any other alternatives for resolving their pain and problems.

Depression. Almost 17% of the U.S. population will meet diagnostic criteria for major depression at some point during their lives (Kessler et al., 1994). It is clear that individuals with depression are at increased risk for suicide. Although different researchers have come up with different numbers, the most empirically supported number for lifetime risk of suicide for people with a diagnosis of major depression is between 3% and 4% (Blair-West, Cantor, Mellsop, & Eyeson-Annan, 1999), giving them a suicide rate that may be as high as 60–70 times that of the general population (Khan, Warner, & Brown, 2000). Depression is linked to completed suicide much more frequently in males than in females. In fact, the male:female ratio for suicide risk in major depression is 5.6:1 in adults. Thus, completed suicide in major depression is primarily a male phenomenon, although women with major depression also have an elevated risk compared with the rest of the female population. Women with major depression also are at greatly increased risk for suicide attempts. There is some difficulty associated with identifying depressed males who are at risk for suicide because males often do not seek psychiatric or medical assistance for their depression.

Thus, increasing help-seeking behaviors by depressed males should be a priority in order to reduce the risk of completed suicide in this highly vulnerable population (Blair-West et al., 1999). Suicide rates among depressed people also vary by ethnicity; depressed Caucasian males have the highest rates and depressed Puerto Rican and Mexican American females have the lowest rates (Oquendo et al., 2001). You will read more about the specifics of suicide and depression in Chapter 7 and the link between suicide and race in Chapter 6.

Anxiety.   Conner and colleagues, in their 2001 review of all the empirical research from 1960 through 2000, identified anxiety as a significant risk factor for suicide. However, there is not universal consensus about this risk factor, as there is with hopelessness, impulsivity, and depression. Studies of people with anxiety disorders have yielded inconsistent results, primarily owing to problems with data collection and the lack of a clear definition in most studies about what constitutes anxiety. Recently, several large-scale studies found that people with anxiety disorders with no comorbid psychiatric problems were at significant risk for suicide attempts and completions. In general, the suicide risk for people with a diagnosed anxiety disorder is more than ten times that of the general population. According to these studies, suicide risk is high regardless of the type of anxiety disorder and is even higher when anxiety disorders coexist with other mood disorders (Khan, Leventhal, Khan, & Brown, 2002; Sareen et al., 2005). You will read more about the specifics of suicide and anxiety in Chapter 7.

Social Disengagement.   Although there is not a lot of research on this factor, what is available supports its relationship to suicidality (Conner et al., 2001). Social engagement is a preference for social interaction (extraversion) as well as the tendency to experience positive emotions. Low levels of extraversion (extreme introversion) have been linked to hopelessness and increased risk for suicide as well as the use of irrational and socially avoidant problem-solving strategies (Duberstein et al., 2001). Low levels of extraversion compromise a person's help-seeking abilities and limit their social support (Van Dras & Siegler, 1997). People with extreme introversion and high rates of hopelessness and helplessness may be unwilling—or unable—to recruit help and benefit emotionally from friendships and family relations (Duberstein et al., 2001). Earlier in this chapter, you read that people who are not partnered (never married, divorced, or widowed) are at higher risk. This is consistent with Durkheim's theory of suicide. He believed that the more socially disengaged individuals were from society, the easier it was for them to take their own lives. In 1897, Durkheim wrote that suicide could result from "society's insufficient presence in individuals" (Durkheim, 1951, p. 258). It is interesting that over 100 years after Durkheim first wrote down his ideas, the most current research still supports this major tenet of his theory.

Related to the concept of social disengagement is the role of self-disclosure in reducing risk. The ability to talk with others about problems and concerns could be a coping mechanism that decreases suicide risk among adult populations. Apter, Horesh, Gothelf, Graffi, and Lepkifker (2001) found that ability to self-disclose significantly differentiated serious attempters from suicide ideators and mild attempters. In other words, individuals who were capable of disclosing their suicidal ideation and talking through their problems were less likely to have high lethality in their attempts. Furthermore, Apter and colleagues noted that the ability to self-disclose is negatively related to both loneliness and social isolation, linking self-disclosure to social engagement. The personality trait of "openness" has been explored by Duberstein and colleagues (2001) in connection to suicide. Openness is a personality characteristic that can be defined as being interested in a variety of both inner and outer experiences for their own sake. Duberstein and colleagues (2001) asserted that individuals with low levels of openness are less likely to report their suicidal ideation and are more likely to complete suicide. They hypothesized that individuals who are more open to expressing their suicidal ideation typically are supported by a mobilization of family and treatment resources, whereas those who are not open are not afforded these benefits.

Shame and Guilt. A final cognitive and emotional risk factor, not identified in the 2001 meta-analysis by Conner and colleagues but discussed in some detail by other authors, is shame and guilt. Hastings, Northman, and Tangney (2000) differentiate and define *guilt* and *shame* in the following manner: "Guilt is an emotional state associated with a focus on a specific behavior involving the perception of having done something 'bad' or 'wrong,'" whereas "shame is much more painful and global, it is a negative evaluation of the whole self." Lester (1997) adds, "While guilt involves psychic conflict, shame involves a deficit: something is missing or lacking; the person finds the self to be flawed." Most authors writing in this area argue that shame is the more important emotion in relation to suicide, as it represents a rejection of self, as opposed to conflict concerning a behavior. However, no systematic study of the role of shame or guilt in suicide has been published.

Environmental Risk Factors

Social Isolation. Suicide appears to be related to social isolation in a direct and fundamental way. Impaired social support may predispose people who live alone and lonely individuals to be at higher risk (Heikkinen, Aro, & Loennqvist, 1994). It is for this reason that many factors that have a common element of loss of social contact—losing a job, getting divorced, moving to a new city, becoming widowed—may all increase risk. Disintegration of existing social support networks, the inability to form social networks, and poor social support all have been theorized as increasing risk because of the lack of protective factors that social relationships can offer (Heikkinen, Aro, & Loennqvist, 1993). Traditionally, it was thought that the protective factor of marriage was particularly salient for men. Among males who live alone, being divorced or separated is a risk factor for suicide (Kposowa et al., 1995). More recently, Stravynski and Boyer (2001) found that loneliness was significantly related to both suicidal ideation and parasuicidal behavior, with little differences between men and women. Thus, whether one is partnered or not does not tend to be the key factor; loneliness and isolation are what increase risk, regardless of married or partnered status.

Geographic Mobility. Related to loneliness and isolation is the risk factor of geographic mobility. Potter and colleagues (2001) found that moving within the last

12 months was positively associated with near-lethal suicides even when depression and alcoholism were factored out. Further, it was noted that characteristics of the move, such as frequency, distance, recency, and difficulty staying in touch with former social supports, were significant risk factors. Geographic mobility may be an important risk factor to consider for populations that are highly mobile, such as young adults, people in the military, those who are moved by corporations, and migrant workers. Again, it appears that loneliness and isolation are important components of this risk factor.

Stressful Life Events/Trigger Events.   A significant body of research has examined the association of suicide with a specific trigger or stressful life event. A study of stressful life events experienced by people who made a suicide attempt found a high prevalence of trigger events (Weyrauch, Roy-Byrne, Katon, & Wilson, 2001). These are listed in the following box.

Further, the study found that in 77% of the sample, acute interpersonal conflict (typically between the subject and his or her significant other) preceded the attempt by one to seven days. This pattern occurred whether or not the suicidal person had a diagnosable mental disorder and regardless of gender or age. What is even more telling is that 96% of the sample, in addition to interpersonal conflicts, experienced more than one of the listed stressors, with 22% having one or two, 33% having three or four, and 37% having five or more. Thus, interpersonal conflict *coupled with* significant stressors increases risk. As would be expected from a complex phenomenon such as suicide, there

BOX 4.1 • *Life Stresses in Failed Suicide*

Life Stressor	*Percent of Sample*
1. Financial Concerns	71
2. Unemployment	63
3. Physical Illness	49
4. Move from Neighborhood	49
5. Psychiatric Treatment	41
6. Other Stress	38
7. Witnessed Violence	32
8. Legal Difficulties	27
9. Divorce or Separation	15
10. Physical Abuse	15
11. Disciplinary Problems	11
12. Parental Conflicts	10
13. Sexual Abuse	10
14. Academic Problems	4
15. Pregnancy or Fatherhood	3

Source: Weyrauch, K.F., Roy-Byrne, P., Katon, W., & Wilson L. 2001. Stressful life events and impulsiveness in failed suicide. *Suicide and Life-Threatening Behavior*, 31(3), 311–319. Reprinted with permission.

is no specific risk factor that emerges from this study, but a constellation of factors that increase risk. The stressors identified in this study, plus countless others (e.g., death of a loved one, jail term, conflict at work), without sufficient protective mechanisms to handle the stressors, all contribute to suicide risk. The number of stressful events, as well as the pace at which stressful life events occur, develop, and change, may lead individuals to feel overwhelmed and unable to cope, increasing their risk of suicide (Riskind, Long, Williams, & White, 2000).

Abuse and Assault.   Abuse in childhood (emotional, physical, and sexual) and adult physical and sexual assaults have been investigated as risk factors for suicide. The pattern of this research, unlike many other areas of suicide research that focus on males, has focused almost exclusively on females. Research has demonstrated that women with histories of sexual assault in childhood and/or adulthood have a higher lifetime risk for suicide attempts (Ullman & Brecklin, 2002). Further, it appears that the more types of abuse (emotional, physical, and sexual) women experience, the higher their suicide risk. In a large sample of African American women, women who experienced one, two, or all three types of abuse were (respectively) 1.8, 2.3, and 7.8 times more likely to attempt suicide (Anderson, Tiro, Price, Bender, & Kaslow, 2002). Results were similar in a sample of 640 college-age women which indicated that experiencing more that one type of abuse was related to increased suicidal ideation in young women (Gutierrez, Thakkar, & Kuczen, 2000). All of these results support the hypothesis that negative life experiences that are seen as violations of personhood have long-lasting effects on an individual's view of life and death.

Family Patterns.   Suicide risk tends to run in families. That is, a family history of suicide can be an important risk factor. A large-scale study of more than 4,000 families with a completed suicide found that a family history of completed suicide significantly and independently increases suicide risk, even when other risk factors, such as mental health diagnoses, were accounted for (Qin, Agerbo, & Mortensen, 2002). One theory that is widely advocated is that once a suicide occurs within a family, it removes some of the stigma of suicide in that family and allows for conceptualization of suicide as a viable option to life's problems. For example, the first author once worked with an adult male who was approaching his fortieth birthday. His grandfather and his father had both committed suicide on their fortieth birthdays, and this man had spent much of his adult life facing this family history and wondering whether his fate would be the same. He believed that he had a legacy to fulfill, even though consciously he was aware that it didn't have to be inevitable. He had typical middle-age problems and stressors, but seen in the context of his family history, he began to wonder whether suicide was the solution—it had "worked" for two generations of men in his family as the solutions to their problems. It took much work to help him find other solutions and to stop the family pattern. Part of the therapeutic relationship involved helping to assuage the guilt he felt for not following in the family "tradition." Clearly, the role of previous suicides in the family must be addressed in a mental health context to allow remaining family members to make healthy choices.

BOX 4.2 • *Adult Risk Factors*

- Gender (males commit suicide more often; females have more attempts and deliberate self-harm)
- Health (males who smoke; females who are obese—may be related to depression)
- Cognitive and emotional risk factors
  - Impulsivity/aggression
  - Hopelessness
  - Depression
  - Anxiety
  - Social disengagement/loneliness/isolation/low self-disclosure
  - Shame and guilt
- Social isolation
- Geographic mobility (may be related to depression and loneliness)
- Stressful life events/trigger events
- History of abuse and assault
- Family patterns

Now that you have read about risk factors in adults, you can see how many risk factors Mike and Marvin had that contributed to their deaths. Reread the cases, and try to identify these specific risk factors.

College Students as a Special Group of Young Adults

College students have been studied more than any other group of adults. This is most likely because many researchers and academics view college students as a convenient sample, as college is one of the few places young adults congregate into a researchable group. College students experience high levels of subjective stress and are vulnerable to many physical and mental illnesses (Chang, 1998). College students have been shown to have high rates of suicide ideation. Amazingly, 90% of college students report that they know of a peer who has suicidal ideations or behaviors (Mishara, 1982); the proximity of the living situation most likely heightens awareness. *Further, 43.7% of college students reported having had suicidal ideations themselves during the previous year* (Rudd, 1989).

Attitudes Toward Suicide in the College Population

In a study of 509 undergraduate college students' views concerning suicide, King and Hampton (1996) found the following:

- 7% had previously attempted suicide.
- Women were more likely than men to have made an attempt.

- No differences were found among racial groups concerning attitudes about suicide.
- Parents' marital status was not related to attitudes about suicide.
- Previous attempters were more accepting of suicide as an option for themselves but not more accepting as an option for others than were nonattempters.
- Students varied in their beliefs about how circumstances can affect suicide acceptability, from a high of 56% believing it was acceptable for someone with a terminal illness to a low of 2% acceptability of suicide for someone with job problems.
- Students who viewed themselves as being associated with a religious group were less accepting of suicide than were those not affiliated with a religious group, both for themselves (8.9% versus 19.3%) and for others (13.8% versus 22.1%).
- Students were consistently more accepting of suicide for others than for themselves.

This study reveals that many college students believe that suicide is a viable alternative for others in certain situations, such as having a terminal illness, but were less inclined to see suicide as a viable alternative for themselves. It is interesting to look at this finding in the context of other research with adolescents that indicates that most (75%) adolescents would not inform a parent, teacher, or counselor if a peer told them that he or she was suicidal. If this collusion carries into young adulthood, then the unwillingness to violate a peer's confidence, even about something as serious as suicide, makes early identification and intervention difficult in adolescent and young adult populations.

Charlie was a 21-year-old college senior who had always been a highly motivated and successful student. He was voted most likely to succeed by his high school class and was admitted to the college of his choice. He had just successfully completed his premed studies at a large midwestern university and had applied to several medical schools and would in all likelihood be accepted to at least one of them on the basis of his excellent grades and outstanding MCAT scores. Charlie had recently been featured in his hometown newspaper as a success and awarded recognition by the town's Rotary Club. Charlie was close to his family; he had several close friends and a girlfriend whom he had been dating seriously for several months. Recently, he and his girlfriend had discussed moving in together while Charlie was in medical school and possibly getting married.

Although on the outside, it appears that Charlie had it all, inside he often found himself depressed and anxious, feelings that he worked hard to hide from his family and friends. His highly perfectionistic tendencies made it difficult for him to generate solutions other than "working harder" or "doing better." When faced with a difficult task, he simply applied himself all the more, often working at an exhausting pace for weeks at a time. As a result, he had never really faced a significant failure or setback.

In applying for financial aid for medical school, Charlie was told that he was ineligible because he had been reported as a dependent on his parent's taxes in the previous year. Charlie knew that his parents, although earning a good living, could not afford the $45,000 a year that it would cost for him to attend medical school. Charlie was informed that he would in all likelihood probably need to wait a year before entering school and then be eligible for student loans and other scholarships.

He was confused when he left his appointment with the college financial aid administrator, with many catastrophic thoughts running through his head. He told himself that he was an idiot for not planning his financial affairs in a more superior manner. He felt shame, embarrassment, and panic—what would his peers, friends, girlfriend, and parents think about him? After all, he was successful and competent Charlie. Once he started thinking about the reactions he would get from others, he came to the conclusion that his girlfriend would undoubtedly leave him (after all, she was interesting in dating a future doctor, not a loser!), his family would be mortified (they had told all their friends that Charlie was going to medical school next year), and the Rotary Club would be sorry that they singled him out for an honor. He would be disgraced and discredited by everyone he cared about.

Charlie was found dead by his girlfriend later that evening. He had drunk a lot of beer and then asphyxiated himself with his car exhaust in his apartment's garage. His family and friends were devastated and shocked by Charlie's suicide. Many of his family and his friends insist that his death must have been some sort of accident. Charlie had always been such a nice, successful, and upbeat kind of guy. He just wouldn't kill himself—would he?

Charlie's case is a difficult one. Although he appears to have had all of the skills needed to manage a crisis, even a particularly challenging one, in reality, he did not. His perfectionistic thinking, an extremely rigid way of viewing the world, and his cognitive catastrophic thinking left him ill prepared. As a result of this tunnel vision, when a crisis occured, he could not problem-solve, and he was left with only one solution.

Risk Factors in the College Population

In general, all the risk factors previously described in this chapter apply to college students as well. In addition, risk factors that are more specific to the college population have been identified and are briefly described here.

Perfectionism.   Excessive self-criticism, doubts about one's own abilities, concerns about meeting expectations of self or others (typically parents), and an excessive focus on organization and neatness are all attributes related to perfectionism (Chang, 1998). Perfectionism can be associated with both constructive and dysfunctional coping strategies and, when used appropriately for motivation, can help to increase college success. However, perfectionism can be a suicide risk factor. High levels of irrational perfectionistic thoughts, socially prescribed perfectionism, and rumination about perfectionism all have been linked to high levels of psychological distress and suicide in college populations (Flett, Madorsky, Hewitt, & Heisel, 2002).

Victimization.   In a study of rape in a college population, both victim and perpetrator were at increased risk of suicide. The trauma of the rape for the victim increases risk, while the antisocial status of the rape perpetrator is in itself a risk factor for suicide (Bridgeland, Duane, & Stewart, 2001).

Interpersonal Relationships.   Although the stress of interpersonal relationships can increase suicide risk in all populations, the unique stressors of interpersonal functioning within a college population may be a particular risk. For example, learning to live with roommates, peer pressure without the context of parental support, long-distance relationships, and finding one's place in a new setting all can contribute to suicide risk.

Changes in relationships with parents also affect risk. In a study of previously suicidal college students, interpersonal relationship problems were listed by the students as a major contributor to suicide risk (Knott & Range, 1998).

Risk-Taking Behaviors.   Substances increase suicide risk in all populations, but the ready access to alcohol and other substances on college campuses and the risk-taking behaviors of this population lead to higher risk. College students with high levels of suicide ideation are significantly more likely to engage in risky behaviors, including carrying a weapon; engaging in a physical fight; boating, swimming, or driving after alcohol use; riding with an intoxicated driver; and not using seat belts (Barrios, Everett, Simon, & Brener, 2000).

Cognitive Vulnerability.   Developmentally, traditional-age undergraduate students are at risk for rigid cognitive functioning. In other words, students of this age are more likely to engage in black-and-white thinking, such as "If I fail at this task, I am a complete failure" or "If the person I love doesn't love me back, then I am worthless." Abramson and colleagues (1998) found high rates of this type of thinking in a college-age population and generalized this rigid thinking pattern into a vulnerability for suicide. Students who are caught in this pattern are not able to generate other options once they decide that suicide is a viable solution to their problems.

Finally, it is important to consider whether attendance at college has a positive or preventive effect on young adult suicide. A ten-year study of 12 "Big Ten" universities, involving 261 suicides of registered students ranging in age from 17 to 49 years, found that college may have a preventive effect on suicide for young adults. The study found that the rate of suicides for the college students was half that of a sample of young adults who were not in college matched on age, gender, and race (Silverman, Meyer, Sloane, Raffel, & Pratt, 1997). However, the authors also noted that older college students (age 25 years and over) have a significantly higher risk than do younger students and that men have a rate of completion that is roughly twice that of women throughout their undergraduate years. Since education does give people advantages concerning achievement in work and career, attending college may have a palliative effect on suicide among young adults.

Summary

Adulthood is a poorly understood time for suicide risk, yet suicide rates continue to be high, with adults in the middle years having higher rates than anyone other than males older than age 75 years. As with all age groups, women have more attempts, and men have more completions. Caucasian males are at the highest risk for completion. Handguns, hangings, and overdoses are the most common methods for both attempts and completions.

The best-supported risk factors for this age group are impulsivity and aggression, hopelessness, depression, anxiety, and social disengagement. The lack of social connections, isolation, and loneliness are particularly salient for adults, and it is one of the reasons why marriage appears to have a preventive effect (although people who are married or partnered can still feel very lonely and be at high risk). Stressful life events (particularly multiple stressors, coupled with interpersonal stress) can significantly increase risk, as can a history of abuse or neglect and family patterns of suicide.

Suicide risk in the adult years is an extremely complicated topic, and there are no specific risk factors that can predict suicide attempts or completions. It appears to be a complex interplay of risk factors—including emotional predisposition, cognitive rigidity, environmental stressors, and resilience—that leads to suicide risk. Very little can be said with any specificity about the adult years in suicide risk, as adults are the least studied of any population. Much more research needs to be done to examine the specific risk factors as constellations of factors that interact in conjunction with each other and in the context of the developmental tasks that define the stages of adulthood.

5

Suicide and Suicide Risk Factors in the Elderly Population

People who are age 65 years and older have been studied in relation to suicide risk. This chapter outlines the specific risk factors for this age group, with attention to developmental risks. The differences in suicide risk by gender and ethnicity are particularly striking in this age group.

Adults, more particularly adult males, 65 years and older, have the highest risk for suicide of any age group. For example, suicide rates for males in this age group are 40 per 100,000, compared with rates of 6 per 100,000 in adolescent males. Although people over 65 make up only 12.7% of the population, they accounted for 19% of the completed suicides in 1998 (Murphy, 2000). Older adults also are much more likely than any other age group to have highly lethal attempts that lead to higher rates of completion. There are probably between 50 and 200 nonlethal attempts for every completed suicide in the adolescent population (McEvoy & McEvoy, 1994). In the 65 years and over population, however, there are only between two and four attempts for every completion (Miller, Segal, & Coolidge, 2000).

Suicide in this age group tends to be well planned and well thought out, not the impulsive acts of many suicidal younger people. Older adults are much less likely than young adults to use suicide as a "plea for help" and more likely to plan their suicide attempts with a "deliberate and single-minded determination" (Miller et al., 2000, p. 358) that does not allow for rescue. In young people, the motivation for suicide is varied, from a desire to stop hurting to cries for attention to attempts to influence others to methods to eliminate feelings of guilt, anxiety, revenge, anger, or depression. In older adults, suicide appears to be a much more focused attempt to release themselves from depression and despair. Older adults who attempt suicide for the most part genuinely want to die, compared to younger adults, who often simply want to alleviate temporary suffering (Atchley, 1991). When older adults attempt suicide, they choose highly lethal methods with less possibility for interventions, such as guns or hanging. Compared with younger adults, older adults make less use of available psychological assistance to get them through a suicidal crisis. They do not tend to make use of suicide hotlines or psychological services, and as a group, they have poorer knowledge than younger people about suicide myths and facts and about available resources and assistance (Miller et al., 2000). Only about 10% of older people with depression receive any type of treatment or intervention. Thus, when older adults are suicidal, they are much more likely to be sure of their intent to die, to develop a very specific plan, and to use highly lethal methods.

Early detection and prevention of suicide in older adults have not been a public health priority. More than 70% of elderly Americans who commit suicide have visited their family physician in the month before their death, 40% within the last week, and 20% on the day they died (National Alliance for the Mentally Ill, 2003). Primary care providers often fail to recognize the warning signs for suicide in this population, including suicide wishes, hopelessness, helplessness, futility, and worthlessness. Physicians and family members of the older adult might believe that depression is an inevitable aspect of growing old and might refuse to believe that the person could seriously consider taking his or her own life. Well-intentioned loved ones might have difficulty believing that mom or dad, grandma or grandpa could ever think about committing suicide and might ignore or minimize the warning signs.

Suicide among the elderly population is generally more accepted by society as a choice to make an intentional ending to a long and productive life. This might contribute to the reason why, although suicides are far less common in younger people, most people would say that teen and young adult suicide is more common. Suicide in the elderly population attracts less media and other attention.

In trying to figure out what places people at risk for suicide, it is also important to understand what protects them. Little is known for any age group about self-perceived reasons for living—what keeps people who think about suicide from moving from suicidal thoughts to suicidal behaviors. Older adults who have suicidal ideation but do not attempt are more likely than younger adults to report both child-related concerns and moral and/or religious objections as reasons for not completing. Older people are also somewhat more likely to list obligations to family in general as a reason for not carrying out a suicide (Miller et al., 2000). Thus, older people who contemplate suicide might never move to behaviors because of strong moral injunctions and a strong sense of responsibility to family members. Those who are able to move past those injunctions to the point of suicidal behaviors appear to have strong motivations to make their attempt a lethal one.

Just as with all segments of the population, suicide in the older adult population is underreported. Many of the methods that are used by this age group make it difficult to determine cause of death. For example, elderly people may take overdoses of prescription medication, mix drugs, fail to take medications, or starve themselves. In these instances, family members often advocate for the official cause of death to be listed as accidental.

Although the older adult population has the highest risk of any age group, within this population, there is a wide range of variability in suicide risk. The most consistent demographic factors associated with suicide in the older adult population are gender, race, and age. As is true for all other age groups, males have considerably higher risk, with more

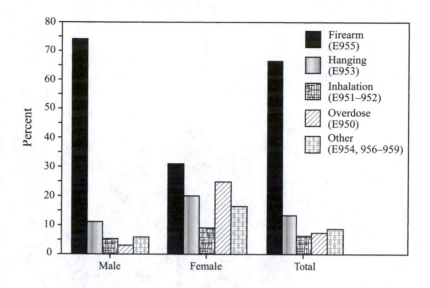

FIGURE 5.1   Percentage of Suicides among Persons Aged ≥ 65 Years, by Sex and Method—United States, 1980–1992. (Identified through *International Classification of Diseases, Ninth Revision*, codes on death certificates.)

Source: www.cdc.gov/mmwr/preview/mmwrhtml/00039937.htm.

than six male completions for every female completion, and males accounting for about 84% of completions in this age group. Suicide rates for elderly males are 40.2 per 100,000, compared with 6.0 per 100,000 for females. Again, similar to other age groups, Caucasians also kill themselves at higher rates in this age group as well. The suicide rate for Caucasians over 65 is 21.0 per 100,000, compared to 8.3 per 100,000 for all other ethnic groups. Finally, within the subgroup of older people, suicide risk increases with age. The suicide rate for Caucasian males over 85 is nearly 70 per 100,000, making this group by far the most likely of any demographic group to commit suicide.

Carlton was a World War I veteran who returned to the United States after the war, got married, and settled down. He worked intermittently, often struggling to find work, but eventually found a job as a local veteran's service officer. His wife Justine worked in a hardware store. The couple tried for many years to have children, but they were unsuccessful. However, they had many friends and an active social life. When Justine was 75, she was diagnosed with breast cancer, and she died within the year. Carlton seemed lost without her, after having spent more than 50 years with her by his side. He struggled along quietly, however, and tried to spend time with his remaining friends. One by one, his friends became ill and died. Last year, at age 92, Carlton found that he could no longer live alone. He had relied on a local bus service to get him around for the few errands he needed to run, and he

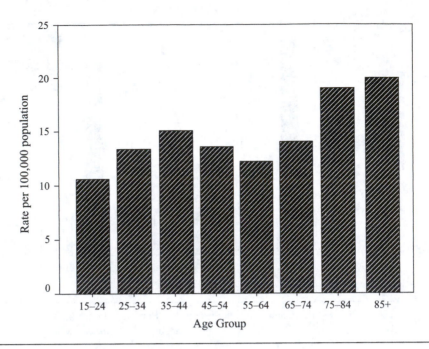

FIGURE 5.2   United States suicide rates by age, 1998 data.

Source: Computed from *2001 Statistical Abstract of the United States.*

made use of Meals on Wheels. Twice a week, a service came in to help him with some minimal household chores and to assist him with his bath. Last year, however, it all became too much for him, and he decided that he needed to move into an assisted living facility. Carlton was still very mentally active and quite capable physically, considering his age. The facility had promised him a lot of activities, and he was looking forward to making some new friends and enjoying some of the social life at the nursing home without the responsibility of caring for his own place. When he came to the home, however, he was soon horribly disappointed. He complained that everyone around him was "old and tired," no one was able to engage in lively political conversations, which he used to enjoy, and the staff treated everyone like babies. Even the activities that were planned he found to be juvenile and not intellectually or socially stimulating. After a year, he started thinking about suicide. He thought he had given the nursing home experience a "fair shake" and found it to be unsatisfactory. When he looked forward in his life, he could see only more of the same and a future in which he became as empty and tired as the people around him. He decided that he didn't want to die that way, old and feeble, and that he would take actions to end his life with dignity before he became unable to do so. It was not difficult for Carlton to hoard the necessary medication. Over the course of several months, he simply slipped a random pill or two from a pill tray into his pocket, doing it infrequently enough that he did not raise suspicion or get caught. One day, when he had collected more than enough pills to kill himself, he spent the afternoon writing a list of how he wanted his few possessions to be distributed, made a detailed description of how and where he wanted to be buried (in a plot he had reserved, next to Justine's), and took out his Bible and prayed. That evening after dinner, he went to bed early, held onto his picture of Justine, and took the pills. The next morning, the nursing home staff commented that they were not particularly surprised by his choice, although they were saddened, because he had "livened up the place."

Carlton had many of the risk factors associated with suicide in the elderly population. As you read the following pages, try to identify what put Carlton at specific risk.

Developmental Considerations of Older Adult Suicide Risk

According to Erikson (1968), people in the older adult stage of development must work to achieve ego integrity rather than despair. Ego integrity, similar to Maslow's concept of self-actualization, allows individuals to feel fulfilled in their lives and not

BOX 5.1 • *Myths About Suicide in the Elderly Population*

- MYTH: Because older adults have successfully navigated earlier developmental stages without committing suicide, they have the coping skills to navigate this last stage as well.
  - FACT: Risk among elderly people is greatly enhanced by depression, loneliness, and social isolation. Older people who are widowed or divorced have suicide rates approximately three times those of their partnered counterparts.
- MYTH: Depression in older adults is almost inevitable. Therefore, there is little that can be done to prevent depression or suicide that may result from it.
  - FACT: About 18% of people over age 65 suffer from clinical depression, but there are very effective treatments. Through medication, counseling, and electroconvulsive therapy, about 80% of people with clinical depression can be effectively treated.
- MYTH: Retirement is a time of relaxation and contentment. Retired adults do not have the stressors of working adults.
  - FACT: Common stressors for older adults include changes in lifestyle and financial status, caring for grandchildren, caring for a sick spouse, death of relatives or close friends, deterioration of health, physical disabilities or chronic illness, worries about being able to live independently, and concerns about institutionalization.
- MYTH: Medical illness, which is common among older adults, causes an increase in suicidality.
  - FACT: As you will read in Chapter 8, some illnesses (HIV/AIDS, some types of cancer, Huntington's disease, and multiple sclerosis) have been linked to higher rates of suicide, but most other diseases have not. It appears to be how one handles the illness— and coexisting depression and anxiety—that increases risk, not the illness itself.
- MYTH: Suicide in older adults is typically a rational decision that is not related to mental health. It is based on a rational belief that life should be ended before one becomes mentally or physically deteriorated.
  - FACT: Old age, in and of itself, is not considered by most people to be a reason for self-destruction. Geriatric depression, which is often the cause of such "rational decisions," is highly treatable.

have major or debilitating regrets about the course that they have taken in their lives. This inner reflection moves people in this stage toward a stance as a philosopher, growing in wisdom through life experiences.

Other developmental theories of aging suggest different developmental tasks:

- Disengagement theory proposes a progressive process of physical, psychological, and social withdrawal from the wider world. Although this theory has been widely defended, the current state of the research does not show evidence to support this theory. It remains a philosophical stance
- Activity theory holds that as disengagement occurs, so too does activity level. With this decline may come decreased feelings of satisfaction, contentment, and happiness. Activity theorists believe that the majority of healthy older people maintain fairly stable levels of activity, with engagement or disengagement depending on past life patterns rather than any inherent or inevitable aging process, but for those who disengage, depression is the almost inevitable result.
- Role exit theory maintains that opportunities for older people to remain socially useful are severely limited as they age, with work roles diminishing from retirement, parenting roles limited, and spousal or relationship roles ending with the death of a spouse.
- Social exchange theory holds that people enter into relationships because they derive rewards from them. In this view, older people have limited ability to engage in new relationships because of a deterioration in their bargaining positions.

Although all of these theories have some strengths and limitations and none can definitively describe old age, they all offer a developmental context for understanding suicide risk in older people. The main point is that there is nothing inherent in the aging process that puts people at risk, but aging and the developmental tasks associated with it, when managed poorly, can significantly impair psychological health, which in turn increases suicide risk.

Specific Risk Factors in Older People

Depending on the researcher's perspective, different factors have been identified as contributing to the high rates of suicide in the elderly population. For example, behavioral scientists argue that depression and other mental health issues are the main contributors to suicide in older people, while sociologists focus on increasing fears of dependency, institutionalization, and unwanted invasive care. Others have argued that a decrease in self-worth and social forces that diminish the value of older persons are the major contributors, while still others attribute high rates of suicide to increased availability of handguns, the most common method for suicide in the elderly population (Kennedy & Tanenbaum, 2000). Just as with suicide risk in all ages, there is undoubtedly a complex combination of many factors that contribute to suicide risk. Overall, people who have survived until old age have a lifetime accumulation of coping methods, social supports, and other methods that would allow them to handle many crises, including those that might lead other, less experienced individuals to suicide (McIntosh, 1995). Suicidal crises are most likely to exist in the elderly population when circumstances or mental health issues overwhelm a person's capacity to cope. The breakdown, failure, or exhaustion of the accumulated resources typically has to occur somewhat simultaneously for an older person who has led a relatively mentally healthy life to reach his or her breaking point and consider suicide.

It is worth remembering that suicide risk in the older population remains (as in other age groups) a primarily Caucasian male phenomenon; 84% of completed suicides in people over 65 are by Caucasian males, with an even higher percentages for people over age 85. The risk factors that are outlined in the remaining pages of this chapter do not make distinctions between males and females (or Caucasians and other races, for that matter) because such information does not exist in the research. Clearly, females and people from non-Caucasian racial groups in this age bracket have some protective factors that mitigate these risk factors, but it is not clear what these are (other than the general listing earlier in this chapter) or how they interact with existing risk factors in some segments of the population. Therefore, as with all risk factors for all age groups, the factors outlined below are meant to stimulate thinking about risk and are not a definitive list.

Biological Risk Factors

The role of specific physical illnesses in suicide ideation and suicide behaviors will be discussed in Chapter 8. However, the role of specific biochemical changes in later life does not always occur in the context of a physical illness. For example, elderly people with suicide risk show lower levels of serotonin and dopamine at their synapses than do their nonsuicidal peers. (This difference between suicidal and nonsuicidal persons is true for all age groups.) Malone and Mann (2003) noted that there is a connection between impaired serotonergic function and increased risk for suicide and suicide attempts. They also raised the question of whether some individuals might be biologically predisposed to have a reduction in serotonergic function and therefore are biologically at higher risk for suicide and suicide attempts. Research also has raised the possibility that aging in and of itself might adversely affect serotonin levels, making older people biologically more at risk than are younger people (Duncan & Hensler, 2002; Stillion & McDowell, 1996). Thus, it is possible (although this is still in the investigatory stages) that the biological process of aging itself increases the possibility of suicide risk, although this does not explain the gender and racial differences in suicide completions that are so evident in this age group.

Emotional Risk Factors

Psychological autopsy studies demonstrate strong links between suicide and psychiatric disorders in elderly people. A consistent body of research over the last 50 years has found that up to 90% of older people who commit suicide had a diagnosable mental health disorder at the time of their death (Conwell, 2001). The most common are depression and alcoholism and substance abuse. Psychotic illnesses, personality disorders, and anxiety disorders appear to play a less significant role, and the role of dementia and delirium in suicide risk remains unclear.

Older people who commit suicide are more likely than people at other ages to have suffered from depression (particularly hopelessness). Although depression/hopelessness is a key factor in suicide risk for all age groups, impulsivity also plays an important role in suicide of young people. Older people do not tend to engage in impulsive suicides, and therefore a higher percentage of suicides in elderly persons can be linked to depression. Different studies produce differing percentages of completed elderly suicides that are linked to depression, from a high of 90% (Kennedy & Tanenbaum, 2000) to 80% to a low of 63% (Harwood, Hawton, Hope, & Jacoby, 2001). Regardless of the number, depression does appear to substantially increase risk. Unfortunately, fewer than one quarter of elderly persons diagnosed with depression receive psychological or psychiatric interventions (some studies show just 10%), and many more go undiagnosed (Brown, Lapane, & Luisi, 2002).

Most studies do not differentiate between bipolar, current episode depressed, and unipolar depression. However, the frequency of depressive episodes, whether in the context of bipolar disorder or as a part of unipolar depression, is related to suicide risk, with people who have had more episodes of depression at higher risk (Harwood et al., 2001). Bellini and Matteucci (2001) noted that the type of depression that an elderly person has might be related to outcome. They found that those with late-onset depression (people who became depressed late in life but had good premorbid functioning prior to the depression) were overall more responsive to medical intervention and, if properly cared for, were less likely to commit suicide than those with early-onset, lifelong depression. However, if late-onset individuals were not identified and no psychiatric intervention occurred, individuals with late-onset depression were at higher risk for suicide than were those with early-onset depression. It appears that people who develop depression later in life have fewer coping skills for handling the depression than do those who have battled with depression on and off throughout their lives.

Alcoholism and substance abuse disorders are relatively common in older adults, particularly males, and up to 16% of older adults have alcohol use disorders (Menninger, 2002). In about one third of the cases, alcohol and substance abuse has late onset and typically begins after a series of changes or losses (e.g., retirement, decline in economic status, deaths of loved ones) in an attempt to reduce psychological, physical, or emotional stress. However, alcoholism and substance abuse is often overlooked in the elderly population, and as few as 20% of elderly alcohol abusers are correctly diagnosed by physicians (Adams, Magruder-Habib, Trued, & Broome, 1992). Alcoholism increases the risk of suicide, and among older people, drinking more than three alcoholic beverages per day was found to be a significant predictor of completed suicide (Conwell et al., 2002). However, alcoholism appears to be a factor in fewer suicides in the elderly population than in the younger age groups. Substance abuse is also a problem among the elderly population, primarily in the form of prescription and over-the-counter medications. The increased risk of suicide for elderly people who abuse substances is little studied and not well understood. It is possible to speculate, however, that substance abuse can impair rational thinking, which contributes to suicide risk.

Cognitive Risk Factors

Just as with suicide in all age groups, elderly people who are suicidal often have limited abilities to develop and consider other possibilities. Limited problem-solving skills and reduced coping skills are always risk factors in suicide. These reduced options may be a result of a lifetime of poor coping but more commonly are the result of a cognitive rigidity that develops in some older persons.

Environmental Risk Factors

Widows and widowers are two to three times more likely to attempt suicide than are married people, although some research suggests that living with another person versus living alone is not the deciding factor in suicide risk; rather, loneliness and isolation are what put people at risk (regardless of age), and it is simply that married people tend to be less lonely than those who are widowed (Seidlitz, Conwell, Duberstein, Cox, & Denning, 2001). Elderly people who are lonely appear to be at higher risk, and older people are more likely than younger people to list loneliness as a major reason to consider suicide, as well as financial problems, poor health, depression, alcohol problems, feelings of worthlessness, and isolation (Kennedy & Tanenbaum, 2000).

The notion of cumulative loss also has been suggested as an environmental risk factor for suicide in older populations. It is not so much the magnitude of any one particular loss, but the seemingly rapid succession of losses—retirement, deaths of friends and loved ones, loss of income, prestige, mobility, health—that allows insufficient time to grieve each loss, and the cumulative effects can lead to a hopeless depression (Stillion & McDowell, 1996).

It is important to mention that many life situations have been hypothesized to be related to suicide risk in the elderly population. Retirement, often anticipated by those who are not yet retired to be a carefree time of relaxation, can be extremely difficult, especially for those who received positive esteem and identity from their careers. The loss of financial freedom that often comes with retirement and old age also has been hypothesized as a suicide risk, particularly for older persons who live at or near the poverty line. Other life circumstances—widowhood, children moving away, diminishing independence (moving into a nursing home or in with adult children and their families), and failing health—all have been linked to suicide risk. It is important to note, however, that none of these life circumstances has been found, in and of itself, to be a significant predictor of suicide; only the person's attitude and beliefs about the event(s) are significant. Hopelessness and depression seem to be the only significant variables in predicting elderly suicide. Those who face new situations and challenges with emotional strength, intact coping skills and problem-solving ability, and a sense of hope are not at any increased risk for suicide. Those who face the challenges with hopelessness, despair, and depression find themselves at a high risk.

Recently, there has been some discussion in the literature about the ability of modern technology to extend life beyond a person's desire or ability to experience it. In what Kennedy and Tanenbaum called the "excesses of modern medicine," an older person may fear continuing to live over fearing death because the person dreads becoming a "prisoner of technology" (2000, p. 352). In these instances, elderly people might attempt suicide while they are still physically able to prevent a future over which they have no control. Clearly, this brings to the surface the topics of rational suicide and physician-assisted suicide. Both are beyond the scope of this book to cover fully, and both involve philosophical issues that are quite different from the typical suicide prevention, assessment, and treatment issues. A brief discussion follows.

Rational suicide and physician-assisted suicide both relate to client-initiated hastened death in people with chronic or terminal illnesses. They are extremely controversial subjects and have inspired much debate both in the scientific literature and in the popular media. In the 1990s, some stances were taken by professional associations and the government in response to an increasing desire among the public to explore these issues. Polls show that between 45% and 59% of Americans support physician-assisted suicide (Braun, Tanji, & Heck, 2001). In 1994, the National Association of Social Workers developed a policy statement that included the mandate that social workers explore rational suicide with terminally ill clients who bring up the issue. In 1994, with the approval of the Death with Dignity Act, Oregon became the first state to legally allow physician-assisted suicide. In 1996, two separate U.S. circuit courts of appeals ruled that states could not prohibit physician-assisted suicide, although the Supreme Court later overturned these rulings, determining that it was up to states to decide what their laws would be (Werth & Holdwick, 2000). The law came under attack by the U.S. Attorney General, who threatened to revoke the licenses of physicians who assisted with suicides, but a federal appeals court reaffirmed the Oregon law in May 2004. In January of 2006, the U.S. Supreme Court voted 6 to 3 in favor of upholding the Oregon law. In addition, the Supreme Court previously had determined that individuals can decide to refuse or end life-sustaining treatments, noting that there is a difference between letting someone to die (e.g., not intervening with life-sustaining treatments) and helping someone to die (e.g., physician-assisted suicide).

Some studies have shown that many terminally ill patients want to discuss the possibility of euthanasia and have assurances that this is an option available to them. However, very few ever take this option. Thus, it appears that the possibility of euthanasia becomes an "escape valve" for these people. That is, by having assisted death as an option, it no longer becomes a pressing issue, and the person can live more fully in the moment, without worrying as much about what will happen in the future. People who promote rational and physician-assisted suicide argue that these choices allow dignity and self-determination.

However, concerns over hastened death have been raised by people who believe that individuals who request aid in dying might be doing so because of depression or another treatable mental disorder or even external coercion. Arguments against hastened death also have been based on religious or ethical grounds. Still others make social arguments, stating that allowing these decisions to be made individually is not good social policy. Many physicians argue that physician-assisted suicide violates the Hippocratic Oath to "above all, do no harm," and the American Medical Association has come out against physician-assisted suicide. Within the mental health professions, rational suicide and physician-assisted suicide are controversial, and many professionals come down strongly on one side of the issue or the other, while many others find themselves caught in the middle, facing competing ethical choices (helping clients to maintain dignity and autonomy versus preserving life). As you work with clients who are terminally or chronically ill, you will need to know the laws in your state regarding rational suicide, and if it is legal, you will need to make an individual decision about whether or not you can work with a client who is making such a decision.

Methods, Warning Signs, and Triggering Conditions for Suicide in the Elderly Population

Older people who want to commit suicide typically use very lethal methods that do not allow for last-minute interventions. Most who complete do not tend to engage in "cry for help" activities or warning signs that would allow other people to recognize the enhanced risk. Because of the link between depression (hopelessness) and suicide risk, it appears that depression is the most significant warning sign, as is an increased amount of alcohol consumption. However, although there are few warning signs, there are some triggering conditions that can be attended to, including all of the life circumstances listed above (e.g., retirement, reduced income, medical illness, loss, and diminished independence). Whenever an elderly person meets these circumstances with a depressed or defeated attitude, intervention is a must.

One final triggering condition for suicide in the elderly population is entrance into a suicide pact. Although suicide pacts are relatively rare, older adults have the highest rates of suicide pacts in the United States (followed by adolescents). Spouses are most likely to enter into suicide pacts, particularly after one spouse has significant loss of function. Just as with adolescent suicide pacts, there appears to be a dominant and a passive member of the dyad, who are extremely interdependent on each other.

BOX 5.2 • *Suicide Risk Factors in the Elderly Population*

- Biological risk factors
  - Reduced serotonin
- Emotional risk factors
  - Mental conditions, primarily:
    - Depression (hopelessness)
    - Alcoholism/substance abuse
  - Loss of coping skills, problem-solving abilities
- Environmental risk factors
  - Loneliness
  - Cumulative loss
  - Life changes:
    - Retirement
    - Loss of friends, income, prestige, independence

Double suicide attempts are almost always fatal, as highly lethal methods are typically employed.

Summary

Suicide rates are the highest for the older population (age 65 years and older) than for any other age group. Suicide in this age bracket remains a primarily Caucasian male phenomenon, although it is important never to minimize or ignore warning signs and risk factors in other segments of the population. Just as with younger people, a complex interplay of risk factors must be considered, and the relationships of these risk factors with protective factors that one has accumulated over a lifetime are poorly understood. Major risk factors (besides gender and race) include older age (for Caucasian males, risk continues to increase as age increases), depression (particularly hopelessness and loneliness), substance abuse (prescription drugs or alcohol), and a rigid cognitive mindset that does not allow for the problem-solving necessary to face new challenges. For older adults, the environmental stressors that come with adjustment to old age appear to be particularly challenging, such as loss of work, financial burdens, death of loved ones, and loss of independent living.

6

Suicide and Suicide Risk in Multicultural Populations

Suicide risk is not universally the same. As you read in Chapters 3–5, there are differences based on age. In Chapters 6–9, you will read about differences based on other factors: ethnicity, mental illness, physical illness, and other high-risk characteristics. This chapter highlights differences—and similarities—in suicide risk of the four major U.S. ethnic groups.

By sheer numbers, completed suicide is primarily a Caucasian male phenomenon. Even in terms of percentages, a higher percentage of Caucasian males complete suicide than any other demographic group. Nevertheless, it is extremely dangerous and unwise to ignore the suicide risk in other cultural or ethnic groups. Suicide rates are high in several ethnic minority groups. For example, Native Americans (both American Indians and Eskimos) have higher suicide rates than the national averages, and there is some evidence that the risk for these populations continues to grow (Group for the Advancement of Psychiatry, 1989). In other populations, suicide is on the rise. Suicide rates among African American adolescent males increased by 114% between 1980 and 1995 (Centers for Disease Control and Prevention, 1998). This is the highest rate increase of any population and suggests that the gap between the suicide rates of Caucasian and African American male adolescents is narrowing (Joe & Kaplan, 2001). Finally, for some cultural and ethnic groups, there are extremely high rates of suicide attempts. Several studies have found that the Hispanic population has the highest levels among all ethnic groups of lifetime suicide attempts (Vega, Gil, Zimmerman, & Warheit, 1993). Thus, although raw numbers—and even percentages—of suicides for many cultural groups do not approach the suicide risk of Caucasian males, there is evidence that (1) suicide risk is high among some subgroups; (2) suicide risk is increasing at an alarming rate among some populations; and (3) suicidal ideation and attempts are high within some cultures.

In determining levels of suicide risk, cultural factors must be taken into consideration. Aside from differences in rates of completed or attempted suicides among the various cultural groups, there are differences in suicide attitudes, levels of acceptability, and appropriate intervention strategies (Range et al., 1999). Some cultures have strong cultural and/or religious injunctions against suicide. Although this can be a protective factor, it also can prevent individuals from reaching out and seeking help. When they do reach out, their suicidal statements might be minimized or shut down by others. Thus, people from some cultural groups might not receive the suicide prevention, assessment, and interventions that they require. Some cultures have strong negative beliefs about the mental health system and are, in general, unlikely to utilize services that are available. When people from these cultures are overwhelmed by life crises or mental illnesses, they might turn to suicide in desperation, given the lack of other options. Finally, some cultures have risk factors inherent in them (e.g., high rates of poverty and alcoholism among some Native American tribes) that put their members at high risk for suicide.

Although there is general agreement in the literature and among practitioners that cultural consideration must be a part of suicide prevention, risk assessment, and interventions, surprisingly little information is available on suicide in a multicultural context. What information is available has been released very recently and remains rather sketchy and inconclusive. Thus, while it is clear that cultural norms can influence suicide risk and suicidal behavior (Orbach, 1997), it is less clear what mechanisms are at play that influence risk in the various cultures and how they can be best used for suicide prevention (Range et al., 1999).

Finally, before beginning a discussion of suicide risk in the four major U.S. cultural groups (African Americans, Hispanic American, Native Americans, and Asian Americans), it is important to remember that any attempts to paint a broad picture of these cultural groups are rather strained at best. Although there is certainly between-group variation in suicide risk, which will be discussed in the sections that follow, there also is much within-group variation within each of these cultural groups. Therefore, mental health practitioners can use this information as offering a context for suicide risk, but *individual factors must always be the overriding principles used in considering suicide risk and possible interventions.*

Suicide Risk in Hispanic Americans

Hispanic Americans are the largest and fastest-growing ethnic minority group in the United States, with approximately 38.8 million individuals, making up more than 13% of the population (U.S. Census Bureau, 2000). Mexican Americans and Puerto Ricans make up more than two thirds of the Hispanic American population, the remaining one third represent a large number of countries of origin, including Cuba, South and Central American countries, Spain, and Portugal. Given the diversity of this population and the varying suicide rates within it, it is impossible to determine a suicide rate for the Hispanic American population (Range et al., 1999). Rather, it is more appropriate to discuss suicide rates for the various subgroups. The rates for the largest groups are discussed briefly below.

Suicide Rates in Hispanic American Populations

Suicide rates vary within the Hispanic culture. Attempts have been made to generalize suicide rates for groups that have immigrated to the United States, based on the suicide rates in the home countries. For example, the Latino countries with the five highest suicide rates (in descending order) are Cuba, Spain, Puerto Rico, El Salvador, and Portugal. The Latino countries with the lowest suicide rates (in ascending order) are Peru, Nicaragua, Guatemala, Brazil, and Colombia (Canetto & Lester, 1995). However, as the following paragraphs demonstrate, suicide rates in home countries are not necessarily applicable to rates of immigrants once they move to the United States or to successive generations.

Suicide attempts appear to be generally very high in the Hispanic American female population (21% lifetime prevalence), more than twice the rate in the Caucasian (10.4%) or African American (10.8%) female population. Hispanic American adolescent females are also twice as likely as their Caucasian or African American counterparts to require medical attention after a suicide attempt (Centers for Disease Control and Prevention, 1996). More than 50% of Hispanic American adolescent females report intermittent suicidal thoughts, and those who report a suicide attempt are between six and eight times more likely to make another attempt compared to those who have never attempted (Zayas, Kaplan, Turner, Romano, & Gonzalez-Ramos, 2000). Each successive suicide attempt increases the chance of a completed suicide, placing these young women at an ever-increasing risk of suicide.

Mexican Americans have a suicide rate that is approximately half that of their non-Hispanic Caucasian counterparts. However, the suicide rate climbs with each successive generation following immigration to the United States (Hovey & King, 1997). It has been hypothesized that the low rate of suicides grows as Mexican immigrants become more acculturated to the United States and take on more mainstream characteristics, moving the suicide rate in the direction of that of the United States in general (Range et al., 1999). The ratio of male to female suicide is 6.3 to 1 (Men's Health America, 2002). Mexicans residing in Mexico have suicide rates that are approximately one fourth those in the United States (3.2 per 100,000 compared to 11.9 per 100,000 in the United States) (United Nations, 1998).

Mexican American adolescents have higher rates of suicidal ideation and suicide attempts than do their non-Hispanic Caucasian counterparts. Rates of suicidal ideation are approximately 25% (e.g., the percentage of Mexican American youths reporting that they had thought about killing themselves on one or more days during the past week), which is approximately twice that of Caucasian youth (Canino & Roberts, 2001).

The *Puerto Rican* population has two major segments: those who live in Puerto Rico and those who live on the mainland. Suicide rates for those living in Puerto Rico are about one- half those of the general U.S. population (Mental Health and Well-Being, 2002). Puerto Ricans have one of the highest ratio of male to female suicide: 10.4 to 1 (Men's Health America, 2002). For those who live on the mainland, recent research indicates that rates of completed and attempted suicides for Puerto Ricans are higher than those for either Mexican Americans or Cuban Americans (Ungemack & Guarnaccia, 1998). However, most of the research on Puerto Rican suicide is more than a decade old and was conducted in New York City, limiting its generalizability. In all populations in the New York City area, suicide rates are higher than the average for the rest of the country. Thus, the elevated rates among Puerto Rican males might be a result of the combination of ethnicity and location. Puerto Rican males in New York City have a suicide rate that is higher than the national average and 40% higher than the rates for African American or Caucasian males living in the same area. The rate is nearly three times higher than for Puerto Rican males living in Puerto Rico. The same holds true for Puerto Rican women, with those in New York City killing themselves at rates almost three times higher than those living in Puerto Rico. The majority of Puerto Ricans who killed themselves in New York City (87%) were born in Puerto Rico, suggesting that the process of acculturation to the mainland contributed to the suicide risk (Group for the Advancement of Psychiatry, 1989). However, other studies found no differences in suicide rates based on place of birth (Fernandez-Pol, 1986). The fact that all of this research was conducted in the 1980s makes it impossible to gain an understanding of the current status of suicide rates in the Puerto Rican population.

Cuban Americans in general have low rates of suicide. This is quite a contrast to Cubans; residents of Cuba have suicide rates approximately twice that of the U.S. general population (20.3% in 1996) (United Nations, 1998). Although suicide rates for Cuban Americans are low, there is one segment of the Cuban American population with particularly high suicide rates: Elderly Cuban American males have suicide rates 1.67 times that of older Americans in general (Llorente, Eisdorfer, Loewenstein, & Zarate, 1996). The male:female ratio among Cuban Americans is very high, three times higher than that in the non-Hispanic Caucasian population. Rates of suicidal ideation, typically higher in the Hispanic American population, are not elevated in the Cuban American population compared with their non-Hispanic Caucasian counterparts. In general, the Cuban American population does not fit the Hispanic American profile with regard to suicide risk. Cuba is the only country of origin where suicide rates are higher than those in the United States, and suicidal ideation and attempts are not higher in the adolescent population. Thus, Cuban American suicides are a primarily male phenomenon, and older males are at the highest risk. This has been attributed to some very distinct characteristics of the Cuban American population (e.g., high socioeconomic status, high education) that make it unique (Canino & Roberts, 2001).

Maria was a 17-year-old first-generation Mexican American, living on the outskirts of Los Angeles. Her father and mother had come to the United States when Maria was just seven years old. Her parents and older siblings worked hard to make a life for the family in their newly adopted home. Neither of her parents spoke any English, and both worked for long hours at low-paying jobs. Nevertheless, they never regretted their move to the United States, where they thought Maria and her younger siblings would have many newfound opportunities. Maria believed that her parents were too entrenched in the customs and mannerisms of the "old country." She was embarrassed by their actions, and she did not want to look or act "like a Mexican." During her early teen years, she became more and more withdrawn. She spent long hours in her room, flipping through fashion magazines and dreaming about the type of family that she wished she had—parents who were more liberal, more understanding, and more willing to let her be who she was.

As Maria became more and more depressed, her mother responded by trying to talk to her more. Her father, on the other hand, became more and more angry. He shouted that he and his family had sacrificed much to give Maria the kind of life she had, and she should be grateful rather than acting like a disrespectful and spoiled gringa. Maria was caught between two cultures, the Mexican culture of her parents that she found too domineering, stifling, and controlling and the American culture that she saw in magazines and looked at "from the outside" at her school. Her mother tried to get Maria's older cousin, Benita, to talk some sense into her. At 19, Benita was perceived by her family as bridging the gap between the two cultures. But when Benita talked with Maria, it was clear to Maria that Benita's answer was just to "obey her parents and find a boy who will marry you." When she thought ahead to a life married to a Mexican American man who would be "just like her father," Maria couldn't bear it. On the day after her sixteenth birthday, Maria slit her wrists and had to be taken to the emergency room. When she spoke with a social worker, she stated that this was her first suicide attempt, but the reality was quite different. Twice before, Maria had taken an overdose of pills, but neither attempt was life-threatening. She had never told her parents.

After the suicide attempt that required medical attention, the social worker helped Maria to make an appointment with her school counselor. Maria met with the school counselor several times but denied that she continued to be suicidal. The school counselor tried to get Maria involved in several school activities in which she could connect with the other students, many of whom were Mexican by birth and living in similar circumstances. Maria showed little interest in or aptitude for any of these activities.

As her seventeenth birthday approached, Maria looked back on the past year since her suicide attempt and realized that nothing had changed for her. As she assessed her situation, she realized with some finality that nothing ever would change and that she was condemned to a miserable life. She had learned from her previous attempts through overdose what it would take to kill her, and this time she was determined to "do it right." On the day after her seventeenth birthday, one year to the day after her last attempt, Maria overdosed and killed herself.

Maria's suicide carried not only the angst of a teenager who had depression, limited ability for problem solving, and hopelessness about the future (risk factors that were outlined in Chapter 3), but also the complicating factor of acculturation. As you read through the next section, consider the risk factors that apply to Maria and how a mental health professional might want to work with Maria and her family to bridge the two cultures and assist Maria.

Specific Risk Factors in Hispanic American Populations

As with all ethnic groups, mental illness and substance abuse increase the risk for suicide in the Hispanic American population, and hopelessness has been found to be a significant risk factor for suicide in Hispanic Americans. Additionally, low socioeconomic status and high rates of unemployment or underemployment, leading to severely impoverished living conditions, appear to contribute to suicide risk (Marrero, 1998). For Hispanic people who have entered the United States illegally, access to mental health care is extremely limited. In addition, even for those who have entered legally, intimidation and confusion surrounding the health care system in general can limit access. Other factors that have been identified are the stressors of a language barrier, discrimination, poverty, and low educational levels (Group for the Advancement of Psychiatry, 1989). Fewer suicide attempts are reported among middle-class Hispanic adolescent females than among those of lower socioeconomic status (Ng, 1996). However, it is clear that these factors in and of themselves do not increase suicide risk, given the high proportion of the Hispanic population who face language barriers, poverty, and discrimination and the relatively low rates of suicide among this population.

Issues of acculturation contribute to suicide risk, and Hispanic Americans from all countries, with the exception of Cuba, have higher suicide rates in the United States than in their countries of origin (Zayas et al., 2000). The interplay of acculturation with suicide risk, however, is not fully understood. It is clear that intergenerational conflict is a contributing factor. For example, among Hispanic female adolescents, as in the case of Maria, intergenerational conflict, particularly between an adolescent acculturated daughter and a foreign-born immigrant parent, has been shown to increase stress that has been associated with higher risk of suicide attempts (Ng, 1996). It is clear that acculturation and generational status are important factors in understanding risk, but how they interact with other risk factors is little understood.

Specific Protective Factors in Hispanic American Populations

Several protective factors have been identified that contribute to the overall lower risk of suicide in the Hispanic American population. The emphasis on family, including extended family, provides social support that has been linked to decreased suicide risk in many populations. Although the family can provide a protective factor, dysfunctional family environments can increase suicide risk. Cultures that are dependent on nuclear and extended families for support have a dual-edged sword. The family provides an important safety mechanism through its strong social support. Conversely, however, a dysfunctional family—one that is neglectful, abusive, or violent—can elevate risk even higher because there is a cultural imperative of what families "should" be. Additionally, when traditional, patriarchal family values are challenged, as when the traditional ways of immigrant parents meet with the acculturated stance of their children, the stressors on the family can increase.

A second protective factor is the influence of the Roman Catholic Church. A strong opponent of suicide, the Church is thought to be a buffer against suicide, as is the role of religion in general. Finally, the Latino concept of *fatalismo* has been linked to a lowered suicide risk. Fatalismo is the belief that divine providence rules the world and individuals have little or no control over their life circumstances. It has been argued that fatalistically accepting one's life circumstances, rather than attempting to change or control the uncontrollable, might lessen suicide risk (Range et al., 1999), although this has not been systematically studied.

Because of the strong influence of family and religion, clinicians who work with Hispanic clients on suicide prevention or intervention should be certain to include both of these elements in their counseling. A narrow, individualistic focus, common to much of the mental health system, would in most cases be inappropriate. However, even extending the intervention to the nuclear family might not be sufficient. Friends, extended family, and church members might need to be included and used as a source of support for suicide prevention (Range et al., 1999). The most important issue in working with Hispanic American clients in suicide prevention is for the clinician to enter into the client's subjective world as fully as possible and to use all of the resources that are available to keep the client alive and well.

Suicide Risk in African Americans

African Americans constitute the second largest ethnic minority group in the United States, with approximately 36.4 million individuals, making up 12.9% of the population (U.S. Census Bureau, 2000). As a group, African Americans have a suicide rate that is lower than that of the Caucasian population, and suicide is not among the top ten causes of death for African Americans as a whole (it is number ten overall for Caucasians). For men, there are 1.75 completed suicides by Caucasians for every 1 completion by African Americans. For women, the difference is nearly 2 to 1 (Range et al., 1999). Of all leading causes of death, suicide is the only one for which African Americans have a lower mortality rate than Caucasians (Allen & Farley, 1986).

The gender paradox in suicide—that females make more attempts but males have more completions—holds true for the African American population. However, the gap in completion rates between males and females is much more pronounced in the African American population than in the general population. There are approximately six completed suicides by African American males for every suicide completion by an African American female, a considerably wider gap than the 4:1 ratio in the Caucasian population (Joe & Kaplan, 2001). In general, suicide attempts in the African American population are associated with young women, while suicide completions are associated with young men. Men account for 84% of completed suicides in the African American population, making African American females, as a group, a very low-risk category. (Of course, individual characteristics can put certain African American females at risk, and it is imperative that practitioners never assume low risk for any individual on the basis of a particular demographic characteristic.)

The overall age pattern that emerges when all races are combined (suicide risk, in general, increases with age) disappears when we look at the African American population. Within the African American population, the highest rates of suicide for men are among the 15- to 29-year-old age group, with suicide accounting for approximately 7–8% of all deaths (National Institute of Mental Health, 2002). For African American men, the rates of suicide "increase sharply in early childhood, peak in young adulthood, decline steadily and level off in middle age, and finally increase moderately in late adulthood (Joe & Kaplan, 2001, p. 107).

For African American adolescents, suicide risk increased throughout the 1980s and 1990s. Between 1980 and 1995, the suicide rate for African American youths increased from 2.1 to 4.5 per 100,000. Because of the sharp increase in rates, the suicide risk for African American teens is quickly approaching the risk for Caucasian teens. However, in the years since 1995, there appears to be a leveling off of the suicide rate for African American teens, and, more recently, even a trend toward a decline. Time will tell whether this decline holds or simply represents a temporary reduction.

The most common method for suicide among African American men is firearms, and research has demonstrated a correlation between gun ownership and African American firearm suicide (Kaplan & Geling, 1998). Firearm-related suicides accounted for 96% of the increase in the suicide rate during the 1980s and 1990s for African Americans aged 10–19 years (Centers for Disease Control, 1998). Suicide rates for African Americans vary by region, and the largest increase occurred in the South

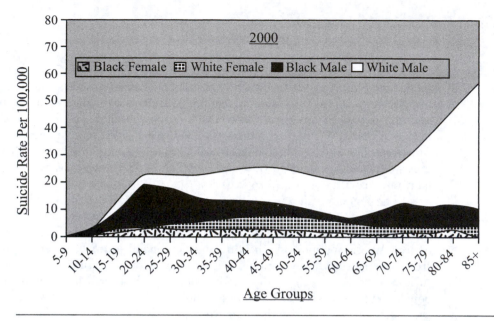

FIGURE 6.1   U.S. Suicide Rates by Age, Gender, and Racial Group.

Source: National Institute of Mental Health. U.S. Suicide Rates by Age, Gender, and Racial Group. Bethesda (MD): National Institute of Mental Health, National Institutes of Health, U.S. Department of Health and Human Services; 2002. http://www.nimh.nih.gov/suicideresearch/suichart.cfm.

(a 214% increase from 1980 to 1995) (Centers for Disease Control, and Prevention, 1998).

Suicide Risk in African American Men

Although suicide risk varies from person to person, in general, African American males are at much higher risk than their female counterparts. Very little is known about this elevated risk, which is most prominent in young men. There is little research or literature about the mental health of young African American men in general. Although always a concern for the mental health profession, this lack of knowledge and understanding exacerbates the difficulty in understanding suicide risk for African American young adults. It becomes even more difficult to uncover what led to an increased risk because young African American men underutilize mental health services. In one large-scale study of young African American men, 14.3% reported suicidal ideation at some point in their lives, and 5.3% reported at least one attempt. Approximately two thirds of study participants who reported a lifetime suicidal ideation or a previous attempt had a history of a mental or substance disorder. However, only 18% of study participants received mental health services at the time of their most recent attempt (Ialongo et al., 2002). Thus, it appears that, in general, young African American men who contemplate or attempt suicide are less likely than their Caucasian counterparts to have a mental health or substance disorder. Additionally, they are less likely to utilize mental health services.

In Ialongo and colleagues' study (2002), the largest one to date of suicide risk in the African American male population, the most common psychiatric diagnoses for African American males who contemplate or attempt suicide are major depression, antisocial personality disorder, conduct disorder, attention deficit hyperactivity disorder, alcohol dependence/abuse, and substance abuse. Interestingly, the affective disorders were more likely to precede the suicide attempt, whereas the alcohol and substance use disorder were more likely to occur after the initial suicide attempt. Although prevention efforts are difficult with this population, given the lack of utilization of mental health services, it is clear that prevention must include screening for affective and substance use disorders. Additionally, since approximately one third of participants who reported suicidal ideation went on to make a suicide attempt, it is important to assess suicidal ideation as well as previous attempts. Finally, mental health practitioners must reassess the mental health services that are provided. If services are available but not utilized, then we cannot lay blame at the feet of those who do not access the system. Rather, we must consider what changes and alterations must be made to make our services more appealing to those who need it most.

Suicide Risk in African American Women

African American women have the lowest suicide risk of any segment of the population (Nisbet, 1996), and rates remain rather steady throughout the life cycle. Suicide rates for African American women are approximately 1.9 per 100,000, compared with the national average of 11.4 for men and women and 4.4 for women of all ethnic groups (Marion & Range, 2003). However, it is important to note that examinations of official suicide statistics have demonstrated that female African Americans have the highest rates of misclassification—that is, deaths that are inappropriately declared to be accidental or natural deaths rather than suicides (Young, Twomey, & Kaslow (2000); therefore, suicide rates for African American women might be artificially lowered. Nevertheless, even high rates of misclassification cannot account entirely for the low rates, and it appears that African American women are indeed at low risk in general.

Because of their low suicide rates, African American women have been studied to determine whether there are any specific buffering factors that, if isolated, could be applied to other segments of the population. Within the African American female population, four significant and interrelated buffers have been identified: social/family support, unacceptable or negative views toward suicide, a belief that overcoming life's difficulties has made them strong, and a collaborative religious problem-solving style (Bender, 2000; Greening & Stoppelbein, 2002; Marion & Range, 2003).

Although social support has been identified as a protective factor for suicide in the general population, it appears to be particularly salient for African American women. Families have long been considered to serve as an important protective barrier against the racism and oppression of the dominant culture (Kaslow, Thompson, Brooks, & Twomey,

2000). Several studies have found that when African American women perceive their families as nonsupportive, they have much higher rates of depression and suicide ideation. Perceived support from friends and lovers also has been demonstrated to serve as a buffer for psychological stress (Kimbrough, Molock, & Walton, 1996; Marion & Range, 2003).

Within the African American community, religion serves as an important buffer for many people (Johnson, 1995), and in general, African American women tend to be more religious than men (Levin, Taylor, & Chatters, 1994). It has been argued that African American religious leaders typically hold the belief that suicide is extraordinarily sinful and pass that belief to their congregations (Early & Akers, 1993). Others have found that African American women are more likely than Caucasian women to endorse the statement "Religion sometimes restricts my actions" (Bender, 2000). These findings suggest that external control, primarily in the form of religious leaders and limitations on behaviors, limit the perception of suicide as an option for African American women. Other findings suggest that a strong internal religious motivation also serves to limit suicidality (e.g., Blaine & Crocker, 1995; Donahue & Benson, 1995; Neeleman, Wessely, & Lewis, 1998). African American women are, in general, likely to endorse beliefs that religion is important and to perceive that religion is integral to self (Greening & Stoppelbein, 2002). Within the African American female population, endorsements of religiosity have been linked to increased psychological well-being and decreased suicidal ideation. The commitment to religiosity as a core, fundamental belief emerges as the strongest protective factor against suicide for this population and supercedes depression and hopelessness as a predictor of suicide (Greening & Stoppelbein, 2002). Finally, using religion to cope with problems, a common problem-solving strategy in the African American female population, also has been linked to fewer depressive symptoms and decreased risk for suicide (Woods, Anotoni, Ironson, & Kling, 1999).

The negative views of suicide within the African American female population—that it is "not an option" or "completely unacceptable"—have been linked to religious beliefs and to the belief that strong women, who have overcome many difficulties in life, do not give up. There are large and significant differences between African American and Caucasian women regarding suicidal beliefs in general. African American women are much more likely to believe that suicide is never acceptable, even under specific circumstances, and is not an acceptable method to end an incurable illness or to end suffering from an incurable and terminal disease. Thus, even though rates of depression in African American women are similar to rates in Caucasian women, and although rates of many medical illnesses are even higher, there is a strongly held belief and social norm that acts as a buffer against suicide even when life is difficult and depressing (Bender, 2000).

Specific Risk Factors in the African American Population

Joe and Kaplan (2001) claim that the topic of suicide is a difficult and awkward one to discuss within the African American population for both cultural and religious reasons. Nevertheless, in their review of the existing literature on suicide risk in the African American population, they identified several important risk factors for this population. These include socioeconomic factors, community and familial violence, and psychopathology. Other authors have added important risk factors, including, for African American women, psychological distress, posttraumatic stress disorder, hopelessness, alcohol and drug problems, low levels of social support, maladaptive coping styles (Kaslow et al., 2000), a history of childhood maltreatment (Young et al., 2000), and marital discord (Kaslow et al., 2000).

Socioeconomic Factors.   African Americans have endured a long history of social, economic, and political disadvantages, but these factors in and of themselves do not appear to place African Americans at risk for suicide. Indeed, given the inequality that has persisted throughout the history of the United States, it would be clear that if socioeconomic factors in and of themselves increased suicide risk, then African Americans would have higher rates of suicide than their Caucasian counterparts. Yet the opposite is true: Rates are lower in the African American population. Although the research has not demonstrated a clear link, there is some evidence that it is not socioeconomic disadvantages per se, but social and economic inequality, that heightens risk. One study found higher rates of suicide among African Americans living in areas with high occupational and economic inequality between races (Burr, Hartman, & Matteson, 1999). Additionally, there is some evidence that suicide rates among African Americans are positively associated with education and wealth (Burr et al., 1999; Lester, 1994a). Clearly, the link between SES and suicide in the African American population requires further investigation.

Community and Familial Violence.   Exposure to violence appears to be an important risk factor for suicide in the African American population. In general, suicide rates for African American youths are higher in urban areas than in rural regions (Group for the Advancement of Psychiatry, 1989). One study found that urban adolescents who knew someone who had been murdered were twice as likely to attempt suicide, and those who had witnessed a stabbing were three times as likely to attempt suicide (Pastore, Fisher, & Friedman, 1996). Other studies have found that a history of childhood maltreatment (Young et al., 2000), childhood sexual abuse, marital discord (Kaslow et al., 2000), early sexual experiences (Walter et al., 1995), and physical abuse (Hernandez, Lodico, & DiClemente, 1993) also can increase the risk of suicide. Joe and Kaplan (2001) note that these are particularly disturbing findings, given the high rates of exposure to violence among African American youths in urban situations. Finally, the connectedness of family—an identified protective factor for African American women—can become a risk factor when families are poorly connected or are violent. Suicide rates among African American young men are negatively correlated with perceptions of older people's sense of parental duty. That is, when young men perceived that older adults in their lives took on a role of parental responsibility and care toward them, they were less likely to attempt or commit suicide (Eckersley & Dear, 2002).

The high levels of violence in many, particularly urban, African American communities have led some researchers to consider the rise in suicide for (primarily urban) young African American males in a postmodern context. In other words, changes in society at the end of the twentieth century—the breakdown of the nuclear family, the destruction of many formalized institutions of social engagement, the increase in hopelessness, the lack of social norms to control and limit behavior—have all led to an increased level of individual stress (Willis, Coombs, Cockerham, & Frison, 2002). The postmodern interpretation is that the breakdown of these important social institutions contributes to a culture in which individuals feel isolated and disconnected. This leaves young African American urban youths particularly vulnerable, given the traditional emphasis on collectivism in the African American culture and the fact that many urban youths live in areas that are resource-poor and cannot compensate for the declining social support from families, religious institutions, and the community. High rates of unemployment and underemployment contribute to feelings of profound hopelessness, despair, loneliness, and depression (Joe & Kaplan, 2001). Thus, this argument concludes that the lack of connectivity in the face of increasing stressors and psychopathology contributes to the steady increase in suicide rates in the young, urban, African American male population.

In discussing violence in the urban community, one more factor must be considered: "suicide by cop." Although by no means a common occurrence, it is nevertheless one that receives considerable media attention and merits a brief discussion here. *Suicide by cop*, the common street term for inducing a police officer to kill one rather than committing suicide, is not limited to urban, African American youths, but it is believed to be much more prevalent in this population than in any other. In general, there is some evidence that young African American males are more likely than other groups to be involved in deadly reactions from police officers and other individuals with weapons (Range et al., 1999). There are no numbers or rates associated with this phenomenon, given the impossible task of assessing the mindset of a person killed by a police officer to determine whether suicide was the true—or at least a partial—motivation. Nevertheless, the perception remains within the suicide literature that suicide by cop is a very real occurrence.

Psychopathology.   As in all segments of the population, psychopathology in the African American population contributes to suicide risk. Of course, not all individuals with an identified psychiatric or substance use disorder are at high risk for suicide; over 90% of such individuals in the African American population never have a suicide attempt. Additionally, whereas more than 90% of individuals who complete suicide in the Caucasian population have a psychiatric or substance abuse disorder, that percentage is only about two thirds in the African American population (Ialongo et al., 2002). Thus, a previous history of psychiatric difficulty is a stronger predictor of suicide in the Caucasian population than in the African American population. Nevertheless, depression, hopelessness, posttraumatic stress disorder, substance use/abuse disorders, and anxiety disorders all must be considered in assessing individual suicide risk.

Reluctance to Admit Suicidal Ideation or Suicide Plans.   Although strong religious and cultural injunctions against suicide can serve as a protective factor, they also can become a risk factor. African Americans might be reluctant to admit to feeling suicidal. One study that assessed suicide risk in university students found extreme reluctance among African American clients to readily volunteer that they were feeling suicidal. In fact, only 1 of the 36 African American clients with suicidal ideation in the study sample voluntarily self-disclosed the suicidal thoughts at intake. In the other 35, the suicidal thoughts were uncovered only through a suicide assessment by a therapist (Morrison & Downey, 2000). Therefore, it is imperative that mental health professionals complete suicide assessments with their African American clients, even if suicidal ideation is not a presenting concern.

Suicide Risk in Native Americans

The Native American Population

With a population of 4.1 million, or 1.5% of the U.S. population, the Native American population is the smallest of the four major ethnic groups in America (U.S. Census Bureau, 2000). Approximately one half of Native Americans live on or near reservations, and the other half live in rural or urban areas (Kaiser Commission, 1997). More than 50% of Native Americans live in Arizona, New Mexico, California, and Alaska (Group for the Advancement of Psychiatry, 1989). Native Americans have high unemployment rates, about 1.6 times greater than the national average, and Native American households are 2.3 times more likely than the rest of the U.S. population to live below the poverty line (Hisnanick, 1994). The population of Native Americans is increasing, and the birth rate for the Native American population is twice the national average. In 1990, there were just over 2 million Native Americans in the United States, and in 2000, there were more than 4 million. Because of the high birth rate, the Native American population is younger than the overall U.S. population, with a mean of 17.3 years, compared to 29.5 years for the rest of the population. Thus, proportionally, there are a greater number of adolescents and young adults in the Native American population, and it is people in this age group who are at the highest risk for suicide (Range et al., 1999). Among Native Americans, suicide is the third leading cause of death for ages 10–14 years and the second leading cause of death for ages 15–34 years (Centers for Disease Control and Prevention, 1998).

The term *Native American* is a global indicator for American Indians and Alaskan Natives from more than 500 different tribes speaking more than 200 different languages, making it difficult to speak of suicide rates in the Native American population as a single figure. Range and her colleagues (1999) note that suicide rates vary widely among the tribes; some tribes report rates more than 150 per 100,000, while other tribes report rates of zero per 100,000. Within the Alaskan tribes, for example, the suicide rate in 1998 was 48.2 per 100,000, compared with 11.3 per 100,000 in the general U.S. population and 23.7 for all residents of Alaska (Indian Health Service, 2002), as shown in Figure 6.2 on page 98.

Taken together, more than 800 Native Americans per year take their own lives. When rates for all tribes are combined, it is clear that the suicide rate among the Native American population is high, around 19.2 per 100,000, or almost twice as high as the overall U.S. rate of 11.9 (Indian Health Service, 2003). There is some evidence

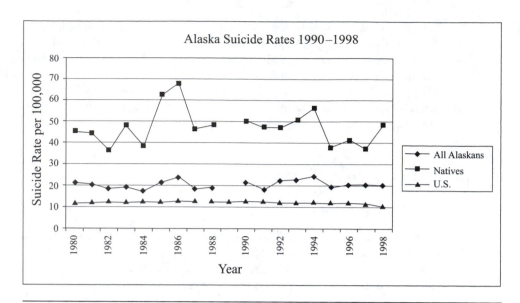

FIGURE 6.2   Alaska Suicide Rates, 1990–1998.

Notes: Rate per 100,000 population, age adjusted to U.S. 1940 population; ICD-9 codes 950–959.

Source: Alaska Division of Vital Statistics.

that these rates have been declining in recent years, but it is difficult to know whether this represents a permanent decline or simply a downward dip in a suicide cycle. There is some evidence that suicide occurs within tribes in a cyclical pattern that last approximately 5–8 years (Van Winkle & May, 1993).

Among Native Americans, just as in the rest of the U.S. population, suicide is a predominantly male phenomenon. The male:female ratio is 12:1 (compared to 3.3:1 in the rest of the U.S. population). It also occurs primarily in the younger population. The median age for suicide in the Native American population is 25 years, compared to the U.S. median age of 64 years (Range et al., 1999).

Specific Risk Factors in the Native American Population

Almost all official data on suicide and studies on suicide risk in the Native American population have been conducted with the population on reservations; little is known about risk for suicide in Native Americans who live in other areas. Additionally, there is some evidence to suggest that risk factors vary by tribe, with no single risk factor correlating to suicide risk in all tribes (Novins, Beals, Roberts, & Manson, 1999). Nevertheless, attempts have been made to identify general risk factors for the Native American population, and these are included in the following discussions. In addition to the specific risk factors identified below, the general risk factors for suicide that are applicable to all populations (e.g., mental and addictive disorders, access to firearms, recent and severe stressful life events, and intoxication) must be considered (Mościcki, 1997). Readers are cautioned, however, that of all ethnic groups, the least is known about suicide risk in Native Americans, and there are undoubtedly great differences between and among tribes. Therefore, suicide risk assessment must be done in a highly individualized context with the Native American population until more research can be done.

Alcohol and Substance Abuse. Just as with all U.S. populations, alcohol and substance abuse is correlated with completed suicide. Alcohol and substance abuse has been identified as a top health problem in the Native American population, and mortality from substance abuse from 1994 to 1996 was more than six times higher in the Native American population than in the general U.S. population (Indian Health Service, 2001). In their review of suicide risk within the Native American population, Range and her colleagues (1999) noted that alcohol has become a "primary and destructive coping mechanism for Native American people" (p. 420). They add that while in many social groups, people drink to create a social bond, the self-reported intention among many Native American men is to "get drunk, to become totally oblivious to their deplorable living conditions." Thus, alcohol is used as an attempt to "alleviate the sense of hopelessness and loss of identity engendered by intergenerational conflict, posttraumatic stress disorder, acculturative stress, and other problems" (p. 420). Between 75% and 90% of completed suicides in the Native American population occur in the presence of alcohol or substance abuse (Van Winkle & May, 1993). In one study, substance abuse emerged as the greatest single predictor of suicide among Native American youths, but it is clear that people who use substances may have other risk factors (e.g., hopelessness, depression, loneliness) that correlate with suicide risk as well (Yoder, 2001). Thus, it may be that substance abuse is not causally related to suicide but simply correlates with many other high-risk factors. Nevertheless, this factor remains significant for suicide risk assessment and prevention because of the high rates of alcohol and substance abuse among the Native American populations.

Family Disruption, Acculturation, and Abuse. Family interconnectedness is, in general, a strong cultural imperative within the Native American community. When the family (broadly defined, often including several generations of individuals) is disrupted, suicide risk increases (Middlebrook, LeMaster, Beals, Novins, & Manson, 2001). This disruption can come about through geographical relocations (e.g., one or several members of a family leaving a reservation), through marrying outside one's tribe, and through varying levels of acculturation (e.g., when members of a younger generation begin to adopt non-Native customs or values). As an example, in traditional Native American tribes, tribal elders often are looked to for guidance and direction. In fact, in some tribes, grandparents were given the role of raising children, on the basis of the belief that parents were not yet wise enough to engage in such an important task. However, the influence of Western culture, which downplays and minimizes the role of elders, disrupts this multigenerational connection, weakening the family.

Sexual or physical abuse within the family also can elevate risk. A national survey by the Indian Health Service found that more than 20% of Native American adolescent females reported a history of physical and/or sexual abuse, and there is a significant correlation between abuse and suicide risk (Blum, Harmon, Harris, Bergeison, & Resnick, 1992). Other studies also have found a correlation between physical and sexual abuse in adult Native American women and negative health consequences, such as depression, substance abuse, and suicide attempts (Bohn, 2003). Thus, it is clear that family disruption and family conflict in the Native American population, regardless of cause, increase suicide risk.

Socioeconomic Factors.   High rates of unemployment and poverty, which are typical on Native American reservations, also might contribute to suicide risk. Some tribes report unemployment rates of 90% with more than 60% of tribal members living below the poverty line. In many of these areas, more than one third of the homes have no running water or electricity (Healthy Start, 2000). In some tribes, as many as 65% of young people never finish high school (Young, 2001). Although no studies directly link poverty to suicide in the Native American population, it is clear that the hopelessness and disenfranchisement contribute to a culture in which suicide is seen as a viable option.

Cultural Beliefs.   One final risk factor that has been identified for the Native American population is a cultural belief about the continuity of life and the nature of life and death (Range et al., 1999). Native Americans, in general, tend be accepting of natural events, to live in harmony with nature, and to understand the cyclical nature of life and death. In this vein, death is viewed as simply a part of the life cycle. Thus, the same cultural attitudes that resist birth control and contribute to extremely high rates of teen pregnancies (in many tribes, more than half of the live births are to girls under the age of 17), because giving life is viewed as a natural extension of life itself, also contribute to an acceptance of death. It has been argued, although not empirically studied, that these cultural beliefs might lessen the social stigma typically associated with suicide. Regardless of the impact of this specific cultural belief, it is apparent that cultural beliefs, values, and customs—and the degree to which an individual views these cultural components as relevant, protective, and/or confining—can play a significant role in suicide risk assessment.

Suicide Risk in Asian Americans

In the 2000 census, Asian Americans and Pacific Islanders made up 4.2% of the population, with 11.9 million people self-identifying in this category. The population of Asian Americans is expected to double in the next 25 years (U.S. Department of Health & Human Services, 2002a).

The term *Asian American* represents individuals from many different countries. The U.S. Census Bureau has identified about 43 different ethnic subgroups with about

100 different languages and dialects, and about 35% live in households in which there is limited English proficiency in those over age 13. Some subgroups have more limited English proficiency than others: 61% of Hmong, 56% of Cambodian, 52% of Laotian, 44% of Vietnamese, 41% of Korean, and 40% of Chinese American households are linguistically isolated. (U.S. Department of Health and Human Services, 2002a). Additionally, Asian Americans tend to represent both extremes on socioeconomic, education, and health indices. The average family income for Asian Americans is higher than the national average, but more than a million Asian Americans live below the poverty line. Asian American woman have the highest life expectancy of any group in the United States, but 21% of Asian Americans lack health insurance (compared to 16% of the U.S. population in general). More than 44% of Asian American adults hold a college or professional degree (compared to 28% of Caucasian Americans), but two out of three Cambodian, Hmong, and Laotian American adults have not completed high school. (All statistics are from the Centers for Disease Control and Prevention, 2003, and the U.S. Department of Health and Human Services, 2002a.) These figures demonstrate the extremely heterogeneous nature of this population.

Along with the extreme diversity in socioeconomic, education, and health indices, there is also diversity based on ethnic origin. Just as with the Hispanic American population, each of the distinct ethnic subgroups has its own customs, values, beliefs, and traditions that make it difficult to talk about suicide risk in the population as a whole. In addition, very little research has been conducted on the mental health of Asian Americans, particularly non-English speakers. What is known, however, is that in general, the suicide rates for the Asian American population are lower than those for the U.S. population as a whole. For example, the U.S. Caucasian suicide rate is 12.8 per 100,000, compared with 5.5 per 100,000 for the Asian American and Pacific Islander population. However, there is wide variation within the ethnic subgroups. For example, the suicide rate for Filipinos is 3.5 per 100,000, that for Chinese is 8.3 per 100,000, and that for Japanese is 9.1 per 100,000. In some subgroups, the rates exceed the national averages. For example, Native Hawaiian adolescents have a suicide rate that is higher than the rate of other adolescents in Hawaii, and older Asian American women have the highest suicide rate for women over 65 in the United States (U.S. Department of Health and Human Services, 2002a). The Asian American population is the only ethnic subgroup that has a method other than handguns as the primary method of suicide. Among the Asian American population, hanging is the most common method of completion.

Just as with all segments of the U.S. population, more Asian American males than females complete suicide (sex ratio: 2.2:1). One notable difference is within the Chinese American population, in which suicide rates for females approach the rates for males (Lester, 1994b).

Suicide risk in the Asian American population differs by age group. In general, women are at the highest risk when they are young or when they are very old. Asian women over the age of 85 years have the highest suicide rate of all women of all ages in all cultures. Young Asian women, ages 15 to 24 years, have the second highest suicide rates for women in their age group (Caucasian women have higher rates) (Foo, 2002). For Asian men, suicide rates peak in the 75- to 84-year age range (Shiang, Blinn, Bongar, & Stephens, 1997).

Specific Risk Factors in the Asian American Population

Within the Asian American culture, there is a widespread belief that mental illness is highly shameful and that one's problems should not be shared outside of the family (Coalition for Asian American Children and Families, 2001). Nevertheless, there is a documented high need for mental health care within the Asian American population, just as in all populations in the United States. Rates of diagnosable mental illnesses in the Asian American population are similar to those in the U.S. Caucasian population, but Asian Americans show higher levels of depressive symptoms, and Chinese Americans are more likely to demonstrate somatic symptoms of depression than is the rest of the U.S. population. Other issues, such as cultural beliefs, acculturation, family conflict, and specific traumatic experiences, also contribute to suicide risk. These are in addition to the general suicide risk factors that have been identified for all populations.

Barriers to Mental Health Services.   Asian Americans appear to have extremely low utilization of mental health services when compared to other segments of the U.S. population. In one study, only about 17% of Asian American who were experiencing problems sought care (Centers for Disease Control and Prevention, 2003). Thus, when outside services are sought, problems might already have reached high levels of severity. There are many reasons for low rates of utilization of mental health services among Asian Americans, and barriers to services can be grouped broadly into four major categories. The first is financial. Lack of health insurance and low or no income among many Asian Americans make access to mental health care difficult. Others work in low-paying jobs (e.g., domestic service) with long and inflexible working hours that make it difficult to seek out care. The second major barrier is cultural and language differences. There are a limited number of bilingual mental health care providers, and approximately one out of every two Asian Americans will have difficulty accessing mental health services because of language barriers (Centers for Disease Control and Prevention, 2003). Other cultural barriers are less tangible and include cultural injunctions against seeking help, admitting to mental difficulties, or discussing problems outside of the family. A third major barrier is fear. Undocumented immigrants and people who perceive governments as hostile or threatening because of their previous treatment in their home countries might fear entering a government-subsidized mental health system (Coalition for Asian American Children and Families, 2001). Finally, a fourth barrier is perceptions of other people about the Asian American population. This perception has been called the "model minority myth" (Foo, 2002), which leads people to assume that all Asian Americans are healthy, intelligent, hard-working, and well adjusted. Thus, people (e.g., teachers, school counselors, and coworkers) who might readily recognize mental health problems among other populations are less likely to assume that a person of Asian descent needs mental health care. For example, among children, Asian Americans are the least likely of any ethnic group to receive mental health care.

Cultural Beliefs.   It is difficult to speak of cultural beliefs within the Asian American population because of the wide diversity of beliefs and practices among this very heterogeneous group. Nevertheless, there are some beliefs that might increase suicide risk, and mental health professionals must ascertain the level of adherence to these beliefs among their clients. For example, Range and colleagues (1999) identifies the three main traditional religions (Confucianism, Buddhism, and Taoism) among Asian Americans and notes that all three of these religions deemphasize the importance of the individual compared to the group. This can have a preventive effect for suicide, as death is considered in the context of relationships, and suicide is discouraged if it will harm the group. On the other hand, in all of these religious/philosophical stances, suicide might be preferable to remaining alive "if the suicide protects the family from shame, exposure, or embarrassment" (Range et al., 1999, p. 422). Suicide even might be considered a dignified choice as a method to express regret or to promote harmony within the family. Some studies have found that in general, Asian Americans believe that suicide is acceptable and that a person has a right to die (Range et al., 1999). One study found that people of Taiwanese descent were more than six times more likely than Caucasian Americans to view suicide as "a normal behavior" (Domino, Shen, & Su, 2000). Clearly, the degree to which an individual accepts these cultural and religious beliefs will affect the person's suicide risk and must be assessed in determining suicide risk.

Other cultural values, such as a reluctance to seek help, also affect suicide risk. Admitting to failure or even difficulties, particularly in work or school, may be extremely hard for Asian Americans. An overall guarded nature might be preferable to revealing weaknesses and putting either themselves or their families at a disadvantage. Thus, Asian Americans might not seek out the help they need, even if it is readily available. Some research has found that Asian American children and adolescents are more prone to depression than are their non-Asian peers and cite pressure to succeed in school as a primary source of stress and anxiety. In a large-scale study of Asian Americans in the state of New York, 30% of Asian American girls in grades 5–12 reported suffering from depression, the highest rate of depressive symptoms among children of all races. Additionally, Asian American teenage boys were more likely than their Caucasian, African American, or Hispanic peers to report physical or sexual abuse (Coalition for Asian American Children and Families, 2001).

Acculturation. Although level of acculturation per se does not appear to affect suicide risk, there is some evidence that acculturation level combines with other factors to influence risk. As a person acculturates, some compromise must be made between traditional values and those of the dominant U.S. culture. Varying levels of acculturation within families can precipitate intergenerational conflict, which increases suicide risk. Acculturation also can affect identity formation. Kwong (2000) noted that ethnic identity development might be particularly difficult for Asian American youth. Adolescents seeking conformity and a connectivity to peers might struggle as they determine whether to follow the path of their non-Asian peers or their Asian American families and subgroups. The pressure to conform to both paths increases depression and suicide risk.

Family Conflict. Conflict within the family has been linked to suicide, particularly in Asian females. Waters (1999) noted that in some Asian subgroups, there are strong cultural beliefs that tolerate violence toward and extreme subjugation of women. In such instances, women can see suicide as the only reasonable solution to a life of extreme suffering with no legal recourse or other viable options. Other research, primarily with Asian Americans, has found that family conflict in general can increase risk. For example, Chung (2000) found that differing expectations of expressing love can increase risk in young Asian women. For these women, the expectation of the American culture, that love and affection would be openly expressed within families, conflicted with the expectation against overt displays of love or affection in traditional Asian families. This intergenerational conflict, primarily between mothers and daughters, increased suicide risk in the young people in her study. Finally, there is evidence that when family conflict occurs, Asian Americans are less likely to use existing resources and will instead try to solve the problems on their own. When problems overwhelm the family system, all members of the family system are at increased risk.

Specific Traumatic Experiences.   Asian Americans who are immigrants or refugees might have particular suicide risk factors. Asian Americans are heavily represented among the refugee population, and many are at risk for posttraumatic stress disorder (PTSD). One study found that 70% of Asian refugees who sought mental health assistance met the diagnostic criteria for PTSD. Another study of refugees from Cambodia's concentration camps under Pol Pot found that more than half met the criteria for PTSD and more than 40% suffered from depression ten years after leaving Cambodia (Centers for Disease Control and Prevention, 2003). Clearly, among populations in which traumatic experiences are more prevalent, such as the refugee population, suicide risk increases.

Because of the great diversity within the Asian American population, including ethnic subgroup, religion and degree of adherence to religiosity, language, level of acculturation, refugee status, income, education, and socioeconomic status, it is difficult to assess suicide risk for the Asian American population in general. What is important to remember is that within the Asian American population, there is a wide range of attitudes and beliefs about suicide—some that serve to protect and some that encourage suicide. A thorough assessment of risk must always include an individual assessment of beliefs and attitudes toward suicide.

Summary

This chapter outlines the suicide risk factors for the four major U.S. ethnic groups. Overall risk factors, such as mental health problems, rigid cognitive styles, and alcohol and drug use, are just as salient for members of these ethnic groups as they are for any other member of the U.S. population. In addition, there are specific risk factors that might be relevant for each of the four ethnic groups. Mental health practitioners are strongly encouraged to consider all of these factors as they make their determinations of risk with individual clients. However, it is always important to remember that there is as much within-group variation as there is between-group variation. This chapter serves primarily as a reminder about factors to consider in assessing risk, but assessment must be done on an individual basis.

Although the four populations outlined in this chapter represent the four largest ethnic minority groups in the United States, it is important for mental health practitioners to know and understand the ethnic diversity within their own communities. For example, in the town in which we live, there has been a large influx of refugees from Somalia. Although few books or articles include information on counseling refugees from this particular country under these particular circumstances, it has been incumbent on us to learn all that we can about the Somali population. The same holds true for all communities. Learning to understand the diversity within your own community is the only way for you to be a truly culturally competent mental health practitioner.

7

Suicide and Suicide Risk Factors in People with Mental and Emotional Disorders

Throughout Section II of this book, you have been reading that depression, anxiety, and other mental illnesses increase suicide risk for people of all age groups and ethnicities. This chapter highlights the specific risks associated with mental illness, regardless of other demographic factors. As you read the chapter, you will want to remember what you read in Chapters 3–6 and how age and race might interact with mental illness to increase—or decrease—an individual's suicide risk.

In any given year in the United States, about 44 million adults have a diagnosable mental disorder. That means that approximately 28–30% of the adult population has either a mental health disorder or an addiction to alcohol or drugs (Satcher, 1999). The presence of a mental and/or emotional disorder is a highly significant risk factor for suicide. Research indicates that in 90% of completed suicides, a mental illness can be identified (Conner et al., 2001). Although only a small percentage of the people with mental health disorders attempt or complete suicide, the vast majority of suicidal individuals have a mental health disorder (Mann, Waternaux, Haas, & Malone, 1999). Individuals with psychotic disorders (primarily schizophrenia), mood disorders (major depression, bipolar disorder), anxiety disorders, personality disorders (primarily borderline personality disorder), substance abuse disorders, and many other disorders have significantly higher rates for suicide than the general population (Conner et al., 2001; Range et al., 1997; Rihmer & Kiss, 2002).

There are several theories about why individuals with mental illnesses are at higher risk for suicide than are other populations. First, mental illness diagnoses are still stigmatizing in our society. Receiving a diagnosis of schizophrenia, for example, carries a social stigma that is more negative in nature than receiving, for example, a diagnosis of heart disease. Typically, people in our society with mental illness are viewed as having a character defect or as lacking in behavioral self-control. As a result, many people with mental illnesses find themselves socially ostracized, isolated, and lacking support from the rest of society and their families. In fact, in interviews with people with mental illness, most people identify the stigma associated with their illness as more destructive and difficult to live with than is the disease itself (BBC Online Network, 1999; Corrigan, 1998). Social stigma, a lack of a supportive social network, and loneliness can contribute to the increased suicide rates for people with mental illness (Reid, 1998).

A second theory to explain the increased risk is that many people with mental illnesses do not receive a high standard of care for their illness. This lack of care may have socioeconomic ramifications leading to the so-called downward drift hypothesis. This hypothesis states that many disabled people end up being unemployed, poor, and dependent on social aid programs that provide just enough for subsistence. Hopelessness is a logical outgrowth for people with mental illness, who are often trapped in impoverished social classes, and hopelessness is in and of itself a risk factor for suicide.

A third theory is that the nature and symptoms of the disorders themselves may lead to impulsive and desperate behaviors. Neurobiological research evidence suggests that in both mood disorders and schizophrenia, low levels of the neurotransmitter serotonin might contribute to impulsivity and aggression (Asberg & Forslund, 2000). Therefore, an increased risk for suicide among people with mental health disorders could be a behavioral result of a biologically based genetic or biochemical etiology. The chronic and as yet incurable nature of many mental health disorders might contribute to feelings of hopelessness and helplessness. The frequent comorbid abuse of alcohol and drugs by people with mental illnesses can contribute to impaired judgment, a risk factor for suicide in all populations (Hufford, 2001). Of course, the symptoms of many mental disorders, such as significant or chronic feelings of depression, might in and of themselves be sufficient cause for individuals suffering from mental health illnesses to perceive suicide as an option to relieve their pain. The research seems to suggest that it is not just having a mental illness that leads to suicide, but the comorbidity of having a mental illness coupled with the realities of the economic and social duress that people with these illnesses must endure and the symptoms of the illnesses themselves that all contribute to the increased population mortality from suicide (Mann et al., 1999; Persson, Runeson, & Wasserman, 1999; Reid, 1998).

There are many outstanding first-person accounts of people with mental illness who are suicidal. One of the more compelling is *Night Falls Fast: Understanding Suicide* by Kay Redfield Jamison. This book is particularly enlightening, as Dr. Jamison includes both a professional and a personal account. She is a professor of psychiatry at Johns Hopkins School of Medicine, and she has bipolar disorder (also sometimes known as manic-depressive illness). Anyone who is interested in the mental health field is encouraged to read this (or another) first-person account in order to more fully understand the subjective world of people whose suffering from mental illness leads them to consider suicide.

Carolyn is a 28-year-old Caucasian female who has a history of bipolar disorder. She was diagnosed in her early twenties when she entered a manic episode. Her family found her, ten days after her first manic symptoms, in Las Vegas. In the space of less than two weeks, her manic symptoms had caused her to spend her life savings, rack up credit card debt in excess of $30,000, and engage in sexual relations with a variety of men she met on the Strip. Soon after her first manic episode, she fell into an extreme depressive episode, and she attempted suicide. She spent three weeks in an inpatient psychiatric unit and the next four weeks in a day treatment facility. In the ensuing six years, she lost her marriage, custody of her two young children, her job, and almost every vestige of her previous life. She was placed on lithium and a series of other psychiatric medications to try to lessen her symptoms, with some success. Nevertheless, three times after her original diagnosis, she took herself off the medications, stating that the side effects were too much to bear. Each time, she quickly entered into a manic phase, always with serious life-changing results.

Carolyn's psychiatrist meets with her every six months for 15 minutes for a medical check. The medications appear to work, but Carolyn uses them inconsistently. She has moved back in with her parents, and her mother tries to monitor Carolyn's medication compliance, but it often becomes a struggle of wills, and her mother tires of the day-in, day-out fights. Carolyn meets periodically with a social worker, who wants her to consider part-time work, but the chaotic inner world in which Carolyn lives makes this difficult. Her psychologist agrees that work would be too stressful for Carolyn.

Last month, Carolyn began a depressive episode. She was extremely tearful, was tired all the time, and could not bring herself to eat. Her mother was worried about her and called Carolyn's psychologist, who placed her in a day treatment program for one week. By the end of the week, Carolyn's energy had improved a bit, but she was still extremely tearful and hopeless. All during the week, she told the mental health practitioners at the day treatment unit that she was tired of living the life she had, and she was completely hopeless about the future. She could foresee a time when she could not live with her disease, and she could not foresee a way for it to end. She told the staff that she repeatedly thought about suicide.

By the end of the week, it appeared the suicide crisis had passed. Carolyn had more energy and, with the help of staff members, made plans to go to the mall over the weekend. When her mother came to pick her up on Friday afternoon, everyone was feeling more hopeful—everyone, that is, except Carolyn, who had gone along with the staff's assessment of her reduced lethality but, inside, recognized that she still felt incredibly hopeless. Later that evening, while her mother was preparing dinner, Carolyn took an overdose. When she did not come downstairs for dinner, her mother went upstairs to see where she was. She found Carolyn, still alive, and called the paramedics.

Carolyn's case represents the tragedy of a life overtaken by a severe and chronic mental illness. Although she was in treatment, Carolyn deliberately worked to hide her suicidality from the treatment staff. The case demonstrates how difficult it is to get into the mind of a suicidal person and do an accurate suicide risk assessment, particularly when the person makes attempts to deliberately deceive others and minimize risk. Like many depressed individuals, as you will read about later in this chapter, the highest risk for Carolyn was when her depression started to lift, and she had the energy to engage in a suicide attempt. As you read the remainder of the chapter, try to identify other risks that Carolyn demonstrated.

The information in the rest of this chapter relates some of the research on the relationship between selected specific psychiatric disorders and suicide. Although almost all mental and emotional disorders increase the risk of suicide, it is beyond the scope of this chapter to cover all of the diagnosable psychiatric disorders. Therefore, the disorders that we selected for this chapter are some of those that have been associated with the highest risk and that present with the most clinical frequency.

Mood Disorders

The relationship between suicide and mood disorders is well established. It has been estimated that 50–80% of all suicides are linked to the presence of a mood disorder (Bottlender, Jager, Straub, & Moller, 2000). Mood disorders include major depression, bipolar disorder, dysthymia (a type of low-grade depression), and other disorders. They are some of the most prevalent of all mental health disorders, second only to anxiety disorders.

The Special Case of Suicide in Children and Adolescents with Mood Disorders

Mood disorders are the most frequent diagnosis for children and adolescents who attempt or commit suicide. Two longitudinal studies of depression in children showed that prepubertal onset of depression increases the risk of adolescent suicide to three times the rate for their nondiagnosed peers. For individuals with onset of depression during adolescence, there was a 14-fold lifetime increase in risk for suicide as compared to the rates for nondepressed individuals (Weissman et al., 1999a; Weissman, Markowitz, & Klerman, 2000). For girls, the presence of a major depressive disorder might be the single most significant risk factor for suicide, whereas for boys who complete suicide, the presence of major depression combined with a comorbid disorder such as conduct disorder or substance abuse may increase the risk up to threefold (Sanchez & Lan, 2001). Further, children with "double depression" (dysthymia and major depression) have significantly more suicidal ideation and attempts than do children with major depression alone (Kovacs, Goldstone, & Gatsonis, 1993). Additionally, many children (20–40%) with depression will go on to develop bipolar disorder later in life, and bipolar disorder is associated with increased mortality.

Children and adolescents with mood disorders and other mental health problems frequently go undiagnosed and untreated. Only about one third of children and adolescents with mental health disorders receive services (U.S. Department of Health and Human Services, 1998). In addition, there is a real paucity of research on the benefits of psychotherapy or medications for reducing suicide mortality in children and adolescents. However, one would expect that if more children and adolescents received treatment, there would be a reduced incidence of child and adolescent suicide (Sanchez & Lan, 2001).

Major Depression

It has been said that depression is the "common cold" of the mental health professions because of high frequency of occurrence of the disorder in the population. Even though major depression is a highly treatable disorder, it is one of the most significant risk factors for suicide attempts and completions. Simply stated, over 50% of suicides occur in the context of a major depressive episode (Oquendo, Malone, Ellis, Sackeim, & Mann, 1999). One study has suggested that suicide risk might be highest during the first three months after the onset of a major depressive episode and also within the first five years after the lifetime onset of the disorder (Malone, Haas, Sweeney, & Mann, 1995). Other research and much common wisdom in mental health suggest that the time of greatest risk is just as depression begins to subside. Some have suggested that this is because a person's physical energy returns before the person feels significant emotional improvement. Thus, the person has the energy to commit suicide and the ongoing emotional pain that makes suicide appealing. Whatever the time frame, however, all people who are diagnosed with depression are at significantly increased risk for suicide and need to be evaluated and monitored on an ongoing basis as a regular part of the clinical management of these cases.

For many years, the rate of suicide for people with major depression was frequently cited as being 15%. This figure was based on the meta-analytic work of Guze and Robins, which was published in 1970. The sample that they used, however, was primarily of people who had depression and/or suicide risk serious enough to for them be hospitalized. Recent authors have criticized this research and sought to analyze the suicide risk not just for the most severe cases of major depression, but also to include the many people who have the disorder but do not ever require hospitalization. When this wider sample is included, the rate of suicides among people with major depression was found to be 3.4% for men and women combined, 7% for men, and 1% for women (Blair-West et al., 1999). Further, there is a significantly lower risk of suicide in cases of unipolar depression (compared with bipolar disorder) and those cases that are not complicated by comorbid substance abuse, personality disorder, or psychosis (Boardman & Healy, 2001). So, the good news is that there are many people with depression who receive treatment in community or outpatient settings who have lower suicide risk than was previously thought. The bad news is that for those who have depression severe enough to warrant hospitalization, as many as 15% will kill themselves over the course of their lifetimes.

There are definite gender and ethnic patterns in the rates of suicide among those diagnosed with major depression. Women have double the rates of diagnosed depression as men. However, just as with all segments of the population, males have a much higher risk for completing suicide than do females, with a ratio of about 7:1. This ratio holds true across all ethnic groups (Oquendo et al., 2001).

A number of theories have been advanced as to why so many people with major depression attempt or commit suicide. Biologically, genetic abnormalities and their resulting effects on neurochemistry have been posited as the cause for the high rates of suicide in major depression (Mitchell, Mitchell, & Berk, 2000). There is some evidence to suggest that a decrease in the activity of the neurotransmitter serotonin is the biological basis of major depression and suicide (Stockmeier et al., 1998). A significant body of research now supports serotonin as a definite biological factor in major depression, although there remains controversy as to what specific areas of the brain are involved and how exactly the binding to neuron receptor sites is disrupted (Stockmeier et al., 1998). In addition to the biological theories, many psychological theories have been posited explaining the connection between major depression and suicide.

BOX 7.1 • *Suggested Reasons for Increased Risk for Suicide in Depressed Persons*

- Clinical symptoms
  - In people with major depression, specific symptoms of hypochondrias, delusional ideas, suicidal thoughts, or previous attempts at the time of hospitalization have been found to be indicators of increasing risk for suicide death after discharge from the hospital (Schneider, Phillipp, & Muller, 2001).
- Personality factors (impulsivity, hostility, aggression)
  - Impulsivity in conjunction with major depression was found to increase suicide attempts, even without the presence of a comorbid Axis II (personality disorder) diagnosis (Malone et al., 1995).
  - The Myers-Briggs types of Introversion (I) and Perceiving (P) were associated with suicide attempters with major depression. People who are introverted may be less likely to seek out social support during depressive episodes, and individuals who are more perceiving are less planful and more impulsive than their counterparts, the J's (Judging) (Janowsky, Morter, & Hong, 2002).
- Previous family history of suicide
  - In terms of family variables, parents of suicide attempters were more likely to have attempted suicide themselves. Suicide attempters had twice as many siblings attempt suicide as did nonattempters.
- Early life loss experiences
  - Suicide attempters were more likely to have had a parent die before the age of 11 than nonattempters (Malone et al., 1995).
- Comorbid disorders (e.g., substance abuse and personality disorders)
  - Both substance use disorders and Cluster B personality disorders (borderline, histrionic, narcissistic) were higher in attempters than in nonattempters (Malone et al., 1995).
- Negative life events and social support
  - For men, the number of negative life events in the year prior, but not the nature of their social support system, were predictors of a suicide attempt (Flint, Hays, Krishnan, Meador, & Blazer, 1998).

Although many factors linking depression and suicide have been investigated, a definitive profile has not yet been developed that would allow clinicians to predict which people with major depression are most likely to attempt suicide and which will probably not. However, although each case must still be taken individually, the research has shown specific risk factors that do contribute to risk. The best-researched and supported risk factors are substance use, impulsivity, previous family history, comorbid Axis II (personality) disorders, experiencing negative life events, and being a Caucasian male. Any one or a combination of these can lead an individual to consider suicide as a method of relief from depression. When working with people who are suffering from major depression and trying to protect them from suicide, the mental health clinician should keep track of these factors and heed the increased message of risk that they can communicate.

Bipolar Disorder

Bipolar disorder is a mood disorder that is differentiated from unipolar (major) depression by the presence of one or more episodes of elevated mood (DSM-IV TR, 2000). Suicide for people diagnosed with bipolar disorder is a significant clinical problem. Some research has found that up to 50% of people with bipolar disorder will have a suicide attempt at some point in their life and that every fifth person with the disorder will complete suicide (Rihmer & Kiss, 2002; Rucci et al., 2002). Despite the high risk for this population, most research on mood disorders lumps all the diagnoses together, and only a small number of studies have independently examined bipolar disorder diagnoses. However, the results from this small body of research are very informative.

The research indicates that the lifetime prevalence of suicide attempts for people who have been diagnosed with bipolar disorder (from 19–50%, depending on the study) is higher than that for people who have unipolar major depression (4%). The high rate of suicide attempts for people with bipolar disorder is important because a previously attempted suicide is a powerful indicator of committed suicide across all populations and even more so among people with mood disorders. Some research has indicated that up to 56% of those diagnosed with bipolar disorder who ultimately complete suicide have had at least one previous suicide attempt.

Depression and, more specifically, the depressive episodes for an individual with bipolar disorder are very significant factors in bipolar suicides. Most suicide attempts by people diagnosed with bipolar disorder take place during a depressive episode. People with this disorder who have a history of suicide attempts have a higher number of depressive episodes than nonattempters (Oquendo et al., 2000). It is important to note, however, that it is a myth that suicide does not occur outside of a depressive episode. Although it is true that suicide attempts rarely occur during euphoric mania, it is relatively common that mixed (dysphoric) and hypomanic episodes can lead to suicidal thoughts and attempts (Rihmer & Kiss, 2002). Individuals diagnosed with bipolar disorder who have a comorbid disorder, like many other populations who are coping with multiple or comorbid illnesses, are at increased risk for suicide. The most common comorbid disorders that elevate risk are anxiety, substance use, personality disorders, or serious medical illness (Rihmer & Kiss, 2002).

Another factor for determining risk for people with bipolar disorder is a family history of suicide. In general, people with bipolar disorder have high rates of suicide in their families (Oquendo et al., 2000). The risks of suicide for a person with the diagnosis are much higher if the person has had a first-degree relative attempt or complete suicide.

A final factor contributing to increased risk that is worth noting is that of the psychosocial stressors (Oquendo et al., 2000). Many people with bipolar disorder create significant problems in their lives as a function of their behavior when manic or hypomanic. Chaotic, impulsive, promiscuous, and often dangerous behaviors may create financial, interpersonal, familial, and legal difficulties for the client. The added burdens of these stressors, including shame, guilt, or anger, combined with the depressed or mixed mood of the person, might contribute to the choice to take one's own life (Rihmer & Kiss, 2002).

It is important to note that treatment, which includes both appropriate medications and counseling, has been shown to significantly reduce the risk of suicide among those with bipolar disorder. Further, some research has asserted that lithium, the most common mood-stabilizing medication for those with bipolar disorder, significantly helps to reduce suicidality in bipolar patients (Ahrens & Muller-Oerlinghausen, 2001; Rucci et al., 2002; Sanchez & Lan, 2001). There is no research on the suicide reduction effects of other types of psychopharmacology used in treating this population. Unfortunately, despite the high rates of mood disorders in the general population, there are still many people who do not receive adequate treatment or comply with that treatment if they should receive it. Treatment should be considered a primary form of prevention of suicide for people with mood disorders.

Now that you have read about risk factors in persons with major depressive disorder and people diagnosed with bipolar disorder, you can see how many risk factors Carolyn had that contributed to her suicide attempt. Reread the case, and try to identify these specific risk factors.

Schizophrenia

Schizophrenia is a severe and chronic mental illness that affects approximately 2.8 million Americans, or about 1.3% of the population (Satcher, 1999).

Suicide is one of the most common causes of premature death among people with schizophrenia (Schwartz & Benjamin, 2001). People suffering from schizophrenia have completion rates that are 20 to 50 times higher than those of the general population (Potkin, Anand, Alphs, & Fleming, 2003). It has been estimated that one in ten people with schizophrenia will kill themselves (Miles, 1977). Although the estimates of these rates vary widely in the research, depending on the methodology, recent researchers have reported the following for people with this disease:

- 60–80% contemplate suicide (Schwartz & Benjamin, 2001)
- 20–42% attempt suicide (Schwartz & Benjamin, 2001)
- 9–15% complete suicide (Potkin et al., 2003)

Interestingly, between 25% and 50% of suicides in people with schizophrenia occur during psychiatric hospitalization (Taiminen et al., 2001). Further, a follow-up study of over 300 participants who had received inpatient treatment for schizophrenia or its spectrum disorders (schizoaffective, schizophreniform, and schizotypal personality disorder) indicated that 40% of the former patients had suicidal ideation, 23% had attempted suicide, and 6.4% had died by committing suicide (Fenton et al., 1997). It is remarkably striking that these people were in relatively close connection with the mental health system at the time of their suicides. Clearly, we all need to work harder to prevent suicides in people with schizophrenia who are in our care.

Several risk factors have been consistently shown to be specific to individuals with schizophrenia, including chronicity of the illness (particularly many acute episodes and remissions), high level of positive symptoms (such as paranoia and delusions), awareness and fear of further deterioration from the illness, substance abuse, and a loss of confidence concerning the successful outcome of treatment (Gut-Fayand et al., 2001; Kreyenbuhl et al., 2002). It is important to remember that people with schizophrenia have to cope with frequent hospitalizations, medication trials, loss of dignity and social status, lack of social support, and a feeling of powerlessness over an incurable disease. So it is not surprising that in many ways, it could be the burden of living with the ramifications of disease that leads to the high rates of suicide among its sufferers. Further, some research has recently indicated that depression and specific positive symptoms, such as paranoia, might be helpful in determining higher risk. In a study of 223 individuals diagnosed with schizophrenia, Schwartz and Cohen (2001) found that the variables that were most strongly correlated with suicidality were depression, younger age, and traumatic stress. These three factors accounted for 38% of the participants' ratings of their suicidality. Fenton and colleagues (2000) also supported the importance of depression, noting that 80% of those who are diagnosed with schizophrenia will experience a major depressive episode at some time during their lifetime. A nationwide study in Finland indicated that in people with schizophrenia, depression was a "highly prevalent" symptom in 64% of the completed suicides (Heila et al., 1997). It is possible that depression contributes to suicides in people with cormorbid depression and schizophrenia (schizoaffective disorder) in that these individuals might lack the ability to cope with a chronic disease, possibly even more so than individuals with other chronic diseases that do not have as their primary symptoms cognitive and perceptual impairments. In other words, people with schizophrenia may be at high risk, owing to their disease, and additionally compromised and adversely affected by depression.

A second risk factor that has been identified is the presence of command hallucinations. Command hallucinations are hallucinations that direct a person to perform an action, and about one quarter of people who experience command hallucinations report that they are unable to resist them (Mackinnon, Copolov, & Trauer, 2004). Their relationship to suicide, however, is poorly understood from a research perspective (Montross, Zisook, & Kasckow, 2005), and it has been argued that command hallucinations are not sufficient to produce action, including suicide, in isolation (Braham, Trower, & Birchwood, 2004). Command hallucinations for violence (including violence toward the self) are most dangerous when they occur in a person who is already feeling hopeless and suicidal, and much clinical lore, if not actual research, suggests that these specific types of hallucination warrant careful monitoring.

A last area of relevant research concerns that of some specific symptoms of schizophrenia as potential risk factors for suicide. Candido and Romney (2002) compared severity of depression in both paranoid and nonparanoid people with schizophrenia, and a group of people diagnosed with major depression. They found that the paranoid schizophrenia group had significantly more depression than did the nonparanoid group. The results demonstrated that the paranoid schizophrenia participants were at greater risk than nonparanoid schizophrenia participants. This study and others have indicated that a critical time for the paranoid schizophrenia participants was the postpsychotic phase of their illness, as this is when they were the most depressed (Candido & Romney, 2002). Several other studies have reported similar findings concerning the increased risk for individuals with paranoid symptoms. Conversely, there appears to be a reduced risk for suicide in people with negative symptoms, such as diminished drive, blunted affect, and social and emotional withdrawal (Fenton et al., 1997; Kreyenbuhl et al., 2002). It appears, then, that prominent paranoid symptoms, especially in the absence of negative symptoms, might help to define a relatively high-risk schizophrenia suicidal group.

The conclusion is that people with schizophrenia who commit suicide have very similar symptomology to that of people with the disorder who do not commit suicide. Therefore, it is difficult to identify clearly any unique high- or low-risk groups. However, recent research has suggested that the interplay of significantly depressed affect combined with positive symptoms and paranoia could create a high risk for suicide in people with schizophrenia.

Anxiety Disorders

There is significant disagreement in the literature about the anxiety disorders and which of these disorders contributes to suicide risk. It is thought that the rates of suicide among those people diagnosed with anxiety disorders (generalized anxiety disorder (GAD), social phobia, panic disorder, post-traumatic stress disorder (PTSD), and obsessive compulsive disorder (OCD)) are probably higher than has been previously reported in the literature. One recent study based on over 20,000 clinical cases estimated that the suicide risk of those with anxiety disorders was greater than the general population by a factor of ten or more (Khan et al., 2002). Other research with more than 7,000 people suggests the increased risk is about three to four times higher for people who have been diagnosed with an anxiety disorder (Sareen et al., 2005). However, considerable controversy still exists in the literature concerning the additive risk of anxiety disorders apart from comorbidity with depression.

Several studies have evaluated the role of panic attacks in suicides, both comorbid with depression and separate from depression. The results are mixed, with some studies finding independent suicide risk for "pure" panic attacks and other studies not finding additive risk for panic apart from depression (Placidi et al., 2000). The presence of a comorbid diagnosis of major depression might play a mediating role by increasing the risk of suicide in those with panic disorder. Stated conversely, when major depression is controlled for as a variable, the risk for suicide among panic disorder cases is substantially reduced (Schmidt, Woolaway-Bickel, & Bates, 2001). Unlike panic disorder, PTSD appears to have a synergistic or additive effect with comorbid major depression. Interestingly, individuals with both PTSD and major depression have higher rates of suicide than do individuals with only one of these disorders, but it does not seem to matter which disorder preceded the other in onset (Oquendo et al., 2001).

There is very little available research on OCD, social phobia, and GAD as they specifically relate to suicide. Most of the research on these disorders discusses them as comorbid with either major depression or bipolar disorder. One study that examined people with social phobia indicated that suicide risk increased when there was a history of previous psychiatric hospitalizations and treatment for depression (Cox, Direnfeld, Swinson, & Norton, 1994). Another study has indicated that individuals with OCD had a low risk of suicide mortality over a 40-year period (Coyell, 1981). However, suicide risk increased when OCD was comorbid with bipolar disorder (Chen & Dilsaver, 1995). Given the lack of research on suicide risk in people who have been diagnosed with anxiety disorders, it is hard to draw conclusions. At present, it seems that while there is widespread clinical acceptance that people with anxiety disorders are at increased risk for suicide, there is still substantial disagreement as to the amount and independence of the increased risk and the links between each anxiety disorder and other comorbid anxiety or mood disorders.

Personality Disorders

A large body of research supports that Axis II (personality) disorders are more common in suicide attempters, especially the Cluster B personality disorders (Kernberg, 2001; Malone et al., 1995). The Cluster B personality disorders are often referred to as dramatic, erratic, and emotional, and they include borderline personality disorder, histrionic personality disorder, and narcissistic personality disorder.

Sarah is a 34-year-old Caucasian female who lives in a small town in the Midwest. She was diagnosed with borderline personality disorder in her late teens. Sarah's entire adult life has been characterized by the extreme pathology of the illness. She has been in and out of state psychiatric hospitals for over ten years and has had dozens of suicide attempts and hundreds of parasuicidal behaviors. Her arms, breasts, and face are covered with the scars from a lifetime of cutting and burning, and she has required skin grafts on both arms after numerous cutting and burning incidents left her with skin that had been too mutilated for ongoing repairs. In group counseling, she is dramatic and erratic, vacillating between angry and tearful emotional outbursts and hours of complete silence. She has worked her way through most of the staff of the inpatient unit and, over the course of several years, has had almost all of them as individual therapists. Although Sarah typically starts out believing that each therapist will be the one to save her, over time, she becomes increasingly angry with the therapist, and her rejection of each therapist ends with a suicide attempt.

Sarah fears her life outside of the psychiatric hospital, recognizing that she cannot monitor her own safety and fearing the isolation and loneliness that she inevitably feels when she is on her own. During her last hospitalization, the staff worked tirelessly to help prepare her for a date for her release. As the time approached, she became increasingly agitated and angry with the staff, including her current individual therapist, because she felt that they were abandoning her and did not care if she killed herself. After a particularly painful meeting with her psychiatrist and her individual therapist, she left the room, ran out into a group room, tore apart a soda can, and sliced her arm open nearly to the bone. Other patients quickly notified the staff, who rushed Sarah to the emergency room for yet another skin graft.

Anyone who works in mental health for a length of time has a story of a client like Sarah, whose mental illness of borderline personality disorder puts her at extreme risk for suicide and parasuicidal behaviors. Whether or not Sarah intended to actually kill herself, whether she was trying to demonstrate how desperate she was not to leave the hospital, or whether she was trying to seek revenge on what she perceived as an unsympathetic staff is difficult to know. The results, however, were that she came dangerously close to a completed suicide. As you read the discussion of borderline personality disorder, consider the risks that Sarah presents.

The diagnosis of borderline personality disorder (BPD) has been shown to be a powerful predictor of suicide both in conjunction with major depressive symptoms and independent of depression (Corbitt, Malone, Haas, & Mann, 1996; Soloff et al., 2000). Studies show suicide rates of up to 9% in people who have been diagnosed with

BPD (Linehan, Tutek, Heard, & Armstrong, 1994). A number of factors have been researched to help explain the high rates of suicide among those who have been diagnosed with BPD. The very nature of the diagnosis seems to logically relate to increased suicide risk. BPD is characterized by impulsivity and emotional feelings of emptiness. Impulsivity and emotional lability contribute to the high risk for self-destructive behaviors.

Parasuicide is the term used for the self-destructive behavior that is often exhibited as a clinical symptom by people with BPD. Parasuicidal behavior can be defined as deliberate self-harm that is not lethal (Sidley et al., 1999). As many as 80% of people with BPD may commit parasuicidal behaviors, such as self-mutilation. Additionally, 39–84% of BPD individuals may abuse drugs (Welch & Linehan, 2002). Parasuicidal behaviors as a clinical symptom of BPD are serious in that they sometimes accidentally lead to completed suicides, they cause extreme emotional pain for the persons who exhibit them and their loved ones, and they cause a large drain on resources of treatment centers and hospital emergency rooms.

A study on parasuicidal behaviors that compared people with other personality disorders (OPD) to people with BPD (Soderberg, 2001) found the following:

- People with BPD were more likely to have multiple Axis II disorders; 71% of BPD individuals met criteria for three or more personality disorders, whereas only 7% of OPD group did.
- 20% of the BPD individuals did not have an Axis I disorder; whereas almost the entire OPD group had a comorbid Axis I disorder.
- 34% of the BPD group had used methods other than drug overdose for parasuicidal behavior, whereas this was very rare in the OPD group.
- Parasuicidal behavior rates were higher for both lifetime and attempts in the past year for the BPD group than for the OPD group.

Individuals with Cluster B personality disorders have unstable and erratic means of relating to others and abnormal methods of coping with stress or trauma. They might therefore be more vulnerable to suffering the effects of trauma and daily stress. It has been shown that sexual abuse as a child of a person with BPD increases the risk of suicide attempt by ten times when compared to someone with BPD who has not suffered childhood sexual abuse (Soloff, Lynch, & Kelly, 2002). It has been suggested that parasuicidal cutting behaviors in those with BPD might be a communication strategy related to the level of interpersonal problems being currently experienced (Welch & Linehan, 2002).

Clinicians must not become complacent or dismiss people with personality disorders who have high rates of parasuicidal behavior, assuming that the behavior will not reach a lethal level. Unfortunately, the presence of a personality disorder, especially BPD, contributes to increased suicide attempts and completions.

Alcohol and Substance Abuse Disorders

Substance abuse disorders present a double danger for suicide risk. First, people who suffer with alcohol and drug disorders are at greatly increased risk of suicide as compared to nonaddicted people. The second danger is intoxication with alcohol or drugs. Intoxication is dangerous because it leads to impulsive behavior and can dramatically increase the risk of suicide in individuals both with and without mental health disorders.

Alcoholics may be at 60–120 times greater risk for suicide than a non-psychiatrically diagnosed population (Hufford, 2001). Some of the reasons that have been proposed to explain this greater risk among alcoholics are the experience of greater negative life events (marital, family, employment problems), comorbidity of depression, high rates of beliefs concerning helplessness and hopelessness about the future, personality characteristics of impulsivity and sociopathy, family history of previous suicide attempt, and genetics (Hufford, 2001; Mitchell et al., 2000; Roy, 1993, 2000). People with alcoholism therefore could be at higher risk because of the long-term damage that the chronic substance abuse disorder exerts on them, both psychologically and socially.

Additionally, alcohol intoxication, apart from the chronic nature of a substance abuse disorder, can function as an acute contributor to suicide. Alcohol intoxication has been shown to contribute to both the increased likelihood of a suicide attempt and the lethality of the attempt. Drinking within three hours of an attempt has been shown to be one of the strongest variables associated with a near-lethal suicide attempt (Powell et al., 2001). Further, a study of patients treated at emergency rooms found that alcohol intoxication might have increased the risk of a suicide attempt by 90% (Borges & Rosovsky, 1996). A wide variety of ideas have been advanced to explain why many individuals attempt suicide while using alcohol. Examples include the belief that alcohol intoxication has a palliative effect on psychological pain, the belief that alcohol will numb the physical pain of an attempt, a high correlation of alcohol intoxication to periods of depression, the use of alcohol to cope with aggressive or helpless feelings, and decreased judgment and inhibition effects (Hufford, 2001).

Not only do substance abuse disorders and acute intoxication represent substantial risk factors, but they are also highly correlated with other mental and emotional disorders, particularly major depressive disorder, bipolar disorder, anxiety disorders, and personality disorders (particularly the Cluster B disorders) (Modesto-Lowe & Kranzler, 1999).

- Approximately, 50% of people who have been diagnosed with a severe mental disorder will develop a substance abuse disorder at some point in their lives (Cuffel, 1996).
- The lifetime prevalence for alcohol dependence was more than double in people with a diagnosed mental illness compared to those without a mental illness.
- Where alcohol dependence was the primary diagnosis, mental illness occurred in 37% of the subjects versus 20% of those without alcohol dependence.
- In people who had a substance abuse disorder for a drug other than alcohol, mental illness was comorbid in 53% of the subjects (Schaar & Ojehagen, 2001).

Many studies have supported the concept that the abuse of substances, when combined with other mental health problems, increases the risk of suicide (Potash et al., 2000). In summary, alcohol and/or drugs are dangerous additives to any at-risk situation because they impair judgment, increase impulsivity, and decrease physical and psychological abilities to cope with danger or solve problems. Clinicians working with anyone with a mental or emotional disorder should always remember to assess for substance abuse. Establishing the substance abuse pattern of an individual may be particularly important when there is a risk of suicide, as alcohol and other drugs can dramatically increase the likelihood of a suicide attempt.

Summary

Mental health and substance abuse diagnoses place people at significantly elevated risk for suicide. Although most people who suffer from a mental illness never commit suicide, more than 90% of those who do take their lives suffer from at least one diagnosable mental disorder. Thus, treatment for people with mental and emotional disorder must always include a comprehensive and ongoing suicide risk assessment.

Five major types of mental disorder have very strong links to suicide: mood disorders (primarily major depressive disorder, bipolar disorder), schizophrenia, anxiety disorders, personality disorders (particularly Cluster B disorders), and alcohol and substance abuse disorders. The research on people who have been diagnosed with each of these disorders is at varying stages of development. Overall, it is difficult to say what separates those who have the disorder and attempt or commit suicide from those who have the disorder and do not attempt or commit suicide. Therefore, clinicians are left without specific risk factors to differentiate levels of risk. As with all suicide risk assessments, determining risk in people with mental disorders is a highly individualized process.

8

Suicide and Suicide Risk Factors in People with Physical Illnesses

Certain groups of individuals are at higher risk for suicide because of their membership in a specific population. In Chapter 7, you read about the elevated risk in people with different types of mental illnesses. In this chapter, we will overview suicide risk in another high-risk group: people with specific types of physical illnesses.

Rates of suicide ideation and attempts in people with chronic or terminal illnesses have not been widely studied. However, it is widely believed that the rates are higher in the medically ill population than in the general public, although not all researchers studying the issue have found a significant correlation. In addition, many studies of this population have not controlled for depression. That is, it is impossible to know whether the physical illness itself places a person at higher risk or whether the illness simply increases the likelihood of depression and hopelessness, which are the mental states that are most associated with suicide risk. Some have argued that suicidal thoughts are normal coping mechanisms when faced with anticipated loss or physical pain (e.g., Beckett & Shenson, 1993; Schnieder, Taylor, Hammen, Kemerry, & Dudley, 1991). Like all risk factors for suicide, it appears that a single factor (in this case, physical illness) cannot solely account for an increased risk. However, like many other risk factors, it probably plays into a complex web of personal and environmental factors that increase an individual's risk.

Regardless of the specific cause(s) of the elevated risk (or even whether the risk is significantly elevated), it is important that mental health practitioners who interact with people with chronic, painful, or terminal illnesses understand the risk and pay particular attention to the risk factors and warning signs. Approximately half of physically ill people who attempt suicide have had contact with a health professional within 30 days before their suicide (Ikeda et al., 2001). Thus, it is essential that mental health care providers know and understand the risk.

It is very difficult to determine what the rates of suicide or suicide risk are in people with physical illness. Epidemiological studies (studies that capture large segments of the population, such as whole cities or counties, asking every adult person about his or her physical and mental health) have had little success in determining the risk associated with different illnesses.

It is somewhat easier to determine the rates of physical illness among those who are suicidal. That is, people who have revealed their suicidal ideations or behaviors can then be asked whether or not they have a physical illness and, if so, what is the nature of that illness. In these studies, between 30% and 40% of persons who completed suicide had a physical illness at the time of death (Hughes & Kleespies, 2001). In one meta-analysis of 15 individual studies, on average, 34% of people who committed suicide had a physical illness at the time of their death (Whitlock, 1986). In another meta-analysis of 11 studies, the average percentage was 43% (Mackenzie & Popkin, 1990). Across all the studies included in the two meta-analyses of physical illness among people who completed suicide, the range was 18–70%. Using another method, rates of physical illness were found to be 4.8 times higher in males and 1.6 times higher in females who had a nearly lethal suicide attempt than in the general population (Ikeda et al., 2001). The variation in these studies suggests that physical illness in itself is not a sole predictor of suicide risk, but the average percentages (30–40%) indicate that physical illness may significantly contribute to risk.

Across many studies, there is consistent support for elevated risk in some medical populations. These are HIV/AIDS, certain cancers (most particularly brain cancer), Huntington's disease, and multiple sclerosis. It should be noted that there are high rates of comorbid depression with each of these medical conditions. There is an uncertain link between suicide risk and several other medical conditions, including Parkinson's disease, ulcers, spinal cord injuries, Alzheimer's disease, vision loss, and chronic pain or fibromyalgia. There appears to be no increased risk of suicide with heart transplant, hypertension, rheumatoid arthritis, cervical or prostate cancer, amyotrophic lateral sclerosis, or diabetes. Finally, there is decreased risk for suicide among people with one medical condition: pregnancy (Hughes & Kleespies, 2001). The medical conditions that are linked to increased risk (or uncertain risk) are discussed in further detail in the following section. Of course, research is ongoing, and this list of conditions represents only the current state of our understanding and is meant only for the purposes of generalizations. People with other illnesses, not identified in the literature as being at particularly high risk, may have considerable risk for suicide. In other words, simply because diabetes appears on a list of "no apparent increased risk" does not mean that a person with diabetes cannot be suicidal or even that, for any particular person, diabetes could not be a substantial contributing factor to suicide risk. Mental health professionals who interact with people with any medical diagnoses must be careful to uncover any increased risk for suicide and perform careful assessments for coexisting mental disorders and suicide risk.

César was a widower, just days away from his seventieth birthday, when he learned that he had early-stage Alzheimer's disease. In retrospect, he told his son at lunch the next day, he wasn't surprised. His own father had developed serious dementia when he was in his sixties, and César watched his father deteriorate, becoming first disoriented, then agitated, and then downright mean. César's mother had been helpless to care for him, and after César's father engaged in too many dangerous activities (e.g., turning on the gas stove and leaving the house, going outside in the winter in his bathrobe), she finally had him put in a nursing facility. César recounted to his son how he tried to visit his father once a week, but eventually, his father did not even recognize him. César's visits became less and less frequent, and finally, they stopped altogether. His father died at the age of 76, nine years after César stopped visiting him.

César knew all too well what he could expect from the disease. He spoke with his son about the future and his desire not to keep living after he had ceased to be aware of those around him. He feared becoming what his father once was, yet he knew that the path was inevitable. César's son sympathized with his father's plight and admitted that if he ever faced the same plight, he too would seek a way to end his life while he still had dignity. However, César's son said that he did not believe that he could assist his father in a suicide when the time came. He was afraid that he would never be able to carry out his father's wishes.

The two discussed possibilities and eventualities, and after several hours of discussion, César developed a plan. He would make up an envelope with a lethal dose of pills and a note. He would put the envelope with the pills on his dresser, where he would be sure to see it every day. On the front of the envelope, he would write, "IF YOU DON'T REMEMBER WHAT THIS IS, THEN YOU MUST OPEN IT." Inside, he would place instructions that would prompt him to take the pills and then call his son.

César's case is a difficult one. Many of us can sympathize with his fear of a debilitating illness, such as Alzheimer's disease, and his desire not to allow himself to deteriorate as his father had done. His expressed desire to kill himself before he got to that stage plays into our beliefs of dignity and individual choice. On the other hand, many people believe strongly in the sanctity of life and would not condone this choice, regardless of César's circumstances. César's case hits at the core of the debate regarding the right to die and physician-assisted suicide (although César did not request the assistance of a physician). Stop and think about what you believe and whether or how you might assist or intervene.

Medical Illnesses and Conditions That Increase Suicide Risk

HIV/AIDS

AIDS is a chronic, life-threatening condition caused by the human immunodeficiency virus (HIV). This virus damages or destroys the cells of the immune system and interferes with the body's ability to effectively fight off viruses, bacteria, and fungi that cause diseases. The HIV virus makes people susceptible to opportunistic infections that the body would normally resist, such as pneumonia and meningitis, and to certain types of cancers. The virus and the infection itself are known as HIV, and the term *acquired immunodeficiency syndrome* (AIDS) is used to indicate the later stages of HIV infection. Thus, both the terms *HIV* and *AIDS* refer to the same disease. HIV is most commonly spread by sexual contact with an infected partner but can also be spread through infected blood and shared needles or syringes contaminated with the virus. Untreated women with HIV can pass the infection to their babies during pregnancy or through breast milk. Although HIV/AIDS was once considered primarily a gay male disease, worldwide as many women as men are living with the disease. In the two decades since the first reports of the disease, AIDS has become a global epidemic. Worldwide, more than 40 million adults and children are now living with HIV. According to the United Nations Program on HIV/AIDS and the World Health Organization, 5.3 million people were newly infected with HIV in 2001 alone and AIDS-related deaths reached a record 3.1 million (World Health Organization 2006). Of those who died, 580,000 were children. Currently, an estimated 800,000 to 900,000 Americans are living with the disease.

Gay males with HIV/AIDS appear to be at higher risk for suicide than do healthy individuals. This finding has been consistent for many years and across many studies, although only the gay male HIV/AIDS population has been studied. People in other demographic categories with this disease have not been included in the research.

In general, it appears that gay males with HIV/AIDS may be at seven times greater risk than the general population (Conwell, 1994). However, most of the studies have not controlled for depression or substance abuse among the HIV/AIDS population. As many 43% of HIV-positive gay males meet the criteria for depression, although depression rates are high in gay males who are HIV-negative as well, with some studies showing no differences in depression rates based on HIV status (Malbergier & deAndrade, 2001). Substance abuse is also quite prevalent within this population, as are other stressors (e.g., having a partner with AIDS, unemployment, lowered social support, and poor adaptive functioning). Therefore, it is very difficult to determine whether the high suicide rates are due to effects of the illness itself or to comorbid psychological and social variables (Komiti et al., 2001).

HIV-positive adults and those living with AIDS are more likely to report having considered suicide as an option if they have high levels of emotional distress (particularly depression) or poor health-related quality of life. As a group, those who have considered suicide are more likely to use escape and avoidance strategies for dealing with their illness and to report receiving significantly less social support from friends and family, compared to the situation before they revealed their illness (Kalichman, Heckman, Kochman, Sikkema, & Bergholte, 2000).

Although most studies do not inquire about the severity or length of the illness and its relationship to suicidal intent, in one study, 25% of HIV-positive men spontaneously reported that they would consider ending their lives if circumstances became intolerable (Rabkin, Remien, Katoff, & Williams, 1993). In another study of family members in the Netherlands after the death of an HIV-positive person, 48% reported that the deceased had made arrangements for euthanasia before their deaths (Van den Boom, 1995). One study of HIV-positive gay men found that the most common reasons cited for making plans to end one's life were to maintain a sense of control, to make one's own decisions, and to prevent suffering. The most common circumstances within which participants could see themselves deciding on suicide were loss of independence, intolerable pain, and no hope of improvement (Goggin et al., 2000).

It is possible that the suicide rate among people infected with HIV/AIDS is declining, as there has been a drop in the rate since 1996, when protease inhibitors were released in the U.S. medical system as a treatment for HIV/AIDS. This drop in rates could be due to these advances in medications and treatments that offer more hope, or it might simply be an anomaly in the data. It is too soon to tell.

Cancer

Cancer occurs when cell division malfunctions. The timing of cell division is usually under strict constraint, involving a network of signals that work together to say when a cell can divide, how often it should happen, and how errors can be fixed. Mutations in one or more of the signals in this network can trigger cancer, whether through exposure to some environmental factor (e.g., tobacco smoke) or because of a genetic predisposition or both. Usually, several cancer-promoting factors have to add up before a person will develop a malignant growth; with some exceptions, no one risk alone is sufficient (Genes & Disease, 2002). Cancer, then, is a disease in which a single normal body cell undergoes a genetic transformation into a cancer cell. This cell and its descendants, proliferating across months or years, produce the population of cells that we recognize as a tumor, and tumors produce the symptoms that an individual experiences as cancer. Almost 1.3 million new cases of cancer were diagnosed in the United States in 2002, and approximately 9 million Americans are living with cancer. In the United States, one in every four deaths is attributable to cancer (Cancer Facts & Figures, 2002).

People who are living with cancer might be at higher risk for suicidal thoughts and behaviors, although this is variable among types of cancers. The most clearly elevated risk is among patients with cancers of the brain or nervous system. A large-scale Danish study of almost 300,000 cancer patients found elevated risk in this group, and a study using World Health Organization statistics found that patients with brain cancer were nine times more likely than the general population and four times more likely than patients with other types of cancer to commit suicide (Hughes & Kleespies, 2001). Again, factors such as depression and hopelessness were not controlled for, and it is possible that people with these types of cancer have higher levels of depression than do people with other types of cancers. Other studies have found that cancer patients have high levels of stress that increase as the illness advances or as the patient experiences more physical pain (Ciaramella & Poli, 2001). Perhaps as many as 40% or more of cancer patients have major depression, including hopelessness, that places these persons at increased risk for suicidal thoughts and behaviors.

Psychological autopsies show that cancer patients who completed suicide have high rates of hopelessness, fear of suffering, concerns about being a burden on others, and fears about loss of independence and autonomy. Many had isolated themselves from persons who could have been a source of social support (Filiberti et al., 2000). These characteristics, more than the type of cancer or the progression of the illness, seem to place cancer patients at high risk.

Huntington's Disease

Huntington's disease is a neurological disorder that is chronic, progressive, and debilitating. The disease typically begins in midlife, and it is characterized by motor impairment, cognitive decline, personality change, and increased susceptibility for mental disorders. Some early symptoms of Huntington's disease are mood swings; depression; irritability; and trouble driving, learning new things, remembering facts, or making decisions. As the disease progresses, concentration on intellectual tasks becomes increasingly difficult, and people with Huntington's disease may have difficulty feeding themselves or swallowing. Many people with Huntington's disease die from choking, infections, or heart disease. There is no cure for Huntington's disease, and eventually, people with the disease become totally dependent on others for all their care. The rate of disease progression and the age of onset vary from person to person.

People with Huntington's disease have high rates of suicidal ideation and attempted suicides. Depression is not just a side effect of living with a debilitating disease but is also a symptom of the illness itself. The biological effects of problems with dopamine in the brain actually cause depression. Aside from the depression that is a common side effect and symptom of the disease, persons in early-stage Huntington's disease often are extremely fearful of the physical and mental difficulties that lie ahead. Genetic testing can determine who will get this disorder, and once a person has been identified as having the gene, it is a near certainty that sooner or later, he or she will develop the disease. Therefore, people who have been genetically tested and are positive for the gene are at greatly increased suicide risk, even before symptoms begin to appear. One study found that among people who tested positive for the gene but did not yet show any symptoms, 35% considered suicide, and almost 18% had had a suicide attempt (Robins et al., 2000). Potential loss of cognitive function and emotional stability appear to be the most significant concerns of those who have tested positive, and counseling is indicated immediately after identification of the gene and throughout the progression of the illness.

Multiple Sclerosis

Multiple sclerosis (MS) is an autoimmune disease that affects the central nervous system, which consists of the brain, the spinal cord, and the optic nerves. Symptoms of MS are unpredictable and vary from person to person and from time to time in the same person. For example, one person might experience abnormal fatigue, while another might have severe vision problems. A person with MS could have loss of balance and muscle coordination, making walking difficult; another person with MS could have slurred speech, tremors, stiffness, and bladder problems.

People with MS appear to be at increased risk of suicide, although just as with HIV/AIDS and cancer, it is unclear whether that risk is attributable to the illness itself or to the higher incidence of psychological problems in this population. In several meta-analytic studies, people with MS were approximately twice as likely as the general population to commit suicide (Kleepsies, Hughes, & Gallacher, 2000), and in general, people with MS have higher rates of suicidal ideation than the general population (Scott, Allen, Price, McConnell, & Lang, 1996). However, it should be noted that MS patients have high rates of depression and/or anxiety (in up to 48% of patients in one study by Nicholl, Lincoln, Francis, & Stephan, 2001) and hopelessness (Patten & Metz, 2002). Depression in patients with MS is linked to decreased self-assessed quality of life (Fruehwald, Loeffler-Stastka, Eher, Saletu, & Baumhackel, 2001). Therefore, it appears that patients with debilitating MS—or patients who perceive their MS to be highly debilitating—are at greater risk.

Overall, the MS patients who at greatest risk are males who have recently experienced a deterioration because of the illness, have moderate to severe disability, are unemployed, are experiencing financial stress, and have an inability to express feelings and ask for help, which results in social isolation and a reduced social support system (Berman & Samuel, 1993; Stenager, Koch-Henriksen, & Stenager, 1996). In fact, lack of social support might be the most significant predictor of suicide in MS patients (Long & Miller, 1991). Male patients who are at high risk also have more impaired mobility, more problems with vision, and more problems with bowel and bladder control (Kleepsies et al., 2000). Different studies have found higher risk either within the first five years of diagnosis or in the late stages, when the illness is more likely to be debilitating. Males with MS who attempt suicide tend to use very lethal methods, such as guns. Much less is known about female MS patients and their risk for suicide. Many more males with MS attempt suicide, and no pattern has emerged for female attempts.

Medical Illnesses and Conditions with Uncertain Suicide Risk

Parkinson's Disease

Parkinson's disease is a chronic and progressive disorder of the brain that primarily affects the central nervous system but also affects thinking and emotions. Between one million and one and a half million Americans, slightly more males than females, have been diagnosed with the disease. Primary symptoms include tremor (of the hands, arms, legs, jaw, or face), rigidity or stiffness of the limbs, slowness in movement, and impaired balance, which often leads to difficulty walking. Other common symptoms include sleep disturbances, depression, anxiety, dizziness, problems with speech, breathing problems, and sexual problems.

There is mixed understanding about the role that Parkinson's might play in suicide risk. One study of the data from almost 150,000 patients with Parkinson's disease found that the suicide risk for this population is more than ten times greater than that for the general population (Myslobodsky, Lalonde, & Hicks, 2000). Several other large-scale studies have examined suicide risk in people with Parkinson's disease, and no consensus has emerged. In one review of several of these studies, no increased risk was found, but in a different review of other large-scale studies, there was a statistically significant increase in risk for suicide among people with Parkinson's disease (Harris & Barraclough, 1994; Stenager & Stenager, 1992). As with almost all research on suicide risk for people with medical illnesses, many of these studies did not control for depression or other coexisting mood states. There is a high rate of depression in people with Parkinson's disease, and the NIMH estimates that as many as half of people with Parkinson's disease also have clinical depression. The disease itself interferes with dopamine in the brain, and the result can be a biological depression. Just as with Huntington's disease, therefore, depression can be both a symptom and a side effect of Parkinson's disease. With Parkinson's disease, some of the antiparkinsonion medications have side effects that affect mood, most notably causing depression and, in some cases, psychosis. Therefore, the effects of the medication, as well as a general depression that is so prevalent with this disorder, all contribute to suicide risk in this population.

Ulcers

Ulcers are sores in the lining of the stomach (gastric ulcers) or the small intestine (duodenal ulcers) and are collectively known as *peptic ulcers*. Ulcers occur when something damages the protective lining and allows stomach acid to eat away at it. People with ulcers experience a burning, aching, or gnawing discomfort from them and often have severe pain, bloating, or nausea. Approximately 10% of the population will have an ulcer during their lifetime, and men are more susceptible than women. There is an unclear link between stress and the development of an ulcer, but stress clearly can exacerbate existing ulcers.

People with ulcers might be at higher suicide risk than is the general population, with some studies showing suicide rates for this population as high as 14% (Knop & Fischer, 1981). One study found gastritis and/or peptic ulcers in more than one quarter of people who committed suicide (Gustafsson & Jacobsson, 2000). Little is known about the link between ulcers and suicide risk, although several hypotheses exist. First, there is a high correlation between ulcers and alcoholism, and alcoholism has been linked to suicide risk. Second, people with ulcers often have coexisting mental disorders (e.g., anxiety, depression) that may contribute to the risk. Given the rather high risk for suicide in this population, it is surprising that so little research has been conducted. What is most pressing for suicide risk assessment, however, is to recognize an elevated risk in this population and to complete screens for depression, alcoholism, and suicide for people who have ulcers.

Spinal Cord Injuries

A spinal cord injury is a lesion of the spinal cord that results in paralysis of certain areas of the body, along with the corresponding loss of sensation. Most spinal cord injuries result in loss of sensation and of function below the level of injury, including loss of controlled function of the bladder and bowel.

Approximately 7,800 people per year in the United States survive a spinal cord injury. Overall, more than 80% of people living with spinal cord injuries are male, and the average age for the injury to occur is 33 years (but the mode, or most common age for an injury to occur, is 19 years) (National Spinal Cord Injury Association, 2002).

Studies show that people with spinal cord injuries have high rates of suicidal ideation, but there are mixed results about actual suicide completions in this population. Some studies have shown suicides to be four to five times more prevalent among people with spinal cord injuries and the second leading cause of death among people with paraplegia (DiVivo & Stover, 1995). Suicide among people with quadriplegia is difficult to complete, as assistance from another person would typically be required. Therefore, suicide rates among people with quadriplegia have not been tracked. The majority of suicide attempts by people with spinal cord injuries occur within one year of injury (Beedie & Kennedy, 2002). As with other medical illnesses, there are high rates of depression, anxiety, and alcohol and drug abuse in people with spinal cord injuries. In many cases, the accidents that cause spinal cord injuries are related to alcohol, drug abuse, and/or failed suicide attempts.

The mediating factor of social support has been hypothesized to be particularly important as a suicide buffer in persons with spinal cord injury, both because it provides generally positive experiences and because social support can enhance perceived control over stressors and barriers. Perhaps more than any other population, people with spinal cord injuries are forced to rely on others for assistance. The degree to which that assistance is forthcoming and provided by supportive others can mediate the hopelessness that might otherwise occur. Kishi and Robinson (1996) found that between 10% and 15% of spinal cord injury patients made suicide plans within the first six months of their injury. In general, these individuals had low levels of social support and high levels of hopelessness. Other studies have confirmed that both high-quality and high-quantity social support is associated with lower levels of hopelessness and depression in patients with spinal cord injury (Beedie & Kennedy, 2002).

Alzheimer's Disease

Alzheimer's disease is really a cluster of several disorders that cause gradual loss of brain cells, leading to dementia. *Dementia* is an umbrella term for several symptoms that relate to a decline in thinking skills, including loss of memory, problems with reasoning or judgment, disorientation, difficulty in learning new information, loss of language, and a decline in the ability to perform routine daily tasks. People with Alzheimer's disease also experience changes in their personalities and behavioral problems, such as agitation, anxiety, delusions, and hallucinations. Approximately 4 million living Americans have Alzheimer's disease. It is most common among the elderly, and as many as 10% of Americans over age 65 years and 50% of Americans over age 85 years have the disease (Alzheimer's Association, 2002).

People with Alzheimer's disease often have little insight into their own cognitive and functional deficits, and this lack of insight often occurs very early in the course of the progression of the disease. In general, suicide attempts are rare in people with dementia, and some people have theorized that cognitive deficits might actually serve as a protective factor in suicide risk. However, there has been little understanding of whether patients with Alzheimer's disease fit the model of low suicide risk that is common with other types of dementia or whether they are at higher risk. Depressive disorders are relatively common in people with Alzheimer's, with perhaps up to one third of those with the disorder demonstrating symptoms of depression. Reviews of studies of suicide risk in this population reveal substantial differences in rates, ranging from 2% to 30%. Overall, preliminary evidence shows that people with Alzheimer's disease who have insight into their cognitive and functional impairments are more likely to be hopeless and to endorse a statement that "life is not worth living" (Harwood & Sultzer, 2002). Other preliminary studies of elderly people who committed suicide used brain autopsies to look for biological signs of Alzheimer's disease in the tissue. These studies found high rates of early Alzheimer's disease in the brains of those who committed suicide (as high as 92%) (Rubio et al., 2001). This research, however, represents only a very few studies of this population, and overall, the effects of Alzheimer's disease on suicide risk are not well understood. It is possible that people with Alzheimer's disease are most at risk early in the course of the illness, when they still have the cognitive capacity to understand what lies ahead.

Vision Loss

There are approximately 10 million to 11 million visually impaired people in the United States and about 1.3 million who are legally blind. The term *visual impairment* covers a wide range of disability, from total blindness to low vision that cannot be corrected to moderate visual impairment. Vision loss is more common among the elderly, and roughly half of the blind or visually impaired people in the United States are over the age of 65 years (American Foundation for the Blind, 2002).

Very little information on suicide and vision loss is available. Two studies appear to support the concept that suicide risk is increased in visually impaired persons, particularly those who have experienced recent vision loss. Impaired vision has been linked to depression in the elderly population (Kennedy et al., 1989). In one study of elderly people who committed suicide, impaired vision was a predictor of suicide (Waern et al., 2002). Another study found that sight loss—and, more particularly, fear of losing sight—could cause otherwise psychologically healthy adults to suffer severe psychological distress that can lead to suicide (DeLeo, Hickey, Meneghel, & Cantor, 1999). The authors of this second study believe that people with progressively worsening sight are at high suicide risk and that ophthalmologists should work in tandem with mental health professionals to refer people who are at high risk. Others argue that individuals with vision loss are at no more risk for suicide than is anyone suffering any type of psychological trauma (Hine, Pitchford, Kingdom, & Koenekoop, 2000).

Chronic Pain and Fibromyalgia

Chronic pain is pain that continues a month or more beyond the usual recovery period for an illness or injury or pain that goes on over months or years as a result of a chronic condition. It may be continuous or may come and go. Approximately 86 million Americans will suffer chronic pain at some point during their lives, the most common type being lower back pain (American Chronic Pain Association, 2002). Between 50% and 70% of Americans will experience lower back pain at some point during their lives, and it is second only to the common cold in prompting visits to doctor's offices. For most people, the lower back pain is temporary, but up to 20% of people with lower back pain develop chronic pain. Many of these individuals become temporarily or permanently disabled, and about 5.2 million American are partly or completely disabled by chronic lower back pain (Witty, Heppner, Bernard, & Thoreson, 2001).

Fibromyalgia (FM) is a chronic pain illness that is characterized by widespread musculoskeletal aches, pain, and stiffness; soft tissue tenderness; general fatigue; and sleep disturbances. The most common sites of pain include the neck, back, shoulders, pelvic girdle, and hands, but any body part can be involved. Other symptoms may include irritable bowel and bladder, headaches and migraines, restless legs syndrome, impaired memory and concentration, skin sensitivities, dry eyes and mouth, anxiety, depression, ringing in the ears, dizziness, vision problems, neurological symptoms, and impaired coordination. FM patients experience a range of symptoms of varying intensities that wax and wane over time. The diagnosis of FM remains controversial, and no laboratory tests are currently available for diagnosis. The web site of the

National Fibromyalgia Foundation claims that approximately 3–6% of the U.S. population has FM, with more women than men affected (2002).

Chronic pain has been linked to increased suicide risk (Hargis, 1997). This increased risk might be due to elevated rates of depression. With chronic pain patients, the intensity of the pain, the chronicity of the pain, and the level of disability all have been linked to depression, lowered levels of social support, and higher levels of catastrophic thinking, all of which may contribute to suicide risk (Fisher, Haythornthwaite, Heinberg, Clark, & Reed, 2001). Other studies have found that suicidal people with chronic pain may have reduced problem-solving ability, which again is consistent with suicide risk (Witty et al., 2001). The source of the pain (e.g., fibromyalgia, chronic back pain, or rheumatoid arthritis) does not appear to affect suicide risk (Amir et al., 2000). However, chronic pain within the course of other debilitating illnesses (e.g., HIV/AIDS, cancer) may compound the suicide risk, particularly for terminal illnesses. As yet, this is simply a hypothesis that has not been tested (Bengesser, 1998).

BOX 8.1 • *The Case of ALS and Physician-Assisted Suicide*

In recent years, there has been discussion about the role of physician-assisted suicide with people who have chronic, debilitating illnesses, such as amyotrophic lateral sclerosis (ALS). ALS (also called *Lou Gehrig's disease*) is a progressive neurodegenerative disease that affects nerve cells in the brain and the spinal cord. The progressive degeneration of the motor neurons eventually leads to death. Voluntary motor activity is progressively affected, and the person eventually becomes totally paralyzed. Nevertheless, for most people, their mind (both cognition and emotion) is unaffected (Amyotrophic Lateral Sclerosis Association, 2005).

The Amyotrophic Lateral Sclerosis Association has found itself in the middle of this very sensitive debate. They argue that they staunchly support the right of people with ALS to make informed decisions, including the decision to die, but they also argue that people need to be fully informed about symptom management and comfort measures. Within the medical field, there are reported "high rates of physician-assisted suicide and euthanasia" for people living with ALS (Appel, 2004), but these are based on clinical lore rather than actual reports, as other than in Oregon, physician-assisted suicide, even in the case of ALS, is against the law. People living with ALS tend to believe (70%) that it is morally acceptable to request physician-assisted suicide, but only 7% indicated that, if it were legally available, they would request such assistance (Achille & Ogloff, 2004).

The current available research on suicide does not indicate high suicide risk for people with ALS. In other words, there is no evidence that people with ALS take their own lives at higher rates than the rest of the population. Nevertheless, the debate about physician-assisted suicide puts people with ALS in the spotlight and raises questions about how society in general, and the health professions specifically (including the mental health profession), work to best meet the needs of the people for whom they provide care.

Summary

After an initial period of adjustment, people with physical illnesses typically move toward psychological adjustment to the new reality of their lives. What is clear is that physical illness in and of itself does not cause suicide. The psychological reaction to receiving a medical diagnosis and living with a medical disease are the key contributors to suicide risk. The most critical aspect of all of the diseases outlined in this chapter are the levels of depression and hopelessness that accompany the physical disorder. There are higher rates of depression in people with these physical disorders than in the general population, placing these individuals at higher risk for suicide. This is why it is critical for mental health practitioners to be aware of the increased risk for people with these physical conditions and to check for depression and suicide even when it is not readily apparent.

9

Suicide and Suicide Risk Factors in Other High-Risk Populations

There are some individuals who are at increased risk for suicidal thoughts and behaviors because they belong to specific subsets of the population; their job, their circumstances, or their lifestyles contribute to their risk. These subgroups have little in common with each other, yet each has been given special attention in the suicide risk literature. Therefore, they have been grouped together, rather artificially, for the purposes of talking about high-risk groups.

This chapter is divided into five sections, discussing suicide risk in the following groups:

1. Gay/lesbian/bisexual/transgendered (GBLT) populations
2. Prisoners or incarcerated populations
3. Law enforcement populations
4. Military and veteran populations
5. Health care professionals

There certainly are other populations whose jobs or circumstances place them at higher suicide risk than the general population, but these five categories consistently rise to the top of the research literature as being worthy of special attention.

James was a 17-year-old Caucasian male who was a member of his high school's varsity wrestling team. He was an average student who had friends in school, primarily members of the team, and his parents were supportive of both his schoolwork and his athletic interest. He was a junior and had begun discussing his future. He had long understood himself to be "not college material," and he was more interested in pursuing some sort of technical career. His parents supported that decision. His father was a plumber, and his mother worked in the high school cafeteria. From all appearances, James was a reasonably adjusted, rather ordinary student who did his work, stayed out of trouble, and enjoyed being a part of the wrestling team. Although he was not a star member of the team, he felt comfortable with the other guys on the team and felt that he fit in.

James's high school guidance counselor had little interaction with James. As a student who neither caused trouble nor was destined for college, James sort of "fell through the cracks," but that was fine with James and his family, who believed that life was progressing as it should.

During the previous wrestling season, James had begun to have a growing sense of uneasiness around his teammates. It started with a sexually explicit dream he had one night about one of the other boys on the team. He woke up startled and upset and lay in bed wondering whether the dream meant that he was gay. He and the other guys on the team had little tolerance for anyone who was gay, and calling someone a "fag" was the worst insult they could offer. For several days, he obsessed about the dream and what it meant, but he did not tell anyone. A few nights later, he had a similar dream, this time involving several boys from the team. Truly frightened now, James started to become extremely conscious about showering with the others boys after practice or touching them as they wrestled. He was convinced that he was gay and that it would just be a matter of time before everyone knew.

Over the ensuing six months, James started using the Internet to look at gay pornography and he chatted on an Internet site with other gay teenagers. One night, he left the house after dark and met with one of the people he had gotten to know on the Internet to engage in sexual activity. By the next morning, he felt extremely confused, alone, and scared. Over the next several weeks, James continued to meet the boy he had first met on the Internet, as well as several other boys, to engage in sexual activity. Most of the time, the boys would drink together, sometimes quite heavily, but James was always careful not to drink too much, which he knew would affect his wrestling. Nevertheless, he always drank some alcohol, as it helped him not to think about what he was doing.

One day after wrestling practice, while they were in the locker room, one of the other members of the team caught James looking at him while he was in the shower, and yelled, "What are you, some sort of fag?" At that moment, James started thinking about all he had gone through in the last six months and the reaction that he was sure others would have to him, and he realized that he could not tolerate being gay. After practice, he went home, took his father's gun out of the bedside drawer, and shot himself. No one in his family or friendship network had any idea of why James killed himself. They noted only that he had been somewhat quiet and introspective lately but did not know why.

Charlie, a 38-year-old husband and father of two, was arrested one Sunday afternoon for driving under the influence. He had a blood alcohol level that was more than twice the legal limit. His wife and children were spending the day at her mother's, and Charlie had gone out with some friends to play golf. After the game, they stopped for lunch and a few drinks, and after his friends left, Charlie stayed and had a few more and then left for home. About six blocks from home, he went through a stop sign and slammed into the side of another car. The children in the backseat of the other car were taken to the hospital in critical condition.

Charlie was mortified about what he had done. He knew that it meant the end of his career as the high-profile president of a local bank, and he was quite certain that his wife would leave him and take the children. Everything that Charlie held dear—his family, his career, and the life he had carefully constructed—would be last.

At the police station, Charlie was devastated and seemed to operate in slow motion. As he was being escorted from the booking area to the cell block, he was crying and told the officers that his life was over. When he was put into his cell, one of the officers noted that Charlie immediately took off his T-shirt. About 30 minutes later, an officer returned to the cell to get Charlie so that bail could be arranged. The officer found him dead, hanging by his T-shirt.

Both of these case studies represent people whose circumstances brought them into life situations that were beyond their ability to cope. Unfortunately, neither person turned to professional help—or even to other laypeople who might have helped them to make other choices. Both are examples of people with tunnel vision, the concrete thinking that is so often part of suicidal attempts and completions.

Gay, Lesbian, Bisexual, or Transgendered People

There are no national or statewide databases on completed suicides that include the sexual orientation of the deceased. However, there is a widely held belief, both in the literature and in the practicing community, that people who are gay, lesbian, bisexual, or transgendered (GLBT) are at particular risk for suicide or suicide attempts. Several studies have confirmed this elevated risk, particularly among GLBT youths. A 1989 Department of Health and Human Services report entitled *Report of the Secretary's Task Force on Youth Suicide* estimated that GLBT youths might account for as many as 30% of youth suicides, putting them at two or three times the risk of their heterosexual peers. When the report was presented to Congress, several members of Congress and high-ranking members of the administration argued vehemently against the report, stating that it was based on flawed data and served to undermine family values (McDaniel, Purcell, & D'Augelli, 2001). This controversy highlights a major difficulty in understanding suicide risk among young GLBT people: It is difficult to obtain reliable data on sexual orientation of people who completed or attempted suicides, particularly for young people. Reported numbers are undoubtedly low, as family members often deny or are unaware of sexual orientation issues in their loved ones. This difficulty is compounded by federal programs that for years have refused to consider sexual orientation as a risk factor about which data should be collected or prevention programs should be designed around. It was not until 1995 that the American Association of Suicidology, the Centers for Disease Control and Prevention, and the National Institute of Mental Health came together to begin a dialogue to increase understanding of suicide in the GLBT population (McDaniel et al., 2001). Since that time, there have been increasing attempts to understand the suicide risk in this population.

Suicide Rates in the GLBT Population

Studies using standardized methodologies have found suicide rates are between 2.5 and 7 times higher in the GLBT population (Saunders & Valente, 1987), although other researchers have found no differences in the rates for the GLBT population when compared to heterosexuals (e.g., Shaffer, Fisher, Hicks, Parides, & Gould, 1995). Several studies have been published that employ more rigorous methodologies than these earlier studies. However, all of the more recent studies have investigated suicide ideation and suicide attempts rather than completed suicides.

In a large-scale study in Canada that included 750 young men (ages 18 to 27), participants were divided into two groups: those who had been sexually active in the past six months and those who had been celibate in the past six months. They were then further categorized into gay or bisexual or heterosexual (based on self-report). The researchers found that lifetime rates of suicide attempts were highest for celibate gay and bisexual men (15.5%), followed by sexually active bisexuals (5.4%), sexually active gay men (3.1%), sexually active heterosexuals (0.5%), and celibate heterosexuals (0%). When combined into one group for analysis, gay and bisexual men were 14 times more likely than heterosexual men to have attempted suicide (Bagley & Tremblay, 1997).

Another study examined a longitudinal birth cohort of children born in New Zealand in 1977 (1,265 participants). This study found that self-identified GLBT individuals were at increased lifetime risk for suicide attempts (32%, compared with 7% of the heterosexuals in the sample) as well as suicidal ideation, major depressive disorder, anxiety disorder, conduct disorder, and nicotine dependence (Fergusson, Horwood, & Beautrais, 1999).

Safren and Heimberg (1999) compared 56 GLBT youths to heterosexual youths ages 16 to 21 and found that more than twice as many GLBT youths (30%), compared with heterosexual youths (13%), reported a prior suicide attempt. They also found that GLBT youths reported a much higher rate of depression and hopelessness, lowered social support, and fewer positive life events than their heterosexual peers did. With further analysis, they found that the increased levels of depression, hopelessness, and social support could account for the higher levels of suicidality in the GLBT population.

These studies help researchers to understand the suicide risk for GLBT individuals. These studies and others support the widely held belief that suicide risk (e.g., suicide attempts, suicidal ideation) is higher for the GLBT population, particularly in adolescence and early adulthood, than in the heterosexual population. However, mental health appears to be a very significant intervening variable. That is, the GLBT population, in general, has been found to have higher rates of psychiatric disorders (most notably depression, anxiety, and substance abuse) in young adulthood than the heterosexual population, and it is these disorders, not sexual orientation, that elevate risk. In other words, once the mental health disorders are controlled for in the research, the suicide risk for GLBT individuals is no higher than that for heterosexual individuals. There is nothing about being gay, per se, that elevates risk; it is the depression, anxiety, and substance abuse the frequently are part of the GLBT world that are the problem.

Specific Risk Factors in the GLBT Population

The same risk factors that have been discussed within the context of the general population also are at play for the GLBT population. In general, over 90% of suicides are associated with a mental illness, and this appears to hold true for the GLBT population as well. However, GLBT individuals appear to be at higher risk for psychiatric illnesses, particularly during certain developmental stages (e.g., adolescence and early adulthood, primarily around the coming-out process). Young GLBT people are at increased risk for substance abuse and other psychosocial difficulties. It has been hypothesized that the act of coming out, both to self and to others, is a developmental stressor for GLBT youths that increases mental health difficulties, which, in turn, increase suicide risk (McDaniel et al., 2001).

Other specific risk factors for the GLBT population are linked to discrimination and homophobia. The widespread stigmatization and institutionalized discrimination against the GLBT population leads both to externally derived hostility and internalized homophobia. Together, the external and internal stressors can lead to shame, hostility, and self-hatred (Herek, 1996). These negative consequences have been linked to substance abuse, familial difficulties, suicidal ideation, depression, isolation, and violence (McDaniel et al., 2001). Violence and victimization, because of sexual orientation, also have been proposed as risk factors for suicide, although others have found that violence and discrimination did not elevate suicide risk. Diminished social support can be linked to suicide, and one study found that among GLBT youths, those who had attempted suicide were more likely than other GLBT youths to have lost a friend after disclosure of sexual orientation (Hershberger, Pilkington, & D'Augelli, 1997). The use of alcohol and drugs by GLBT people, particularly during adolescence and young adulthood, contributes to increased risk. Some research shows that as many as three in ten GLBT individuals have a significant problem with drugs or alcohol (Granello, 2004). Although the research is mixed, it is clear that the greatest risk for psychiatric difficulties among the GLBT population occurs in early adolescence and young adulthood and that by the time people reach middle adulthood, there is no difference is mental health pathology rates between the GLBT and heterosexual populations. Therefore, writers have hypothesized that by the time GLBT persons reach middle adulthood, most have developed a variety of coping strategies to deal with discrimination and homophobia and to minimize its negative consequences (Muehrer, 1995).

Finally, several authors have suggested that conversion therapy might increase suicide risk, and anecdotal studies have supported this claim. Conversion therapy is based on the belief that homosexuality is pathological, is undesirable, and can be changed, and therapies that attempt to change the sexual orientation of GLBT individuals tend to reinforce homophobic stereotypes. It is possible that this process increases internalized homophobia and may increase suicide risk, and it is also possible that persons who are motivated to undergo conversion therapy have other characteristics that may elevate their suicide risk (McDaniel et al., 2001). Systematic research on the possible suicide risk of conversion therapy does not exist.

Concluding Remarks: Suicide and Suicide Risk in the GLBT Population

Overall, then, it appears that research supports generally higher rates of suicide attempts and suicide ideation in the GLBT population, and there is some evidence that there are higher rates of completed suicides as well. The highest risk appears to be for adolescents and young adults and might be connected to the coming-out stage of development. Young GLBT individuals have higher rates of psychiatric disturbances (most notably depression, anxiety, and substance abuse disorders) than those of the heterosexual population, and these mental health problems appear to be the mechanism that increases the suicide risk. That is, being gay, lesbian, bisexual, or transgendered in and of itself does not elevate risk for suicide. Mental health problems in the GLBT population, which may be linked to discrimination, homophobia, and violence, increase risk. There is some evidence that once a GLBT person reaches middle age, the incidence of mental health problems decreases and matches the level of psychiatric disturbances in the heterosexual population. Once this occurs, there appears to be no greater risk for suicide in the GLBT middle-aged and older adult population than in the heterosexual middle-aged and older adult population.

Prisoners and Incarcerated Populations

In 2001, nearly 6.6 million adults were on probation, in jail or prison, or on parole; that is, 3.1% of all U.S. adult residents or 1 in every 32 adults. Prison inmates accounted for nearly 1.5 million people: 1,264,437 under state jurisdiction and 161,681 under federal jurisdiction. Additionally, local jails held or supervised 737,912 people awaiting trial or serving a sentence (U.S. Department of Justice, 2002). Over 100,000 juveniles were held in residential placement facilities (U.S. Department of Justice, 2002). In general, incarcerated people tend to be young (about 44% are under age 25), male, single, and poorly educated. Racial minority groups (particularly African American, Hispanic, and Native American) are overrepresented.

Overall, the incarcerated population has higher rates of completed suicide and suicide attempts than does the general population. Although estimates vary, approximately 20–30 inmates per 100,000 commit suicide each year (compared to approximately 12 per 100,000 in the general population). However, just as in the general population, suicide rates among the incarcerated population vary significantly by age and circumstance. The most notable difference is among types of holding facility.

Suicide Rates in the Incarcerated Population

Suicides in jail and prison populations tend to occur toward the beginning of the incarceration. About 60% of the suicides occur within the first six months, and about 90% occur within the first three years (Blanc, Lauwers, Telmon, & Rougé, 2001). It is for this reason that the majority of suicides occur in jails, where inmates are typically held during the pretrial portion of their incarceration and sometimes for the initial posttrial holding period.

Suicide rates in jails are much higher than rates in prisons. In fact, several studies have demonstrated suicide rates in jails as high as 132 per 100,000, more than ten times the national average for the general population of similar age, sex, and race (Winfree, 1988). Those who commit suicide in jail typically have committed a serious or violent crime (e.g., murder, rape, felonious assault) and will commit suicide either within a few days after incarceration or a few months later, when a trial is approaching or sentencing has just been completed. Thus, suicide in jails tends to be a decision based on acute crisis. The most common method for suicide in jail is hanging, using whatever means might be available (e.g., shoelaces, underwear, bedsheets) (Lester, 1993c).

Suicide rates also are high in police lockups, before an initial meeting with a judge to set bond or to be held over for trial in a jail. Although specific statistics are difficult to uncover, there is evidence of suicide risk for a particular subset of the population in police lockup. The individuals who are at highest risk are white males with no history of criminal behavior, who are under the age of 22, and who have been arrested for a relatively nonserious crime. It appears that the risk is highest for these individuals within three hours after booking, as they come to understand the seriousness of their situation or the embarrassment they have caused their families. The most common method is by hanging (Lester, 1993c).

Suicide rates in prisons, although somewhat higher than in the general nonincarcerated population, are much lower than the rates in jails. Prison suicides typically occur at maximum-security institutions among inmates with long sentences (more than eight years). Prisoners on death row are at the highest risk among the prison population, in spite of the tighter security measures that are in place for that specific population.

Rates of suicide attempts in the incarcerated population are higher than rates in the general population. Although it is extremely difficult to determine the number of attempts in jails and prisons, in general, it is thought that suicide attempts occur at rates about seven times higher than in the general population matched for age, race, and gender (Bland, Newman, Thompson, & Dyck, 1998). In a large-scale study of all incarcerated people in a single catchment area, 22.8% of male inmates reported that they had made a suicide attempt since their incarceration (Bland et al., 1998).

Just as in all groups with high suicide risk, there is an increased rate of psychiatric disorders in the prison population compared to the general population. Many mental health care workers have noted that jails and prisons are increasingly becoming "hospitals of last resort" for people with mental illnesses (Barr, 1999). That is, as access to good-quality mental health care is decreasing for people with chronic mental illness, many of whom are poor, unemployed, and people of color, more and more people with mental illness are finding themselves involved in the legal system. For example, not long ago, a person with schizophrenia who was causing a public disturbance would be admitted to a residential facility. Today, few such facilities exist, and those that do often have long waiting lists. The same person with schizophrenia today would likely find himself or herself in a jail. Jails—and, to a lesser extent, prisons—become the place where people with mental illnesses are removed from a society that does not tolerate them. As many as 20% of people in jail have a serious mental illness, and many more have a substance abuse disorder.

Inmates who are at higher suicide risk tend to have poorer coping skills than the rest of the prison population. Just as in the world outside of prisons, inmates with poor coping skills have few alternatives for handling their intrapsychic pain. Because incarceration itself limits the variety of coping skills that can be employed, inmates must work to adapt coping skills that they utilized in the outside world to their imprisoned selves. For example, successful coping skills in the prison population tend to focus on distraction, cognitive reframing, acceptance, seeking social support, and relaxation (Dear, Slattery, & Hillan, 2001). Inmates who either cannot adapt their coping styles to fit the limitations imposed by their incarceration or did not have coping skills to begin with find that the stress of living in prison can place them at high risk for suicide.

Inmates, in general, also have higher rates of traumatic life events than the nonincarcerated population, and suicidal inmates typically have suffered even more trauma than the average prisoner. For example, one study found that almost one third of male suicidal inmates had been sexually abused, more than half had been confronted with a suicide attempt or completed suicide of a significant other, and an even higher proportion had experienced physical maltreatment, emotional maltreatment, or abandonment (Blaauw, Arensman, Kraaij, Winkel, & Bout, 2002).

Finally, there is some evidence that people who attempt or commit suicide while in prison have higher rates of being bullied by other inmates than do those who do not attempt suicide (Blaauw, Winkel, & Kerkof, 2001). As many as one third of inmates who completed suicide had notes in their prison files documenting their perceptions that they were being bullied by other inmates. Inmates who are the victims of serious bullying (e.g., actions that made them fear for their lives or the lives of family members) are at higher risk than those who are victims of less-serious offenses (e.g., being ridiculed, being called names, or having their property destroyed).

Specific Risk Factors in the Incarcerated Population

In the 1970s, Danto (1971) identified a typology of suicidal inmates. Although this typology has not been empirically validated, it does offer some general guidelines for people who work with this population.

Morality Shock. People in this category become suicidal rather quickly after confinement (often in a police lockup or jail, typically before they reach prison). They realize the magnitude of their problems and the consequences of their actions. Often, these individuals have no significant criminal history and typically have stable marriages, responsible careers, and families. Crimes range from crimes of passion (first- or second-degree murder) to sexual offenses that will be made public to white collar crimes, such as embezzlement. The individual's own sense of morality is offended by his or her actions, and they are deeply ashamed of the embarrassment they have caused their families.

Chronic Despair. Incarcerated people who attempt or commit suicide from a place of chronic despair typically have already been sentenced and are living in a jail or prison. These individuals have a deep and ongoing sense of hopelessness and futility about their futures. They have been incarcerated long enough to feel rather disconnected from the world outside, including their families and their previous lives. People in this category might or might not have served a previous prison term. They use suicide to escape what they perceive as a hopeless future.

Manipulation. Just as there are people in the outside world who use suicidal threats and attempts to get their needs met, so too are there people in jails and prisons who use suicide as a manipulative gesture. People who attempt suicide might get transferred to a prison hospital, which could result is getting away from problems with cellmates or being assigned to an easier work schedule. They also might use suicide simply as a mechanism to get some attention or to relieve their chronic sense of boredom. In the case of manipulative attempts, the goal is not death (unlike those with morality shock or chronic despair), but improved living conditions.

Self-Punishment.   A small percentage of suicidal inmates believe that they justly deserve to be punished for their behaviors, and they use suicidal threats, attempts, or completions to make themselves as miserable as possible. These individuals have a deep and pervasive sense of guilt for their crimes, and they use violence against themselves as atonement.

The Special Case of Incarcerated Juveniles

With more than 100,000 juveniles in residential placement facilities, the population of juvenile offenders warrants brief mention. In general, incarcerated adolescents are at high risk for suicide threats, attempts, and completions. The rate of completed suicides for incarcerated juveniles is estimated to be between four and five times higher than that for their nonincarcerated peers (Memory, 1989). Just as with the nonincarcerated adolescent population, attempts are higher among the female incarcerated population. Unlike the general population, however, there is some evidence that completed suicide also is more prevalent among incarcerated adolescent females, although this population is extremely difficult to study (Rohde, Seeley, & Mace, 1997). Nevertheless, it is not surprising that the incarcerated adolescent population, in general, would be at high risk. Many of the at-risk behaviors, cognitions, emotions, and environmental risk factors that were outlined in Chapter 3 are extremely prevalent in this population. For example, the juvenile offender population has high rates of psychiatric disorders (often conduct disorders and substance abuse disorders), poor coping skills, deficits in their social support systems, and problems with anger and impulsivity and lives in an extremely stressful environment (Rohde et al., 1997). Just as with the nonoffender population, depression and hopelessness contribute to suicide risk, and incarcerated juveniles typically have very little hope about the future.

Concluding Remarks: Suicide and Suicide Risk in the Incarcerated Population

People who are incarcerated have a higher risk for suicide, when matched for age, race, and gender, than the general population. In general, the highest risk occurs in the weeks and months following the initial arrest, with crisis points occurring immediately after arrest, just before the trial, just before or after sentencing, and in the initial adjustment to prison life. Many factors contribute to the increased risk, including high rates of psychiatric disorders among inmates, high stress levels, and high rates of trauma, both before and during incarceration. Inmates who are at higher risk for suicide are primarily those who are experiencing moral shock (what they have done has offended their own moral code) or those in chronic despair who see no hope for their future. Inmates also make suicide attempts to manipulate prison staff and to receive special privileges. Finally, a smaller number may use suicide as a form of self-punishment. Little is known about suicide risk in the juvenile offender population, but all available research suggests that this population, as a group, also is at high risk for attempts and completions.

Law Enforcement Populations

There has been a long-standing belief in the mental health community that police officers have a higher rate of suicide than do people in other professions. Each year, in the United States, an estimated 300 active-duty police officers commit suicide (Seligman, Holt, Chinnit, & Roberts, 1994). The high-stress nature of the job, full of potential life-threatening situations, contributes to high rates of alcoholism, divorce, marital strain, and general decline in overall health (Marzuk, Nock, Leon, Porter, & Tardiff (2002). As recently as 1996, Violanti called suicide in the law enforcement profession an "epidemic," and other authors have suggested that the suicide rate for law enforcement professionals is two to three times the rate for the general population (Hem, Berg, & Ekeberg, 2001).

The problem with making determinations about the suicide risk for the law enforcement profession is that the studies use widely varying methodologies, and many have poor generalizability to the police profession at large (Hem et al., 2001). For example, many studies are conducted in a specific locality, and rates can vary widely by geographic location and urban or rural settings. Additionally, many such studies are conducted after a local epidemic of police suicides in a particular area. Studies often have very small sample sizes. For example, one study in Wyoming focused on ten police officers who committed suicide and then concluded that the suicide rate for police in Wyoming was 203.7 per 100,000—about 17 times the rate for the general population (Nelson & Smith, 1970). Finally, most studies do not differentiate the type of assignment for the police officers who are involved, and there is undoubtedly wide variability in the stress levels of people assigned to routine or desk jobs or public education and outreach and those assigned to street-level enforcement in urban areas.

In 2001, Hem and colleagues conducted a comprehensive review of the research on police suicides. They included 20 studies from 1950–2000 in their review, each study with a minimum of ten police suicides. From their review, they concluded that there is not sufficient evidence to substantiate the claim that suicide rates are higher among law enforcement professionals than in the general population. Studies vary widely in their results, some finding that there is decreased risk, others concluding that there is the same risk, and still others with results that support increased risk. In the face of the current research, then, it appears premature to report that police and law enforcement officials have an increased risk for suicide, although there certainly are specific individual studies that support the elevated risk.

Even though the latest research supports no elevated risk overall, mental health practitioners should be aware of several concerns. First, specific police departments, cities, or jurisdictions may have high risk associated with them. There is some evidence that police suicides occur in local epidemics. Second, the high-stress nature of the job of many law enforcement officials and the easy access to handguns make suicide a potential option that must always be seriously considered in assessing risk. Third, because police officers undergo psychiatric evaluations that are designed to weed out psychiatrically disturbed recruits, it could be argued that rates that are similar to the general population are in fact *effectively higher* for the police population, given that the incidence of suicide occurs within generally psychologically healthy individuals (Marzuk et al., 2002). Fourth, because of the strong loyalty that develops within the closed systems of most police departments, it is possible that there is an even higher incidence than normal of underreporting and misclassification of suicides (Mohandic & Hatcher, 1999).

Specific Risk Factors in the Law Enforcement Population

Just as with all populations, suicide risk in the law enforcement profession has multiple determinants. Several of these have been identified, including exposure to trauma and death, difficult administrative policies, changing assignments, irregular work hours, poor equipment, public mistrust, government criticism of police actions, and judicial decisions that are perceived to undermine police work (Marzuk et al., 2002). Others have noted a culture of violence in the law enforcement profession that might increase risk for suicide. This culture of law enforcement might support the belief that violence is a way of solving problems. There also is a pervasive belief that individuals must fall back on their own self-reliance and inner strength to solve problems. Reaching out to others for support might be perceived as a weakness (Mohandic & Hatcher, 1999).

Concluding Remarks: Suicide and Suicide Risk in Law Enforcement Populations

At this point, it is difficult to say from a research perspective whether law enforcement personnel overall have a higher suicide rate than the general population. What is clear is that there are circumstances that can elevate risk—both occupation-based and individual risk factors. Additionally, suicides among police personnel can sometimes occur in clusters within departments or jurisdictions (such as the much-publicized case of two police partners who committed suicide within several months of each other in Los Angeles during 1997). Overall, mental health practitioners who work with law enforcement personnel must be intimately familiar with the special culture that exists within a particular police department and the extreme pressure that officers face on a daily basis—not just the stress of their jobs, but also the added stress of trying to live up to a societal ideal of individual strength, resiliency, and morality. Whether the statistics demonstrate increased risk at a societal level is, in fact, somewhat immaterial. Mental health practitioners must calculate the risk factors for these professionals at an individual level.

Military and Veteran Populations

Overall, rates of suicide in the active military population have been lower than those in the general population. According to the Department of Defense 1998 data, approximately 4% of active military personnel report that they have considered suicide as a mechanism to relieve their stress and/or depression (U.S. Department of Defense, 1998). Before the second Iraq war, rates of completed suicides in the active military were approximately 12 per 100,000—lower than the general population when matched for age and gender (U.S. Department of Defense, 1999). Data from the separate branches of the military do not show significant differences in suicide risk or rates of completed suicides. Historically, there is a significant body of research that demonstrates that suicide rates in the military (as well as in the general population) are lower during periods of war (Lester, 1993d). However, this trend might not be holding true for the Iraq war. During a one-year period from April 2003 to April 2004, 24 soldiers killed themselves, making the suicide rate approximately 17 per 100,000, or higher than that in the general population. In addition, seven soldiers killed themselves on returning home to the United States. If this rate holds, then the suicide rate for active-duty soldiers in the Iraq war will be higher than that during the Vietnam War (15.6 per 100,000) and the 1991 Persian Gulf War (3.6 per 100,000). Some in the military have noted that the ambiguous nature of the daily decisions in the Iraq war are particularly difficult for men and women in the military who have been trained to view war in black-and-white terms (Miller, 2005). Others have stated that decisions to extend the deployment of troops have played a major factor. According to military analyst James F. Dunnigan (2002), "the higher suicide rate in Iraq can be attributed to the higher percentage of married and reserve troops, and the lower amount of stress training and screening in basic training for non-combat troops."

The historically lower rates of suicide does not mean that the military does not have significant mental health problems among its members. Given the high rates of stress inherent in military life (military personnel rate separation from family and deployment as most stressful), it is perhaps not surprising that members of the armed services have high rates of stress-related mental health problems, most commonly alcoholism. Approximately 8–10% of veterans suffer from posttraumatic stress disorder (PTSD), which may increase suicide risk (Berkowitz, 2004). In suicide autopsy studies, the leading cause of the suicide was loss of "love object" (Military and Veterans Health Coordinating Board, 2000; Rothberg, Fagan, & Shaw, 1990), and approximately 75% of the active military personnel who completed suicide in 2000 had "significant relationship problems in their personal lives" (DC Military, 2001).

One reason that has traditionally been given for the lower rates of suicide in the military than in the general population is the psychological screening of recruits that occurs and the ongoing mental health assistance that is available to everyone in the military. However, in 1998, almost 18% of active military stated that they believed that they needed mental health care, but only 9% reported that they received such care. The most common reason for not seeking help was a belief that such behaviors would negatively affect the military career. In 2003, an Army report noted that under newly enacted war policies in the Iraq war, soldiers with preexisting mental health problems were inappropriately deployed to the front. The report stated "variability in pre-deployment screening guidelines for mental health issues may have resulted in some soldiers with mental health diagnoses being inappropriately deployed." That could "create the impression that some soldiers develop problems in theater, when, in some cases, they actually have pre-existing condition" (Berkowitz, 2004). Clearly, there is room for significant improvement in access to and use of mental health care in the military. Both the Air Force and the Army have begun large-scale efforts aimed at suicide prevention, and there is some preliminary evidence from both of these branches that the suicide rate has dropped even further since the initiation of the programming (DC Military, 2001; U.S. Department of Health and Human Services, 2002b), although these results were released before the Iraq war, with no follow-up data available.

Specific Risk Factors in the Veteran Population

In general, veterans who had longer periods of exposure to combat, had more survivor guilt, were prisoners of war, or were wounded in combat have higher rates of PTSD, which has been linked to higher suicide rates (Bullman & Kang, 1996). One study of World War II veterans found that those who were war amputees had suicide rates that were 37% higher than those of the general population (Bakalim, 1969). Another found that suicide rates were double the average rates in a population of veterans with spinal cord injuries (Nyquist & Borg, 1967). World War II prisoners of war were more likely to commit suicide than the general population when matched for age and gender (Cohen & Cooper, 1955; Keehn, 1980). There is also some evidence that Vietnam era military personnel serving in the Army were more likely to commit suicide than were those serving in the other branches (Adams, Barton, Mitchell, Moore, & Einagel, 1998).

The media have reported high rates of suicide among Vietnam veterans, with numbers ranging from 50,000 to 100,000. In fact, there is a movement in some segments of the veteran population to erect a Vietnam veterans' suicide wall next to the Vietnam veterans' memorial in Washington, D.C., to highlight to enormity of the tragedy. However, a *New England Journal of Medicine* study reports suicide rates among Vietnam era veterans to be 65% higher than that of nonveterans (Hearst, Newman & Hulley, 1986), a figure that, while alarming, does not approach the numbers that are generally reported in the media. The CDC is conducting a large-scale follow-up study of postwar mortality of Vietnam era veterans to increase our understanding of suicide rates in this population. What is evident is that there are high rates of PTSD and alcoholism among veterans, particularly Vietnam era veterans and these factors can contribute to higher rates of suicide attempts and completions. MacNair (2002) found that although PTSD is often associated with being a victim of trauma, Vietnam era veterans who had killed others reported higher rates of PTSD than did those who had not, suggesting that the act of killing can increase susceptibility to PTSD. Other mental health disorders, such as major depression and borderline personality disorder, have been linked to higher suicide rates among subgroups of veterans (Reich, 1998).

Recent studies in Australia, an ally of South Vietnam that had 8,000 troops in Vietnam during 1968 and lost more than 500 men, found high rates of suicide among the children of Vietnam era veterans. In fact, after numerous validation studies, it appears that the suicide rate for veterans' children is more than three times the national average, when matched for age and gender. Most of the deaths occurred when the children were between the ages of 15 and 29 years (Australian Institute of Health and Welfare, 2000). Although similar work has not yet been conducted in the United States, it is possible that this risk factor exists in the United States as well.

Concluding Remarks: Suicide and Suicide Risk in the Military and Veteran Populations

In general, the suicide risk in the military has historically been lower than that in the general population, but initial results from the Iraq war show an increased risk for active military. Recent programming in several military branches has had the effect of reducing the number of completed suicides, but the latest figures are from before the Iraq war and might be changing. Unlike the civilian population, military personnel appear to be at particularly high risk for suicide after the breakup of a relationship. The combination of the stress of deployment and separation from family, with the added stressor of a loss of a love object, greatly increases risk. Although mental health services are available to all U.S. military personnel, there is still stigma attached to using those services.

The picture for military veterans also is difficult to understand. There appear to be several factors that can increase risk, including length of time in combat situations, type of combat experienced, being wounded, and having high rates of survivor guilt. High rates of PTSD and alcoholism among some subpopulations of veterans also might increase risk. There is currently no comprehensive information available about the suicide risk of veterans of the first or second Gulf War.

Suicide and Suicide Risk in the Health Care Professions

The final population to be considered in this chapter is members of the health profession. There is some evidence that people in the health care professions are at higher risk of suicide than is the general population.

Dentists

Dentists have the highest rate of suicide of any profession. When compared to others of the same age, gender, race, and marital status, dentists are more than five times as likely to kill themselves (odds ratio: 5.43) (Stack, 2001a). The suicide rate among dentists has not been fully explained, although it has been hypothesized that it might be attributable to high occupational stress factors, such as hostile patients, the relatively low status of dentistry in the medical profession, and the economic difficulties of running a small business in a competitive environment (Stack, 1996). In interviews with practicing dentists, Hilliard-Lysen and Riemer (1988) found that dentists perceived their high levels of occupational stress to be due to (1) economic problems, (2) the feeling that they were perceived as second-class doctors in the medical profession, and (3) the pain that is inherent in much dental work that keeps dentists from cultivating a close doctor-patient relationship. They concluded that the occupational stress of dentistry leads to high rates of alcoholism and substance abuse, marital problems, and extreme depression. It is also possible, although it has not been studied, that the profession of dentistry attracts people who may have personality characteristics that predispose them to an increased suicide risk. Anecdotal reports note that the field of dentistry tends to attract people who are highly perfectionistic, detail oriented, and socially introverted, which might work together with the factors highlighted above to increase risk.

Physicians and Nurses

Medical doctors have a suicide rate over twice the national average, when gender, age, race, and marital status are controlled for (odds ratio: 2.31:1) (Stack, 2001a). When compared to the gender risk in the general population, female physicians are at higher risk than are male physicians (Lindeman, Heinänen, Vaisänen, & Lönnqvist, 1998). An estimated 1.5% of female physicians have attempted suicide, and 19.5% have a history of depression (Frank & Dingle, 1999). Specific risk factors that increase risk for female physicians include cigarette smoking; histories of poor mental health, alcoholism, and/or drug use; working too much; career dissatisfaction; chronic fatigue; and severe sexual harassment.

The American Medical Association and the American Psychiatric Association conducted a study of physician deaths by suicide, investigating both personality and psychosocial factors in a suicide autopsy study. They found higher rates of social problems in physicians who had committed suicide than in their control group of physicians and found that most of these social problems were attributed to alcohol and drug addiction and personality problems. Physicians who completed suicide tended to be very critical in their personal relationships, dissatisfied with their professional abilities, dissatisfied with their families and personal lives, and workaholics. (AMA Council on Scientific Affairs, 1987).

Lindeman and colleagues (1998) identified risk factors for medical doctors. They noted that many of the same risk factors that occur in the general population exist for people in the medical population (e.g., alcohol, substance abuse, depression) but at a higher rate. A specific risk factor for medical doctors was the lack of treatment of their somatic and mental disorders. Physicians tend to self-diagnose and self-treat rather than seeking the assistance of others, and they tend to do so rather poorly. It also is possible that other physicians see them as colleagues rather than patients, and therefore treat them differently. A second risk factor is the availability of drugs and the knowledge of how to use them. When physicians commit suicide, they use drug overdoses at higher rates than are seen the rest of the population, and physicians use doses that they know will be lethal. A third risk factor is knowledge of physical health that might contribute to more pessimistic views of their own physical health in the future. That is, physicians might understand the magnitude of their chronic health concerns earlier in the process and choose to end their own lives rather than losing autonomy and independence to an illness in its later stages. Finally, medical doctors might have attitudes toward life and death that allow them to consider suicide as an appropriate end, particularly when faced with an illness that might limit functioning or cause chronic pain.

There is also evidence of a higher suicide risk for nurses. When compared to others in their age, race, gender, and marital status categories, nurses are 1.58 times more likely to die of suicide. Very little information is available about the specific risk factors that contribute to the higher rate of suicide in nurses. What information is available suggests that nurses who are at risk for suicide have higher rates of smoking and serious alcohol abuse (Hawton et al., 2002). A large epidemiological study of nurses found that nurses who were experiencing the combination of high stress at home and high stress at work had a fivefold increase in suicide risk (Feskanich et al., 2002).

Social Workers

Social workers, when compared to others in their age, race, gender, and marital status, are 1.52 times more likely than the general population to commit suicide. It is possible that jobs such as social work (as well as nursing, as mentioned previously) contribute to stress because of high occupational stress levels. Certainly, social workers are often overburdened and underresourced. In general, social workers and psychologists have higher rates of lifetime prevalence of thoughts that life is not worth living, of death wishes, and of suicidal thoughts than the general population (Ramberg & Wasserman, 2000), but no data are available on suicide rates in other mental health professions (e.g., counselors, psychologists, chemical dependency specialists).

Concluding Remarks: Suicide and Suicide Risk among Health Care Professionals

Some occupations within the health care profession have a higher suicide risk than the general population. The most notable is the profession of dentistry, with rates more than five times the national average. Medical doctors, nurses, and social workers also are at higher risk. It has been hypothesized that the constant reminders of life's problems that are inherent in many health care occupations might contribute to suicide risk (Ramberg & Wasserman, 2000). The high-stress nature of these occupations in general also might elevate the risk, although people in other high-stress occupations (e.g., firefighters, air traffic controllers) do not appear to have elevated risk. Thus, it is probably a combination of the stress, the coping mechanisms used (or not used), and the personalities of people who are attracted to these positions to begin with. Clearly, this is an area of research that is open to much further study.

Summary

This chapter outlines suicide risks in five specific populations that have elevated risk: the GLBT population, people in law enforcement, prisoners and incarcerated individuals, active-duty military and veterans, and certain members of the health professions. Each of these subgroups carries an elevated risk that has been substantiated by research. Clearly, people in each of these categories deserve special attention in assessing suicide risk. However, it is worth repeating that inclusion in one of these categories heightens risk only to the extent that coexisting conditions (e.g., depression, hopelessness, impulsivity, alcohol and substance abuse, anxiety) exacerbate perceived problems. Conversely, people who are not in these high-risk categories can be individually at very high risk. Therefore, mental health practitioners are reminded to engage in prevention, careful assessment, and treatment for all people, and it is this aspect of suicide study that Section III of the book addresses, starting in the next chapter.

10

Suicide Prevention

Section III of this book addresses what mental health professionals can and should do to help prevent suicide deaths. The five chapters in this section are meant to be the "action" section of the book. In other words, you learned in the preceding section (Chapters 3–9) about who is at risk and why; this section is focused on *what to do*. To prevent suicides, there are three major activities in which mental health professionals can engage: prevention (for the most part what is called *primary prevention*, or working with groups of people to give them skills to help prevent suicide), assessment (primarily with individuals who have elevated risk), and intervention (for those who have been identified as being at risk). This section also contains a chapter on the legal and ethical issues surrounding suicide. The section begins with a chapter on prevention, with the goal that we all engage in as many prevention activities as possible to give people the skills they need to minimize individual risk.

The term *prevention* has been used to define very different approaches to the delivery of services. Traditionally, the public health care model has divided the construct of prevention into three subtypes: primary, secondary, and tertiary (Silverman & Felner, 1995). Primary prevention services are those services delivered to populations who have a potential for a particular problem but as yet do not demonstrate the targeted health problem. In the case of suicide, primary prevention involves providing services directed to general populations, for example, an entire class or building of schoolchildren who, as a whole, are not exhibiting signs or symptoms of suicidality. In the case of suicide, primary prevention programs frequently employ education as a method for increasing awareness, reducing the stigma around the discussion of suicide, and providing training on basic interpersonal skills. The education model for primary prevention education should be designed not only to raise awareness, but also to empower people to seek assistance for themselves or others. For children, this means teaching them where and how to access care from concerned adults. For adults, this includes empowering them through information, screenings, and encouragement for at-risk individuals to get help with an appropriate and accessible mental health professional.

Secondary prevention programs or services are those directed at subpopulations that can be identified as distinct in some way from a general population (Foster & Bilsker, 2002). These subpopulations are considered at risk when they possess qualities or characteristics that increase potential of acquiring the health problem. Many of these at-risk populations were discussed in some detail in Section II of this book. Examples of at-risk populations include the following:

- Native American adolescents living on a reservation where there are high rates of alcohol abuse
- Elderly Caucasian males who are isolated from social support systems
- Individuals who have families with genetic predisposition for mood disorders and with a history of suicide

These at-risk subpopulations usually have already developed problems or characteristics that make them a particularly important target for prevention programs. In many cases, providing education and counseling about how to reduce the impact of risk factors, such as family history, substance abuse, and depression, can be valuable prevention strategies. Thus, reducing risk and severity of risk in populations who are identified as having high risk is the objective of secondary prevention programs.

Finally, *tertiary prevention* is really another name for clinical treatment of those who have a full-blown case of the health problem. Tertiary prevention includes efforts to provide rapid access to services that will lessen the severity or duration of the illness and might also reduce the cost of providing health care (Stillion & McDowell, 1996). For a completed suicide, of course, there is no opportunity for tertiary care of the individual. Tertiary care for suicide, then, can be thought of as services provided to suicide attempt survivors. Intervention and treatment for underlying depression and hospitalization intended to prevent future suicidal behaviors are part of tertiary prevention. In addition, services provided to suicide survivors (e.g., family, friends, or peers) and intended to minimize contagion of a suicide constitute another type of tertiary prevention. Timely high-quality care is the key for successful treatment, not only of the immediate suicidal crisis, but also of the underlying risk factors that brought the individual to the desperate place of a suicide attempt. However, provision of high-quality care at the level that most suicidal individuals need is, sadly, rarely given. Many suicidal individuals are discharged from emergency rooms without having had a thorough psychiatric assessment, and the discharge process that is in place in most emergency care settings leads to poor follow-up appointment compliance (King, Hovey, Brand, Wilson, & Ghaziuddin, 1997). High-quality care requires advocacy on the part of the clinician for the client, coordination with both inpatient and outpatient providers, and a solid knowledge of crises management skills.

As we saw in previous chapters in this book, many suicide attempts and completions are the result of both unrecognized and untreated mental health and substance abuse disorders. Consequently, an important key to preventing many suicides is to gain the ability to detect and treat people who are exhibiting signs of mental and emotional distress at the earliest possible occasion and take action to get them help. Logically, then, the main reason for advocating for prevention is as an important intervention strategy: to improve the ability of gatekeepers in the school and community to detect suicide risk in others and to link those at-risk people to intervention services. To do this, most of the programming for suicide prevention would be primary preventive in nature, with the goal of preventing new cases of completed suicides.

Unfortunately in the United States, most medical and social service systems are often designed to respond only after a problem (i.e., a suicide attempt) has taken place. At present, most "prevention" programs in the educational, medical, and community services system focus on delivering services that at best could be characterized as secondary or tertiary in nature (Maris, 2002). Although there is a great spectrum nationally concerning the provision of high-quality care, many communities simply do not have adequate mental health care programs or resources available to provide effective primary prevention programs. Sadly, even when a child or adolescent with increased risk has been identified and secondary prevention is called for, often little or no treatment is provided to them in a timely manner, especially to those who are dependent on health care programs provided in the public sector (Kataoka, Zhang, & Wells, 2002). Fewer than 20% of depressed adolescents (American Academy of Child & Adolescent Psychiatry, 2005) and 10% of depressed older people (Miller et al., 2000) receive any type of mental health intervention.

We argue that progress in preventing suicides must challenge this current approach of only responding to crises or providing a minimal social safety net to public health issues, such as suicide. To achieve the goal of preventing new cases of suicide, an increase in resources (time, money, professional energy) must be directed toward primary and secondary prevention programming. To place emphasis on the importance of preventing new cases of suicide, this chapter will focus on primary and secondary prevention programming, specifically as it relates to prevention programs for schools and

BOX 10.1

- FACT: Younger age children are attempting suicide at increased rates.

- FACT: Adolescents complete suicides at the rate of about 11 per day, or 4,000 per year. About 3,500 adolescents attempts suicide *each day*. Suicide is the second leading cause of death of those 15–24 years of age.

- FACT: Depression and conduct disorders are a serious and pervasive mental health problem in our schools. In one study, 95% of school age suicide victims in had at least one diagnosable psychiatric disorder (Shafii & Shafii, 2003).

- **Fact: The majority of schools do NOT have *any* suicide prevention programming.**

community settings. Tertiary prevention (treatment) is discussed in much greater detail in Chapters 12 and 13, which focus on interventions for suicidal individuals.

Suicide Prevention in Schools

The first three facts in the accompanying box simply do not logically fit with the last fact. Unfortunately, the absence of suicide programming in schools remains a reality, in spite of a consistent and clear need. In one survey of 1,200 educators, only 20% indicated that their school had any suicide prevention plans (Speaker & Petersen, 2000). Furthermore, when they were asked, "What were the reasons for not having a suicide prevention program in school?," the number one response was "do not know the reason." In other words, there appears to be no logical reason for this oversight, other than that no one has taken it on as a responsibility. In another very disturbing study of high school health teachers, only 9% believed that they could identify a student at risk for suicide (King, Price, Telljohann, & Wahl, 1999). Clearly, school personnel need more and/or improved training in suicide screening, assessment, and referral.

Difficulties in Providing Suicide Prevention Programs in Schools

It might seem odd to start a section on suicide prevention programming with the reasons why people perceive that it will not work. We do this intentionally. We want you to think about what preconceptions you might have or might have heard about suicide prevention programming in the schools. Then we intend to spend the rest of the chapter telling you why we think these difficulties can easily be overcome. We believe strongly that unless we take a proactive stance toward suicide prevention programming in schools, we will never make significant headway in reducing suicide risk. The challenges are real, and we do not deny them, but we have conducted suicide prevention programming in enough schools to know that these challenges can be overcome if people are committed to the goal.

A small, coed, religiously affiliated high school had three completed suicides within the space of four years. The school was known for its high standards, its top-quality students, and the career trajectories of its graduates (most of whom went on to highly prestigious colleges). Each year, the school would post the list of seniors in the front atrium and list the name of the college that the student would be attending. For students who had not yet been accepted to a college, "TBA" was listed. Students knew this to be code for "didn't get into the school of his/her choice." Parents and families of the students at the school tended to be wealthy and prominent citizens in the city and state. The three students (two males and one female) who committed suicide were good students. One was a freshman; the other two were seniors. An additional suicide was completed by a recent graduate of the school within the first month of starting to attend college away from home.

Faculty discussions with administration about the completed suicides revealed that there was a widely held belief within the school that although these were good students, there was a lot of pressure to succeed, and students did not appear to know where to turn for help. Although there was a guidance counselor at the school, she was focused primarily on college applications and testing and had little time for personal and social interventions. Several high-ranking members of the administration (including the principal) worried aloud that staff members were making too big a deal of these suicides and that calling attention to them might increase the likelihood of more suicides. They also noted that parents might get upset if they learned that the school took time from academics to talk about suicide and mental health. Finally, they worried about the image of the school, the reaction of alumni, and their own competence to handle the mental health concerns that students might raise.

What do you see as the major stumbling blocks to suicide prevention programming in this case? As you read through the chapter, consider what difficulties are in place in this example and what might be done to overcome them.

There are many reasons why schools do not engage in suicide prevention programming. There is, of course, a general stigma surrounding mental health issues, particularly suicide, and most people have difficulty in talking about the topic. It makes all of us feel uncomfortable to talk about suicide. It is much easier to pretend that it doesn't happen. In general, stigma comes from misinformation, fears, and myths. Thus, the only way to overcome stigma is through education, often in the form of primary prevention.

Other reasons for difficulties in arranging primary prevention may be idiosyncratic to a specific school system, such as the lack of awareness about youth suicides on the part of administrators and staff (often until after a student commits suicide) or perceived lack of resources. Other reasons may be more general and apply across our schools as institutions (Herring, 1990). Anton Leenaars (2001), a leading suicide expert, believes that many popular misconceptions might be behind the reluctance of schools to engage in primary prevention programming. Examples of these misconceptions include the following:

- Suicide prevention has no place in schools.
- Talking about suicide will cause suicide.
- Schools can be sued if they have a suicide prevention program.
- Suicide prevention programs lead to contagion and copycat suicides.

Stop and consider: Have you heard any of these misconceptions before? Are there others that could get in the way of developing programming in the schools?

It is important to examine these and other misconceptions or myths in detail, because having ready responses to these concerns can assist those practitioners who want to develop suicide prevention programs in the schools. In addition to the many myths and personal biases or resistances that serve as roadblocks to providing mental health programming in schools, there are also complex and competing demands being placed on educators today. However, when mental health professionals are educated about and sensitive to these issues, they will be better prepared to advocate successfully for the provision of suicide prevention programs with school administrators and principals. Let's look at these myths again, with some responses based on research.

- MYTH: Suicide prevention has no place in schools.
  - FACT: Our nation's schools, in partnership with communities and families, are the obvious places to identify suicidal youths and to provide information to all children and their families. The 1999 Surgeon General's Call to Action, the 2001 National Strategy for Suicide Prevention, and the 2003 New Freedom Commission on Mental Health (all of which you will learn about in this chapter) call on schools to be active partners in supporting and maintaining the mental health of young people. Several key reasons have been identified for schools to be the primary place for primary prevention (Lazear, Roggenbaum, & Blase, 2003).
    - In schools (rather than home or community), students' problems with academics, peers, or other issues are more likely to be evident.
    - Suicide warning signs might appear with greater frequency at schools than at home.
    - At school, students have the greatest access to multiple helpers, such as teachers, counselors, nurses, and classmates, who have the potential to intervene.
    - Students who feel connected to their schools (e.g., they believe that teachers like and care about them, feel close to other students, and feel part of the school) are less likely to engage in suicidal behaviors.
    - Research has found that schools are the ideal place for primary and secondary prevention activities.
- MYTH: Talking about suicide will cause suicide.
  - FACT: This is a particularly dangerous myth. The reality is that talking about suicide and the feelings surrounding suicide can greatly reduce the distress of a suicidal person. Talking to people about suicide helps them understand that someone cares—that they are not alone. A study of more than 2,000 teenagers found that not only were depressed teenagers not more likely to consider suicide after it was brought up in a class, depressed teenagers who had attempted suicide in the past reported that they were *less likely* to be suicidal or upset after the discussion (Gould et al., 2005). We do not give people morbid ideas if we bring up the topic. In fact, most people consider suicide, at least fleetingly, at some point in their lives. Giving permission to talk about those feelings and find other solutions than suicide can be extremely beneficial. Of course, if by "talking about suicide," you mean simply discussing methods of committing suicide or providing web sites with "how-to's" for suicide, then yes, this kind of talk can be dangerous to people who are at risk. But, of course, that is not the kind of talk we are promoting through primary prevention programming.
- MYTH: Schools can be sued if they have a suicide prevention program.
  - FACT: As you will read in the following section, the opposite is true. Schools can be successfully sued if they ignore this important component of student life.
- MYTH: Suicide prevention programs lead to contagion and copycat suicides.
  - FACT: Copycat suicides do exist, and if someone is already vulnerable (e.g., depressed, showing warning signs, has made a previous attempt), then one suicide in a school system can trigger another. However, it is not the primary

prevention programming that leads to copycat suicides; it is the existence of other completed suicides in a young person's life (either in the school system or elsewhere in the community). Thus, primary prevention programming is intended to mitigate the already existing danger of copycat suicides in the schools.

Legal Implications of Providing Suicide Prevention Programming in Schools

One of the barriers to suicide prevention in the schools that is often presented is the fear that providing information about suicide prevention will imply that the school staff is now responsible and liable for detecting all student suicides. Several legal cases have dealt directly with these issues and point to the conclusion that primary prevention training actually lessens the legal liability of schools.

> *Kelson* v. *The City of Springfield, Oregon, 1985*: In this case, a judge ruled that an inadequate response of the school staff resulted in the death of a 14-year-old student. This case established the precedent that parents of a student who commits suicide can sue the school if the death allegedly resulted from inadequate school-based prevention. Further, the findings in this case demanded that all school staff (e.g., janitors, lunch room personnel, secretaries), not just teachers and administrators, are responsible for protection of the student (Miller, 1996). Therefore, primary prevention training must include school staff in order to reduce legal liability.

> *Wyke* v. *Polk County School Board, 1997*: In this case, a 13-year-old student had attempted suicide twice at school before completing suicide at home. Two school administrators who knew about the school attempts failed to notify the parent or secure any kind of mental health care for the child. The court found that the school district was negligent and further that "If a person of ordinary prudence would recognize an emergency health need, we see no reason why as part of their duty to supervise, school officials, and teachers should not also recognize them." (Milsom, 2002). The judgment in this case is significant because it indicates that school administrators and teachers can be held liable for not recognizing and reporting a student who is at risk for suicide. The courts have clearly found that negligence on the part of professional personnel, inadequately developed prevention policies, and poor compliance with those policies are grounds for and may result in successful lawsuits against a school system (Rittenmeyer, 1999).

There are important legal principles that arise from these two cases and serve as precedents for schools. First, a school has a responsibility to both recognize and respond to the mental health needs of students in their custody. Second, all schools and *all staff* employed by schools are responsible for the safety of their students. The responsibility for safety includes informing parents and the appropriate community agencies to ensure the students' safety. Failure to comply with either of these principles can be the basis for legal action. In advocating for suicide prevention in schools, it is important that school administrators and all staff clearly understand the risks in not providing adequate suicide prevention training to faculty, administrators, and staff.

An ethical note seems in order to conclude this section. Clearly, there are strong legal arguments to be made in favor of suicide prevention training in schools, but there is also an ethical or moral imperative. No educator who has experienced the death of a student by suicide would ever argue against the provision of these programs as the right thing to do. The authors have met countless teachers and school administrators who emotionally recount the stories of completed suicides in their schools and lament their lack of training or understanding in how to prevent them. All too often, however, schools and school systems fail to take preventive action, and it takes the loss of a child and the effects of that loss on an entire community to make this point.

Government Demands on Schools

Another concern raised by schools is the difficulty in finding time for anything other than academics. School systems are under constant and increasing pressure from government agencies to demonstrate their effectiveness related to student academic achievement (Loesch & Richie, 2005). In the past decade, schools have been deluged by state and federally mandated achievement tests, primarily under the provision of the No Child Left Behind Act of 2001.

Understandably, school administrators and teachers feel a need to stress the academic program components that they hope will produce the "magic numbers" needed on these tests. Given this trend in education, the non-test-related educational curriculum has suffered. Arts programs, music education, physical activity, and programs that are concerned with the students' holistic and mental health development have been deemed less important by many school systems. When all available instructional time must be used to stress the subjects that will be tested, primarily reading and math, it becomes increasingly difficult to provide programming that cannot be demonstrated as contributing directly to improved test scores (Isaacs, 2003).

Given the government and public demands for increased academic accountability in schools, it is somewhat ironic that there are also new government policies that emphasize the need for an increased role of schools in the safety and mental health of children. As of 2005, there were no states that mandated suicide prevention programming in the schools, and it is up to individual schools and districts to decide what type of suicide prevention programs, if any, students will receive. Nevertheless, there has been a push for other types of mental health programming in the schools. Some of these pro–mental health policies are also promoted as essential to increasing academic achievement.

In 1999, Dr. David Satcher, in his role as the Surgeon General of the United States, issued the first report on children's mental health, entitled *The Surgeon General's Call to Action* (U.S. Public Health Service, 1999). That report included two important goals and statements that directly relate to schools, which are outlined as follows:

> *Goal 6:* Implement Training for Recognition of At-Risk Behavior and Delivery of Effective Treatment
>
> • Key gatekeepers (in need of training) include **teachers and school personnel**.

Goal 8: Improve Access to and Community Linkages with Mental Health and Substance Abuse Services

- Providing training for clergy, **teachers and other educational staff,** correctional workers, and attorneys on how to identify and respond to persons at risk for suicide. . . .
- Defining and implementing screening guidelines **for schools, colleges,** and correctional institutions, along with guidelines on linkages with service providers. . . .

Following the Surgeon General's report, a national strategy for suicide prevention was developed. The National Strategy for Suicide Prevention: Goals and Objectives for Action was developed by the U.S. Department of Health and Human Services (2001). It also specified an important goal specifically related to the role of schools in suicide prevention:

Goal 4: Develop and Implement Suicide Prevention Programs

- Increasing the number of evidence-based suicide prevention **programs in schools, colleges and universities,** work sites, correctional institutions, aging programs, and family, youth, and community service programs, ...
- Individuals from a variety of occupations need to be involved in implementing the plan, such as health care professionals, police, attorneys, **educators,** and clergy.
- Institutions such as community groups, faith-based organizations, **and schools** all have a necessary part to play.

A special commission was ordered by the president to evaluate the current state of the mental health care system in the United States and to recommend goals for improvement. The New Freedom Commission on Mental Health (2003) indicated that one of its main goals for improving the mental health system would be to improve and expand school mental health programs. Three important statements, taken from the commission's final report, support this goal:

1. "By 2005, increase the proportion of school districts and private school associations with evidence-based programs designed to address serious childhood and adolescent distress and prevent suicide."
2. "Schools should have the ability to play a larger role in mental health care for children. Growing evidence shows that school mental health programs improve educational outcomes by decreasing absences, decreasing discipline referrals, and improving test scores. The key to improving academic achievement is to identify mental health problems early and, when needed, provide appropriate services or links to services. The extent, severity, and far-reaching consequences make it imperative that our Nation adopt a comprehensive, systematic approach to improving the mental health status of children. Clearly, school mental health programs must provide any screening or treatment services with full attention to the confidentiality and privacy of children and families."
3. "The Commission recommends that Federal, State, and local child-serving agencies fully recognize and address the mental health needs of youth in the

education system. They can work collaboratively with families to develop, evaluate, and disseminate effective approaches for providing mental health services and supports to youth in schools along a critical continuum of care. This continuum includes education and training, prevention, early identification, early intervention, and treatment" (pp. 62).

Thus, from one side, schools are being pressured to focus almost exclusively on academic learning, and from another side, they are being pressured to attend to the underlying health and social needs of children, particularly as these needs affect academics. The reality concerning youth suicide is that amid all of these competing social pressures and conflicting government policy demands, each day children and adolescents take their own lives in increasing numbers. Efforts must be made by responsible and ethical school principals, counselors, faculty, school nurses, and staff to address this real-world problem before many more young lives are lost. Fortunately, in response to the realities of youth suicide, many school counselors and staff (especially the ones who have lost a student) are no longer questioning the value of implementing school-based suicide prevention programming. Instead, they are grappling with the steps of the implementation process, including how to create a program, overcome barriers to programming, focus and evaluate their efforts effectively, decide on specific content, and determine to what audiences to deliver their prevention messages. In the next section, we will take a more personal approach to examining some specific models for implementing a primary suicide prevention program in a school setting. Through the examples provided by these models, we hope that counselors and other school staff will make the determination that such programming is both desirable and possible. The goal of this section is to answer as many questions as possible to reduce the barriers—real or perceived—that are preventing such programming in the schools.

Developing a Comprehensive School Suicide Prevention Program

Developing a school suicide prevention program might seem like a daunting task to professionals with already demanding schedules. Fortunately, you do not need to reinvent the wheel. Many good resources and guidelines have been developed to assist in this process, and most are available free of charge. We will focus on three main components of programming in the next section. The first is a checklist of tasks that you can use to assess your current school system's suicide prevention program. On the basis of the assessment derived from this checklist, you might wish to develop goals related to the tasks indicated on the checklist that you will need to accomplish.

The next resource in the section is a table consisting of important web sites related to developing a suicide prevention program in a school setting. You might want to bookmark these sites and use them as reference materials. Several of these sites offer free (or very inexpensive) downloadable files that provide all the information you would need to establish a suicide prevention program in your school.

The third component provided contains models for implementation of a school-based suicide prevention program. These models are not intended to be exhaustive. One model that is provided is one that the authors have used; it is provided to help you think about the collaborations and constituents that you will want to work with in setting up your program. By using the materials contained in this book and the references provided, you will be well equipped with useful materials to assist you in developing your own school suicide prevention program.

Checklist for Components of a School Suicide Prevention Program

In a comprehensive review of the literature on school-based suicide prevention programs Malley and Kush (1994) developed a 16-point list of those components most commonly recommended for inclusion. The components have been adapted here, and added to them are some questions relating to each that you might wish to consider. As

BOX 10.2 • *Components of School-Based Suicide Prevention Programs*

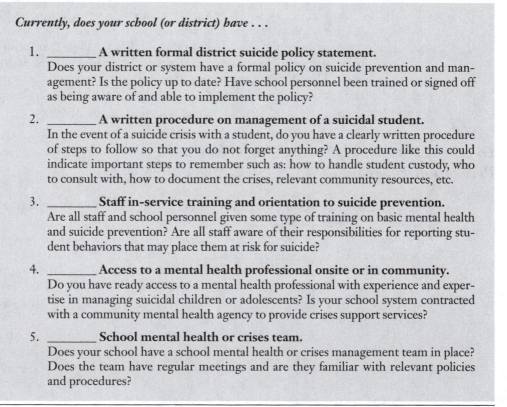

Currently, does your school (or district) have . . .

1. _____ **A written formal district suicide policy statement.**
   Does your district or system have a formal policy on suicide prevention and management? Is the policy up to date? Have school personnel been trained or signed off as being aware of and able to implement the policy?

2. _____ **A written procedure on management of a suicidal student.**
   In the event of a suicide crisis with a student, do you have a clearly written procedure of steps to follow so that you do not forget anything? A procedure like this could indicate important steps to remember such as: how to handle student custody, who to consult with, how to document the crises, relevant community resources, etc.

3. _____ **Staff in-service training and orientation to suicide prevention.**
   Are all staff and school personnel given some type of training on basic mental health and suicide prevention? Are all staff aware of their responsibilities for reporting student behaviors that may place them at risk for suicide?

4. _____ **Access to a mental health professional onsite or in community.**
   Do you have ready access to a mental health professional with experience and expertise in managing suicidal children or adolescents? Is your school system contracted with a community mental health agency to provide crises support services?

5. _____ **School mental health or crises team.**
   Does your school have a school mental health or crises management team in place? Does the team have regular meetings and are they familiar with relevant policies and procedures?

BOX 10.2 •   Continued

6. _____ **Prevention materials for distribution to parents.**
Are materials available for parents concerning students' mental health and warning signs for depression and suicide?

7. _____ **Prevention materials for distribution to students.**
Are materials available for students concerning mental health and warning signs for depression and suicide?

8. _____ **Psychological screening prevention programs that identify at-risk students.**
Are any programs provided for depression screening? Are any monitoring programs in place for students who may have demographic or other characteristics that may place them at risk?

9. _____ **Prevention classroom guidance discussions.**
Are any classroom guidance activities or presentations concerning mental health, depression, or suicide organized and delivered?

10. _____ **Mental health counseling for at-risk students.**
Are treatment services adequately provided to students either at school or in the community? Are there any preventative groups or counseling services for students who may be at risk?

11. _____ **Suicide reference materials for counselors.**
Do you have access to recent information about suicide that might help you when dealing with a crisis or with a student with suicidal ideation?

12. _____ **Suicide prevention and intervention training for school counselors.**
Has the school district's primary counseling staff been adequately trained not only in awareness and screening but in crises management and intervention?

13. _____ **Faculty training in detection of suicide warning signs.**
Is your faculty [including staff] able to name and identify the key warning signs for suicide? Do they know what to do if a student communicates that they are suicidal?

14. _____ **Post intervention procedure in the event of an actual suicide.**
In the event of a student suicide, is there a plan in place for how the system or district will respond to the other students, school personnel, media, and community at large?

15. _____ **Written procedure for assessing the lethality of a student who is suicidal.**
Is there a district approved method of assessing a student who is suicidal? Are there approved screening interview procedures, instruments, or documentation requirements?

16. _____ **Written policy that describes how the school-based adolescent suicide prevention and intervention program is evaluated.**
How is the suicide prevention program evaluated? What are the goals and outcomes that will be used to determine the benefits of the program?

BOX 10.3 • *World Wide Web Resources for Suicide Prevention Programming in Schools*

- **Guideline for School-Based Suicide Prevention Programs.**

  Developed by the American Association of Suicidology, 1999
  www.suicidology.org/ associations/1045/files/School%20guidelines.pdf

- **The Youth Suicide Prevention School-Based Guide**
  Funded by the Institute of Child Health Policy at NOVA Southeastern University, 2003
  http://theguide.fmhi.usf.edu

- **Technical Assistance Sampler on School Interventions to Prevent Youth Suicide**
  Developed by the Center for Mental Health in the Schools
  http://smhp.psych. ucla.edu/pdfdocs/Sampler/Suicide/suicide.pdf

- **Suicide Prevention: Why and How Should Schools Get Involved**
  Developed by the Center for Mental Health in Schools
  http://smhp.psych.ucla. edu/qf/suicide qt/suicide school involvement.pdf

- **SOS Signs of Suicide® Program**
  Commercially available training program supported by National Association of School Psychologists
  http://www.mentalhealthscreening.org/highschool/

- **Some Things You Should Know About Preventing Teen Suicide**
  Published by the American Academy of Pediatrics, 2003
  www.aap.org/advocacy/ childhealthmonth/prevteensuicide.htm

- **About Youth Suicide. Facts, Risks, Signs, Acting, and Prevention**
  Published by the American Foundation for Suicide Prevention, 1998
  www.afsp. org/about/newyouth.htm

- **National Strategy for Suicide Prevention Suicide: Cost to the Nation**
  Published by the U.S. Department of Health and Human Services
  www.mental health.org/suicideprevention/costtonation.asp

- **National Strategy for Suicide Prevention**
  Developed by the U.S. Department of Health and Human Services
  http://www. mentalhealth.org/suicideprevention/strategy.asp

- **Preventing Suicide: A Resource for Teachers and Other School Staff**
  Developed by the World Health Organization
  http://www.who.int/mental health/ media/en/62.pdf

- **TeenScreen**
  Developed by the Carmel Hill Center at Columbia University
  http://www.teen screen.org/index.htm

you read through the list, you might want to check off the components that are currently in place in your school system and take notice of the components that you might need to implement.

A school-based checklist also is provided on the Web, under the Youth Suicide Prevention School-Based Guide, at http://theguide.fmhi.usf.edu/. The 19 items in Youth Suicide Prevention checklist have much overlap with the list provided above but also include a general assessment of the climate of safety and attention to overall mental health concerns than the Malley and Kush (1994) checklist.

Models for Implementation of a School-Based Prevention Program

Suicide Prevention in Elementary Schools. Suicide prevention programming at the elementary level should focus on primarily on enhancing the overall well-being of the children rather than the specifics of suicide. Those who implement this programming must recognize the developmental stages of the children for whom the programming is intended and construct programming that is responsive to the developmental tasks that each child must navigate. Prevention programs at this level are typically broadly construed as primary prevention for mental health (not just suicide and/or depression) and should focus on building self-esteem, self-efficacy, social skills, problem solving, negotiation, and emotional identification and expression. The development of the concept of resiliency has been a useful one related to primary prevention programming for elementary school children. Resiliency programs teach children the protective skills that they need to adapt and respond to the demands and stressors that exist in their home and community environments. The rationale is that the promotion of protective factors at an early age will have long-term benefits in equipping students for the trials of the middle and high school adolescent years.

Secondary prevention program at the elementary level could target children who are at risk because of factors such as loss (e.g., a parent or sibling death), trauma (e.g., a house fire), or existing mental health issues (e.g., a diagnosis of ADHD or another impulse disorder). Just as with primary prevention, the programming might focus not specifically on suicide but rather on making sure that the child has the opportunity to learn healthy coping, problem solving, and emotional expression. When children feel that they are able to communicate and solve problems using non-violent means, they are more likely to avoid the mental health and stress related problems that can lead to an eventual suicide (Stillion & McDowell, 1996).

Suicide Prevention in Middle and High Schools. Suicide prevention programming in middle and high schools has two major goals. At the conclusion of such programs, students should know the following:

1. What to do if they come into contact with a person (primarily a peer) who is suicidal (i.e., identify a person at risk, respond appropriately, know how to get help, and be willing to seek help for the person)

2. What to do if they feel suicidal or depressed (i.e., know how to seek help, know to whom they can turn for help, and be willing to utilize that help as an alternative to suicidal behaviors)

The first of these goals is based on the very real and very alarming statistic that only 25% of teens say that they would tell an adult if they knew of a suicidal peer (Helms, 2003). Adolescents might believe that they are being loyal to their friend by keeping this secret. They need to fully understand that the best way to help a friend is to get an adult involved. Trying to keep the secret or trying to be the friend's therapist is not in anyone's best interest. In a training session that the first author conducted with eleventh grade boys, one of the participants summed it up beautifully when he said, "So, what you're saying is that it is better to lose a friendship than to lose a friend." Yes, that is exactly the message we want to communicate.

The second goal is to help young people recognize that help is available and they need not face a crisis alone. In Chapter 3, you learned that many suicidal young people develop tunnel vision—they cannot think of alternatives to suicide, but they do not really want to die. They just want the pain to end. Bringing in other people to help is essential. In one study of more than 1,500 high school students, 87% stated that depression and suicidal thoughts and attempts were a problem among teenagers, and 73% said that they needed more information on where to go for help if they felt depressed or suicidal (Washington County Department of Public Health & Environment, 2001).

With these two goals in mind, a school professional can access several good resources for developing a suicide prevention program at the middle or high school level. The American Association of Suicidology (AAS) has published a very useful document entitled *Guidelines for School-Based Suicide Prevention Programs* (1999) (the document is downloadable from their web site: www.suicidology.org). The AAS guidelines are divided into five sections: Conceptual Basis for Prevention Approaches, Requirements for Effective Prevention Programs, Requirements for Effective Implementation, Requirements for Institutionalization of Programs, and Comprehensive School-Based Suicide Prevention Programs. These topics provide an overview of the entire process for implementing a primary suicide prevention program in a school setting. In addition to the general topical discussion, the AAS document gives an example for a school-based suicide prevention program that includes six components: administrative consultation, school gatekeeper training, parent training, community gatekeeper training, student classes, and postvention interventions.

A second resource was developed by Capuzzi (2002). He presented an almost identical six-stage model for the development of a suicide prevention program for middle and high schools. Capuzzi's model not only includes the stages suggested by the AAS, but also recommends individual and group counseling and the preparation of crisis teams.

Finally, one of the best (and completely free!) resources for a comprehensive school-based program takes a slightly different approach from those of the two stage models listed above. It is called simply "The Guide." The Guide is an informational packet developed by the University of South Florida that provides extensive practical information for school personnel who want to develop a suicide prevention or postvention program. The Guide is organized into topical briefs with supporting checklists, handouts, annotated

BOX 10.4 • *Models for Suicide Prevention: Components of the Programs*

American Association of Suicidology	Capuzzi Model	Florida Guide Model
Administrative consultation	Communication with administrators	• School Climate • Risk Factors: Risk and Protective Factors and Warning Signs • Risk Factors: How Can a School Identify a Student At-Risk for Suicide? • Administrative Issues • Suicide Prevention Guidelines
School gatekeeper training	Faculty and staff in-service	• Intervention Strategies: Responding to a Student Crisis
Parent training	Parent education, preparation of crisis teams	• Family Partnerships • Intervention Strategies: Crisis Intervention Teams
Community gatekeeper training		• Intervention Strategies: Establishing a Community Response • Culturally and Linguistically Diverse Populations
Student classes	Classroom presentations	• Information Dissemination
Postvention interventions	Individual and group counseling options	• Preparing for and Responding to a Death by Suicide: Steps for Responding • Preparing for and Responding to a Death by Suicide: Responding to and Working with the Media

bibliographies, and a literature review. Each of the topical briefs focuses on a specific subject, such as "School Climate," and provides detailed information and a checklist for implementation of the specific program component. School personnel can obtain a Guide Packet that organizes and collates all of the information into a manageable folder (the Guide can be accessed at http://theguide.fmhi.usf.edu).

The above chart provides an overview comparison of the AAS, Capuzzi, and Florida Guide models for suicide prevention program development. The important issue is not which model to utilize in developing a suicide program, but to use a systematic approach that will ensure that all necessary components have been addressed and then to actually take action to implement a prevention program in the school.

As is evident from the chart, there is much overlap in the models. Differences are primarily in terminology, not in actual practice guidelines. In the following section, each of these components of the models will be discussed in greater detail to assist with implementation.

Administrative Consultation.   In developing a suicide prevention program, it is important to consult with school administrators and to have their support. School administrators may have important information concerning the population of the school, school resources, and the ability to promote the program with the faculty and staff of the school (Kalafat & Ryerson 1999). Before the meeting, it is important to have the basic details of your proposed program in writing (including a needs statement, goals, evaluation strategy, and a list of required resources) so that when you meet with your school administrator, he or she has something tangible to which to respond. This

---

BOX 10.5 • *Sample Outline for Staff Suicide Prevention Training (1.5 hours)* *

- Provide background information on suicide (10 minutes).
  - Suicide as a major public health problem.
  - Current statistics related to your population.

- Discuss the importance of early intervention in suicide prevention (20 minutes).
  - Share general risk factors.
  - Share risk factors specific to your population.
  - Discuss the importance of ASKING about suicide.

- Provide overview of suicide assessment (10 minutes).
  - Provide information on reliability and nature of suicide assessment.
  - Share specific examples of informal suicide checklists.

- Provide overview of crisis management (30 minutes).
  - *Practice* how to ask a student whether she or he is suicidal.
  - *Practice* how to communicate with a suicidal individual.
  - Provide information on whom to seek for consultation in a crisis.
  - Teach how to properly document a suicidal crisis.
  - Review the policies and procedures that apply in your setting.

- Summarize, and stress the importance of ASKING about suicide and the need to act early to help prevent suicides (10 minutes).

- Question and answer time (10 minutes).

*This is a model employed by the authors in school settings. Remember, this is for teachers, administrators, and all staff. It is assumed that the person who will receive the referral (e.g., the school counselor or school nurse) has more advanced training in suicide prevention, assessment, and treatment.

might be the best time to bring administrators up to speed about the legal and ethical imperatives of being well prepared for preventing a student suicide.

Training All School Personnel   A key component of your suicide prevention program will be to hold staff and faculty in-services to raise awareness concerning child mental health, depression, and suicide. Davidson and Range (1999) demonstrated that teachers were positive about and responsive to such in-services and, after such training, became more proactive concerning suicide prevention. As a result of this training, individuals in the school who come into contact with students should be able to identify those who exhibit warning signs for suicide and be willing to refer them to a school counselor, nurse, or administrator for assessment and, if necessary, referral to mental health care. It boils down to this message: "If you are worried about a child, let the appropriate people know." In the case of depression and suicide, it is truly better to be safe than sorry.

Parent Training an.d Community Gatekeeper Training

In a large-scale study (2,722 adolescents), self-reported suicide attempters had lower parental involvement than did nonattempters (Flouri & Buchanan, 2002). Suicide attempters were also more likely to report conflict in their families. Students who reported higher parental involvement were less likely to have made suicide attempts. To include parents in the suicide prevention program, a prevention presentation can be made on children's mental and emotional health issues. Parents can be made aware of the normal developmental issues to be expected in their children and adolescents as well as the warning signs of potential mental and emotional problems. Depression, substance abuse, suicide, and other child and adolescent risk behaviors can be discussed. The program for parents may also contain many of the same training elements as the educators' training, stressing the importance of asking children about suicidal ideation and how to get help in the community. Studies have shown that more than 86% of parents are unaware of their children's suicidal behaviors (Carlyon, Carlyon, & McCarthy, 1998). Not surprisingly, more than 85% of teenagers say that parents need more training in how to recognize depression in their teens and to take it seriously (Washington County Department of Public Health & Environment, 2001).

Parents can be told that a higher level of involvement with their children does have a protective influence on suicide risk. Also, parents should be informed that they will be contacted by the school if there is reason to believe that their child is having mental or emotional difficulties that might be placing themselves or others at risk.

On-site presentations to parents are not always possible. In several school systems with which the first author has worked, parent newsletters (including e-mails for school systems with active e-mail lists) were used for communication purposes. Informing parents that their children will be discussing suicide and depression at school is an important "heads-up," and teaching parents what to do if they believe that their child is at risk is essential. It would be inappropriate to teach children to talk with their parents if they are feeling suicidal but not help parents know what to do if their children approach them. The Florida Guide provides information for parents (available at http://theguide.fmhi. usf.edu/pdf/IB-8.pdf). A sample parent newsletter that

BOX 10.6 • *How to Talk with a Suicidal Adolescent*
(Information for School Staff and Parents)

It is difficult to talk with a person who is contemplating suicide. It is tempting to problem-solve for the person or to minimize the problems. As adults, it is often easier for us to see that the problems that seem so important and insurmountable to a young person are, in the greater scheme of things, not worth getting so upset about. Nevertheless, it is *essential* that we stay calm, *really listen*, and help the young person to feel heard. Some tips:

- Always ask. Ask about suicide in definite and concrete terms. Sometimes people speak in euphemisms ("They'll be sorry" or "I'm going to be with my grandmother"). Ask, "Are you thinking of hurting/killing yourself?" (More on suicide assessment is discussed in Chapter 11.)
- Stay calm and listen. The more agitated the person becomes, the more calm you need to be. People who are suicidal may come across as angry or unlikable. Don't escalate, don't become emotional, just listen.
- Don't minimize, ridicule, or problem-solve. Emotional ventilation (telling the story) is an essential component of preventing suicide. Validate their emotions ("I understand that you feel really upset and hopeless and you don't know where to turn"). You don't have to agree with the person's assessment of the problem. (You could say, for example, "Well, I don't think suicide is the only option" but do not say, "That's not worthy of being suicidal" or "It's stupid to feel suicidal over something so minor!")
- Take suicide threats seriously. Evaluate the risk, or refer the person for evaluation from a qualified individual.
- Be active. Do something. Have a plan to help. Validating the suicidal feelings *does not mean* allowing the behavior to occur ("I understand that you're really upset, and now that I understand how serious this is for you, I plan to help.") and then do something.
- Tell the person that you are going to make every effort to keep him or her alive and to marshall every resource possible to do this. Help the person to understand that this is because you care about him or her and that even though the person does not currently believe that life is worth living, *you do!* You are going to make every effort to get the person through this crisis. He or she is worth it!

contains information about mental health in children also is available at the following web site: http://www.wphf.org/ pubs/newsletterpdfs/F2005hktHS.pdf.

Community gatekeepers include adults other than school staff or parents who regularly interact with children or adolescents. These people may include clergy, sports coaches, scout leaders, 4-H leaders, or other adults. Children often trust these individuals, and they might be the individuals to whom young people disclose their suicidal ideation or intent. A presentation or even communication through a newsletter should help these individuals to understand their important role in early detection and their responsibilities to report any concerns or information they might have to the child's parents, a mental health agency, or school personnel.

Suicide Prevention as a Classroom Guidance Activity

Classroom guidance is a valuable method of communicating to a large number of students without extensive staff time (Ciffone, 1993). The content of a suicide prevention guidance activity can include information about how to recognize warning signs, where to go for resources to help, and how to respond to a troubled friend. Often classes involve the use of stimulus media, peer-led discussion, or role-plays. An important focus of classroom guidance activities for adolescents is to lessen the stigma concerning the seeking of help and to stress the importance of sharing about a fellow student they may be concerned about to a school counselor, nurse, or administrator (Kalafat & Elias, 1995). Further, students should be helped to see that suicidal thoughts and feelings might be part of a mental illness, such as depression that needs to be treated, and that adolescents should understand that emotional crises do occur and that adult help should be sought out (Ciffone, 1993). Finally, they need to understand that feeling sad and even fleeting thoughts of suicide are normal (and it does not mean that you are "crazy" if you think about suicide), but acting on those suicidal thoughts is not okay. In other words, normalize the idea that many people feel frustrated and overwhelmed but that does not mean that they kill themselves.

According to the Washington County Department of Public Health and Environment (2001), teenagers say that they would like to see the following in school-based suicide prevention programming:

Teach teens that depression is a form of illness that can be treated   65%

Inform teens how common depression is   56%

Teach teens how to tell if someone is really depressed, or just in a mood   68%

Teach teens how to recognize depression in oneself or others   74%

Teach teens where to go for help if they or a friend is depressed or suicidal 73%

Teach teens how to talk to a friend who is depressed or considering suicide 81%

Teenagers say that they want to learn this information through the use of guest speakers (93% ranked this as one of their top-three choices for a source of information), on TV (60%), from a caring adult (54%), or through peer education (53%).

When asked what adults could do to help, the overwhelming response from teens is nothing complicated or expensive: just "talk and listen to youth."

In general, we cannot yet speak from a research perspective about which prevention programs actually reduce suicide risk. In 2003, the Suicide Prevention Resource Center (SPRC) contracted with the American Foundation for Suicide Prevention (AFSP) to begin to develop an online registry of evidence-based programs for suicide prevention. Extensive reviews of programs has resulted in four practices deemed effective and eight deemed promising. Of those rated "effective," none are primary prevention or gatekeeping in nature. One (C-CARE/CAST) is a type of targeted intervention for high-risk children, one (PROSPECT) is targeted to primary care physicians and high-risk elderly, and two address means restriction. Of the eight labeled "promising," three (Columbia University Teen Screen; SOS: Signs of Suicide; and Lifelines) are

BOX 10.7 • *Sample Outline of Classroom Guidance Activity for High School Students*

This training, which has been used by the first author, typically takes place over two days, with a few days in between to allow students to think about what they have learned and prepare questions for the following class period. The training is about two hours—an hour each day. There is some emerging evidence that training provided over a two-day period is more useful than "one-shot" training, but this evidence is anecdotal and not yet supported by empirical research.

Day 1:

 Introduction to the topic
 Why is the topic being presented to students?
 Suicide myths handout and discussion of thoughts relating to suicide
 Brief presentation of statistics, risk factors, and general information
 Discussion of protective factors
 Role-play: the difference between feeling sad and feeling depressed
 Role-play: how to approach a friend who may be suicidal

Day 2:

 Begin with questionnaire about previous session:
  One thing you learned
  One thing that surprised you
  One thing you already knew
  What questions or concerns do you still have?
 Review information from previous day
 Discussion (with video clips, if available)
  Depression
  Anger and stress
  Suicide
  Helping a friend
 More role-plays this time in pairs: how to help a friend
 Generate list: What adults could you tell if you or a friend felt suicidal?
 Generate specific names from the school and community

Handouts provided with the student training:
- Information entitled "Suicide Is Not About Death" available from www.education.osu.edu/dgranello
- Information entitled "Understanding and Helping the Suicidal Individual" available from the American Association of Suicidology: www.suicidology.org
- Information on Adolescent Depression, available from the National Mental Health Association: http://www.nmha.org/infoctr/factsheets/24.cfm
- Computer-generated business cards with phone numbers for local suicide help and hotlines. Tell students to take out their purses or wallets and put these cards in them. That way, there is no stigmatizing effects that differentiate students who make a visible effort to keep the cards versus those who throw them away.

school-based primary prevention programs intended for the entire student body. As more data is collected and more evaluations completed, these may receive ratings of effective. In the meantime, these three programs offer the most extensively studied efforts at wide-scale suicide prevention programming in the schools.

For more information on evidence-based practice in suicide prevention, visit the Suicide Prevention Resource Center at http://www.sprc.org.

Program Evaluation.   In today's evidenced-based and data-driven world, all programs should have an evaluation component as part of their design. Suicide prevention programs can be evaluated in a variety of ways, most commonly through the use of structured interviews, open question surveys, and quantitative surveys (Mackesy-Amiti, Fendrich, Libby, Goldenberg, & Grossman, 1996). Collecting data before and after program delivery on quantitative variables such as number of students referred for help, type of problems that led to referral, and types of community resources referred to will allow for the impact of the program to be assessed. Qualitative data, such as the results of asking students what they learned from the training, how their thinking about suicide has changed, or whether they are more likely to seek assistance, can be invaluable sources of information. We caution against using the quantitative measures of completed suicides or suicide attempts requiring medical attention on school or district levels. The reason is that although suicide is a large-scale concern, on a smaller scale, such as a school or district, there might be very few completed suicides in any given year. For example, suppose that in the year prior to the training, there was one suicide in a school. After the training, a suicide rate of 0 would not necessarily mean that the training has been effective; the numbers are simply too small to make those kinds of comparisons. Or if there were two suicides after the training, it would not mean that the training was not successful; perhaps there were extreme and extenuating circumstances in those students' lives that the training could not mitigate. The point is that unless there are more than about 100,000 people in a study, rates of completed suicide are too imprecise a measure to use.

Kalafat and Ryerson (1999) have written an excellent and very useful article illustrating step by step how they have implemented a suicide prevention program of their own design called the Adolescent Suicide Awareness Program (ASAP). The ASAP contains the six components that are contained in the models illustrated previously and also includes a methodology for conducting a program evaluation. Mackesy-Amiti and colleagues (1996) have developed a 25-item knowledge test to be given as a pretest and posttest evaluation of participants who have attended postvention training. In the training that we conduct with high school students, we use two open-ended questions to assess what they have learned, a question that asks what questions they still have (so we can get them answered), and then some specific questions about their reactions to the resources, the presenters, and so on. Remember, the goal of training is twofold: know how to and be willing to help a friend and know how to and be willing to help yourself. The first two questions, with sample responses from a class of eleventh grade boys, appear in the accompanying box. It is worth noting that we did not go through the answers and select the "best" ones; we just chose the first several answers from each question in our database. You can see that in this example, the students whom we trained were able to take away exactly what we wanted from the training.

BOX 10.8

1. What is one main point or message that you have taken from these two presentations?
- Suicide needs to be discussed.
- Suicide is a common problem that accounts for many needless deaths in the world.
- Suicide is never the answer.
- We have to actually do something if a friend confronts us with suicide and not keep it bottled up.
- Suicide has so much effect on others.
- You should talk to people close to you when they seem to be going through a tough time or have not acted normally.
- Talk to others about your feelings.
- That suicide is a large problem but I have the power to help.
- That you always have someone to turn to; you can always get help
- Suicide is a permanent solution to a temporary problem.
- That no matter what, you need to tell adults.
- Suicide is not worth it. You can always get help.

2. Do you think, because of these presentations, you view suicide/depression or anyone dealing with suicide and/or depression differently? How?
- Yes, I see that suicide is preventable if you look for the warning signs.
- Yes, I learned that depression is a disease that you can recover from.
- Yes. I know it is very important to be open about this topic.
- Yes. Having examined the idea, it seems less likely that suicide is an answer.
- No, it only reinforced what I already knew.
- Yes, I believe that I will try and talk to my friends more.
- Yes, I know the mindset of the person depressed.
- Yes, I now know more about it.
- Yes, people need to find help.
- Yes, I realize now that suicidal people aren't just crazy, but in a lot of pain and need help.
- Not really. I've had to deal with friends before. However, I did become aware of more facts than before.
- Yes, the firsthand stories helped me see how many people are affected by a suicide.

Postvention: Responding to a Suicide in a School

So far, this chapter has stressed the need for prevention programming. Mental health professionals need to make efforts to help organize and advocate for suicide prevention programs in their school districts, workplaces, and communities in general. However, primary prevention is only part of the effort. Even with primary prevention and care, completed suicides are part of the world in which we live. Once a suicide has occurred, every effort must be made to reduce contagion and to give those who are left an opportunity to process their loss. In this section, we discuss the need for postvention preparations and management of the media.

Even in schools that are actively engaged in prevention programming, a student suicide might occur. A suicide death in a school is a complex event that affects many groups, including school personnel, parents, the media, and of course the students. Children and adolescents who experience the suicide of a peer may experience a traumatic reaction, sometimes with many of the symptoms of PTSD (Mauk & Rodgers, 1994). Individuals who are directly affected might require individual or family counseling, and this is covered in Chapter 15, "Suicide Survivors." This section addresses larger-scale postvention programming for schools and larger communities.

Postvention is the term that refers to interventions that occur after a student suicide. Postsuicide interventions have three purposes: to allow students, staff, faculty, and community members to process their reactions to the event, to help facilitate grief work, and to prevent suicide contagion among identified vulnerable peers (Thompson, 1995). The key to managing the many loss and grief issues that arise after a suicide death is to be prepared in advance with a functional district or school suicide postvention policy and procedure. Once a suicide has occurred, it is too late to begin planning for postvention, as programs must be implemented immediately. Preparation of such a policy before a crisis enables school personnel to get into action rather than figuring out what to do while the crisis is occurring. Trying to throw together an adequate system response after the suicide death has already occurred is simply not possible.

Postvention programs are designed to indicate the roles and responsibilities, as well as to coordinate the activities, of multiple school personnel including administrators, counselors, teachers, and staff. A very useful web site for helping to develop a postvention plan is hosted by the state of Maine: http://www.state.me.us/suicide/sinfores.htm. In addition, the American Association of Suicidology has a downloadable model postvention program (available at www. suicidology. org).

Good postvention plans indicates who will brief parents, the media, and the students and who will provide services to affected students. The plan indicates what resources will be needed and how and where those resources will be allocated. For example, it is common in school districts with good suicide postvention plans to increase the counseling personnel or provide personnel in the form of crisis response teams to a school after a suicide has occurred for a set period of time. The postvention policy might indicate, among other things, how crisis teams will be formed, how other school personnel will be deployed, who is in charge of the crisis response, how the media will be informed and worked with during the crisis, and how concerned community members can be utilized. It is also important to think about the scope of the postvention plan, how long the plan will be in operation, and what measures will be used to determine the outcomes of the program. Once the plan is developed, it is essential for key personnel to be aware of it and trained in how to implement the policy in a time of crisis (Mauk & Rodgers, 1994).

School personnel should be aware of their communities' mental health resources and understand how to refer students at risk to those resources. This means that school personnel must reach out to community agencies in the locations where they are situated and invite these agencies into the school setting. This ensures that clinicians in those agencies become familiar with the needs of the school before the crisis.

In general, postvention programs must be implemented quickly (often within hours of the death) as well as over a longer period of time. Immediately after a death, students who are affected might emerge as needing additional support and counseling. For some students, this happens on the day after the suicide, and they immediately self-select, or are identified by others, as being directly affected. Other students may emerge days or even weeks later and might not be readily identified by teachers and staff as being directly affected. It may be beneficial to conduct a brief screening of all potentially affected students rather than to rely on self-selection. Postvention programs need to be in place long enough for all affected students to receive assistance. All students must be made aware of how they can take advantage of support and counseling, and various opportunities should be put in place (individual, small-group, and classroom sessions). Finally, it is important to give factual information and not to dramatize or romanticize the suicide. This means helping students to recognize that the deceased child made a bad choice (but was not a bad person) and that other, more effective choices are available to them.

Suicide Prevention in Community Settings

Primary prevention services for suicide have traditionally been very limited in most communities. Suicide prevention programs in the general community, just as in school programs, must cope with the stigma surrounding the topic of suicide, historic, and economic factors. Economically, there exists a general lack of private, state, or federal resources allocated to provide for any type of prevention programming in the U.S. health care system. Although the United States spends more on health care per individual than any other country in the world, only 1% of total health care expenditures are spent in prevention efforts. It was not until the 2004 Garrett Lee Smith Memorial Act (Public Law No: 108-355) that funds were directly earmarked for suicide prevention on the federal level.

Another reason for the lack of suicide prevention programming is that traditionally, suicide was seen as the exclusive purview of the mental health fields. Therefore, suicide prevention was focused on treatment of an individual with a specific mental health disorder rather than on large-scale prevention efforts for large segments of the population. However, this might be changing. In recent years, there have been efforts to conceptualize suicide more broadly as a public health issue. The application of the public health model to suicide prevention has presented its own challenges. Suicide, unlike some phenomena in health care, has proven to be complex, with multiple and unclear etiological pathways. The complexity of variables that may contribute to a suicide makes the design, training, implementation, and evaluation of prevention programs very difficult. In spite of these limitations, some attempts have been made to provide several different types of suicide prevention programs in the community. In the next section, we review several models for suicide prevention in the community and give examples of each.

Approaches to Suicide Prevention in the Community

Three approaches to suicide prevention programming in the community have been implemented with varying levels of success: the public health model, the operational model, and the injury control model.

The public health model that was briefly described at the beginning of this chapter uses primary, secondary, and tertiary categories for prevention programs. This model is strongly connected to the traditional medical model and has some limitations that make its application to the behavioral sciences somewhat limited. The first of these limitations is the premise that there are identifiable sources that can be traced as the basis of a disease. The complexity of environmental and individual risk factors in behavior like suicide frequently makes it difficult to identify a specific source. The second limitation of the public health model is that it assumes that early manifestations of a condition are preventable once they have been identified. Again, in behavioral health it is not always easy to detect the very earliest manifestations of a problem. However, in spite of these limitations, the public health model has been used as the basis for design and delivery of a variety of suicide prevention programs. Examples of successful public health model prevention programs for suicide include education for parents to increase awareness of mental health issues and increase involvement with adolescents (Flouri & Buchanan, 2002), education for community primary health care providers concerning depression and the risk factors for suicide, and training in proper crisis intervention techniques for mental health workers and emergency room staff (Foster & Bilsker, 2002; Litman, 1995; Luoma, Martin, & Pearson, 2002; Rutz, 2001).

The operational model (sometimes referred to as the IOM, or Institute of Medicine model) was first advanced by Robert Gordon (1983) and became widespread through its inclusion in the Institute of Medicine's 1994 report on prevention in mental health (Mrazek & Haggerty, 1994). The IOM model uses three levels of prevention (universal, selected, and indicated) that are classified by the degree of risk that exists in a given population. The universal level of prevention targets whole populations that are at average levels of risk. An example of a universal program for suicide would be to hold depression screening events at community events, such as fairs or sports events. Next, selected prevention programs would target identified groups that are at higher risk than the total population. An example of a targeted program for suicide could also be depression screening for a group with higher risk than that of the general population, such as college students or geriatric groups. The last level is indicated programs that target those individuals with the highest risk. An example of an indicated program might be a suicide symptom monitoring process for clients with schizophrenia at a local mental health center or with incarcerated populations (Hayes, 1997). The IOM model is the one used by the American Association of Suicidology model for prevention programs in the schools, with universal prevention (information given to all students), targeted programs (e.g., groups for children who have experienced loss), and prevention for indicated populations (specific interventions and monitoring for adolescents who have a prior attempt). This model allows mental health professionals to specifically target groups on the basis of their estimates of risk and conceptualizes prevention programs on a continuum of care.

The last model, the injury control model (also called *means restriction* or the *ecological model*) utilizes preemptive control of the environment to remove the means for suicide (Silverman & Maris, 1995). The rationale behind this approach is that by making the environment less conducive to suicide, suicide rates can be reduced. Examples of ecological suicide prevention programs would include the passing of legislation that restricts access to firearms, a hospital's installing fencing around potential jumping places such as parking garages, or a government agency policy for tracking and regulating access to poisons (Lester 1998).

Using prevention models can help mental health practitioners to decide what populations they are trying to serve and also may provide a link to the research on their efficacy. In addition to the models described above, the Centers for Disease Control and Prevention (1992) has published a very useful resource for community and school practitioners who currently deliver or want to deliver prevention programs. The following examples are listed as types of prevention programs in the guide, along with illustrative programs, research findings, and evaluation needs:

- School gatekeeper training: Provide training on suicide risk factors and prevention to key gatekeepers in schools and other institutions that provide services to populations of children and adolescents. It is important that these gatekeepers know where to find mental health resources in the community when a crisis arises.
- Community gatekeeper training: Provide training to key gatekeepers in institutions that serve at-risk populations such as the elderly, people with mental illness, or substance-abusing populations. Provide information on how to manage a crisis situation with an individual and how to get professional support.
- General suicide education: Provide information in the community to destigmatize the issue of suicide, raise awareness, and normalize help-seeking behavior. Information should illustrate that suicide is a public health issue that crosses racial, gender, and socioeconomic lines.
- Screening programs: Organize and provide depression, anxiety, and other types of mental health and substance abuse–screening programs in the community. Provide a visible presence at community events for mental health, and provide information on how to get services if a screening result is of concern.
- Peer support programs: Provide programs that support at-risk populations and those who have been affected by a suicide death. Social support networks of survivors and volunteers can provide a valuable resource for public speaker bureaus, screening programs, or other services.
- Crisis centers and hotlines: Individuals in crisis should be able to readily access help. Organize community mental health providers and volunteers to staff a 24-hour-a-day, 7-day-a-week crisis line. The numbers to these hotlines should be posted in many locations, including physicians' offices, hospital waiting rooms, emergency rooms, schools, churches, community phone books, and any other location that is frequented by the public. A resource card with the crisis hotline numbers should be distributed to every client of community mental health centers, private mental health providers, and substance abuse treatment providers as well as to students in schools
- Means restriction programs: Community mental health providers should advocate with local governments and institutions to help control and make safe the community environment. Examples of this type of activity include advocating for legislature that controls easy access to handguns by adolescents or working with the local college or university to reduce substance abuse in the dormitories.

In a study that asked adolescents what type of suicide prevention programming they thought was needed, 39% said that they needed more education about mental health issues. This need was poignantly stated by one student, who said, "Have speakers

... I know it can be difficult to gather assemblies, but if we can have [a] sports rally, we really should be able to have an assembly to save our kids' lives." Another said, "[Make it] part of the curriculum from grade school on. Make people aware of mental health issues from little to big. Every year drugs are addressed, why not depression?" In the same study, 23% said that they needed a person who they could talk with. One student said, "The easiest way to reach tends to make help very easy and available. People want help, but they shy away if it is difficult to get" and "Have a special place teens can go just to have someone to listen to them. Many times teens don't want their parents to know about their problem and would rather talk to anyone qualified in the area of stress and depression." Another said, "I don't know how adults can reach teens. Whenever I try to get help, money gets in the way. I don't have money," and one suggested, "Pay counselors to offer services to people that can't afford counseling." Finally, 14% said that the media should be employed. One student suggested, "Through television. All kids do is watch TV. There could be some public service announcement type of stuff and that might help kids realize what to do, and come out about their problems." Others suggested, "Make videos, posters, commercials, and programs for teens and adults in the school and community" and "I would advertise and try to make the program more socially acceptable so kids don't feel embarrassed or ashamed if they think they have depression." (All figures and quotations are from the Washington County Department of Public Health & Environment, 2001.) Clearly, adolescents and members of the community have good ideas about what types of prevention programming they need.

Although presented in a very simplified form in the following box, the process steps to develop a suicide prevention plan for Ohio can provide some valuable tips for others who wish to develop programs in their states, municipalities, school districts, or agencies. Some of the tips are as follows:

- Design a program with a manageable scope. Volunteer advocacy groups could be of any size and related to the scope of the program: city sections, blocks, or other designated zones.
- Build a widespread volunteer base for encouraging business, community, and political leadership to take notice and take action. There are many suicide survivors who are willing and motivated and are looking for a way to contribute to suicide prevention efforts.
- Organize your most active volunteers into a cohesive working group with a clear objective for developing a business plan to map out exactly how, when, and what the cost will be for developing your program.
- Get some start-up funds. You do not have to fund the entire program initially; just get the planning stages funded. Once you have your business plan, you will have something to sell to state agencies and business leaders.
- Get some expertise. Community business leaders or entire civic organizations can be tapped to provide business expertise for developing the plan for the suicide prevention program. Business leaders can provide pro bono time for needed legal or accounting support and will receive a tax deduction for this.
- Get some media attention, hold a kickoff event, or involve the media with news briefs about the development of your program. Include information about how interested volunteers or donors can contact you.

BOX 10.9 • *Community Prevention: Developing a Statewide Suicide Prevention Program: Example: The Ohio Suicide Prevention Foundation*

The evolution of Ohio's statewide suicide prevention program, after several years of work by many concerned community volunteers and governmental support, has resulted in the development of a nonprofit foundation called the Ohio Suicide Prevention Foundation (OSPF).

This is the first time in the history of Ohio that a centralized statewide resource for suicide prevention has existed. The purpose of the foundation is to provide a stable agency to coordinate, train, develop, and disseminate information and programming to prevent suicide in Ohio. The creation of a separate foundation apart from existing state agencies has two major advantages: The OSPF will be able to solely focus and specialize on its primary suicide prevention function, and its charitable status allows for the development of an endowment that will enable the foundation to eventually become fiscally independent.

How did Ohio go from no statewide program to an independent foundation for suicide prevention? In a very simplified form, here are some of the critical events:

1. The Ohio Department of Mental Health, directed by Dr. Michael Hogan, established a small office for prevention programs in 1995.
2. Directed by Ms. Elnora Jackson, the prevention office organized volunteer suicide advocacy groups in 50 of Ohio's 88 counties. These advocacy groups were largely made up of suicide survivors. The volunteers were given basic gatekeeper training and encouraged to promote the prevention of suicide in their home counties and to the Ohio legislature.
3. To further coordinate the county advocacy group, members of the county suicide prevention advocate groups were invited to join a statewide organization called the Ohio Suicide Prevention Team. The efforts of this team would serve as the backbone for planning and developing a business plan for creating a new statewide suicide prevention foundation.
4. The prevention team worked with a business consultant, with the support of the Ohio Department of Mental Health, to develop an extensive plan for creating and implementing the OSPF. One of the key steps in this plan was to find a community partner to house and provide support to the foundation in its first years of functioning. A Request for Proposal offering a contract to potential partners by the suicide prevention team for the administration of the foundation was sent out.
5. The Ohio State University Department of Counselor Education (Dr. Paul Granello) responded to the RFP and was selected as the partner to house and oversee implementation of the new foundation. Partnering with a university meant that there was an existing infrastructure for grant development and management, human resources, and research efforts.
6. A large kick-off event was held with the media in attendance and the OSPF opened its doors in 2005. The foundation received start-up funds from the Ohio Department of Mental Health, and private charitable contributions.
7. A chief executive officer was hired and, along with the board of directors, began work on developing an annual strategic plan and a three-year strategic plan to guide the foundation's prevention and research activities.

Postsuicide Interventions in the Community

Postvention suicide services are those that are intended to help survivors affected by a suicide death cope with their loss. Survivors of suicide may be considered to include anyone who was connected in the social network of the deceased individual. Examples of those who might be affected include family members, friends, coworkers, classmates, or fellow church or club members. In short, anyone who thinks that he or she has been affected by the suicide of another can be considered a survivor. These people may experience shock, denial, and severe grief reactions when learning about the suicide.

These individuals need understanding and support to help them get through the very real emotional, cognitive, economic, and social aspects of their loss. Because suicide is still considered a very abnormal way to die, many individuals have not been prepared by previous experiences, cultural context, or social scripts with how to respond mentally or behaviorally. It is not uncommon to hear, "I never thought this would happen to our family" or "I never dreamed that I would ever have to deal with anything like this." Survivors often simply state that they cannot accept or believe that someone they know or love would ever have committed suicide.

Mental health professionals must respond empathically and provide a safe place for suicide survivors to process their grief and loss. Psychotherapy models for treating other populations who have been through a posttraumatic experience might have value in helping individuals who experience significant distress from the suicide, but little information is available on postvention models outside of the school setting. The types of services that are needed as part of the postvention response may include group and individual crisis debriefing sessions, group and individual counseling, assessment of at-risk individuals (e.g., friends of the deceased person), and appropriate referrals to mental health providers for ongoing care. Services also might be required not only for the initial crisis period but also for several months, as a community may be deeply affected by the loss of one of its members. In one situation that the second author was involved with, after the suicide death of a coworker, times were set up for coworkers to meet in groups and talk about the person who had died and to get information from counselors about depression, grief, and suicide. Individual appointments also were available by request.

Working with the Mass Media: Prevention and Postvention

Evidence has emerged that broadcasting different types of media messages can have an influence on suicide rates. The influence of the media has been shown in both a positive direction, contributing to a reduction in suicide, and a negative direction, as contributing to contagion and copycat suicides (Bale, 2001; Etzersdorfer & Sonneck, 1998). Media stories about suicide in both electronic and print formats that are repeated frequently, describe in detail the method of suicide, are sensationalized or given prominence, and neglect to mention underlying psychiatric illness all can increase suicide contagion (Bale, 2001). Conversely, media stories that encourage people to find other solutions to problems can reduce suicide. In Australia, for example, media coverage of the death of Kurt Cobain was highly critical of his choice to take his life, and suicide deaths by 15- to 24-year-old males fell dramatically in the month following his suicide (Martin & Koo, 1997). Thus, it appears that the way in which suicide is reported can have an effect. The frequency and duration of suicide reports also can affect suicide rates. Gould, Jamieson, and Romer (2003) reported a dose-response relationship, with the amount of copycat suicides related to the intensity and duration of the media coverage. Further, they found that news coverage of real suicides is more likely to produce imitative suicides than is a suicide portrayed in fictional stories. Finally, their research found that celebrity suicides are more likely to produce copycat effects.

Given the potential role of the media, it is important that mental health professionals, regardless of practice setting, learn to influence the messages that the media broadcasts in their communities. It is not sufficient to say that the media are irresponsible in reporting suicides. We must all learn to work with the media in a positive fashion. In general, according to the American Association of Suicidology (1999), the media should *not* do the following:

1. Simplify the cause of the suicide. Suicide is not the result of a single factor, and although it is not necessary to list all the precipitating factors, acknowledging that they existed is important.
2. Engage in repetitive, ongoing, or excessive reporting of the suicide. Repetitive coverage increases risk in the 15- to 24-year-old age group.
3. Provide sensational coverage of the suicide. Morbid descriptions and/or photographs should not be used.
4. Report how-to descriptions of the suicide. General descriptions might not increase risk, but specifics regarding how many pills were needed or how to build the device that led to a carbon monoxide death are risky.
5. Present suicide as an effective tool for accomplishing certain ends. Suggesting that the suicide was a way to cope with a difficult problem (e.g., a breakup of a relationship, not getting into college) might inadvertently suggest that suicide is an effective method for problem solving.
6. Glorify the suicide. Although well intentioned, dramatic eulogies and remembrances (e.g., flying flags at half staff, setting up shrines around lockers in schools) should not be conducted, and when they are done, they should not be displayed in the media. This can send the message to vulnerable people that the suicide death, rather than the person, is being honored.
7. Focus on the deceased person's positive attributes without full recognition of the problems that led to the suicide. Again, although well-intentioned and designed to comfort family members, focusing on the deceased person as "a good kid with a bright future" minimizes the reality of the situation and may encourage vulnerable populations to look up to the deceased person and copy his or her death.

Summary

A lot of important information was covered in this chapter, and it is worth a quick glance back over the chapter to reinforce the main point: In spite of the very clear need, the reality is that primary or secondary prevention programs are rarely implemented in either schools or community settings. The reasons for this lack of prevention programs are many, and examples include lack of governmental support, economic constraints, and lack of skills in mental health providers, as well as the continuing public stigma concerning the topic of suicide. Neverthess, prevention programs do not have to be costly or time-consuming to implement. Progress in preventing suicides in schools and communities must come from our increased willingness to both initiate and bear the economic costs of primary prevention programs. It is only through the early detection and appropriate treatment of children and adults for underlying mental and emotional problems that the unfortunate consequence of suicide will be diminished.

11

Suicide Risk Assessment

The assessment of suicide risk is a difficult and complex task. There is no way to predict with absolute certainty who will commit suicide, but the belief that at least some suicides are preventable, if they are foreseeable, is what drives the desire to continually improve our risk assessment capabilities. Mental health professionals use risk assessment to predict the future, and although prediction is neither easy nor 100% accurate, it is the best (and only) way we know to keep people safe. Suicide risk assessment can help us identify acute, modifiable, and treatable risk factors (Simon, 2002), and help us recognize when clients need more concrete methods to help them manage their lives. Suicide risk assessment requires knowledge, training, and experience.

Because suicide risk assessments are about prediction, they can be wrong. Attempts to determine individual risk will lead to many false positives (predicting that people will attempt suicide when they will not) as well as false negatives (predicting that people will be safe from self-harm when they will not). False positives have some unintended consequences, such as utilizing valuable resources or limiting individual freedoms for persons who do not plan to hurt themselves. False negatives, however, have much more serious consequences: People die. Therefore, a fundamental rule of suicide risk assessment is to err on the side of caution.

In the following section, some of the major components of risk assessment are discussed. They are also summarized in a table with the hope that you will consider each of these factors when you are determining suicide risk. In the second section of the chapter, risk factors and warning signs are reviewed. These risk factors were discussed in very specific ways in Chapters 3–9, and here they are simply listed as a reminder and to consolidate many of the risk factors into one place. Readers are encouraged to spend time reviewing Chapters 3–9 for a more complete discussion of these factors. In the third section of this chapter, informal risk assessment instruments are discussed, and a listing of formal or commercially available risk assessments are available in Appendix A. Finally, the chapter ends with some resources for suicide risk assessment.

The Components of Suicide Risk Assessment

For all mental health professionals, the assessment of suicide risk is a stressful topic. We work hard in all that we do to keep clients safe and well, and our goal is always helping them improve their well-being. The topic of suicide is a frightening one, particularly for beginning professionals, but even seasoned professionals find themselves stressed and uncertain when it comes to the assessment of suicide risk. Making a final determination about what should be done raises our anxiety levels because we are determining a concrete action (e.g., send the person home, call in family members, recommend hospitalization) based on an imperfect ability to predict.

Kenny was a 45-year-old Caucasian male with a history of depression and anxiety. He worked manning a small donation collection site for a charity organization in the parking lot of a local mall. His mental health had been a problem for most of his adult life, and he had had several previous suicide attempts, the most recent one about a year ago.

During December, Kenny's work became busier and more stressful, and he found himself frequently overwhelmed by the long line of cars waiting to drop off donations and the general impatience of the donors. During a routine appointment with his counselor at a local community mental health agency, Kenny confessed that lately he had begun to consider suicide. He choked back tears as he told his counselor that the increased stress at work and the constant reminders of Christmas at the mall made him feel very hopeless about the future. Kenny had been divorced for more than 15 years and had no children, and both of his parents were deceased. About two months earlier, he had stopped taking his medication for depression because he could no longer afford it, as he had no health insurance through his job.

The counselor engaged in a comprehensive suicide evaluation of Kenny, and there were many factors that put him at elevated risk. He had prior attempts, had current suicidal feelings, had access to lethal methods (he owned a gun), was feeling hopeless, smoked two packs of cigarettes a day, had a history of depression and anxiety, and had no real support system. In addition, although he was not a heavy drinker, he had a plan for suicide that involved drinking (e.g., he would drink the whiskey that he kept in his house and kill himself with his gun). Perhaps most important, Kenny stated that he was not sure he would be able to keep himself safe. He was unable to generate solutions—or agree to solutions presented by the counselor—if he started to think about killing himself.

Kenny's counselor asked whether Kenny would be willing to remove his gun from the house, and he said that he might consider it but, when pressed, stated that if he felt suicidal, he could easily come up with other methods to kill himself. He had read in the news about a man who committed suicide by jumping from the top of a local parking garage, and he said that if his gun were removed, he might use jumping from the mall parking garage as his backup plan.

Kenny's counselor decided that Kenny might well need to be hospitalized to keep him safe, and Kenny agreed that this was probably true. The counselor notified her supervisor and made plans to have Kenny transported to the local emergency room for an evaluation. With Kenny in the room, she called the emergency room and gave them notice that he was on his way. When she hung up, she agreed to meet Kenny at the emergency room, where she could give corroborating information and support him through the process.

In this case, Kenny demonstrates many risk factors (Caucasian male, divorced, no support system, history of psychiatric illness) that were discussed in Section II of this book. In addition, he had a specific plan, available means, no one to stop him if he felt suicidal, and little or no belief in his ability to stay safe. As you read the remaining part of the chapter, consider how a risk assessment with Kenny would lead to the decision that was made.

Here is another, very different case to consider:

This case is based on the experiences of the first author. Because it was her first time making the final determination of risk for suicide, it stands out in her mind, even years later, as a pivotal professional moment.

I [Darcy] was midway through my doctoral internship, working at a private psychiatric day treatment clinic. Clients came to the facility for the day and returned to their homes or to supportive housing environments for the evenings and weekends. Because clients were at the facility eight hours each weekday, staff at the clinic knew the clients fairly well. In this instance, I had worked with "Doris" for the week and a half she was at the clinic, and I had direct contact with her (group or individual counseling) approximately five hours per day. Doris had borderline personality disorder, a personality disorder that is characterized by, among other things, extreme emotional lability, impulsivity, a fear of real or perceived abandonment, a history of suicidal behaviors and attempts (cutting, taking pills), and unstable relationships. She was at the clinic because a recent breakup of a relationship had spiraled her into depression. She had been in and out of the clinic about five times over the last two years, each time staying in treatment about two to four weeks until she was stable enough to return to outpatient therapy. Doris constantly made thinly veiled suicide threats, and she had made several rather low-level attempts in the past couple of months.

One Friday, I was sitting with the psychiatrist as he did medical rounds with the clients. He saw each of the clients individually for about 15 minutes, and I was there to offer any information or perspective that I saw after spending many hours with the clients each day. Doris had been talkative and engaged in group all morning and was interacting well with the other clients. She discussed how she hated going home to her empty house and was dreading the weekend. Her fears of abandonment and her feelings of emptiness made it extremely difficult for her to be alone, yet she had few friends. On the suggestion of another client, she started making plans to go to the local mall and walk around in the air condition-ing on Saturday, although she wasn't sure how much that would help her to feel better.

When Doris came into the psychiatrist's office for medical rounds, she was extremely lethargic, depressed, and initially noncommunicative. Because I had seen her just a half-hour before and she had been talkative and engaged, I asked what had happened. Doris mumbled that she had got into a fight with another client who had called her a "fat pig." She teared up, stated that she had no reason left to live, and said that she planned to kill herself over the weekend. She could no longer handle the stress of her life and her chronic feelings of emptiness and unworthiness.

Doris, the psychiatrist, and I engaged in a discussion to try to determine her lethality. She had many risk factors: depression, hopelessness, the recent breakup of a relationship, previous attempts, loneliness/isolation, and impulsivity. On the other hand, she had a history of seeking attention through suicidal threats and behaviors and a real desire to be sent to the hospital, where others would take care of her and interact with her rather than her having to be alone. She had made suicide threats on previous Fridays and had been sent to the hospital to keep her safe. I asked her some very specific questions: Did she have a plan? (no, but she might take some pills, she supposed). Did she have access? (she could go buy over-the-counter medicines). Could she use an emergency plan, if she needed to? (she thought she could, depending on what it was). Did she have any available social support? (one of the other clients said that Doris could call her if she needed to talk, and she gave Doris her phone number).

Doris was sent from the room for a few moments, and the psychiatrist looked at me and said, "Well, you decide. Do we hospitalize her?" I was stunned. He had never done that before, and I tried to profess, "I'm not ready for that kind of responsibility." He said, "It's never easy to make that decision, and it's not any easier for me just because I'm the doctor. You spend the most time with her, use all the information and your clinical judgment, and decide." I was frightened that I would make the wrong choice. The local hospital had very few psychiatric beds, and putting Doris in one of them might mean turning away someone who really needed assistance over the weekend. Hospitals and clinics also must have a close working relationship. If a psychiatrist commits someone, the hospital must believe that the client really is in danger. If there are too many false negatives, the hospital will begin not to trust the doctor's assessments.

In the end, I decided to recommend that Doris not be hospitalized. I believed that she was making suicidal threats without real suicidal intent, and although I had no doubt that she felt hopeless at that moment, I believed that it was a transitory state. I knew she had been in a good mood all day and that this depression occurred right after an insult. I would watch her for the rest of the day and see whether the depression and hopelessness continued and possibly reassess her late in the day. In addition, I knew that she did not have readily available means (she would have to go to the store), and I knew that she would consider using a well-thought-out emergency plan.

So instead of hospitalizing her, I made a deal with her. If she would agree to stay safe on Friday night and during the day Saturday, perhaps going to the mall as suggested or calling the other client for support, then at 5:00 P.M. Saturday night, she could, if needed, call the respite house and stay there on Saturday night and the remainder of the weekend. Of course, if she felt unable to make it through the night on Friday, she could utilize the emergency room. She was given emergency numbers, and we developed a safety plan. I tried to weigh the risk factors with what I knew about the client and develop a plan that would keep her safe and give her some feelings of empowerment. In this case, she recognized that she could stay safe on her own, and the carrot of the respite house gave her something to look forward to, creating some hope.

As it turned out, Doris was safe. She stayed alone Friday night and went to the mall on Saturday. At exactly 5:00 P.M. on Saturday evening, she called the respite house and spoke with the person on staff. After talking for about ten minutes, she decided that she wanted to stay at her home on Saturday night, too, just to prove to herself that she could do it, but she reserved the right to come to the respite house on Sunday morning and stay for the remainder of the weekend. She did not, however, need to exercise that option and remained safe throughout the weekend.

On the other side of town, I spent the weekend holding my breath and praying that I had made the right decision. I felt as though I had a tremendous weight on my shoulders until I saw Doris again on Monday morning. It turned out to be the right decision—to give her a combination of responsibility and independence with a safety net. When I think of this case, I am reminded of how risk factors play a role in suicide risk assessment, but so do clinical acumen and relationship. Doris had many risk factors, yet my clinical skills told me that her threats were her way of conveying to us that she felt lonely and afraid, not that she was really suicidal. My experience with the client confirmed this. But I would not have made this decision if I did not know the client very well and understand her patterns of interacting. In addition, I would not have just sent her home, as she easily could have made a suicide attempt just to show me how wrong I was. Instead, I used my relationship with her to reassure her that I cared about her, I wanted her to be safe, and I wanted her to be successful. I set her up to be able to do both, with a safety net in case she could not.

This case demonstrates many of the difficulties and nuances of suicide risk assessment. In all cases, determination of suicide risk involves a combination of risk factors, protective factors, and individual circumstances. Therefore, there is no universal measure of risk.

Assessment of Each Person Is Unique

There is no "one size fits all" when it comes to suicide risk assessment. Although there are some formal and informal measures that can be used to guide assessment (these will be discussed later in the chapter), the unique situation of each person needs to be considered. In the first case example above, Kenny had many risk factors, and an assessment of his current functioning led the counselor to worry for his safety enough to have him assessed for hospitalization. In the second example, the general risk factor categories were offset by the personal characteristics of the client and the components of the counseling relationship. In other cases, given the same risk factors and the same client diagnosis, the outcome could be very different. It is the interplay of the risk factors, the protective factors, and the individual client that must be assessed.

Clearly, to do an individualized risk assessment, it is important that the person doing the assessment have as much information as possible about the client. In many cases, even if you are not the person making the final risk assessment, you will be asked

---

BOX 11.1 • *Essential Features of Suicide Risk Assessment*

- Assessment of each person is unique.
- Assessment is complex and challenging.
- Assessment is an ongoing process.
- Assessment uses multiple perspectives.
- Assessment tries to uncover foreseeable risk.
- Assessment relies on clinical judgment.
- Assessment is treatment.
- Assessment errs on the side of caution.
- Assessment takes all threats, warning signs, and risk factors seriously.
- Assessment asks the tough questions.
- Assessment tries to uncover the underlying message.
- Assessment is done in a cultural context.
- Assessment is collaborative.
- Assessment is documented.

for your opinions about the client, your understanding of the situation, and your recommendations. Just be as honest and forthcoming as possible. If you know the person, then your perspective is important and provides critical information. Simply sending a person to a crisis center or hospital for a risk assessment means that the assessor might not have access to vital information. Clients might choose not to share all of their plans with a stranger, particularly if they have already determined that they will commit suicide. Everyone in the field has a story of a client who threatens suicide but, when sent for assessment for hospitalization, gives all the "right" answers and is released, only to go on to complete suicide. It is the responsibility of the person conducting the assessment to learn as much information as possible about the client in order to provide the most accurate prediction of suicidal risk for that person. It is the responsibility of everyone who knows the client to be forthcoming with all the information they have. Remember, when a client is potentially suicidal, confidentiality agreements no longer apply. If you are conducting the assessment, get all the information you can. If you are referring a person for an assessment or are contacted for your opinion, give all the information you know.

Assessment Is Complex and Challenging

Suicide risk assessment is difficult for several reasons. First, it is difficult—if not impossible—to determine with 100% accuracy the risk of specific behaviors from what are often more vague and tumultuous emotional states and irrational cognitions. Clients who are suicidal are often ambiguous. They typically do not want to die; they just want the pain to end. That ambiguity is important for treatment—it gives clinicians a way "in." We tap into the ambiguity to allow us to keep clients alive, to give them a sense of hope. That same ambiguity, however, makes risk assessment complex. Clients may fluctuate in their suicidality. They might feel suicidal at one point but feel more hopeful the next. They might feel confused with competing emotions—hopelessness that drives the suicidal feelings while, at the same time, guilt about causing pain toward their loved ones if they complete the suicidal act and a longing for things to be better. Therefore, suicide is difficult to assess because, most of the time, even the client does not know whether or not he or she will attempt. So it is not simply a matter of understanding the mind of the client to get the answer; understanding the mind of the client will help to clarify only the issues, not the results. People who are suicidal are rarely of a single determination, and those who are can often be identified and hospitalized (although it is worth noting that some people who are determined to die will deny suicidal intention in order to prevent hospitalization and the removal of access). More common are people who are torn, who are in inner conflict about their suicidality, and these individuals are much harder to assess.

Suicide risk assessment also is complex because there are no absolutes. There is no checklist or instrument that a clinician can complete that yields an answer. Most beginning practitioners (and many who have been in the field for a long time) yearn for an answer. If a checklist yields this score, hospitalize the client. If it yields another score, send the client home. Realistically, although you might recognize that this is not possible, it probably does not keep you from wishing it were that easy!

A final complexity in suicide risk assessment is the stress that it causes in the clinician. When clients talk about suicide, it raises the practitioner's anxiety level, particularly for those who are just beginning in their field. It is difficult to remain rational and calm when your thoughts are racing and you are scrambling to remember what areas to assess. Keeping notes, lists, or guided interview protocols handy to refer to can be useful, but the reality is that suicide assessment is always stressful. Someone's life is at stake, and most of us are uncomfortable with that level of responsibility. This is part of the reason why suicide assessments are conducted by clinicians who have been trained and who have some experience, and consultation with other professionals is an important component of all suicide risk assessments. We also must remind ourselves that although we must take appropriate precautions to assess client risk and keep at-risk clients safe whenever possible, we ultimately are not responsible if we take all the appropriate precautions and someone still chooses to take his or her own life. All we can do is make sure we have done all we can. Suicide assessments offer no guarantees.

Assessment Is an Ongoing Process

There is probably no type of mental health assessment in which this is more true than the process of suicide risk assessment. Suicide risk is not static, and suicide risk assessment is a process, not an event (Simon, 2002). Suicidal thoughts and behaviors can change from day to day, even from moment to moment, and completed suicide assessments in a client's file quickly become useless. Suicide risk assessments must be completed frequently throughout the course of treatment. Even among clients who are not suicidal, it is important to reopen the question throughout treatment, particularly if there has been a stressor in the life of the client, such as a breakup with a boyfriend or girlfriend, divorce, or sudden financial crisis. The important concept here is that suicide risk assessment is never completed; it is always an ongoing component of any counseling or therapeutic process. This does not mean that a full-blown risk assessment must be conducted at every interaction with the client, but the question should always be raised and should be investigated more thoroughly whenever there is cause.

When assessing risk, clinicians must understand both the immediate risk and the ongoing risk. It is not uncommon to hear a clinician say, "I consider Bob to be an ongoing suicide risk." That is, there are risk factors that increase Bob's overall propensity to consider suicide as an option. Therefore, the clinician checks in with Bob frequently to determine whether there is an immediate occurrence that has raised his risk for the immediate future. Some clients, on the other hand, have short-term suicidal crises. In assessing a client for suicide, it can be helpful to ask, "Did you feel suicidal this morning? Yesterday? Last week?" to uncover whether suicidal thoughts are ongoing or acute.

In chapters 3–9, you learned that impulsivity is related to suicide risk. The difficulty is that when clients are impulsive, they make permanent decisions on the basis of temporary mood states. Thus, when clients are at elevated risk and they enter into a mood state that makes them feel hopeless, they are more likely to engage in suicidal behaviors. Therefore, clients who have an elevated ongoing risk must be monitored for impulsivity. If they are impulsive, their risk for suicide is higher, they will need more frequent monitoring, and more safeguards must be put in place to keep them alive.

Assessment Uses Multiple Perspectives

There are many ways to collect information about suicide risk. Interviews and interactions with a client are the most common methods to assess suicidal risk, but there are many other methods than can—and should—be used to understand risk. Paper-and-pencil tests or checklists can provide some information but are never appropriate if used alone. Consultation and collaboration with other mental health practitioners who interact with the client can help to fill in gaps and give a more complete picture of the client's risk. Interviews with the client's family, friends, and significant others also can provide useful insights. In schools, teachers, counselors, and other adults who interact with the student can report on ways in which a child interacts with others. Client records often chronicle past suicidal thoughts and attempts. The point is, there are many sources of information, including different people and differing sources of data. The most successful risk assessors use all the information they can to form the most complete picture possible. All of this leads to the greatest possible chance of successful prediction.

Assessment Tries to Uncover Foreseeable Risk

Suicide risk assessment is based on the belief that at least some suicides are preventable. Most clinicians believe that many, if not most, suicides could be prevented. Acute suicide risk tends to be a relatively time-limited event, and if a person can be kept alive during the acute stage of the crisis, the chances are good that the person will not kill himself or herself. Of course, there are people who are acutely suicidal for long periods of time, but the majority of individuals pass through a suicidal crisis more quickly, often in a period of days or a few weeks. Therefore, assessment is typically focused on suicide risk in the foreseeable future.

Suicide is preventable only to the degree that it is foreseeable. In rare cases, people attempt or commit suicide without warning. However, it is much more common for people to make their suicidal intentions known to at least one other person (Ruddell & Curwen, 2002). Once a client is identified as having a risk for suicide in the foreseeable future, then appropriate action must be taken.

Assessment Relies on Clinical Judgment

Although checklists, tests, and structured interviews for suicide exist, they never replace clinical judgment. Clinicians use their clinical experience, the rapport and relationship they have with their clients, and their knowledge and training in suicide risk assessment to make decisions about levels of intervention. Suicide risk checklists, if followed blindly, can lead clinicians to unsound decisions. For example, in the SAD PERSONS checklist, a client can receive a score of 4 (and a recommendation of "close follow-up, consider hospitalization") simply by being a 50-year-old divorced male with diabetes and no thoughts of suicide whatsoever! On the other hand, a person could receive a score of 2 (and a recommendation of "send home with follow-up") if she was a 35-year-old female with severe depression and an organized plan. Clearly, in the first instance, there is no specific reason to believe that the person is suicidal, while in the second instance, clinical judgment would deem the person to be at high risk. As another example, in the second case study in this chapter, Doris had many risk factors, but sound clinical reasoning determined that she did not appear to be in imminent danger. These examples illustrate how risk factors and checklists can provide direction and context, but they can never take the place of clinical judgment.

Assessment Is Treatment

The moment a mental health professional begins to assess someone for suicide, treatment has begun. A major part of suicide assessment is emotional ventilation, allowing people to tell their stories and to feel heard and understood. Yalom (1975) noted that the telling of one's story in and of itself is curative. Feeling heard and understood, experiencing empathy from another human being, and feeling valued (unconditional positive regard) are cornerstones of Carl Rogers's client-centered therapy and most clinicians would agree that although they might not be sufficient conditions for change, they are valuable nonetheless. Williams and Morgan (1994) note that the skilled clinician will recognize "the immense value of reaching out and listening to resolve a suicidal crisis, no matter how complex and apparently insoluble the individual's problems may seem" (p. 16). One of the most important skills that nonmental health professionals (e.g., teachers, police, resident advisors in dormitories) learn when working with suicidal people is to *listen*. The act of listening and making someone feel heard can help the person through the suicidal crisis. It is never useful to interrupt or shut down a suicidal person with comments such as "That's foolish for you to feel that way" or "Don't talk that way—you have so much to live for." The simple act of listening not only helps assess the seriousness of the situation, but also takes the important first steps toward a healthy resolution of the crisis.

Assessment Errs on the Side of Caution

This point was made repeatedly throughout the first part of this chapter (and will continue to be emphasized in the remainder of the chapter and the book), but it bears repeating and listing as its own key point. It is far better to have a false positive (acting as though someone is suicidal when the person is not) than a false negative (acting as though someone is not suicidal when the person is). It cannot be emphasized enough that although the consequences for the first case (the false positive) may be lost time or resources, the consequences for the second case (the false negative) can be death. Sometimes mental health professionals who have been in the field for awhile can get jaded. They start to think certain types of clients or people with certain types of mental disorders are not at serious risk. They might begin to take shortcuts in their assessments or allow their frustrations with clients to determine risk, rather than a combination of all available information as well as clinical judgment. This is never appropriate.

Assessment Takes All Threats, Warning Signs, and Risk Factors Seriously

This point ties in with the previous: to err on the side of caution. When clients make threats or engage in suicidal behaviors (e.g., cutting, taking pills), we must take these actions seriously. Clients must know that their actions have consequences. Sometimes, a suicidal threat or low-level attempt is a method to demonstrate how desperate a person is feeling, a method to seek reassurance that someone would care, or a way to get attention. Whatever the cause, each threat or behavior must be thoroughly investigated.

There are times when family members or others want to minimize the threat. Many school counselors tell stories of how principals discourage them from investigating a threat of suicide or how parents deny that their son or daughter could possibly be considering suicide or need professional care, even in the face of significant evidence to the contrary. Family members might dismiss suicidal talk—or even suicide attempts—as insignificant. Mental health professionals must never make that mistake.

Assessment Asks the Tough Questions

There is a prevalent myth that interferes with suicide risk assessment. Many people believe that asking a person about suicidal ideation increases risk by planting the idea in the person's mind. This myth is not true. Asking a person about their suicidal thoughts *does not* increase suicide risk. In fact, the opposite is true, provided that the person who is asking is empathic and sensitive rather than judgmental (Ruddell & Curwen, 2002). There is strong evidence that asking someone about his or her intent to commit suicide actually has a very positive effect on people in suicidal crises. Most people feel relieved that someone is interested enough and cares enough to ask and is willing to talk with them about their ideas and plans (Doyle, 1990). People who are at risk for suicide must feel free to talk about their feelings and their suicidal thoughts.

To assess risk, suicide assessments must be in clear and frank language. Direct questions are necessary to elicit the level of the threat. Does the person have a specific plan? Sometimes people will use euphemisms (e.g., "I just want to be with the angels" or "I won't be around for them to pick on anymore"). It is important that suicide assessment take the conversation to a concrete level. "Are you thinking of killing yourself?" or "Are you planning to commit suicide?" or "How will you do it?" brings the discussion to a level that allows for a more accurate assessment. In our clinical experience, we have found that clients sometimes think of suicide in very peaceful, gentle terms, such as "slipping away into peace." The reality of death by suicide, however, is typically very brutal and ugly. It is much more difficult for a person to think of suicide as a peaceful and calm ending to a difficult situation if the assessor reminds the person of the harsh reality of the act he or she is considering and engages in a very real discussion that is honest (but never judgmental) about the consequences of the decision. For a client to say, "They'll be sorry" implies a level of abstraction that does not allow for true assessment to take place.

Assessment Tries to Uncover the Underlying Message

There are as many reasons why people attempt or commit suicide as there are suicidal individuals, but most can be summed up in three major categories: **communication**, **avoidance**, or **control**. Persons who threaten, attempt, or commit suicide use their suicide as a way to communicate something to those around them, as a way to avoid a painful situation, or as a way to control their environment or other people. A thorough suicide risk assessment will uncover the underlying message or messages, and these become the crux of the intervention. Here are three brief examples:

Communication.   A couple came to an outpatient clinic to meet with a counselor because they had been referred by a hospital social worker. The woman had had a suicide attempt during the previous weekend when she took several handfuls of pills before bed, lay down next to her husband, and then changed her mind and told him what she had done. He took her to the hospital for treatment, and when she was discharged, the hospital social worker insisted that they see a counselor. The husband denied the need for counseling and minimized the attempt, stating that she often engaged in erratic behavior. But the social worker insisted, and he finally relented. During the first counseling session, it was clear that the couple had very different views of their relationship. He stated that everything was fine, that they had their "ups and downs" but that she was just an emotional person who "blew things out of proportion." She had a completely different story. She stated that she felt "suffocated" in the relationship, that he never listened to her, and that he made her feel insignificant and childlike whenever she tried to talk with him about her feelings. It was clear by the end of the first session that her suicide attempt had been a way for her to communicate to her husband just how desperate she was feeling and how badly she wanted him to take her concerns seriously.

Avoidance.   One of our students was completing her internship in a high school when she was asked to work with a senior who had expressed suicidal intent to his girlfriend. The girlfriend reported it to the school counselor. In the student's interactions with the young man, she learned that he planned to kill himself on the day before graduation. He had a plan, a method, and the means and had even written his obituary. With more discussion, she learned that he was failing a class that he needed to pass to graduate, but he could not handle telling his parents. He was the first person in his family to go to college, and his parents were planning a huge graduation party for him. Relatives were flying in from all over the country to be there to help the family celebrate. He planned the suicide as a method to avoid what he saw as an unbearable situation. With work and consultation with his teachers, the counseling student was able to help the boy make up work and pass his class. However, he was referred to an outside counselor to help him learn to make more effective choices in the future when faced with difficult situations.

Control. We once worked with a woman in her late fifties who had had a suicide attempt. In a group counseling situation, we did a dynamic family sculpture (based on the work of Virginia Satir). In this case, we put the woman in the middle of the room and had her use the other members of the group to represent members of her family and place them around her in a way that represented their emotional attachment to her. Because her children were grown, scattered about the country, and busy with their own families, the woman placed her children very far away from her (several even in another room), facing away from her, and attending to their own families. She placed herself in the middle of the room, looking desperate, with her arms reaching out to her children to no avail. We then asked her to resculpt the family as it looked after the suicide attempt. In this case, she brought all the children into the room, placed them in a circle around her, hands linking and supporting her from underneath. The visual impact was stunning. She came to recognize how she had used the suicide attempt to control her family to get them to respond to her needs. We could then work in therapy on other methods she could use to get her needs met.

Assessment Is Done in a Cultural Context

In Chapter 6, you read about specific suicide risk factors for the four major cultural/ethnic minority groups in the United States. Suicide risk assessment must take these cultural risk factors as well as individual risk factors into account. Recall, for example, that in a study of university students, only one of the 36 African American clients with suicidal ideation in the study sample voluntarily self-disclosed the suicidal thoughts at intake. The other 35 were uncovered only through a complete and culturally competent suicide assessment by a therapist (Morrison & Downey, 2000). In this example, it becomes clear that simply asking a client, "Are you thinking of killing yourself?" might not be sufficient. Mental health professionals must understand the culture of their clients and interact with the clients appropriately. A culturally sensitive risk assessment asks questions and interacts with clients in ways that make them feel heard, understood, and respected.

Assessment Is Collaborative

One of the fears that practitioners face when conducting a suicide risk assessment is the fear that they will miss something, that they will make a wrong decision or have inaccurate assessment data. Earlier, we said that getting multiple perspectives (multimodal assessment and multiple sources of information) is one way to improve chances of gaining a complete perspective. Another important way is through collaboration and consultation. When a client is at risk for suicide, bringing in other professionals to help evaluate the risk is always a good idea. Different professionals brings different perspectives, all of which can be extremely valuable. Many times, we operate under the assumption that new professionals need supervision and benefit from collaborative efforts but more seasoned professionals do not. Suicide risk assessment is no time to go it alone.

Assessment Is Documented

Client suicides are one of the most frequent malpractice claims against mental health professionals. Although we have taken a stance in this book that focuses on the therapeutic side of suicide prevention, assessment, and treatment, completed suicides (or even suicide attempts) among clients can become legal issues for clinicians. The single most important thing any mental health professional can do to protect themselves against litigation is to document their work (Simon, 2002). Courts recognize that not all suicides are preventable, and they tend to support clinicians who make consistent and systematic efforts to keep their clients safe. The only way for the legal system to determine these efforts (or lack of them) is through documentation. According to the law, a completed suicide risk assessment that is not documented did not happen. In other words, it is not sufficient for a mental health professional to *say* that a client was not suicidal, the professional must document that he or she did some sort of assessment and the results of that assessment (Simpson & Stacy, 2004). This must be done every time the assessment occurs.

In his comprehensive work on suicide assessment, Shea (2002) argues that documentation not only fulfills a legal obligation, but also in and of itself improves client care. He notes that thorough and accurate documentation can be useful if the client becomes suicidal in the future. A future clinician can look at the case file and know precisely what happened in the previous suicidal crisis. As a second point, Shea notes that sound documentation can help us to improve review and recall our assessments and make changes as appropriate. The mere act of writing down exactly what was done becomes a built-in checklist for high-quality care.

The Role of Risk Factors and Warning Signs in Suicide Risk Assessment

Risk factors are typically thought of as ongoing client characteristics that increase risk (e.g., depression, substance abuse, loss of relationships, isolation, impulsivity). Warning signs, on the other hand, are behaviors that clients engage in that warn of imminent risk (e.g., giving away possessions, acquiring a means, withdrawing). Both risk factors and warning signs (as well as protective factors) for different segments of the population were outlined in the second section of the book. The following table summarizes the overall risk factors and warning signs that have been most supported through research. Remember, however, that these tables are only a guide, and suicide risk assessment must be individualized to be effective.

Risk Assessment Instruments

A comprehensive suicide risk assessment typically is multimodal, involving several types of assessments as well as several different sources of information. A complete psychiatric history and an examination of both demographic and individual risk factors are always

BOX 11.2 • *Factors Associated with Increased Risk of Suicide*

Risk Factors
- Male
- Single
- Widowed
- Divorced/separated
- Elderly
- Psychiatric illness (in decreasing order of risk)
  - Depression*
  - Schizophrenia
  - Alcoholism*
  - Drug addiction*
  - Organic cerebral disorder (e.g., epilepsy, brain injury, mild dementia)
  - Personality disorder (especially sociopathy, impulsivity, aggression, lability of mood)
  - Anxiety disorders
- Psychosis*
- Hopelessness/helplessness*
- Previous suicide attempt(s)/self-harm (parasuicide)*
- Social isolation*/rejection by others
- Physical illness (life-threatening/chronic/debilitating)*
- Unemployed/retired
- Family history of affective disorder, alcoholism, or suicide*
- Bereavement/loss (recent); preoccupation with anniversary or traumatic loss*
- Childhood bereavement
- Social classes at the extremes (either the poorest or the wealthiest)
- Family destabilization due to loss, personal abuse, violence, sexual abuse*
- Recent trauma (physical/psychological)*
- Specific suicide plan formulated*
- Exhibits one or more uncharacteristic intense negative emotions*
- Preoccupation with earlier abuse*

Warning signs
- Giving away prized possessions/putting personal affairs in order*
- Radical changes in characteristic behaviors or moods*

* Gilliland and James (1997) have suggested that individuals should be treated as high risk if four to five or more of the factors shown with an asterisk are manifested. The mental health professional is reminded always to use clinical judgment in assessing risk.

Source: Ruddell, et al. (2002) Understanding suicidal ideation and assessing risk, *British Journal of Guidance and Counselling*, vol. 20, pp. 363–372. Taylor & Francis Ltd., www.tandf.co.uk/journals.

part of a comprehensive assessment (Cochrane-Brink, Lofchy, & Sakinofsky, 2000). In addition, many mental health professionals make use of risk assessment instruments. There are two major types of assessments: informal (unstructured) and formal (structured). Informal or unstructured instruments are discussed in this chapter. The more

BOX 11.3 • *Warning Signs Associated with Imminent Risk*

- Isolating from and avoiding others and/or withdrawal from activities that they were previously involved in
- Deterioration in work or school performance, or deterioration in activities of daily living
- Reading books on methods for committing suicide and/or obtaining materials (e.g., gun, poison, rope, pills) that could be used for suicide
- Increased use of drugs/alcohol, gambling, food, sex, etc., as if they are desperately trying to lose themselves in these activities
- Direct or oblique references to when they will be dead, including joking about their dying
- Preoccupation with the negativity and tragedy in the world
- Self-demeaning statements (e.g., "I am no good," "I'd be better off dead")
- Openly expressing hopelessness about their situation and their future
- Preoccupation with death in talk, writing, or other activities (e.g., movies and books)
- Making final arrangements, preparing a will, making amends, giving away prized possessions
- Increased hostility, negativity, or defensiveness toward others
- Disinterest or avoidance of making future plans, neglecting responsibilities
- Discussing one's life as if it were over
- Inexplicable sudden attitude change from one of sadness or negativity to one of calmness and certainty

Source: Drab, K. J. (2001). Ending the pain. Workshop presentation. p. 10.

formal or structured (and commercially available) assessments are listed in Appendix A. Because there are no suicide risk assessment instruments that have been universally supported as being effective in determining risk, only the most commonly used assessments will be reviewed. Readers should know that hundreds of suicide risk assessments are available (some commercially, some through research literature, and some that have been developed by practitioners for use at different schools, hospitals, and agencies), and all assessment tools must be appropriate for the population for which they are being employed (e.g., sensitive to cultural differences, age, situation).

Informal or Unstructured Assessment Interviews

The most common method to assess suicide risk is simply to ask. Sometimes, beginning practitioners get so caught up in all the complexity of the risk assessment that they forget to ask the question (something like "Have you thought about suicide?" or "Are you considering killing yourself?"). Other times, clinicians let their assumptions, rather than their clinical judgment, dominate the assessment. One student in her practicum told a story of a high school girl who was a very popular student, a cheerleader, and on her way to a top-quality college. As the student told the story of the girl's depression, she kept emphasizing how much the girl had going for her—looks, popularity, intelligence. It was clear, however, that the girl was very depressed, and the practicum student was asked what sort of suicide assessment she had done. The practicum student quickly exclaimed, "Oh, she's not suicidal!" With some exploration, however, we soon learned that the practicum student simply *assumed* that a young woman like this, who did not look like a candidate for suicide, could never be suicidal, so a suicide risk assessment never entered her mind. If the girl had been less popular, overweight, or sullen in her mood, the practicum student might have made very different assumptions. We immediately made plans for a suicide risk assessment, and it turned out that the girl had a very serious and organized plan. She actually was relieved when someone finally asked her. She said that it was the first time that someone had looked at her for who she was underneath rather than through all the trappings of success. Once she felt heard and understood, we could get started on the process of treatment. The "take-home" message is: *Always ask.*

Assessments, whether formal or informal, are an important component of suicide risk assessment. There is evidence that with simply a standard clinical interview, suicide risk can easily be overlooked, even by very experienced professionals (Mays, 2004).

Interviews.   A comprehensive suicide risk assessment interview does more than just ask a simple question. Clients are led through a series of topic areas that should include the following (at a minimum):

- Suicidal intent—present/recent thoughts about killing oneself.
- Details of the suicide plan—the more specific, the more dangerous.
- The means by which the person plans to commit suicide (e.g., a gun, hanging, overdose, etc.). Be sure to consider the lethality of the means (e.g., a gun is more lethal than ingesting several over-the-counter aspirin).
- Accessibility of those means to the suicidal person (how easy is it for the person to obtain the means). In other words, saying that one will shoot oneself is less of an immediate threat if one does not have access to a gun, compared to someone who says, "I will shoot myself using my dad's pistol, which is in his dresser drawer and the bullets that are in the garage."
- History of suicidal thoughts and attempts (including parasuicidal attempts).
- Stability of the current mood (e.g., did the person feel suicidal yesterday? Last week? This morning?).
- Family history of suicide attempts or completions as well as family history of mental disorders.
- Client's mental state (through a mental status examination).
- Assessment of warning signs and specific risk factors.

The following list was devised by Dr. D. J. Palmiter, Jr., as a list of items that should be included in the documentation of a thorough suicide assessment:

- Previous attempts
- Current suicidal feelings
- Current suicide plan (include access to lethal means)
- Feelings of hopelessness
- Sleep problems
- Appetite problems (include weight gain or weight loss)

- Concentration problems
- Current substance abuse (include smoking)
- Psychiatric and substance abuse history
- Evidence of impulsivity (e.g., sexual promiscuity, fighting, gambling)
- Knowledge of suicide
- Family history of suicide attempts
- Relevant family psychiatric and substance abuse history
- History of runaway behavior (for minors)
- Available support system
- Estimated IQ range
- Negative life events/stresses (including whether or not has been or feeling victimized or rejected and the degree of vocational satisfaction/frustration)
- Evidence of mania
- Client states willingness to comply with emergency procedures
- Documented consultation
- Documented above items and rationale for the plan employed to keep the person safe

Source: Reprinted by permission of the author, copyright © 2003. http://www.helpingparents.net/workshops.html.

Acronyms.   Several systems are available that make use of acronyms to help clinicians to remember the major areas that need to be covered in a suicide risk assessment interview. Some clinicians find these helpful them to remember the major topical areas. Some of the major acronyms are:

S.L.A.P.
S – What are the *specific* details? (S = specificity)
L – How *lethal* is the plan (e.g., guns, pills, rope)? (L = lethality)
A – How *available* is the method of choice? Where is it? (A = availability)
P – What is the *proximity* to help? Who will find the person? How long will it take to be found? (P = proximity)

P.L.A.I.D.
P – Previous attempts
L – Lethality
A – Access
I – Intent
D – Drugs/alcohol

P.I.M.P.
P – Plan
I – Intent
M – Means
P – Prior attempt

M.A.P.

M – Mental state for suicidality (thinking)
A – Affective state for suicidality (emotions)
P – Psychosocial state for suicidality (circumstances)

N.O. H.O.P.E. (Shea, 2002)

N – No framework for meaning
O – Overt change in clinical condition
H – Hostile interpersonal environment
O – Out of hospital recently
P – Predisposing personality factors
E – Excuses for dying are present and strongly believed

Suicide Checklists. Many checklists are available to guide questioning around suicide risk. Again, just as with the acronyms, these checklists are intended only as a guide for the interview, not as a definitive suicide risk assessment. A caution is necessary: The "objective" scoring of some of the checklists can encourage inappropriate use. Remember, these are *general guidelines only*. Nevertheless, research shows that mental health professionals who have been trained in the use of the checklists such as SAD PERSONS had improved ability to evaluate suicide risk than those who had not (Juhnke, 1994).

Sad Persons

The SAD PERSONS scale is a semistructured interview, developed by Patterson, Dohn, Bird, and Patterson (1983). The acronym SAD PERSONS was created by using the first letters of ten suicide risk factors:

S – SEX (males receive one point)

A – AGE (19 years or younger and 45 years or older receive one point)

D – DEPRESSION (people who are depressed receive one point)

P – PREVIOUS ATTEMPT (people with a previous attempt receive one point)

E – ETHANOL ABUSE (DRUGS) (people who abuse alcohol or drugs receive one point)

R – RATIONAL THINKING LOSS (people who demonstrate impaired judgment, are delusional, or experience hallucinations receive one point)

S – SOCIAL SUPPORT LACKING (people who isolate themselves, have few significant others, and do not regularly interact with others receive one point)

O – ORGANIZED PLAN (people with a specific, organized suicide plan receive one point)

N – NO SPOUSE (people who are separated, divorced, widowed, or single parents receive one point)

S – SICKNESS (people who have a chronic, debilitating, or severe illness receive one point)

Scoring: In general, the higher the score, the higher the suicide risk. Remember, however, that this is only a general guideline. Shea (2002) gives the example of a woman with postpartum psychosis. She hears voices that convince her that if she doesn't kill herself, her newborn daughter will be haunted by demons for the remainder of her life. Although the woman in this example scores only ONE POINT (low risk), she is clearly at high risk for suicide. Research has found that scores ≥ 6 indentified the need for hospitalization with a sensitivity of 94% (Hockberger& Rothstein, 1988)

Scoring Guideline:
0–2: Consider sending home with follow-up
3–4: Close follow-up, consider hospital
5–6: Strongly consider hospital, depending on quality of follow-up arrangement
7–10: Hospitalize or commit

Source: Reprinted with permission from Psychosomatics, copyright © 1983. American Psychiatric Association.

Adapted Sad Persons (A-SAD)
In 1996, Juhnke adapted the SAD PERSONS checklist for use with adolescents. The adapted scale can be used to assess immediate suicide risk factors and provide general intervention recommendations for school counselors.

S – Sex (males = 10 points; females = 0 points)
A – Age (older students are at higher risk and receive more points)
D – Depression or affective disorder (the more serious the disorder, the more points)
P – Previous attempt (score recent attempts and more lethal attempts higher)
E – Ethanol/drug abuse (students using alcohol or drugs are at higher risk)
R – Rational thinking loss (any student experiencing rational thinking loss is at risk)
S – Social supports lacking (50% of adolescent suicide completers had no close friends)
O – Organized plan (specificity and lethality increase risk)
N – Negligent parenting (neglect, abuse, family stress, and suicidal modeling increase risk)
S – School problems (aggressive behaviors, vandalism, or deterioration of academic performance signal increased risk)

Scoring Guideline: Assign points (0–10) to match severity for each risk factor. Total scores can range from 0 to 100.

0–29: Students who are perceived to be at risk should be encouraged to participate in counseling services and be given information about crisis counseling. Consider a no-suicide contract.

30–49: Students should be strongly encouraged to receive counseling and close follow-up services. School counselors should contact parents or guardians and make sure a thorough suicide assessment occurs.

50–69: Students in this range should be strongly considered for an evaluation for hospitalization.

70+: Scores in this range suggest both environmental turmoil and severe emotional distress. Scores at this extreme end of the continuum warrant immediate hospitalization. Child protective services should be contacted in cases in which family turmoil does not allow adequate assurance of care.

In general, even students with low scores on the Adapted SAD PERSONS warrant counseling if they present with mood disorder, alcohol or substance abuse, rational thinking loss, and/or an organized suicide plan.

Source: Reprinted with permission. American School Counselor Association, www.school counselor.org

Los Angeles Suicide Prevention Center Suicide Checklist

1. Sex and age – higher suicide potential with increased age. Also, men are more likely to complete a suicide than are women. Be sure to recognize differences in sex and age risks based on culture.
2. Suicide plan – the most important factor in assessing suicide risk. There are three major elements:
   a. Lethality of the suicide method
   b. Availability of means
   c. Degree of specificity
3. Stress – the level of subjective stress the client experiences — the more severe the stressors, the greater the likelihood of completed suicide.
4. Symptoms – the existence of depression, agitation, and/or psychosis increases the probability of suicide completion — especially agitated depression.
5. Resources – the presence of a supportive family, friends, pastors, doctors, and mental health care providers lessen the probability of completed suicide.
6. Lifestyle – sporadic work histories, unstable interpersonal relationships, and personality disorders indicate a higher level of suicidal risk.
7. Communication – the level of seriousness rises as the client isolate him/herself from others.
8. Reactions from significant others – lethality risk rises when an individual's significant others are perceived by the client as responding to his/her suicide gestures in an unhelpful or rejecting manner.
9. Medical status – the suicide lethality rises with serious medical conditions and a simultaneous sense of hopelessness that the client will experience release from them.

Source: Los Angeles Suicide Prevention Center

Suicide Assessment Checklist

A scorable checklist is available for research purposes. However, the broad general categories are useful in a practical setting to make sure many of the major areas of assessment are covered. For information on the scorable form, see Rogers, Lewis, and Subich, (2002).

Part I.

CLIENT HAS A DEFINITE PLAN – Has the client formulated a plan to commit suicide other than a vague "I'm going to kill myself"?

METHOD – If the client does have a concrete plan, which method has she or he chosen?

METHOD ON HAND – Is the method one that is readily available to the client as opposed to one that needs to be obtained?

PREVIOUS PSYCHIATRIC HISTORY – Psychiatic history is used here as a broad term to include the range from inpatient psychiatric care to outpatient psychotherapy.

MAKING FINAL PLANS – Is the client taking care of "unfinished business" and/or giving away prized possessions?

PRIOR ATTEMPTS – Has the client admitted to having previously attempted suicide or described situations that may have been "hidden" attempts?

SUICIDE NOTE – Has the client written or is s/he planning to write a suicide note placing blame for the action, leaving instructions for survivors, or saying goodbye?

SUICIDE SURVIVOR – Has the client had a close friend or relative who has committed suicide?

DRUG/ALCOHOL USE – Does the client use alcohol or drugs at any level?

MALE 15–35 OR 65 AND OLDER – Is the client a male in either of these age categories?

DEPENDENT CHILDREN AT HOME – Does the client have one or more children 18 years or younger living in the household?

MARITAL STATUS – What is the marital status of the client?

Part II

Ratings of the following items are to be based upon your impression of the client's status or "feelings." For example, how hopeless does the client "seem" to feel as opposed to how hopeless do you think the client "should" feel given the circumstances.

SENSE OF WORTHLESSNESS – To what degree does the client "feel" that she or he has no personal worth or value to him or herself and others?

SENSE OF HOPELESSNESS – To what degree does the client "feel" that there is no hope for improvement in his or her situation in the future?

SOCIAL ISOLATION – To what degree does the client "feel" that she or he has no friends and relatives to whom she or he can turn?

DEPRESSION – To what degree does the client exhibit signs of depression (i.e., inactivity, lack of interest, disrupted eating, and/or sleeping habits, etc.)?

IMPULSIVITY – To what degree does the client exhibit impulsive behavior (i.e., acting with little rational thought to outcomes)?

HOSTILITY – How much anger does the client seem to have toward himself or herself, others, or institutions?

INTENT TO DIE – To what degree does the client seem determined to carry out his or her plans to their conclusions?

ENVIRONMENTAL STRESS – To what degree does the client "feel" that events in his or her life are "overwhelming," painful, humiliating, or are providing insurmountable obstacles?

FUTURE TIME PERSPECTIVE – To what extent is the client able to focus on the future or positive future events as opposed to focusing on only the present or negative future events?

Source: Reprinted from Rogers, J.R., Lewis, M.M & Subich, L.M. (*Journal of Counseling and Development*, 80, 2002), page 502. ACA. Reprinted with permission. No further reproduction authorized without written permission from the American Counseling Association.

Association for Adult Victims of Child Abuse (2003) Suicide/Harmful Behavior Checklist

1. Do you feel chronically depressed?
2. Do you have recurring thoughts of killing yourself?
3. Do you have a specific plan to kill yourself?
4. Have you acquired the means to kill yourself, such as a supply of pills or a gun?
5. Do you intend to carry out this plan to kill yourself within a specific time frame?
6. Do you have thoughts of actually killing or harming others?
7. If yes, have you made specific plans or arrangements for this to occur?

Source: Association for Adult Victims of Child Abuse, (2003). *Reprinted with permission.* http://www.havoca.org.

American Academy of Pediatrics (2003) Suicide Checklist for Parents of Teenagers

- Has his or her personality changed dramatically?
- Is she or he having trouble with a girlfriend or boyfriend? Or is she or he having trouble getting along with other friends or with parents? Has she or he withdrawn from people she or he used to feel close to?
- Is the quality of his or her schoolwork going down? Has she or he failed to live up to his or her own or someone else's standards (when it comes to school grades, for example)?

- Does she or he always seem bored, and is she or he having trouble concentrating?
- Is she or he acting like a rebel in an unexplained and severe way?
- Is she pregnant and finding it hard to cope with this major life change?
- Has she or he run away from home?
- Is your teenager abusing drugs and/or alcohol?
- Is she or he complaining of headaches, stomachaches, etc., that may or may not be real?
- Have his or her eating or sleeping habits changed?
- Has his or her appearance changed for the worse?
- Is she or he giving away some of his most prized possessions?
- Is she or he writing notes or poems about death?
- Does she or he talk about suicide, even jokingly? Has she or he said things such as "That's the last straw," "I can't take it anymore," or "Nobody cares about me"? (Threatening to kill oneself precedes four out of five suicidal deaths.)
- Has she or he tried to commit suicide before?

Source: Used with permission of the American Academy of Pediatrics, 2003, http://www.aap.org/advocacy/childhealthmonth/prevteensuicide.htm

Concluding Remarks About Informal or Unstructured Assessments. The point of all suicide risk assessment is to make sure that clinicians cover the major areas of risk assessment, cover them thoroughly, and do not take shortcuts. During times of crisis, when clients are agitated, it is easy to get flustered or skip components of assessments, even if we have memorized them. Interview protocols, acronyms, and checklists are there to remind us of the major areas to cover. Therefore, it is less important that clinicians all use the same one than it is that they find one that they like and will use. You will notice that all of these informal assessments have overlap; that is because they are all trying to measure the same thing. We recommend that you pick one (with advice and guidance from more seasoned practitioners if possible), keep a copy of it someplace where it is easily accessible, and use it.

Formal or Structured Assessments

There are dozens of published standardized suicide risk assessments and hundreds of unpublished questionnaires and assessments. Standardized assessments can be useful in providing adjunctive information that helps to give a clearer picture of the situation. Standardized assessments also can be useful to provide additional support for clinical decisions in working with insurance companies or managed care companies. Research has shown that standardized assessments are especially helpful for professionals with limited psychiatric training (Patterson et al., 1983). However, at best they can only provide an estimate of suicide risk.

Standardized assessments that are used for suicide risk assessment come in two major categories: those that measure suicidal risk directly and those that measure emotional states (e.g., depression, hopelessness, anxiety) that correlate with suicide risk.

The resource list provided in Appendix A focuses on the direct assessment of suicidality, as it is beyond the scope of this book to list all psychological instruments that either have just a small percentage of the questions related to suicide (e.g., the MMPI) or measure constructs that are simply correlated with suicide (e.g., depression or anxiety inventories). The list of resources provided in Appendix A is not intended to be exhaustive of all published suicide risk scales, but only a representation of some of the major assessment instruments. We recommend that you take a moment to look over the list and the brief synopses that appear under each of the instruments to familiarize yourself with the type of assessments that are available.

Summary

Because this is a rather long chapter with a lot of information, it is important that the reader take a moment to consider the main points. Suicide risk assessment is a critical component of suicide prevention. Knowing who is at risk and the specific severity of the risk is essential before intervention can begin. Review again the box that outlines the essential features of suicide risk assessment (on page 184). Next, take another look at the risk factors (on page 194). Finally, recall that suicide assessments include both formal and informal methods.

12

Interventions with Suicidal and At-Risk Children and Adolescents

In this chapter, we move to a discussion of treatment issues. Whereas all adults who come into contact with children and adolescents should be aware of the basics of suicide prevention and assessment, some (although certainly not all) of the treatment issues in this chapter apply primarily to those adults who will intervene in a therapeutic context. There is, however, a lengthy section of this chapter dedicated to treatment issues as they relate to children and adolescents in schools and the school personnel who interact with them.

Suicidal behavior and ideation are of great concern to all people who work with child and adolescent mental health issues. Suicide is the second leading cause of death among adolescents over 15, and suicidal behaviors and ideation are extremely common among young people. Many young people are at risk, and all professionals in schools and communities who work with children and adolescents must have an understanding of the basic guidelines for prevention, intervention, and treatment of suicide.

As you might recall from the previous chapter, people who attempt or commit suicide are making a desperate attempt to say something (communication), to alleviate suffering either now or in the future (avoidance), or to take control of situations over which they feel helpless (control). Although these major categories of reasons for contemplating suicide (communication, avoidance, control) offer some guidance in organizing our thinking, each suicidal situation is unique, and there are as many specific causes of suicide as there are individuals who attempt. Because there is no universal cause for suicide, there is no universal stance to counseling the suicidal person. We do not apply treatment to all suicidal people in a general way, and there is no standard of care that applies universally to all people who are in treatment. Rather, working with people who are at risk for suicide or who have made an attempt means identifying and treating the underlying causes for that person. Each person is unique, and the situation that brought the person to the brink of death is unique. The extent to which we can identify the underlying causes is the extent to which we can offer help. This is one of the reasons why suicide assessment is so vital. Proper suicide assessment helps us to identify the reasons why suicide appears to be a viable solution for that person. It is one of the reasons why, in Chapter 11, we talked about assessment as the first step in treatment. A suicide assessment that identifies *why* the person is at risk will be critical in determining *how* we can help. Although these assessment and treatment generalities also apply to adults, we will focus in this chapter on the treatment of suicidal young people.

In many cases (upward of 90%), children and adolescents who attempt suicide have preexisting psychiatric disorders. These disorders can add significant levels of stress to their lives as well as making them particularly vulnerable to extreme reactions to typical social or other psychological stressors. As a result, when stressors occur, the young person's coping mechanisms are taxed beyond the capacity to handle the situation. Stressors such as the loss of a romantic relationship, disciplinary actions taken at school, trouble with the law, sexual identity issues, and academic or familial difficulties often precede the suicide attempt. Whether the stressor is directly or indirectly related to the psychiatric disorder (as in academic problems or trouble with the law) or is an unrelated stressor (such as moving to a new community), the results can be the same. The child or adolescent who is unable to cope with the level of stress might look for alternatives (Shaffer & Pfeffer, 2001). Counseling that addresses only the preceding stressor as a treatment for suicidal ideation or behaviors might get the person through the immediate crisis but still leave him or her at risk when the next stressor occurs. Therefore, treatment must address both the acute crisis and the underlying psychological vulnerability that allows the person to perceive suicide as a viable option.

Risk factors for child and adolescent suicide were discussed in Chapter 3. As a general reminder, they are included as well. Specific warning signs can cue adults and mental health practitioners to more imminent risk, and Box 12.2 provides reminder of these.

Suicidal Thoughts, Ideation, and Threats

Suicidal thoughts are relatively common in young people, particularly adolescents. Clearly, not all suicidal thoughts lead to a suicidal crisis. Nevertheless, suicidal thoughts typically come to the attention of a mental health professional when the thoughts are verbalized as threats or when nonverbal behaviors raise alarm.

In preadolescent children, disruptive disorders, such as ADHD and oppositional defiant disorder, can increase the presence of suicidal thoughts and threats. In addition, as with all age groups, depression and, more particularly, hopelessness increase the suicide risk. Finally, family dysfunction, including abuse and neglect, increases risk. (See Chapter 3 for a more complete discussion of suicidal risk in children.) In adolescents, mood disorders, anxiety disorders, substance abuse, hopelessness, impulsivity, and isolation appear to increase the presence of suicidal ideation and threats.

The lifelong work of Pfeffer and her colleagues on suicide in children gives us the best insight into suicidal ideation in preadolescents. She has found that suicidal ideation—persistent thoughts about suicide—is the single best predictor of suicide attempts in children (Pfeffer, Solomon, Plutchik, Mizrushi, & Weiner, 1982). However,

BOX 12.1 • *Child and Adolescent Risk Factors*

- Demographic risk factors
  - Male
  - Caucasian

- Biological risk factors
  - Impulsivity
  - Aggression
  - Hyperactivity
  - Brain damage

- Emotional risk factors
  - All mental disorders, but most prevalent are:
    - Depression (particularly hopelessness) and other affective disorders (particularly bipolar disorder)
    - Schizophrenia
    - Substance abuse
  - Identity problems
  - Anger and impulsivity
  - Antisocial personality disorder/conduct disorder
  - For children: *Expendable child syndrome*

- Cognitive risk factors
  - Rigid cognitive structure
  - Limited problem-solving ability
  - External locus of control
  - Inability to envision a future
  - Immature views of death and suicide
  - Attraction to death and repulsion from life
  - Perfectionism

- Environmental risk factors
  - Family dysfunction, including:
    - High levels of conflict
    - Parental alcoholism or substance abuse
    - Physical or sexual abuse
    - High levels of medical or psychiatric problems
    - Suicide within the family
  - Early loss
  - Social isolation
  - Poor peer relationships
  - Bullying (among boys) and victimization

although suicidal ideation is the best predictor of suicide attempts, ideation does not necessarily indicate risk. This is because suicidal ideation occurs with some frequency in nonsuicidal children. In one study, for example, approximately 12% of normal school-age children reported having suicidal thoughts (Pfeffer et al., 1984). Other studies have

BOX 12.2 • *Child and Adolescent Warning Signs*

Early Warning Signs:
- Withdrawal from friends and family
- Preoccupation with death
- Marked personality change and serious mood changes
- Difficulty concentrating
- Difficulties in school (decline in quality of work)
- Change in eating and sleeping habits
- Loss of interest in pleasurable activities
- Frequent complains about physical symptoms, often related to emotions, such as stomachaches, headaches, fatigue, etc.
- Persistent boredom
- Loss of interest in things one cares about

Later Warning Signs:
- Actually talking about suicide or a plan
- Exhibiting impulsivity, such as violent actions, rebellious behavior, or running away
- Refusing help, feeling "beyond help"
- Complaining of being a bad person or feeling "rotten inside"
- Making statements about hopelessness, helplessness, or worthlessness
- Not tolerating praise or rewards
- Giving verbal hints with statements such as "I won't be a problem for you much longer," "Nothing matters," "It's no use," or "I won't see you again."
- Becoming suddenly cheerful after a period of depression. This might mean that the young person has already made the decision to escape all problems by ending his or her life.
- Giving away favorite possessions
- Making a last will and testament
- Saying other things, such as "I'm going to kill myself," "I wish I were dead," or "I shouldn't have been born."

Source: Doan, J., Roggenbaum, S., & Lazear, K. J. (2003) *Risk and protective factors and warning signs* (The youth suicide prevention school-based guide series, no. 218–3a). Tampa, FL: University of South Florida, The Louis de la Parle Florida Mental Health Institute. Funded by the Institute for Child Health Policy at Nova Southeastern University through a Florida Drug Free Communities Program Award. Available online at http://pubs.fishi.usf.edu.

reported higher numbers. As many as 25% of children under age 14 years and 40% of children over age 14 years have considered suicide (Bolger, Downey, Walker, & Steininger, 1989). In contrast, as many as 85% of those who attempted suicide had expressed ideation before the attempt. The point is that many children think about suicide without actually making an attempt, and although a significantly higher percentage of children who attempt suicide express their ideation, the level of ideation in normal, nonsuicide attempts, also is quite high. Thus, suicidal ideation occurs in relatively high rates in the general population of children, at higher rates in the nonsuicidal psychiatrically disturbed population of children, and at the highest rate in children who commit suicide (Wise & Spengler, 1997). That means that suicide ideation is an imprecise predictor of suicide at best.

Research has tried to uncover any differentiation between children who express ideation but do not attempt and children who express ideation and then make a suicide attempt. Kosky and colleagues found no difference between ideators who do not attempt and ideators who attempt on rates of psychiatric difficulties (e.g., depression, anxiety, sleep disorder, conduct disorder, or irritability) or parental divorce. However, they found the combination of suicidal ideation and chronic family discord, drug use, and, for boys, disruption of major attachments, to be more highly correlated with children who move from ideation to attempts (Kosky, Silburn, & Zubrick, 1990).

Suicidal ideation, then, appears to be a good clinical indicator of risk in children when it is combined with other risk factors (Wise & Spengler, 1997). A careful evaluation of all risk factors, included stated ideation, is essential. Because the thought of a young child who is deliberately expressing a wish to die is so disturbing to even the most seasoned of clinicians, it is tempting to ignore it, wish it away, or recast it as something other than a suicide threat. Ignoring the suicidal ideation just because it comes from a child or because it is seen as a way to get attention can result in a fatal error. Wise and Spengler (1997) note that the first step toward accurate suicide assessment in children is accepting the reality of childhood suicide.

In adolescents, suicidal thoughts, threats, and ideation are even more common than they are in children. A large-scale study of high school students found that over 20% of adolescents had seriously considered suicide within the past 12 months and almost 16% had a suicide plan (Centers for Disease Control and Prevention, 1998). With these very high percentages, it might be tempting to minimize suicidal threats in adolescents, classifying them as "typical teenage angst." Clearly, many teenagers express ideation and never escalate to a suicide attempt. Suicidal ideation is itself not necessarily indicative of a high level of psychopathology or of an imminent suicide (Shaffer & Pfeffer, 2001). However, just as with children, suicidal threats and ideation must be taken seriously. In one study, 77% of suicide victims reported suicidal ideation to at least one other person in the three to five years before completion (Klimes-Dougan et al., 1999). This means that more than three quarters of adolescent suicide completers talk to other people about their suicidal ideation, and many do it years in advance of their actual completion, indicating that the suicidal process is a long-term one for them. However, these numbers also mean that 23% of adolescents in this study who completed suicide did not express suicidal ideation to another person. Therefore, although reported ideation is a strong indicator of risk, it is just one piece of data in overall risk assessment. Other risk factors, including affective disorders (depression, bipolar disorder, anxiety disorders), substance abuse, parental psychopathology, and family dysfunction, must be assessed as well (Weller, Young, Rohrbaugh, & Weller, 2001). (See Chapter 3 for a more complete discussion of risk factors in adolescents.) Overall risk assessment places suicidal threats and attempts in the context of the overall risk picture.

Just as with children, it is difficult to know what causes some adolescents to move from thoughts of suicide to suicidal behaviors. Weller and her colleagues (2001) hypothesized that access to firearms or weapons, recent exposure to suicide, an agitated or excited state, and weak societal taboos about suicide might facilitate a suicide attempt in a young person who has an underlying psychiatric condition, suicidal ideation, and a stressful life event. Thus, it is the combination of several factors that may serve to escalate suicidal thoughts to suicidal behaviors. On the other hand, a strong support system, the presence of others, and strong taboos about suicide can lessen the possibility of escalation of thoughts to attempts.

Suicidal Behaviors and Attempts

A previous suicide attempt places a child at high risk for a completed suicide. It is difficult to know the exact rates of previous attempts among children who commit suicide, as attempts might be misclassified as accidents, given the strong prevailing (erroneous) belief that children do not attempt or commit suicide. Thus, many attempts, misclassified as accidents, do not result in appropriate treatment. When attempts are correctly classified and the child receives the appropriate intervention, it might be possible to reduce the probability of a future completed suicide (Wise & Spengler, 1997). Although we know little about suicide attempts in children, there is some evidence that suicide attempts in prepubescent children are predictive of suicide attempts during adolescence (Pfeffer, Klerman, Hurt, & Kakuma, 1993).

The single biggest predictor for a completed suicide in adolescents is a previous attempt. One third of adolescents who commit suicide have made a previous attempt, and adolescents who have made a suicide attempt are 18 times more likely to make a subsequent attempt (Lewinsohn, Rohde, & Seeley, 1993). Boys who have a previous attempt are 30 times more likely to make a future attempt (Shaffer & Pfeffer, 2001). In general, adolescents who make suicide attempts have higher levels of psychopathology than do their peers who have suicidal ideation (Shaffer & Pfeffer, 2001). Yet for being the single biggest predictor, previous attempt is clearly an insufficient one. These same data indicate that two thirds of adolescents who complete suicide do not have a previous attempt. Additionally, many more adolescents attempt suicide than complete suicide. The Centers for Disease Control and Prevention study (1998) of high school students found that almost 8% of high school students (almost 12% of girls and 5% of boys) had made an attempt in the last 12 months. Thus, it is a variety of factors that increase risk, and sometimes suicide attempts occur in the context of a relatively brief adjustment reaction rather than as part of an ongoing cycle (Shaffer & Pfeffer, 2001). Combinations of risk factors appear to be better predictors. Approximately two thirds of adolescents who commit suicide have at least one of these three risk factors: prior attempt, mood disorder, and substance and/or alcohol abuse (Shaffer et al., 1996a). In addition, many adolescents who attempt or commit suicide have a life stressor that precedes the attempt. Common stressors are disciplinary crises, loss of a relationship, child abuse, teenage pregnancy, conflict with or between parents, trouble at school or with the law, physical or sexual abuse, a recent move, and exposure to suicide (Weller et al., 2001). Unfortunately, we know very little about suicide attempts in children and adolescents, since only those that warrant medical attention are ever brought to the attention of the mental health community, and it has been only very recently that any of this information has been systematically tracked (Shaffer & Pfeffer, 2001).

Responding to Threats and Attempts: Treatment Options for Suicidal Children and Adolescents

When the school counselor arrived back at her office from a middle school classroom guidance activity, she found Melissa waiting for her. Melissa was a Caucasian female seventh grader who had suffered from depression since anyone could remember. She was sluggish, easily brought to tears, and withdrawn from the other children. On this day, she mumbled that she had been sent to see the counselor because of a drawing she had produced in class. She held out the drawing, which showed a young girl in a casket surrounded by adults and one small boy, all standing with their backs to it. When pressed, she mumbled that it was her in the casket and this was her funeral, but her family did not even care enough to look at her. She started crying and said that she drew the picture because she felt really sad and wanted to die, but she was worried that if she killed herself, no one would come to her funeral. She said she did not have any friends at school, and even her family did not really care about her.

The counselor and Melissa talked for about a half-hour, with the counselor listening and validating what Melissa had to say. Toward the end of the discussion, the counselor told Melissa that she would call Melissa's mother and talk with her about how sad Melissa felt. Her mother immediately came to the school, met with Melissa and the school counselor, then met with the counselor individually, and took Melissa home. Within days, a counselor in the community called, stated that she had a release to talk with the school counselor, and worked to learn more about Melissa's situation. Melissa remained out of school for about a week. Before she returned, the community counselor again called the school counselor and discussed the plan for reintegrating Melissa into the school. The school counselor was asked to do a daily check-in with Melissa (just five minutes or so) and to ask the teachers to tell her if they noticed anything wrong. By working as a team, the school, the parents, the community counselor, and Melissa provided wrap-around care to help keep Melissa safe.

In this case, there were many caring adults who wanted to help Melissa, and a teacher appropriately alerted someone to the cry for help. Action was taken immediately, and Melissa's parents were given the responsibility to make sure that Melissa had appropriate care. If they were unaware of community resources, the counselor could provide assistance and referrals. When Melissa returned to the school, she did so in an environment that was making extra efforts to keep an eye on her. Note that none of these interventions required much time or resources on the part of the school personnel—just added monitoring and an ongoing reminder to Melissa that someone in the school cared enough to check in with her.

In general, treatment of suicidal children and adolescents (and, in fact, of all suicidal people) is based on a two-tiered system. The first level is crisis intervention. The goal of crisis intervention is to prevent death or injury by restoring a young person to whatever equilibrium existed in his or her life before the suicidal crisis. Young people who are at imminent risk for suicide are provided with resources and support to make it through the period of overwhelming crisis. If the young person is chemically dependent, then reducing immediate danger also means receiving treatment for substance abuse. Suicidal young people who are substance abusers will continue to have cognitive and perceptual distortions that lower inhibitions, decrease problem-solving abilities, and encourage impulsivity (McEvoy & McEvoy, 1994). The second level addresses the underlying vulnerability that not only gave rise to the current crisis, but will also undoubtedly allow future crises to occur. This intervention is more long-term than crisis intervention (Berman & Jobes, 1997). A wrap-around treatment model that includes all levels of care (inpatient, short- and long-term outpatient, and emergency intervention) is used to make sure that whatever type of treatment is most warranted is available to the suicidal young person (Rotheram-Borus, Walker, & Ferns, 1996). Ideally, suicidal children and adolescents would be placed in a seamless system of care in which they receive appropriate crisis intervention, individual and family counseling, and a supportive school environment that supplements the formal counseling process. Each part of the process would exist to assist the special needs of the young person as he or she worked through the suicidal recovery process.

The Suicidal Crisis: Acute Management

Each year, approximately two million children and adolescents attempt suicide, and 700,000 attempts are serious enough to warrant medical intervention, most often with a visit to a hospital emergency room (Shaffer & Pfeffer, 2001). When attempts reach medical significance, emergency room personnel typically try to establish a relationship with both the suicidal young person and the available family members. The goal is both to assess ongoing risk and to emphasize the importance of entering treatment. Attempters who continue to express a desire to die or who have a clearly abnormal mental state should be admitted for inpatient treatment. This includes people who are unable to form an alliance with the clinician; people who are dishonest, deceitful, or unable to discuss or regulate emotions and behaviors; people with psychotic thinking or current intoxication; those with rapid cycling with irritability and impulsive behaviors; and those with command hallucinations (Shaffer & Pfeffer, 2001). All attempters should be evaluated thoroughly before they are allowed to return home.

The major goals of crisis intervention are to reduce lethality; to make plans for safety; to provide support; to treat anxiety, mania, or insomnia that increase irrational thinking; and to replace the client's tunnel vision with a broader perspective. Tunnel thinking, which leads the young person to see suicide as the only alternative, must be challenged. This can be done by (1) encouraging a future orientation; (2) decreasing egocentricity and isolation; (3) giving information about the typical course of suicidal crises, possible diagnoses, and the expected outcomes of treatment; and (4) establishing a problem-solving strategy that includes exploration of problems, generation of alternatives, hypothesis testing, and a resolution or reframing of the immediate crisis (Berman & Jobes, 2001).

It is tempting for family members of a child or adolescent who makes a medically mild attempt to try to minimize the significance of the event. It is imperative that both the suicidal person and the family members be made to understand the importance of the event, the consequences, and the meaning that it had for the person who attempted. Mental health professionals must feel secure that they can provide adequate psychoeducation to family members to help them through the immediate family conflicts and difficulties in communication. In other words, releasing a child or adolescent who has attempted suicide back into a hostile or blaming environment will only increase the likelihood of another attempt. Family members must be given information on how to accommodate the needs of the suicidal young person in ways that lessen risk. Sometimes, there are unavoidable ongoing stressors in the family that elevate risk, and family members might need education and guidance to help their child or adolescent handle these crises.

Outpatient treatment is more successful if the treatment recommendations are congruent with the family members' expectations (this underlies the importance of good psychoeducation), if they are economically feasible, and if the parent is sufficiently mentally healthy and available enough to support the treatment. Mental health professionals should use their skills to predict how a family might respond and always use a cautious approach, keeping the person in the custody of the hospital if they believe that the person will further decompensate at home (Shaffer & Pfeffer, 2001).

Evaluation for discharge should include, at a minimum, a thorough evaluation to assess the ongoing suicidality of the individual and the security and stability of the home environment. Third-party information, in interviews that take place out of earshot of the suicidal person, is imperative to either corroborate or challenge the information that is being presented. People who are intent on suicide might minimize their risk in order to be released to make another suicide attempt. Children and adolescents should never be released from the emergency room until the mental health personnel believe that adequate supervision and support will be available over the next few days and until a responsible adult has agreed to "sanitize" the environment by removing access to potentially lethal methods, such as guns, knives, or pills (Shaffer & Pfeffer, 2001). Additionally, because of the potential for alcohol or substances to lessen inhibitions, access to these should be removed as well. Parents and family members must clearly understand the importance of this responsibility. There is some empirical evidence that parents must be told directly to remove access to lethal methods as they will not, on their own initiative, take the necessary precautions (McManus et al., 1997). Additionally, it is helpful to remind parents that they need only limit access to firearms, perhaps giving them to trusted friends or family for temporary safekeeping. There is some evidence that when parents are told to remove firearms completely from the home, they will not follow through (Shaffer & Pfeffer, 2001). However, simply hiding weapons or pills is not sufficient, as there is some evidence that suicidal adolescents will engage in relentless efforts to find them (Davis, 1983).

No-suicide contracts are sometimes used as an adjunctive intervention. Contracts are negotiated between the suicidal person and the mental health professional with the premise that the suicidal young person agrees not to engage in suicidal behavior and to inform parents, his or her counselor, or another responsible adult if he or she has thoughts of suicide or develops a suicide plan (Simon, 1991). The contract always stipulates a certain amount of time and may be rewritten numerous times, often with longer and longer fixed periods of time (perhaps going from one or a few hours to a day to several days or a week). Although no-suicide contracts are commonly used, there is no empirical research that demonstrates their effectiveness. They are best used to increase both the young person's and the family's commitment to treatment, but they should never be seen as a substitute for other types of interventions. Additionally, no-suicide contracts are not used with people who have disturbed mental states (e.g., severe agitation, psychosis, active substance use (Fergusson & Lynskey, 1995). No-suicide contracts are best used as an adjunct to the management of people with low intent (Shaffer & Pfeffer, 2001).

If the child or adolescent is discharged from the emergency room, there should be closely spaced follow-up appointments that allow for flexible scheduling if emergencies arise. Parents or guardians should be reminded about follow-up appointments with telephone calls, and if appointments are missed, the young person and the parent should be contacted to emphasize the importance of follow-up treatment (Shaffer & Pfeffer, 2001)

High-Risk Children and Adolescents: Inpatient Care

If a person is not discharged from the hospital after an emergency room visit, the next step is inpatient hospitalization. Young people come into inpatient care either from the emergency room after a suicide attempt or when a decision is made that the only way to prevent a suicide attempt is through the round-the-clock care that an inpatient unit provides. Inpatient treatment is a frequently chosen intervention for suicidal children and adolescents, and there is evidence that more and more young people are being hospitalized each year for suicidal intent (Stewart, Manion, & Davidson, 2002).

Suicidal children and adolescents undergo a thorough clinical examination before they are admitted for inpatient care. Assessment is a complex process that includes diagnosis, symptom severity, personality characteristics, family functioning, social supports, and lethality of the attempt or plan. Pragmatic decisions, such as the availability of beds and a review of other treatment options, also play a role in determining hospitalization (Morrissey et al., 1995). Although many factors contribute to making the decision to hospitalize a young person, clinical judgment plays a large role. Research shows that there is only about a 50% agreement among clinicians (psychologists, psychiatrists, and social workers) about which young people require inpatient hospitalization (Morrissey et al., 1995; Ullman, Egan, & Fiedler, 1981). Less experienced clinicians tend to hospitalize more frequently, preferring to err on the side of caution (Dicker et al., 1997). Overall, clinicians seem to place the most importance on depression, previous attempts, alcohol or substance abuse, and family functioning (presence or absence of family support). When asked, clinicians rate their most significant factor in deciding to hospitalize a suicidal child or adolescent as the presence or absence of family support (Morrisey et al., 1995).

Other studies have shown family support to have a significant impact on the quality of follow-up care. In a study that followed 66 hospitalized suicidal adolescents and their families for six months after their release from the hospital, compliance with follow-up treatment was shown to be rather low. Only about two thirds (66.7%) followed through with recommended medication, and about half (50.8%) followed through with individual therapy. Only one third (33.3%) complied with the recommended parent education and/or family counseling sessions. Families with high levels of dysfunction; those with the least involved or affectionate father–child relationships; and those with a depressed, paranoid, or hostile mother had the poorest follow-through (King et al., 1997). Noncompliance rates also are high among urban suicidal females, with fewer than one third (32%) attending more than two follow-up outpatient appointments (Stewart et al., 2002). Given these rates of follow-up, it is understandable that clinicians are more reluctant to release suicidal adolescents from inpatient care when they have poor family support.

Finally, caution should be used in assuming that hospitalizing a suicidal person will alleviate the suicidal crisis. There is no research that demonstrates that hospitalizing a suicidal young person prevents a high-risk person from making another attempt or completing suicide. In one study, more than 20% of hospitalized adolescents subsequently made another attempt, the highest risk being between 6 and 12 months after the hospitalization (Goldston et al., 1999). Another study found that 12% made a subsequent attempt and 30% continued to have suicidal ideation (Rotheram-Borus et al., 2000). A third study found that nearly one third (32.6%) of suicidal children and adolescents who had been admitted for emergency treatment had returned to the emergency room for another suicidal crisis within six months, and nearly one quarter (24.1%) had another documented suicide attempt (Stewart, Manion, Davidson, & Cloutier, 2001). Thus, it is clear that once a suicidal crisis has passed and a young person has been discharged, follow-up is imperative.

Containment within a Supportive Environment: Partial Hospitalization

Partial hospitalization (also called day treatment) is another treatment alternative for youths who are at risk. It offers "intensive, multidisciplinary treatment and skilled observation and support" (Shaffer & Pfeffer, 2001, p. 40S). In other words, the young person is in a structured and safe environment during the day and receives intensive counseling, medication management as needed, and the assistance of an entire treatment team. In some cases, in which there is a safe, supportive, and structured home environment, partial hospitalization can be used in place of inpatient care. In other situations, it is used as a step-down between inpatient and outpatient care. Finally, it can be used as a preventive measure to try to stop a suicidal person from escalating into an attempt or into the need for inpatient care. In cases in which a child or adolescent is escalating, it can be used as a step-up—a more intensive treatment when outpatient care is not sufficient and attempts are being made to prevent the need for inpatient care.

Partial hospitalization makes sense only when there is a structured and safe environment to return to in the evening. Shaffer and Pfeffer (2001) warn that it is an alternative to inpatient care only when "the child or adolescent is considered to be disturbed but containable in a supportive home or other residential setting" (p. 40S). Because treatment in a partial hospital setting tends to be longer than that in inpatient care, it can provide more time to stabilize the emotional problems and address the environmental situations that increase stress.

Management of Ongoing Risk: Outpatient Care

Once an acute suicidal crisis has passed, or to keep suicidal ideation from escalating into a suicidal crisis, outpatient counseling can be used. Outpatient counseling is effective when a child or adolescent is unlikely to act on the suicidal thoughts, when there is adequate family support at home, and when a responsible adult is available to intervene if the young person's behavior or mood deteriorates (Shaffer & Pfeffer, 2001).

In outpatient treatment, the underlying causes of the suicidal crisis can be examined. Many suicidal young people bring difficult issues to treatment, such as mental illness, familial difficulties, drug and alcohol use, and possible parental psychopathology (Berman & Jobes, 2001). Clinicians must be ever-vigilant for signs that the suicidal threat has escalated and the young person requires more intensive interventions.

Integration into the School System

Children and adolescents spend the majority of their waking hours in school; therefore, schools must become a partner in suicide intervention. Chapter 10 focused on suicide *prevention* in schools with a more general approach to helping students make good decisions. In this section, we discuss suicide *intervention* in the schools. Suicidal children and adolescents will require intervention by schools at three major points: during a suicidal crisis when the young person is imminently suicidal; during a longer period of time when a student has an ongoing, lower-level risk but still must be monitored; and after a suicidal crisis, when the student returns to school. During each of these times, schools provide an additional layer of care for suicidal students. Suicide intervention is done best when this layer of care is integrated with other supports—family and community—that are available for the student. Thus, suicide intervention in the school involves all school personnel, families, and community resources, all working together, supporting and informing each other, all with the ultimate goal of keeping a student safe.

Suicide risk assessment in the schools is extremely difficult. As we noted earlier, many children and adolescents report suicidal ideation, but completed suicide is actually a relatively rare occurrence, given the large number of students with very serious mental health problems. Labeling a student as "suicidal" when the student is actually at low risk not only uses up scarce resources, but also can engage a series of actions that might be inappropriate and could even escalate the student's risk by producing a self-fulfilling prophecy of risk (McEvoy & McEvoy, 1994). Therefore, although we always advocate erring on the side of caution, it is important that school personnel not overreact to every implied threat but instead complete a thorough suicide risk evaluation (or refer to an outside source for that evaluation) before engaging in elaborate suicide interventions.

Suicidal children and adolescents might talk about their problems with peers, teachers, school counselors, or other school personnel. Therefore, it is imperative that all school personnel receive training on how to handle a suicidal student and that all students be informed about what to do if they believe that a classmate is suicidal. (See Chapter 10 for a more complete discussion of suicide prevention and programming within schools.) Once a student has expressed suicidal intent or has been identified as being at high risk for suicide, then steps need to be taken quickly to limit the possibility of an attempt. School counselors clearly play a role in the identification of suicidal children, but children who are at high risk will need family interventions and supportive community services as well (e.g., ongoing counseling, hospitalization). If a student is imminently at risk, then crisis intervention models should be used. School counselors should immediately begin to apply counseling and crisis management skills to help prevent a suicidal crisis (Capuzzi, 1994). In these cases, it is important to remain calm, encourage self-disclosure, listen to the student without judging, assess lethality, and contact other professionals for assistance. Parents of minors must be notified and participate in decisions regarding their suicidal child or adolescent. If the student requests that parents or others not be told, it is extremely important *not* to honor this request. Confidentiality is not possible in suicidal crises, and everything must be done to ensure the child's safety. Parents or guardians must be contacted as soon as possible (Capuzzi, 1994). Whenever possible, informing parents of their child's suicide risk should be done in a face-to-face meeting and by the school crisis team member who did the actual assessment. Because contacting parents in this situation can be stressful for both the school professional and the parents, McEvoy and McEvoy (1994) recommend that another crisis team member, particularly an administrator, be in the room during the meeting or on an extension during a phone conversation to document the contact.

Sometimes a young person will need to leave the school environment for hospitalization or other forms of intensive treatment (e.g., partial hospitalization). In those instances, parents will work with hospital staff or other clinicians for admission. Parents or guardians might be reluctant to admit the extent of the suicidal crisis and might even demand that the school personnel withdraw their involvement from the crisis. Given the high levels of stress that are experienced by a family with a suicidal child, this denial or anger is not unexpected. Parents might feel threatened. They might perceive that their parenting skills are being questioned, or they might have limited emotional capacity to handle their child's crisis. Working together as a team, school personnel often can help parents to understand the seriousness of the issue. Again, the most important determination is the welfare of the child, and school personnel must agree to do everything they can to keep the child safe. In cases in which the parents are uncooperative even after attempts to get them to participate, schools should consult with legal counsel to understand the liability issues and to make sure that everything that is legally possible is done to keep the child safe (Capuzzi, 1994).

More common in schools than a suicidal crisis that requires immediate hospitalization is the situation of a young person who has an ongoing, rather low-level risk for suicide. These students are typically in outpatient counseling. If the student is not in outpatient counseling, the counselor will want to make a referral to the parents for a community agency or counselor to get the child the assistance she or he needs. School counselors should have a list of referral options that they can use when faced with a suicidal student. In most schools, it is unrealistic to assume that the school counselor has the time or availability to provide the personal counseling that a suicidal student requires. School counselors typically do not have schedules that allow for this type of intensive therapy, even if they have the counseling skills to handle the situation. Additionally, school personnel typically are not available on evenings or weekends, and outpatient counseling would have provisions made for crises at all hours. Thus, school counselors are seldom the primary therapists for these students. In instances when the

BOX 12.3

When assessing a child or adolescent who is believed to be an immediate risk:

- Establish rapport.
- Speak slowly and calmly, appearing confident and in control, providing security to the young person. The demeanor of the helping professional is critical to the safety of the young person. Be calm and supportive.
- Use basic terms (*sad, angry, hurt, scared, confused*), and label and reflect the student's feelings ("It sounds like you feel . . . " or "What I hear you saying is that you feel . . . ").
- Never minimize or ridicule the person's feelings or shut down the conversation. Comments such as "I'm sure you don't mean that" or "You'll grow out of this" are never helpful. Take every complaint seriously.
- Never act judgmental. Do not suggest that the young person is acting irrationally or selfishly.
- Do not immediately problem-solve. Listen and reflect that you hear and understand. Begin to broaden the young person's perspective on the situation. This is not the time for in-depth counseling.
- Be positive in your own outlook about the future.
- Accompany the student to the counselor or other crisis intervention specialist. Get other people involved. Never leave a suicidal person alone, even for a moment.

Source: Capuzzi (1994), McEvoy and McEvoy (1994).

school counselor is providing an adjunctive role in working with the suicidal student, the role of the school counselor is to help provide a supportive environment and monitor the student for any changes in their risk level. It is important to have releases signed between the outpatient therapist and the school counselor so that they can communicate freely with one another and the school counselor can report any changes in behavior. Because the lack of follow-through with outpatient and family treatment is such a significant problem for suicidal youths, school counselors can use their influence to encourage the student (and his or her family as appropriate) to attend their follow-up sessions.

No-suicide contracts, mentioned earlier as an adjunct to treatment of suicidal youths, are sometimes used in school settings. According to Capuzzi (1994, p. 55), a no-suicide contract should require the young person to do the following:

- Agree not to attempt suicide
- Get enough food and sleep
- Discard items that could be used in a suicide attempt (guns, weapons, medications, etc.)
- Specify the time span of the contract
- Call a professional (counselor, crisis center or some other agreed-upon resource) if he or she is tempted to break the contract or attempt suicide
- Write down the phone numbers of people to contact if the feeling of crisis escalates
- Specify ways in which time will be structured (e.g., walks, talks, movies)

No-suicide contracts might have a role in helping keep children safe, but *there is no evidence that no-suicide contracts actually reduce suicide attempts.* The danger, of course, is that once a no-suicide contract is signed, the school counselor might be led to believe that the child is no longer at high risk for suicide. It is imperative that when no-suicide contracts are used, they are never relied on as a method for safety. They are only an adjunct to more intense interventions that are best used when there is a strong relationship between the school counselor and the student and when the student is at low risk (Shaffer & Pfeffer, 2001).

If the student is to remain in the school setting, the outpatient therapist and the school counselor should, together with the parents and other school personnel, decide what necessary accommodations need to be made to help the student stay safe in school. In a recent case on which the authors consulted, this included allowing the student a pass to come see the counselor whenever she needed. Although there were fears that the student might take advantage of this situation, the reality was that it provided her a safety net. She knew that she could go to class (or lunch or whatever her schedule demanded) but leave without having to go through any bureaucratic steps if she felt overwhelmed or unsafe. She used the pass once, possibly to test whether or not it was real, and never needed it again. Nevertheless, she kept the pass for much of the school year, and it became worn and faded. Fingering the pass when she started to feel anxious provided sufficient relief, and she was able to stay in school.

The final type of suicidal situation in a school that requires intervention is when a young person returns to school after a suicide attempt or a period in a hospital or other intensive program. The key is to provide a supportive environment and to monitor for any changes in behavior that may signal elevated risk. In most school systems, news of the attempt travels quickly throughout the student body, and many students, even those who do not know the affected student well, know of the attempt. Chapter 10 discussed postvention efforts for the school—how to handle the emotional responses of other students, including the risk for suicide contagion. However, in working with a student returning to school after an attempt, there also is concern for the reintegration of the affected student. Thus, while there may be efforts to educate and counsel students after the attempt (or after a suicide completion), there also need to be efforts to reintegrate the affected student after the crisis is over—attending to the needs of the individual, as well as the student body. Unfortunately, very little information is available on how best to handle this reintegration.

Young people who attempt suicide face varied reactions from their peers as they attempt to reenter school and reintegrate into the community. There is some evidence that young males view persons who attempt suicide with less sympathy and empathy than they view the same troubled young males who do not attempt suicide (Stillion & McDowell, 1996). It appears that attempting suicide (and not completing) is seen as a sign of weakness, while a completed suicide is viewed as a sign of strength. Young males who attempt and then want to reintegrate into their peer group might suffer from rejection and ridicule. Clearly, education is needed both for the attempt survivor and for the peers. Young females, by contrast, tend to view the person who attempted with high levels of sympathy. They are more willing than males to discuss suicide with suicidal people, and they are more likely to provide emotional support. However, some have voiced concerns that this higher level of emotional support could contribute to higher attempt rates among adolescent females. Young girls might deliberately engage in nonlethal attempts to receive emotional support from their peers and achieve a type of elevated social status in their peer group (Stillion & McDowell, 1996).

Although school personnel cannot provide long-term treatment for students as they reintegrate to the school, it is important to have one member of the crisis team responsible for acting as a liaison to agencies working with the student and to the student's parents. This person should monitor how the student is doing at school and at home and make sure lines of communication remain open between the school, the treatment personnel, and the family. This team member may serve a sort of case management role for the student, organizing any follow-up activities provided by the school. At a minimum, this should include meetings with the student's teachers, counselors, and other appropriate staff to consider ways to reduce school stress and to meet the student's needs for safety, structure, and acceptance (McEvoy & McEvoy, 1994). Teachers in particular should be encouraged to look for any changes in the student's academic performance, attitudes, and peer interactions and report them to the case manager, who should then report this information to the parents.

As for the emotional climate, students who have attempted suicide must return to a school environment that can be incredibly stress-provoking, including facing peers, teachers, and others who know what has happened. Johnson and Maile (1987) noted that in these situations, the school needs to shift to a "holding environment" that focuses on offering these students a sense of normalcy, consistency, predictability, and acceptance. They recommend making sure that school staff members are warm and friendly to the returning student, without being overly attentive or asking probing questions. Additionally, the "case manager" should meet periodically with the student to monitor behavior, to ensure that the level of risk is not increasing, and to help provide a supportive and caring environment. The goal is to keep open the lines of communication between the student and caring adults

Psychotherapy and Psychopharmacology

Psychotherapy with suicidal people of all ages focuses on the underlying conditions that led the person to believe that suicide was an appropriate option. Once the immediate crisis has passed, ongoing psychotherapy is required to work through these underlying problems. Most commonly, the suicidal threat or attempt is used for communication, avoidance, or control, and the therapy addresses these issues as well as any underlying psychological problems (e.g., depression, substance abuse, bipolar disorder). Because ongoing therapy for suicidal young people is tailored to the needs of the client, there is no universally accepted psychotherapy for suicidal youths. In general, psychotherapy is designed to decrease the intolerable feelings of pain, depression, worthlessness, anger, anxiety, and/or hopelessness that led to the attempt. Psychotherapy with suicidal youths is best done by trained clinicians who are available to the suicidal client and his or her family, have skill and training in managing a suicidal crisis, can relate to the client in an honest and consistent way, can objectively understand the young person's attitudes and life problems, and can convey a sense of optimism and hope (Katz, 1995).

Regardless of the specific modality of treatment employed, in general, young people who are at risk for suicide must be taught basic coping skills. These include (but are not limited to) the following:

- Problem-solving skills, including problem clarification, generation of multiple solutions, goal setting, and implementation
- Depression management skills, particularly methods to handle hopelessness
- Anger and aggression management skills
- Loneliness prevention
- Interpersonal skills, including conflict resolution, reading and interpreting social cues, using steps for problem solving and decision making, understanding the perspectives of others, and understanding behavioral norms
- Identification and expression of feelings, including management of difficult feelings, delaying gratification, controlling impulses, and understanding the difference between feelings and actions
- Critical viewing skills, including understanding the media and how the lifestyles of media figures and fictional characters might or might not be representative of real-world situations and problem-solving skills
- Help-seeking behavior skills

In the following paragraphs, some of the major psychotherapies that have been used with suicidal children and adolescents are discussed briefly. However, none of these therapies has been validated through research for use with suicidal youths. A comprehensive overview of any of these therapies is beyond the scope of this book, and they are presented below very briefly.

Cognitive-Behavioral Therapy

Cognitive-behavioral therapy (CBT) has been shown to reduce depressive symptoms, such as the depressive triad (negative view of self, negative view of the environment, negative view of the future) common in suicidal persons (Beck, 1997). Although research on the effects of CBT in reducing depression in children and adolescents is limited, it appears that some of the basic techniques of CBT (challenging cognitive distortions and negative self-concepts, cognitive reframing, modifying automatic thoughts, and choosing active rather than passive coping strategies) may be beneficial in treating suicidal youths (Shaffer & Pfeffer, 2001). CBT has been used with suicidal adolescents to increase self-esteem, reduce negative thinking, enhance coping abilities, limit substance abuse, and reintroduce the ability to seek and enjoy pleasurable activities with peers (Rittner & Smyth, 1999).

Interpersonal Psychotherapy

Because suicidal behavior in children and adolescents is often associated with interpersonal conflicts, there is some support for the use of interpersonal psychotherapy (IPT) to reduce suicide risk. IPT is a time-limited intervention that addresses interpersonal problems, which are categorized into issues of loss, interpersonal role disputes, role transitions, and interpersonal deficits (Weissman, Markowitz, & Klerman, 2000). Although originally designed for working with depressed adults, IPT was modified for use with depressed adolescents (Mufson, Weissman, Moreau, & Garfinkel, 1999). IPT focuses on current interpersonal relationships and on the immediate social context and helps clients to change the style and effectiveness of their interpersonal interactions.

Dialectical Behavior Therapy

Dialectical behavior therapy (DBT) was originally designed by Marsha Linehan and has been demonstrated to reduce suicidality in adults with borderline personality disorder. DBT focuses on developing problem-solving skills to increase distress tolerance, emotion regulation, interpersonal effectiveness, and the use of both cognitive and emotional inputs in decision making (Shaffer & Pfeffer, 2001). In 1997, Miller and colleagues adapted this approach for use with suicidal adolescents. DBT for adolescents (DBT-A) requires both the suicidal youth and a parent or other responsible adult to attend treatment to improve both the skills of the young person as well as the overall home environment. DBT-A focuses on goals in five areas: (1) building on current capabilities, (2) increasing motivation to change, (3) encouraging generalization of new capabilities from therapy to everyday life, (4) impacting the environment (e.g., home, school), and (5) supporting the therapist's capabilities and motivation to treat their clients effectively. DBT-A has been found to reduce suicidal ideation and general psychiatric symptoms in suicidal adolescents, but has not been found to reduce actual suicide attempts, when compared to other types of psychotherapeutic interventions (Rathus & Miller, 2002).

Psychodynamic Psychotherapy

Psychodynamic therapy has been used with suicidal children and adolescents to help resolve internal conflicts related to early childhood experiences with separation, severe discipline, and abuse (Shaffer & Pffefer, 2001). However, one of the major criticisms of psychodynamic therapy is the lack of research to determine whether or not it is effective (Granello & Granello, 1998), and psychodynamic therapy with suicidal children and adolescents is no exception. There is no research to support its use. However, it remains a widely used intervention for suicidal persons, and clinicians who employ this theory believe that it is useful for suicidal persons.

Family Therapy

After a suicidal crisis with a child or adolescent, families, particularly parents and guardians, play a large role in making sure their children receive follow-up care. As noted earlier, dysfunctional families often have poorer rates of follow-up care, an essential component of treatment. Parent education and/or family counseling that helps family members recognize the seriousness of the suicidal crisis and the importance of follow-up care are vital components to treatment.

In most instances, it is not just the affected young person who will require treatment. Children and adolescents become suicidal within the context of their families, and in most cases, family dynamics will have to change to alleviate the problems causing, or contributing to, the suicidal crisis. Thus, ongoing family counseling is an important treatment component of a child or adolescent suicidal crisis. Suicidal adolescents report higher levels of family discord, poor communication, disagreements, rigidity, disparate goals and values among family members, and irregular routines and activities than do their nonsuicidal peers (Miller, King, Shain, & Naylor, 1992). Family interventions are designed both to improve the overall safety of the family environment and decrease the problems that have been identified in the family that might have contributed to the suicidal crisis. Family counseling in these situations often focuses on developing effective problem-solving techniques, conflict resolution, and a reduction in blame toward the suicidal member (Shaffer & Pfeffer, 2001). Cognitive-behavioral interventions as well as pychoeducational approaches have been used with some success. Additionally, there has been some support for the idea of time-limited, home-based family interventions for suicidal children and adolescents. Working with the family in their home allows the therapist to more fully understand the family dynamics and the complexities of the home environment and to more closely tailor the interventions to the family's needs (Harrington et al., 1998). Whatever interventions are used, the key is that the family must become part of a team that works to keep their affected family member safe. Clinicians will develop family-specific interventions to work through the barriers that exist within a specific family. The main goal, however, is always to have all family members working to ensure the safety of everyone in the family.

Group Counseling

There is a strong body of evidence that supports the use of group counseling with children and adolescents, given the centrality of peer relationships to these age groups. In fact, disrupted or dysfunctional peer relationships have been linked to depression and suicidal ideation in adolescents (Rittner & Smyth, 1999). Thus, group counseling adds a critical interpersonal component that could be particularly useful for young people with suicidal ideation and behaviors.

Group counseling should be offered only if there is an opportunity for a homogenous group, that is, young people of similar developmental stage who have contemplated or attempted suicide. Placing a suicide attempter in a group of young people with less extreme reactions to stress could be counterproductive, and the peers could end up isolating, ignoring, or, conversely, glorifying the suicide attempter. When opportunities arise for more homogenous groups (most commonly in institutional settings), group therapy can offer an important adjunct to individual and family counseling. Groups emphasize verbal expressions of affect, communication and listening skill development, peer support, and role modeling (Berman & Jobes, 2001), all of which are skills that are commonly underutilized among suicidal youth. There is anecdotal evidence that a group counseling intervention that targets issues of self-esteem, cognitive rigidity, social skills deficits, and substance abuse may be beneficial (Rittner & Smyth, 1999).

Psychopharmacology

Children and adolescents who are suicidal or who have attempted suicide will benefit most from treatment that utilizes all available resources, including an evaluation for the possibility of a psychopharmacological intervention. As with psychological interventions, pharmacology must focus on the underlying causes of the suicidal intent. Thus, mood stabilizers (such as lithium, valproate, and cabamazepine) might be a necessary component of treatment for children and adolescents with bipolar disorder, although these medications must be carefully monitored by a third party, given the lethality of overdoses. To date, lithium has been shown to reduce the recurrence of suicide attempts in adults with bipolar disorder or other major affective disorders (by as much as an eightfold reduction), but this finding has not yet been replicated in children or adolescents (Shaffer & Pfeffer, 2001).

Other pharmacological interventions for underlying psychological disorders may be part of the treatment regime, but to date, there is no evidence that these interventions reduce the risk of later completed or attempted suicide. In fact, in the past decade, there has been controversy over whether the use of certain antidepressants, most notably selective serotonin reuptake inhibitors (SSRIs), can induce suicidal behavior or intent in some people. Another concern is that the use of an antidepressant can raise the energy level of a depressed person before the depression has lifted, thus giving the individual the physical energy to complete a suicide. Finally, any medications that reduce self-control or inhibition (such as benzodiazepines) or could be lethal in an overdose must be used with extreme caution. The question of pharmacology is always complicated, and decisions are even more complex in situations surrounding suicide. Although guidelines are still emerging, in general, it appears that lithium or a mood stabilizer may be appropriate for youths with bipolar disorder and should be administered before an antidepressant. Antidepressants, particularly SSRIs, are used in children and adolescents with mood disorders, but the person must be closely monitored for any increase in agitation or suicidality. With children and adolescents, it is extremely important that a responsible adult administer the medications and monitor the young person for any unexpected change in mood, any increases in agitation, or any unwanted side effects (Shaffer & Pfeffer, 2001). The National Institute of Mental Health (NIMH) has released information on antidepressant use with adolescents. Rather than repeating that information here, we suggest that the reader access the most up-to-date information on this ongoing controversy. Readers are encouraged to go to the NIMH website (http://www.nimh.nih.gov/) and type in "adolescents and antidepressants." The National Mental Health Association has similar information, available in printable information sheets for parents (http://www.nmha.org/).

Summary

When a child or adolescent is suicidal, parents or guardians, family members, school personnel, and community agencies must all work together to form an intervention team that is designed to ensure safety. In general, treatment of suicidal young people has two levels: immediate crisis intervention and longer-term treatment to address the underlying vulnerabilities that allowed the suicidal crisis to occur. There are three primary levels of

BOX 12.4 • *If a Child or Adolescent Is Suicidal*

When a young person is considering suicide, here are some things to remember:

1. Engage in crisis management. This differs from typical counseling in that the helping professional is directive and active, and the goal is only to keep the young person safe.
2. Be calm and supportive. A calm demeanor will help to deescalate the crisis and lower the emotionality of the child or adolescent.
3. Be nonjudgmental. The hopelessness or stress that the young person feels should be validated as feeling very real to the person (not validated as a reality) and never dismissed or minimized. Listen and make sure the young person feels heard.
4. Encourage self-disclosure. Talking about the situation is an important first step. It will help with assessment of risk, but it also is the critical first step in treatment.
5. Acknowledge the reality of suicide as a choice, but do not normalize suicide as a choice. Help the young person to know that although suicide is one possible outcome, there are many other, better choices.
6. Do not attempt in-depth counseling. Crisis management is only about getting through the immediate crisis. Long-term counseling will be a necessary next step, but attempting to engage in nondirective in-depth counseling during a crisis can increase risk.
7. Never engage in suicide assessment alone. Always bring in other people to assist with the assessment and with the decision making.
8. Assess lethality. Refer to some of the questions in Chapter 11 to help determine the level of risk.
9. Make decisions. If the young person is potentially suicidal, take steps to ensure safety. This might mean a referral to an outside agency or commitment to a hospital.
10. Notify parents. Suicide is one time when confidentiality does not exist. Parents must be involved.
11. Refuse to allow the young person to return to school until he or she has been assessed by a qualified practitioner.
12. Document everything.

Source: Adapted from Capuzzi (2002).

treatment: inpatient care, day treatment programs, and outpatient treatment. Within each of these levels, ongoing assessment is necessary to continue to monitor suicide risk. Once a student has been reintegrated into a school, schools must work with community partners to ensure an environment that maximizes the student's chances for success and safety. There is no treatment intervention of choice for suicidal children and adolescents. Rather, treatment that addresses the underlying cognitive and emotional risk factors, including mental illnesses, is employed. This may include individual, group, and family therapy, as well as the use of pharmacological interventions.

13

Interventions with Suicidal and At-Risk Adults

The foundation of suicide intervention is the belief that suicidal people in general do not really wish to die. In fact, suicidal crises are typically the result of a temporary, reversible, and ambivalent state (Stillion & McDowell, 1996). Suicide intervention works on the premise that the suicidal crisis, if successfully navigated, need not be fatal. Most clients in a suicidal crisis experience suicide ambivalence: the simultaneous desire both to live and to die. If this were not the case, then the person would not be sitting in front of you or engaging in a discussion, he or she would already have made an attempt or completion. Mental health practitioners capitalize on that ambivalence in their work with suicidal clients. Recognizing the nature of the ambivalence, helping clients to recognize and acknowledge that ambivalence, and finding other ways for them to express the underlying meaning of the suicide (communication, control, avoidance) become the core components of suicide intervention. Clearly, the focus for suicide intervention is short-term stabilization. Thus, although helping clients "choose to live" rather than "choose to die" might help them through the immediate hours and days, longer-term treatment must address the underlying issues that brought them to the suicidal state.

Suicidal thoughts, behaviors, or ideation are not, in and of themselves, a diagnosis or problem that can be treated. Rather, the suicidal thoughts, behaviors, and ideations are symptoms, and the underlying problem must be the focus of treatment. That is why information written about working with people in suicidal crisis typically focuses on management (of the suicidal crisis) rather than treatment. Once the person is stabilized, then treatment of the underlying problem can begin (Fremouw, dePerczel, & Ellis, 1990).

The underlying problems that can lead to a suicidal crisis are extremely varied, and clients will come to experience a suicidal state through many different paths. More than 90% of people who complete suicide have preexisting psychiatric difficulties that make them particularly vulnerable to stress (Conner et al., 2001). With these people, either the psychiatric illness itself or the limitations imposed by the illness on the person's coping ability, problem-solving capacity, or social support network can cause chronic suicidal risk or an acute suicidal crisis. Other people are at risk because a trauma or extreme stressor has challenged their ability to find hope for the future or to cope with the current situation. Still others have impaired thinking or have unchecked impulsivity exacerbated by drugs, alcohol, or organic brain damage. There also are people who become suicidal after a lifetime of behaviors and ineffective coping strategies that leave them at chronic risk. Clients can find themselves being assessed for suicide with any or all of these contributing factors. In each case, the primary goal is to get the client through the immediate crisis so that work can begin on the underlying cause. Because of the diverse nature of suicidal clients, it is difficult to describe a "best" method for intervention that is most appropriate for all clients. Nevertheless, there are some general guidelines for intervention that can lay the groundwork for ongoing treatment.

Dan is a 23-year-old Caucasian man who was diagnosed with schizophrenia at age 19. The combination of medication and supportive therapy that he receives has allowed Dan to remain living at home, working part-time in a sheltered workshop. Dan's parents keep a close eye on him and notify his psychiatrist immediately whenever they perceive an impending escalation. One Friday night after work, they noticed that Dan was more withdrawn than usual. Over the weekend, it became clear that Dan was becoming more withdrawn and paranoid. The last time Dan had become paranoid, he had tried to hang himself in his bedroom, so his parents began to fear for his safety. After Dan spent all Sunday in his room, sitting on the floor behind his bed (with very frequent checks by his parents), his parents decided that they could not wait until the community treatment facility opened on Monday, and they took him to the emergency room. When the emergency room personnel attempted to interview Dan, he refused to speak to them. He appeared to be listening intently to voices that others could not hear, and Dan's parents wondered whether he might be hearing command hallucinations that were telling him to harm himself. His mother told the staff at the emergency room why she believed that Dan was at imminent risk of suicide, and they agreed with her assessment and admitted Dan into the hospital.

Marco is a 63-year-old Italian immigrant. He has lived in Little Italy in New York since coming to the United States at age 27, and he is part of a large Italian family. He has worked in the family butcher shop since coming to the United States, and he is married with children and grandchildren. Most of his adult life, Marco has struggled with alcoholism. In fact, this is why their father gave the butcher shop to Marco's younger brother, Frank, instead of to Marco, who, as the oldest, should have inherited the shop. Periodically, Marco has attempted to curtail his drinking, but these attempts never last more than a few weeks. The close-knit family covers for Marco, and when he misses work or is violent with his family because of the drinking, they make excuses for his behavior.

In addition to his alcoholism, Marco suffers from a low-level, ongoing depression (dysthymia). It is difficult to know how much of the drinking is an attempt to self-medicate (that is, to make him forget about the depression) and how much of the depression is caused by the alcohol (which is, of course, a depressant). Sometimes, when Marco is drinking, he becomes tearful, talks about the "old country," and says that he can no longer tolerate life in the United States. During those times, he threatens to kill himself so that he can be with his long-lost relatives. However, no one in his family takes these threats very seriously— "That's just Marco," they say.

Several weeks ago, Marco traveled to Florida to visit his daughter and her family. His wife had gone to stay with her ailing sister, and Marco was looking forward to a break from the New York winter. One day, while his daughter and her husband were at work, Marco went to a local bar to have a few drinks. By midafternoon, he was sitting at the bar, tearfully telling the bartender about his plans to commit suicide. The bartender became alarmed and called 911. The police came and questioned Marco. Marco could not remember the name of the company where his daughter worked, and he figured that she would be mad if the police called her at work anyway, so he refused to give the police any information about who he was or where he was staying. Marco was used to life in Little Italy, where no one took his threats seriously and the most the police ever did was drop him off at home. Eventually, the Fort Lauderdale police took Marco to the emergency room for a suicide assessment.

Kate is a 39-year-old Caucasian female who is going through a divorce from her husband of 19 years. They have four children, and Kate is worried because her husband plans to fight for custody of the children. Her husband told her that she has no chance of keeping the children, since Kate has a history of depression and drug use, and the event that led to their divorce was that her husband found out she had been prostituting herself to get money to pay for drugs. Kate believes in her heart that her husband is right and that no judge in the world would let her keep her kids. She believes that she is fundamentally unworthy of continuing to live. She was picked up by police after a person in a passing car saw her cutting through the chain-link fence of an overpass with wire cutters. She had planned to jump to her death onto the highway below.

These three cases represent three very different paths that all led to the same result: assessment for suicide by emergency room personnel. As you read this chapter, consider how the treatment received by these three individuals might be very different, in spite of the similar notation on their respective charts that might simply say, "Complete a comprehensive suicide risk assessment."

The Nature of Crises and Emergencies

Regardless of what path a person traveled to get to a suicidal crisis, when the crisis occurs, the person's capacity to cope has been overwhelmed, and the person's normal methods of coping are ineffective (Kleepsies et al., 1999). In his seminal work on crisis in psychiatry, Caplan (1964) noted that an individual comes to any given crisis with a preexisting level of functioning. Whether a person typically has a high level of functioning, just average, or barely gets by, a crisis occurs when he or she can no longer sustain the preexisting level of functioning. During a crisis situation, a person feels overwhelmed, disheartened, frightened, and exhausted, and his or her level of functioning drops precipitously. For people in a suicidal crisis, this time is accompanied by a danger of self-harm. Most crises are time-limited, as the crisis state cannot remain indefinitely without either successful resolution or a further spiraling downward if efforts at coping remain unsuccessful. Most suicidal crises are self-limiting, and after 24–48 hours, most people (although not all) will go into an adaptive period of emotional exhaustion.

As an individual works through the crisis situation, one of three main trajectories can occur. The first option occurs when the crisis has so beaten down the individual that he or she never recovers. In this trajectory, the individual remains at the lowered level

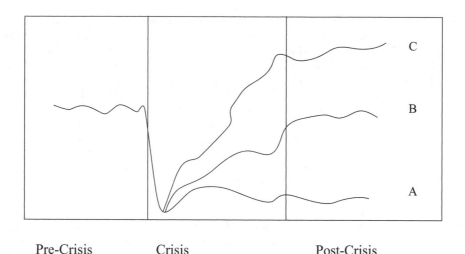

Pre-Crisis   Crisis   Post-Crisis

FIGURE 13.1   Level of Functioning.

Source: Echterling, Lennis G. Presbury, Jack, McKee, J. Edson, *Crisis Intervention: Promoting Resilience and Resolution in Troubled Times,* 1st edition, (2005). Reprinted by permission of Pearson Education, Inc., Upper Saddle River, NJ.

of functioning even after the crisis has passed. This lowered functioning becomes the new "preexisting" level at which the person will enter the next crisis (trajectory A in Figure 13.1). The second option is that the person will successfully navigate the crisis and return to the previous level of functioning (trajectory B in the figure). The third and more hopeful trajectory occurs when a person learns from a crisis and develops new coping skills and a renewed sense of self-efficacy from the experience. The person actually emerges from the crisis at a higher level of functioning than before the crisis occurs and is in a better frame of mind to encounter any future crises (trajectory C in the figure).

Thus, a crisis is an emotionally significant event that may lead to a turning point, for better or worse. However, a crisis does not necessarily imply suicide risk. When people are in a suicidal crisis, they are at elevated risk for suicide, and a thorough assessment must be done to determine risk.

An emergency occurs, however, when an individual "reaches a state of mind in which there is an imminent risk that he or she will do something (or fail to do something) that will result in serious harm or death to self or others, unless there is some immediate intervention" (Kleespies at al., 1999). It might seem that we are splitting hairs with this distinction, but it is important to differentiate between crises and emergencies in suicidal risk management.

Clients who are in a state of crisis may be at high risk, and they might see suicide as an—or perhaps the only—option. Clearly, intervention is essential. Clients can stay in a state of extreme crisis for a few hours or a few days, or they might be in an ongoing low-level crisis for long periods of time. Clients who are in a suicidal emergency, however, are at immediate, imminent risk. These are people who have a plan, and without intervention, they will make an attempt within minutes or hours. A suicidal emergency, then, is one possible culmination of the suicidal crisis.

In this chapter, we will discuss intervention during a suicidal crisis. We will focus on ways to contribute to client safety and to management of the crisis. Later in the chapter, we will address the issue of suicidal emergency and give clinicians some basic steps to help manage these emergencies.

Goals of Intervention

Crisis intervention models have been developed to assist health and mental health professionals involved in these situations. Roberts (1991) synthesized many of these models into a seven-stage crisis intervention model, which serves as the basis for crisis intervention work. These stages are as follows:

1. Assess lethality
2. Establish rapport
3. Identify major problems
4. Deal with feelings
5. Explore alternatives
6. Develop action plan
7. Follow-up

This model serves as the foundation for what appears in the following pages. However, because of the specific nature of the suicidal crisis, some of the steps are expanded. The model that we present is a bit more complex and more specific to suicide. Here is Robert's model again, with a bit more information for suicidal crises:

1. Assess lethality
   a. Ensure immediate safety
   b. Contain the person for safety

2. Establish rapport
   a. Develop a therapeutic relationship
   b. Use congruence, unconditional positive regard, and empathy

3. Identify major problems
   a. Slow things down
   b. Listen, understand, and validate (LUV)
   c. Identify the message

4. Deal with feelings
   a. Encourage emotional ventilation

5. Explore alternatives
   a. Engage social support
   b. Restore hope
   c. Assist the client to envision possibilities and develop resiliency

6. Develop an action plan
   a. Evaluate the risk to determine intervention

7. Follow-up
   a. The type of follow-up needed will depend on the intervention plan

Crisis Intervention Step 1: Assess Lethality

Ensure Safety.   Of course, the primary goal of suicide intervention is immediate safety. As we discussed in Chapter 11, suicide intervention really begins with suicide assessment, and the primary goal of assessment is to ensure safety. Thus, the first critical steps in any interaction with a suicidal person all focus on keeping the person alive through the immediate crisis. Long-term treatment, instilling hope for the future, and providing alternative methods for managing future crises are clearly the desired eventual outcomes, but none of those things matter if the immediate crisis is not managed effectively and the person attempts or commits suicide. Therefore, all first steps are focused on safety. It is for this reason, for example, that a suicidal person is never left alone—not even for a moment. Someone who is interacting with a suicidal individual should never step out of the office to get another person to help or make a phone call, leaving the client alone. Suicide can happen quickly. Do not give the person an opportunity to attempt.

The primary importance of safety and what is physically required to keep a person safe through the crisis will also, in part, determine the type of intervention. For example, a client who is imminently suicidal (in an extreme suicidal crisis or a suicidal emergency) might very well need to be hospitalized because of the necessity of round-the-clock care and monitoring. Hospitals have the ability to put patients on a "suicide watch" that increases their supervision to nearly constant. Even in the best of circumstances, this is rarely available in a home environment. Some medications or medical interventions (e.g., electroconvulsive therapy) can be administered only in a hospital setting or are best administered there, and these medical interventions might be necessary to inhibit impulsivity or lower risk. Hospitals also provide care in the absence of a stable home environment or family support to people who are at risk. Finally, hospitals can provide immediate medical intervention in the event of another suicide attempt. In all suicide interventions, the client's safety needs, as determined from a thorough assessment of the client, the environment, and the risk factors, are the critical factor in determining the types and levels of intervention.

Crisis Intervention Step 2: Establish Rapport

Develop a Therapeutic Relationship.   In helping a client through a suicidal crisis, whether the encounter is a one-time crisis assessment and intervention session or a longer-term treatment relationship, it is important to establish a caring, consistent, and credible therapeutic relationship. Clients need to know that they have an ally, someone who cares about them and will listen to them without judgment. Too often, the pain that suicidal people express is minimized by others (e.g., "Don't be silly—you have so much to live for!") or met with harsh judgments (e.g., "I'm tired of your threats!" or "That's crazy talk!"). The pain is real to the person who is experiencing it, and it may be sufficient to motivate them to attempt suicide.

Research has demonstrated that one of the most significant factors in assessing suicide risk and determining the prognosis for success of suicide interventions is the quality of the therapeutic relationship (Bongar, 2002). The therapeutic relationship plays a major role in determining a client's willingness to seek help, and clients indicate that a strong alliance with a helping professional has a significant impact on helping them through a serious emotional crisis. Just as research has found that a positive therapeutic relationship is a major indicator of treatment success, research also has found that a lack of a therapeutic relationship actually has a negative impact on outcomes (Maltsberger, 1986). In other words, the absence of a therapeutic bond actually harms a suicidal person.

Therapeutic relationships that are characterized by honesty, trust, and compassion can provide key leverage to help people get through a crisis period. Basic counseling skills (e.g., active listening, empathizing, summarizing, paraphrasing, and reflecting feelings) are utilized within the context of a strong relationship. The core of this relationship is best articulated through the work of Carl Rogers. Rogers believed that people who work with those in crisis are at their best when they are warm, real, understanding, and nonjudgmental. His core conditions for a therapeutic relationship—congruence, unconditional positive regard, and empathy—remain as the basis for developing therapeutic relationships.

Congruence refers to congruence between thoughts and behaviors. People who are congruent are genuine in their behaviors. They act how they feel. They do not put up a professional front or distance themselves from their clients. Rogers described congruence as "the feelings the counselor is experiencing are available to him, available to his awareness, that he is able to live these feelings, be them in the relationship, and able to communicate them if appropriate" (Rogers & Stevens, 1967, p. 90).

Unconditional positive regard is the constant and unwavering respect that the counselor has for the client. Clients can present themselves in a multitude of ways, with a variety of problems and varying levels of insight or intelligence, and the counselor always respects and values the client. Counselors distinguish between people and actions; that is, even when the person in front of you has committed terrible actions or is considering taking an action (e.g., suicide) that you find horrifying, the value of the person is not diminished. Unconditional positive regard is what allows mental health practitioners to work with people whose values are very different from their own. Valuing the basic worth of the person and differentiating the person from the behavior allow us to have empathy (Hazler, 1988).

Empathy is the desire to fully understand the world view of the person in crisis, to have a profound interest in sharing the "client's world of meanings and feelings" (Raskin & Rogers, 1989, p. 157). Empathy involves both *understanding* and *communicating that understanding* to the client. True empathy involves the moment-to-moment experiencing of the client's inner world. It is not merely acting as if one understands or using a standard phrase or expression that labels the client's feelings without true understanding. Clients recognize when counselors are using empathetic words but have no real empathy behind the words (Young, 2004). Rogers acknowledged that complete empathy was probably unattainable but saw the ability to empathize as a lifelong goal that should always be under development for those who work with people who are in crisis.

The goal of the therapeutic relationship is a genuine caring and nonjudgmental rapport that allows the mental health practitioner and the person in suicidal crisis to work together—to collaborate—to discover the best way to keep the person safe. A therapeutic alliance such as this helps to instill hope for the future, something that suicidal people desperately need.

Crisis Intervention Step 3: Identify Major Problems

Slow Down.   When clients are suicidal, they are in a state of crisis. The role of the mental health practitioner in this immediate circumstance is crisis intervention, which in some ways is different from traditional counseling. A major challenge in crisis counseling is avoiding the sense that the crisis is taking over and that the client will inevitably be overwhelmed and succumb to self-harm. In general, interactions during this time are focused on slowing the client down. This conveys the message that if suicide is the only solution to this crisis, then it will still be available later on; it does not have to happen right now. The hope, of course, is that when the client is given time to slow down, consider other options, and find hope, the urgency of the current crisis will have passed. This is not a long-term solution, but buying time is a critical

BOX 13.1 • *A Few Words about Managing Ourselves with Suicidal People*

When we interact with people who are in a suicidal crisis, it is easy to become anxious or flustered ourselves. When we are faced with a client who is in crisis, our emotional state and behavior are of critical importance in effective assessment and intervention. We must present a calm demeanor that conveys to the person in crisis that we are comfortable helping him or her through this emotional turmoil. A professional manner that is calm, demonstrates empathy and care, and displays a reassuring confidence in one's ability to help the client through the crisis will go a long way. There is no one right way to be, but we encourage you to take time to consider how you will respond. A stance that is overly clinically detached will not help to establish rapport, but becoming overly enmeshed in the client's emotionality will not evoke confidence. Establishing a professional manner will enhance the person's ability to exercise self-control and to begin to consider other possibilities for the future.

The goal with a suicidal client is to remain calm while expressing empathy for the feelings of desperation that are leading him or her to consider suicide. "You must deal with your clients' thoughts and feelings in a matter-of-fact manner; this suggests to them that you've dealt with such issues previously, and it reassures them, to some degree, that their experiences are not all that unusual. In some situations, you may want to be openly reassuring and supporting, even acknowledging that suicidal urges are sometimes a natural response" (Sommers-Flanagan and Sommers-Flanagan, 1999, p. 262). Obviously, this is a situation that requires practice, observation, and supervision.

component of managing the suicidal crisis. Remember, the focus in initial crisis intervention is on helping the client to survive the first several days so that longer-term treatment can focus on alternative mechanisms for problem solving and coping.

Listen, Understand, and Validate.   In their book on crisis intervention, Echterling, Presbury, and McKee (2005) promote a model for helping persons in crisis express their emotions and tell their story. They utilize the acronym *LUV*: listen, understand, and validate.

   Listening implies active listening—strategies that help the person to feel heard. Many clients in crisis have told their stories to countless others, but they often are still left with a sense that they have not been heard. Active listening strategies include many basic counseling skills, including the use of minimal encouragers, reflections of feelings, paraphrasing, and summarizing. Appropriate nonverbals are an essential component of listening. An open, inviting posture, a slight lean forward, and appropriate eye contact all convey interest and attention.

   Understanding involves using basic counseling skills to communicate to the person in crisis that you understand what the person is feeling—that you have empathy. Remember, in Carl Rogers's description, empathy involves both understanding and communicating that understanding to the client. Basic skills, such as paraphrasing, clarifying, reflecting feelings, and using the language and metaphors of the client, all help to communicate understanding.

   Validating implies not only indicating a belief in what the person is expressing (e.g., "I hear how desperate you feel. I understand what brought you to this place."), but also implying that you believe in the person's abilities, strengths, and resilience. Minimal encouragers (e.g., nodding, small utterances that encourage disclosure) are ways to communicate your interest in the person. Most important is a stance that is respectful, allows the person to speak freely, and does not judge. Stepping in with advice or quick solutions discourages disclosures and communicates a lack of confidence in the person's ability to get through the crisis. In a suicidal crisis, it is tempting to want to step in and solve the problem for the client, but this is seldom appropriate (or possible). Adopting an approach that listens, understands, and validates will encourage the person to tell his or her story and, in time, be ready to consider other solutions.

Identify the Message.   Earlier in the book, we noted that the underlying message for most people who threaten, attempt, or commit suicide can be categorized in one of three ways: communication, control, or avoidance. Suicide becomes a method to tell something to others in a dramatic way with the hope that one will finally be heard (communication), or it is a problem-solving strategy of last resort (control or avoidance). In working with a suicidal individual, helping the person to identify the underlying message (even the person might not know what it is!) allows the focus to begin to shift away from expressing the feelings (emotional ventilation) and telling the story (listen, understand, and validate) and on to assisting the client to ask for help and to learn alternative problem-solving strategies.

   Of course, each person moves through a suicidal crisis in a unique way, on his or her own timetable, and each combination of life history, current level of functioning, and social support determines how this is done. Therefore, with some clients, identifying the message can mean a rather quick and seamless move into fostering resilience and problem solving, while others will take much more time and much higher levels of intervention before the tide turns from problem-focused work to solution-focused work. It is because of this variability that we highlighted the importance of the therapeutic relationship earlier in this section. The ability to understand the client will play a key role in determining how to move through the crisis and what supports to put in place.

Crisis Intervention Step 4: Deal with Feelings

Encourage Emotional Ventilation.   One of the primary tenets of crisis intervention is emotional ventilation (Callahan, 1994). People who are in suicidal crisis often feel overwhelmed by their emotions. Because of the ambiguity that is frequently part of the crisis (e.g., not wanting to die but wanting the pain to end), it is not unusual for many different emotions to occur simultaneously. Of course, anxiety, fear, anger, exhaustion, guilt, and helplessness are common, and people can feel overwhelmed by any emotions. Emotional ventilation allows individuals to experience and express these emotions in a safe place, with another person to listen and without the fear of being judged. Sometimes, clients will say that they are afraid of their emotions. They might say something like "I'm afraid if I let the tears start, they'd never stop" or "If I told you what I really felt, you'd think I was crazy." The goal of emotional ventilation is to allow clients to say those words out loud and to fully experience their feelings. Emotional expression is a form of self-disclosure that has been linked to reduced suicidal intent (Apter et al., 2001). The goal of emotional ventilation is not to escalate a client and amplify the emotions, but rather to allow the person to express the feelings that they have.

There is some preliminary evidence that emotional ventilation can sometimes defuse a suicidal crisis enough to allow for other interventions, such as contracting and problem solving (Westefeld et al., 2000). Although emotional ventilation is typically not sufficient to defuse a crisis, it appears to be a critical component of any crisis.

Finally, emotional ventilation allows the mental health practitioner to more fully understand the mindset of the suicidal person in order to better assess risk and make intervention decisions. Some common themes have been identified regarding the state of mind of suicidal persons (Shneidman, 1981):

1. Acute perturbation or an exacerbation of the already-troubled state of mind. People in suicidal crisis tend to see every situation they face as more extreme, more serious, and more in need of an immediate solution than do people who are not in crisis.
2. Increased negative emotions, such as self-loathing, guilt, or shame.
3. Cognitive restriction, or the inability to generate multiple options or to engage in problem solving. People who have come to the conclusion that suicide is the only way to solve their problems typically will stop trying to generate other solutions.
4. Focused attention on the thought of suicide as a way to end the emotional pain.

Crisis Intervention Step 5: Explore Alternatives

Engage Social Support.   Regardless of the level of intervention that is eventually decided on (outpatient, partial hospitalization, or inpatient), mental health practitioners should help individuals to engage their social support systems to help them through the crisis period. People who are suicidal are often lonely and isolated and have lost the ability to fully engage all of their supports (or never had it to begin with). Some people have "used up" their support systems; that is, the people in their lives have expressed frustration with the suicidal person and can no longer be counted on for support. Still others do not have a support system to engage. Nevertheless, to the extent that it is available as a resource, people working with those in suicidal crisis need to know how to engage the individual's support system.

It is worth noting (and it will be discussed in depth in Chapter 14) that when someone expresses danger to self, normal limits on confidentiality no longer apply. Therefore, when a person threatens suicide, mental health practitioners do not have to worry about telling others. In fact, the ethical imperative is to tell everyone who they have reason to believe can help. This does not mean, for example, that everyone at a person's workplace or even in the person's family automatically is told, nor does it sanction gossip. The point is that when a person has been identified as a source of potential support and/or safety, that person should be brought into the suicide management plan. Clients should be encouraged to develop lists of support people and to fully explore their social support networks for possible assistance. Mental health practitioners should not make assumptions about the client's support network. Sometimes family can provide excellent support, but in other situations, certain family members can exacerbate the stress. Take care not to assume that a spouse or partner (or child or parent) is necessarily a positive link in the support network. Allow the client to determine who she or he finds to be supportive.

Depending on the person and the situation, there are individuals who might be called immediately to come in for assistance with getting through the crisis (e.g., parents, partners, grown children, or neighbors), while other names are listed as possible resources for the future. Clients can be encouraged to consider who might be available at different times of the day or night or in different situations. For example, is there a neighbor nearby? Or is there someone at work in case feelings escalate there? Is there a clergy member who can help? The purpose of engaging the support network is both to get the person through the immediate crisis (a safety approach) and to broaden the person's perspective on the available network to get through the longer-term problems.

Restore Hope.   Because hopelessness has been found to be one of the best predictors of suicide risk, restoring hope is critical to lessening the crisis. Restoration of hope can be considered the goal or outcome of immediate intervention, or it can be the byproduct of a wide variety of interventions targeted as suicidal thoughts and behaviors in general (Ellis, 2001). How the restoration of hope is conceptualized will depend on the therapeutic and theoretical stance of the clinician. Clinicians should work to restore hope without appearing to minimize the crisis. In other words, a clinician who comes across as too hopeful can be perceived by the suicidal person as inauthentic, unempathetic, or glib. Hope is essential, but it must be mixed with the demonstration of empathy and understanding. Nevertheless, all mental health practitioners are reminded to keep hope at the forefront of their work with suicidal people.

Assist the Client to Envision Possibilities Other Than Suicide.   Fortify reasons for living. This concept has been part of the suicide literature for more than 100 years and William James wrote about it in his 1947 essay "Is Life Worth Living?" During a suicidal crisis, people may engage in what cognitive therapists call *selective abstraction*, or using a set of filters to make generalizations about the world or themselves. People who are at suicide risk often fail to recognize the reasons they have for living. An emphasis on resilience and the many ways in which these individuals have faced other problems throughout life and persevered can become an important method to explore alternatives.

There is much evidence that people in suicidal crisis have diminished problem-solving skills. Providing assistance to solve current problems (e.g., financial, legal, employment, relationship) can be an important step in crisis intervention. In the longer term, however, helping clients to restore their problem-solving abilities (or to develop new ones) is an important component of treatment.

Crisis Intervention Step 6: Develop an Action Plan

Evaluate the Risk to Determine the Immediate Intervention.   There is clearly a continuum of risk with people in a suicidal crisis, and individuals are typically divided into three categories: low risk, moderate risk, and high risk. These categories are general guidelines only, and there is clearly much room for clinical judgment within each of these categories. Obtaining all available information (e.g., previous psychiatric records, collaborative information from other treating professionals, input from family or other supports, and participation from supervisors and/or colleagues) is an important aspect of determining risk. An exhaustive suicide assessment (outlined in Chapter 11) includes all of these components and helps to determine risk level.

Fremouw and colleagues (1990, p. 93) listed five areas to help clinicians determine level of risk:

1. The imminence of the behavior (e.g., the immediacy of the risk and whether the person is a clear and imminent danger to self at the present time)
2. The target of the danger (e.g., whether the suicidal behaviors occur in the context of angry interchanges with others, as is often the case, and whether there is the possibility of concurrent homicidal and suicidal thoughts and impulses)
3. The clarity of the danger (e.g., whether and to what degree the person is specific in what he or she plans to do; the intensity of the impulses; and whether the person has selected the method, time, or place)
4. The intent of the behavior (whether there is a clear determination of both the person's intention and his or her motive to die)
5. The lethality or probability of death

In general, there are three options for level of care: outpatient, partial hospitalization (also called *day treatment* or *intensive outpatient*), and inpatient/full hospitalization.

Most people with suicidal ideation can be managed with outpatient counseling and do not require hospitalization. Even with the presence of suicidal ideation, hospitalization typically is not required unless the person states that she or he will not be able to let someone know (e.g., the clinician, a family member, emergency care clinicians) if the risk escalates or there is a strong desire to die or impulsivity that overrides a person's ability to seek help (Yu-Chin & Arcuni, 1990). Other factors, such as recent past attempts with plans for future attempts, hopelessness, psychosis, absence of social support, and substance abuse, may also be indicators for higher levels of care (Bongar et al., 1998).

Persons who are at low to moderate risk are typically treated in an outpatient setting, while those in moderate- and high-risk categories may require partial or full hospitalization. Mental health care professionals should always make these determinations only when they have thoroughly reviewed all available information, done a risk assessment, and consulted with colleagues or other professionals when necessary. Inexperienced clinicians may consider referring a suicidal client, depending on level of experience, setting, and supervisor discretion. Remember, there is no shame in seeking consultation in working with suicidal clients, even for clinicians with years of experience. Every client is unique, and we all benefit from additional perspectives in our work.

Crisis Intervention Step 7: Follow Up

How the crisis is managed and what type of care will be offered for follow-up are determined by level of risk.

Levels of Risk

Low Risk

People who are deemed to be at low risk have suicide ideation but no specific or concrete plans (Sommers-Flanagan & Sommers-Flanagan, 1995). These people typically are managed in outpatient settings. To assess the level of risk, both an initial and an ongoing suicide risk assessment must be conducted. Remember, suicide risk assessment is not a one-time event, and clinicians must always ask about suicidal ideation and suicidal plans. Therefore, suicide evaluation recurs with each meeting until the suicidal thoughts subside and periodically thereafter (Bongar et al., 1998).

When a person is assessed as having a low suicide risk, the primary goals are obtaining a commitment to treatment and developing a risk management plan. A client's commitment to treatment is based on the belief that therapy can help him or her through the crisis and typically directly capitalizes on the strength of the therapeutic relationship. Clients who do not see the value in counseling or therapy to help them through their suicidal crisis are, by definition, not considered to be at low risk. Treatment for individuals who are at low risk is based on treating the underlying disorder or problem and finding new ways for generating alternatives or solutions. Other treatment mechanisms include all of the issues discussed above (e.g., ensuring safety, allowing for emotional ventilation, identifying the underlying message, using active listening skills, and engaging social support). Clients in the low-risk category typically need to have the frequency of counseling visits increased until the crisis period is over. They also might need referrals for more intensive therapy or for a psychiatric evaluation. Research has shown that during a suicidal crisis, clients in the low-risk category benefit most from (1) intensive follow-up, including case management, telephone contacts, and possibly home visits; (2) a clear crisis plan for the client to follow if the risk escalates; and (3) short-term cognitive-behavioral therapy to improve problem solving and reduce suicidal ideation (although this has not been demonstrated to be effective for long-term risk reduction) (Rudd, Joiner, Jobes, & King, 1999).

Friends and family represent important components of treatment for people in the low-risk category. Family counseling might be required, and engaging social support systems can be particularly important. People in the low-risk category also may benefit from engaging appropriate community resources that are appropriate to the client's presenting problems. For example, a person with an underlying substance abuse issue might benefit from a referral to Alcoholics Anonymous or Narcotics Anonymous. Other community support groups or counseling groups that address stressors that helped to precipitate the suicidal crisis also may be appropriate. For example, linking a person to a Parents without Partners group or an HIV support group may be indicated. However, the clinician must remember that not all people will benefit from these types of supports, and in no case should these groups be considered to take the place of individualized treatment.

A risk management plan should be put in place to help the clients know what to do when they have suicidal ideation or an increase in suicidal risk. This is not the same as a no-suicide contract. Rather, a risk management plan helps clients to understand the steps they should take if their risk elevates. A no-suicide contract is meant to dissuade people from making a suicide attempt, but such contracts have not been shown to be effective and therefore might or might not be part of an individual's outpatient treatment. A risk management plan, however, is essential for all potentially suicidal people who are being seen outside of the context of an inpatient hospital.

Risk management plans should be in writing and typically include names and contact numbers of support people the individual has agreed to call if needed. Some clinicians will include their own emergency contact information, but more often, community emergency contacts are included. This means contact information for local emergency mental health, including the number and location of the nearest emergency room and a reminder that calling 911 is an option if the individual believes that he or she is imminently suicidal and has no other safety mechanisms to call on.

Moderate Risk

In general, moderate risk has been assumed to mean that suicidal ideation and a general plan exist and there are some risk factors in place. However, self-control is intact, the client can identify several reasons to live, and there is no imminent intent to commit suicide (Sommers-Flanagan & Sommers-Flanagan, 1995). People in this risk category will require ongoing assessment to determine level of care (outpatient, day treatment, or inpatient hospitalization). Gliatto and Rai (1999) offered the following algorithm to help

BOX 13.2 • *A Note about No-Suicide Contracts*

No-suicide contracts elicit promises from clients that they will not engage in suicidal behaviors for a specified time frame and include emergency contact information. The clinician and the client each keep a signed copy. It has been recommended that no-suicide contracts, when used, should be individually tailored to the specific client (Westefeld et al., 2000).

There is widespread use of no-suicide contracts among clinicians, based primarily on several possible potential benefits. These include using the contract as a way to conduct a mental status examination about suicidality, communicating to the client that the suicidal danger has been heard, thus communicating a sense of caring and strengthening the therapeutic relationship; and slowing down the pace of the suicidal crisis, thus allowing the client to focus on the meaning of his or her choices. Further, there is some evidence that clients (particularly those without prior suicide attempts) view no-suicide contracts as generally positive; therefore, these contracts might be acceptable to clients in a strong therapeutic relationship (Davis, William, & Hays, 2002).

However, although they are used frequently and often relied on by clinicians, there is *no evidence* that no-suicide contract actually reduce suicide attempts, and these contracts *do not guarantee client safety*. In fact, they might lead the clinician into a false sense of security, believing that the client who signed the contract is now somehow safe from self-harm. In one study, 41% of clinicians had a client commit or make a serious attempt at suicide *after* entering into a no-suicide contract (Kroll, 2000). Additionally, anecdotal reports suggest that no-suicide contracts may increase legal liability. After all, if a clinician perceives enough of a risk to use a contract, then why weren't further precautions implemented?

What has become more and more apparent in the research literature is that these contracts might be useful, but only in the context of a strong therapeutic relationship in which there is mutual trust and respect. In these situations, the negotiation of the contract, not the contract itself, becomes a therapeutic element. However, it is not meant to be (nor is it) a legally binding document.

In summary, there is no evidence that no-suicide contracts are therapeutically harmful, but neither is there evidence that they are, in and of themselves, therapeutically helpful. They are useful only in the context of a strong therapeutic alliance. Mental health practitioners who utilize no-suicide contracts should do so with the full understanding of their limitations and with no illusions that they provide for client safety.

clinicians determine level of care. However, as with all other components of suicide risk assessment (e.g., suicide risk instruments, demographic contributing factors), sound clinical judgment must play a large role in determining level of care.

Although mental health practitioners might be inclined to hospitalize persons at moderate risk, there is evidence that most people who are at moderate risk for suicide can be successfully treated on an outpatient basis, with appropriate safety mechanisms in place. Outpatient management does not work, however, if the client is unable to firmly agree to report any escalating risk to the clinician or to another responsible adult caregiver (Kleespies et al., 1999).

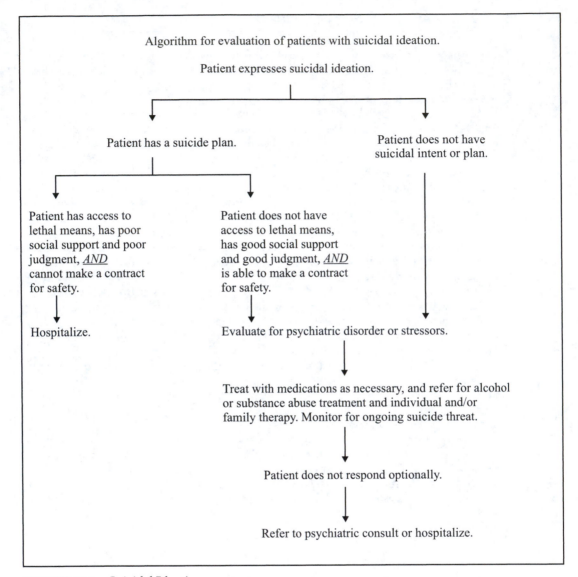

Algorithm for evaluation of patients with suicidal ideation.

Patient expresses suicidal ideation.

Patient has a suicide plan.

Patient does not have suicidal intent or plan.

Patient has access to lethal means, has poor social support and poor judgment, *AND* cannot make a contract for safety.

Patient does not have access to lethal means, has good social support and good judgment, *AND* is able to make a contract for safety.

Hospitalize.

Evaluate for psychiatric disorder or stressors.

Treat with medications as necessary, and refer for alcohol or substance abuse treatment and individual and/or family therapy. Monitor for ongoing suicide threat.

Patient does not respond optionally.

Refer to psychiatric consult or hospitalize.

FIGURE 13.2   Suicidal Ideation.

Source: Reproduced with permission from "Evaluation and Treatment of Patients with Suicidal ideation," March 15, 1999, American Family Physician. Copyright © 1999, American Academy of Family Physicians. All Rights Reserved.

High Risk

People who are at high risk of suicide (also called *severe risk*) have frequent and intense suicidal ideation; a suicide plan that is specific, lethal, and available; few social supports; questionable self-control; and many risk factors (Sommers-Flanagan & Sommers-Flanagan, 1995). Ruddell and Curwen (2002) note that a precise plan with a lethal method that is planned for the next 24–48 hours constitutes high risk and indicates hospitalization. People who are at moderate risk escalate to high risk, and therefore require hospitalization, when there is no therapeutic relationship or the therapeutic alliance disintegrates, attempts at crisis intervention fail, and the person remains acutely suicidal (Kleespies et al., 1999).

When a person is evaluated for hospitalization intake, it is extremely important that the clinician who referred the individual be involved in all aspects of the intake and the initial treatment plan. Schutz (1982) points out that hospitalization cannot be considered the end of the clinician's responsibility. The mental health clinician must provide adequate information to allow the hospital staff to make a complete assessment of suicide risk. Any clinician who has referred a client for a suicide assessment for possible hospitalization knows all too well how clients can present much differently to hospital staff or "know all the right things to say" to reduce the likelihood of admission. Remember, suicide risk assessment is best done within the context of a therapeutic relationship, and hospital staff have no prior relationship on which to base the interview or to elicit accurate responses. Clinicians should (optimally) be present during these interviews or, at the very least, initiate dialogue with the hospital staff about the client. If the clinician withholds important information, does not ensure that the hospital is the type of facility that is capable of securing the client's safety, or does not ensure that the suicide risk assessment was completed, the clinician may be liable.

Once a person has been admitted to a hospital for high suicide risk, the hospital staff is, in effect, "on notice that a patient has suicidal tendencies, [and] the hospital assumes the duty of safeguarding the patient from self-inflicted injury or death" (Robertson, 1988, p. 193). Thus, at the point when the client is admitted, the clinician hands off responsibility to the hospital. If the client is not admitted to the hospital, the client continues to be under the care of the clinician.

Whenever possible, it is therapeutically wise to secure voluntary commitment to a hospital. People who voluntarily seek care have already bought into the therapeutic possibility. These people are, in effect, taking a side in their own ambivalence and are willing to explore the possibility of receiving help. Clinicians are cautioned to assess and document the client's level of cooperation in risk assessment as well as the client's competence to participate in the decision for voluntary commitment. It is possible for a client to voluntarily admit to a hospital only to leave against medical advice and fulfill the suicidal intent. Thus, voluntary commitment, although ideal, is not appropriate for all people (Bongar, 2002).

Involuntary hospitalization occurs under a state's civil commitment guidelines, and it is the final recourse for people who are imminently suicidal and will not or cannot commit themselves to hospital care. The criteria for involuntary commitment is generally considered to be imminent danger to self or others (Simon, 1988). Clinicians who participate in involuntary commitment must have a complete understanding of the laws of their state regarding this issue.

Inpatient treatment has three primary goals: to ensure safety, to reduce or eliminate suicidal intent while treating the underlying disorder(s), and to improve coping skills and resiliency (Bongar, 2002). Inpatient clients typically receive high levels of support, encouragement to use social support networks, and interventions (pharmacological, psychological, and/or biological) to treat the underlying disorder. Although suicides are far less likely to occur in a hospital setting than in the community, it is worth noting that no hospital or setting is completely suicide-proof (Kleespies & Dettmer, 2000).

Within the hospital, suicidal people may encounter different levels of observation and privileges, depending on imminent risk. For example, continuous observation (one on one or remaining in sight of staff members) is necessary for suicidal emergencies. Other options might include restricting the person to an area where he or she can be seen at all times by the staff or, when safety permits, restricting the person to public areas (e.g., not allowing the person to be alone in a room). Less restrictive observations might include checks at regular intervals (e.g., 5 minutes, 10 minutes, 30 minutes), and then a step-down to periodic checks at more than 30-minute intervals. Regardless of the timing of these checks, there will undoubtedly continue to be certain activities that will require constant supervision, such as the use of sharp objects (e.g., nail cutters, razors, scissors), the use of matches or lighters (e.g., cigarette smoking), or the use of poisons (e.g., cleaning supplies, nail polish remover). Staff supervision also might be necessary when the person is engaging in certain activities (e.g., bathroom, kitchen, occupational therapy).

People who have been in the hospital for a suicidal crisis should not be discharged until it has been determined, through direct and ongoing assessment, that the suicidal crisis has been controlled, that the person can function outside the confines of the hospital, that the person is able to seek assistance if the risk begins to escalate, and that the person's remaining psychiatric needs can be adequately addressed in follow-up care (Bongar, 2002). It is essential that people who are discharged receive follow-up care, as the posthospitalization period is a time of elevated risk (Fawcett & Rosenblate, 2000). Follow-up care may involve day treatment or outpatient treatment, and suicide risk must be monitored on an ongoing basis.

Suicide Emergency

People who are at extreme risk are in a suicidal emergency. These people express a clear intent to commit suicide whenever the opportunity first presents itself (Sommers-Flanagan & Sommers-Flanagan, 1995). As a general stipulation, clinicians should approach all situations of suicide risk as a potential suicide emergency until they obtain sufficient information to be convinced otherwise (Kleespies et al., 1999).

People in suicide emergency require swift and directive intervention, and they must *never* be left alone, as they will use any opportunity to make an attempt. Mental health practitioners should inform the person, in a caring and firm manner, that they are going to make every effort to ensure the person's safety. Contacting the local police or a county mental health professional might be necessary. Personally transporting a person in suicide emergency should be avoided, as the person might jump from a moving vehicle or throw himself or herself into traffic to avoid hospitalization (Sommers-Flanagan & Sommers-Flanagan, 1995).

Ethical and legal obligations regarding working with suicidal individuals are discussed in depth in Chapter 14. Nevertheless, it is worth noting here that in suicide emergencies, the typical formal and explicit provider/client contract (e.g., conditions of treatment and fee for services) might not be established, but the clinician is nevertheless under the same legal obligation to care for the client. For example, in an emergency room or in an outpatient setting when someone calls or comes in who is in a suicide emergency, the clinician might not have established a formal contract with a client. Nevertheless, the courts have ruled that because of the life-threatening nature of the situation, the clinician must undertake treatment, even if the client does not consent to treatment (Kleespies et al., 1999). This has been called "interim first aid" (Wheeler, 1989, p. 482), and the assumption is that the nature of the emergency creates a professional relationship and imposes a duty of care on the clinician.

All clinicians who work with high-risk clients should have a predetermined set of steps to determine actions during a suicidal emergency (Kleespies et al., 1999). A predefined plan of response and decisions at each point will help to ensure that the high stress and chaos that are inherent in emergency situations do not negatively affect the clinician's ability to make decisions. The first step typically is containment. What will the clinician do if the client attempts to leave the building while agitated and in a suicidal crisis? Who are the people or resources the clinician will call? What internal mechanisms are in place in a hospital or agency to communicate to other professionals that assistance is needed? Once the client is contained, a typical next step is to attempt to develop a working alliance so that a thorough assessment can be completed. If sufficient rapport or an alliance cannot be obtained, then it is impossible to ensure safety, and hospitalization is necessary. Having thought through the basics of handling a suicide emergency ahead of time helps to reduce stress on the clinician and greatly improves client care (Turner & Hersen, 1994).

Essential Components of Management of Suicidal People

Clinicians who work with suicidal people must have clear processes in place regarding assessment, treatment, and managing the risk. What follows is a list of essential components of care with suicidal people, adapted from the work of Slaby (1998), King, Kovan, London, and Bongar (1999), and Rudd and colleagues (1999).

1. Conduct assessment:
   a. Conduct initial and ongoing assessments for both ideations and plans.
   b. Consider demographics that contribute to risk.
   c. Perform a mental status examination.
   d. Evaluate the client's level of perturbation (how upset, disturbed, agitated, or decompensated the person is).
   e. Evaluate the client's level of hopelessness and helplessness.
   f. Assess and address substance abuse issues.
   g. Ascertain the client's psychiatric history and obtain appropriate records.

2. Activate social support and other networks:
   a. Determine whether or not the client has a support system to help.
   b. Assess the client's marital and family relationships.
   c. Activate the client's social support network.

    d. Have the client sign a consent form so that the clinician can talk with significant others, family, friends, other professionals, and so on.

3. Develop and implement a treatment plan:
   a. Develop and chart a formal axis diagnosis.
   b. Assess the strength of the therapeutic alliance.
   c. Determine whether there is a need for hospitalization. This can change over time and is directly related to the ongoing assessment of risk.
   d. Provide individual, ongoing counseling, and provide family counseling when appropriate.
   e. Refer for a medical consultation if needed.
   f. Consider psychiatric evaluation for medications to treat the underlying disorder.
   g. Use psychoeducation with clients and significant others to help manage the suicidal crisis and to provide prevention for future crises.
   h. Consider increasing the number of treatment sessions or other contacts (e.g., telephone contact, concurrent individual and group treatment).
   i. Use a standardized follow-up and referral procedure (e.g., letters or phone calls) for those who drop out of treatment prematurely, in an effort to enhance compliance.
   j. Monitor and respond to countertransferential reactions, and routinely seek consultation, supervision, and support for difficult cases.

4. Develop a risk management plan that addresses emergency coverage:
   a. Give the client a 24-hour crisis or emergency number information.
   b. Provide informed consent regarding limits of confidentiality in relation to suicide risk.
   c. Determine the client's ability to manage recurring suicidal feelings.
   d. Let the person who is doing backup coverage for the clinician (while on vacation or unavailable) know specifically about the case.
   e. Eliminate or reduce environmental factors that contribute to risk.
   f. Help clients to set realistic goals for managing suicidal crises.
   g. Evaluate the appropriateness of a no-suicide agreement or contract.

5. Manage clinician liability:
   a. Keep current and accurate records.
   b. Utilize consultation.

6. Assess outcomes:
   a. Use a consistent approach to assessing treatment outcome, incorporating both direct (e.g., suicidal ideation, suicide attempts) and indirect markers of suicidality (e.g., general levels of symptomotology).
   b. Assess treatment outcome at specified intervals.

Now that you have read about levels of care, suicide risk, and emergency room care, it should be clear that the three people in the cases earlier in the chapter have very different levels of imminent risk and require very different interventions. Reread the cases, and consider what emergency room personnel might decide to do with these individuals. It might be tempting to dismiss Marco's risk, but recall from Chapter 7 that alcoholism represents a very real ongoing risk factor, which will only become more severe as Marco gets older and his overall risk increases. Nevertheless, it is clear that unless Marco reveals something in his risk assessment that has not previously been demonstrated, he is probably not at imminent risk. Kate, on the other hand, represents a suicide emergency. She was in the process of killing herself when the police found her, and there is reason to believe that, if left on her own for any length of time, she would kill herself. Complicating factors—depression and drug use—make her cognitive abilities impaired. In her case, even promises to refrain from suicidal activities probably should not be believed, and she might require involuntary hospitalization. Dan also requires hospitalization, but in his case, the underlying psychiatric disorder of schizophrenia is clearly what puts him at risk. These three cases are excellent examples of why it is impossible to have one standard treatment for suicide. Imagine trying to implement a treatment that would be effective for all three of these people. Instead, treating (or managing) the underlying disorder (Marco's alcoholism, Kate's drug use and depression, and Dan's schizophrenia) is what is required to lessen the ongoing risk.

Treatment Issues for Suicidal Adults

Whether before a suicidal crisis, to keep risk from elevating, or after a suicidal crisis, to reduce the possibility of a return to the suicidal state, psychological intervention is essential. There is, however, no standardized treatment for suicide. Clinicians are reminded that therapy with suicidal people addresses the underlying disorders, problems, or conflicts that led to the escalation. An understanding of the purpose of the suicidal threat (e.g., communication, control, or avoidance) helps provide another important layer to the treatment. Thus, in ongoing treatment, clinicians employ therapeutic interventions to reduce risk. Unlike the brief, crisis-oriented treatment that occurred during the period of risk, this therapy is generally longer-term.

Psychotherapy and Pharmacotherapy

Cognitive-Behavioral Approaches. Cognitive-behavioral approaches hold some promise in the treatment of suicidal persons because they address underlying cognitive distortions that are inevitably part of the suicidal crisis. The lifelong work of Aaron Beck has contributed greatly to understanding how these cognitive distortions can maintain and exacerbate problems, particularly in the areas of depression and hopelessness. Cognitive distortions were identified in Chapters 3, 4, and 5 as contributing to suicide risk in all age groups. These distortions can include arbitrary inference (assuming something to be true without supporting evidence), overgeneralizations, selective abstraction (looking only at details and specifics and making inferences), personalization

BOX 13.3 • *Recommendations for Level of Care*

Outpatient Management

1. Outpatients at mild suicide risk can usually be managed with recurrent evaluation and monitoring of suicidality.
2. Outpatients at moderate risk usually need intensified treatment such as increase in visits, 24-hour emergency availability, frequent assessment of risk, frequent evaluation for hospitalization, etc.
3. An outpatient approach aimed at problem solving and adaptive coping has been found to be effective with those at mild to moderate risk.

Decision to Hospitalize

1. Hospitalization is needed when the establishment of a treatment alliance and crisis intervention fails and the patient remains acutely suicidal.
2. The decision to hospitalize, whether voluntarily or involuntarily, is based on the clinician's estimate of the risk-benefit ratio.
3. The accepted protocol for patients at imminent suicide risk is inpatient care.

Inpatient Management

1. Patients in imminent danger of suicide require a structured environment with a clinically trained staff.
2. Assessment of imminent risk of self-harm should be conducted as soon as the patient is admitted.
3. Clinical staff need to be aware of their negative feelings and attitudes toward difficult patients so as not to underestimate suicide potential.
4. Because of shorter hospital stays, psychopharmacology and psychotherapeutic intervention are introduced as early as possible in the hospitalization.
5. Reduction of anxiety and agitation or antipsychotic medications can lessen the risk of impulsive suicidal behavior.
6. Psychopharmacology may be used to target specific high-risk symptoms (e.g., insomnia), thus reducing potential for self-harm.
7. Psychotherapeutic approaches best suited for short hospital stays include crisis intervention, problem solving, and focused cognitive-behavioral treatment.
8. Continuity of care from inpatient to outpatient treatment is necessary to mitigate against the possibility of suicidal behavior in the high-risk postdischarge period.

Sources: Kleespies, P.M. Deleppo, J.D, Gallagher, P.L, & Niles, B.L, Managing suicidal emergencies: Recommendations for the practitioner. *Professional Psychology: Research & Practice*, 30(5), 454–463, 1999. Published by APA. Reprinted with permission.

(assuming that general negative comments are directed at oneself), dichotomous thinking (all-or-nothing/black-and-white thinking), magnification (making small problems big), and minimization (minimizing successes or compliments) (Westefeld et al., 2000). Others have included cognitive rigidity, cognitive tunnel vision, and other cognitive vulnerabilities as being particularly salient for suicidal persons (Fremouw et al., 1990). With each of these problems, the client and the mental health professional collaborate to challenge these faulty beliefs by examining the relevant data. This process is called *collaborative empiricism*. "It is collaborative because the therapist and client work together in partnership to understand and solve the client's problems. Empiricism refers to the process of collecting data to evaluate evidence for and against current and alternative beliefs" (Dattilio & Padesky, 1990, p. 3). In this approach, then, the client's life becomes a sort of laboratory in which hypotheses are tested and are either supported by evidence or dismissed.

Related to suicidality, cognitive therapy has at its core the belief that the "central pathway for suicidality is cognition; that is, the *private* meaning assigned by the individual. Suicidality is secondary to the maladaptive meaning constructed and assigned regarding the self, the environmental context, and the future (i.e., the cognitive triad)" (Rudd, 2004, p. 62). Rudd argued that the best way to assess this meaning was to ask six simple questions:

1. What about the client's history facilitates his/her suicidal behavior?
2. What triggered the suicidal crisis?
3. How does the client think about suicide (cognitive suicidal belief system)?
4. What does he/she feel during the suicidal crisis (affective system)?
5. What type of arousal symptoms is the client experiencing (physiological system)?
6. What preparatory or active suicidal behaviors have been observed or planned (behavioral system)? (Rudd, 2004, p. 67).

The next step is to implement strategies that address all the belief systems that maintain the suicidal thoughts. Cognitive restructuring, cognitive flexibility and problem solving, affective distress tolerance, and suicidal behaviors are all targeted.

Cognitive therapy is particularly appropriate for short-term crisis intervention work. It is active, directive, structured, collaborative, and psychoeducational in its approach (Calvert & Palmer, 2003). There is evidence that cognitive behavioral approaches are effective in helping suicidal people. Several research studies have found fewer suicidal acts (Rudd et al., 1996; Tyrer, 1999) and reduced hopelessness (Jacobson, 1999) among those who received cognitive interventions.

In 2003 and 2004, a series of articles on using cognitive therapy for young suicide attempters appeared in the professional literature (Henriques, Beck, & Brown, 2003; Berk, Henriques, Warman, Brown, & Beck, 2004). These articles outlined a conceptual framework based on cognitive therapy that has been implemented for adolescents and young adults that focuses on addressing hopelessness and target suicidal behaviors, engaging clients quickly in treatment to reduce dropout, coordinating with other health services, and increasing adaptive social support. The intervention consists of a ten-session protocol with specific strategies developed for each phase of treatment. The intervention uses a set agenda, including checking symptoms, monitoring substance use, monitoring compliance with other treatments, linking past sessions to current behaviors and beliefs about suicide, making summaries, eliciting feedback, and assigning homework. The cognitive therapy emphasizes the development of a cognitive case conceptualization, in which both the client and the therapist work to make sense of the specific beliefs associated with the suicide attempt. From there, modeling and teaching problem-solving strategies become the major goal of the cognitive interventions. Although the authors note that an ongoing research study will determine the effectiveness of this intervention and these results have yet to be published, the intervention shows initial promise, and readers who wish to implement this protocol are directed to these studies for further information.

Cognitive therapy also has been advocated for older suicidal adults. Older people often find appeal in the practical nature and psychoeducational orientation of cognitive behavioral therapy, as well as its inherent efforts to empower clients. Further, although there are no outcome studies on cognitive therapy in suicidal elderly people, a large body of research on the effectiveness of cognitive behavioral therapy in depressed older adults makes the application of this model to the suicidal population worthy of note. The directive, time-limited, and structured approach is designed to give older adults skills that are immediately applicable to their daily lives. Coon, DeVries, and Gallagher-Thompson (2004) discussed the application of cognitive-behavioral therapy with older adults, and they also provided adaptations for cultural minority, disadvantaged, or medically fragile persons. Coon and colleagues also noted that the therapy can be adapted for people with cognitive impairment, particularly those in the early stages of dementia, when the client can still fully understand the meaning and consequences of a diagnosis.

In general, then, although outcome research is still lacking, it appears that the cognitive behavioral approach holds promise for interventions with suicidal adults. It should be noted that affective and behavioral work should not be ignored, and there is no evidence that cognitive therapy can be used successfully in isolation (Bongar, 2002).

Family Therapy.   As in working with suicidal children and adolescents, family therapy with suicidal adults can be an important component of treatment. Family environments influence individual behaviors and beliefs, and working to ameliorate family dysfunctions can make significant strides in reducing suicidal crises (Ellis, 2001). It is important to note that family therapy does not imply that people are not responsible for their own suicidal actions and does not remove individual responsibility. Family therapy for people in suicidal crisis typically has several major components: focus on behavior (take responsibility for actions), specificity (improve communication and accountability among family members without generalizing or assigning blame), reciprocity (behavioral contracts for interactions among family members), goal directedness (family members lend direct support to the suicidal member's goal attainment to encourage success), positive interchanges (reverse negative interchanges and destructive communication), and focus on the present and future (only the present and the future can be changed) (McLean, & Taylor, 1994).

Chamberlain (1995) noted that suicidal behaviors are not just an outcome, but are an event "embedded in a more complete and complex pattern of interaction in some families" (p. 117). Within this more complex definition, suicidal behaviors and threats can actually be mechanisms to restore equilibrium or prevent change. They also can be ways to destabilize a family that is not responding adequately to change. Within this framework, family therapy becomes a method in which the therapist helps to establish a new reality within the family. Chamberlain notes several important aspects of this dynamic therapy. First, the process of being observed, by necessity, changes the family. Second, families cannot go back in time. That is, a goal of "returning things to the way they were" is not helpful. Third, families are extraordinarily complex. Trying to make things orderly and simple will inevitably cause a spontaneous reorganization into an entirely new order. Fourth, change occurs not slowly and linearly, but often in leaps and bounds, with periods of quiet in between. Fifth, there is a butterfly effect: Small changes can lead to large-scale results. Sixth, when families become too far out of equilibrium, they approach critical moments when change must take place. It is impossible to predict how this change will occur or when it will occur again. Seventh, families are unpredictable. Thus, it is impossible for therapists—or even families—to predict the future. The best possible result of therapy is to give family members the tools that they can use and then be prepared for ongoing and as-needed interventions. The complexity of Chamberlain's axioms, which are based on chaos theory, underscore the complexity of suicidal behaviors and beliefs within families.

A review of the literature on family therapy with suicidal people has found some broad support for the inclusion of families in treatment (Brent, 1995), but many of the studies have been problematic from a research perspective. This is particularly true for adult clients, and the literature and research in family therapy are much more developed for suicidal young people (see Chapter 12 for review). Therefore, it is difficult to say with any certainty how family therapy affects suicidal outcomes for adults.

Group Therapy. Suicidal people are often depressed and hopeless, and treatment of depressed people in groups has much scientific and clinical support. Nevertheless, almost no research is available on the effectiveness of treating suicidal adults in groups. Ellis (2001) notes that this might be because clinicians fear the overpowering emotions that can occur when suicidal persons are in a group together. Nevertheless, the idea that a time-limited, outpatient group could be a beneficial aspect of treatment for reducing suicidal thoughts and behaviors has appeal. Rudd and colleagues (1996) found a group format that employed cognitive therapy (primarily problem-solving skills and general social competence) for high-risk people had positive effects, and initial gains were mostly maintained at 12-month follow-up. Further, people who were considered at very high risk owing to very poor problem-solving abilities appeared to gain the most from these groups. The group counseling intervention consisted of nine hours per day at a day treatment unit for approximately two weeks and thus was rather intensive. Nevertheless, although more study is certainly warranted, it is possible that group therapy could be an important adjunctive component of treatment.

Psychodynamic Theory.   The focus of psychodynamic theory is to help clients find the meaning behind the suicidal thoughts and attempts. Therapists work to help the clients uncover the messages that are being sent through the suicidal behaviors. To do this, therapists look for the conscious and unconscious origins of the problem and are likely to see the suicide attempt as aggression turned inward. This has been described by Bongar (1991) as having the therapist "help patients work through and understand their sense of murderous rage with a self-object that has disappointed them" (p. 126). Although psychoanalytic therapists are traditionally trained to be objective and to provide a blank slate for the client, this is not recommended for suicidal people, who need to experience strong therapeutic relationships with empathy at their core (Ellis, 2001). Shneidman (1981) noted that suicidal people in general require a different therapeutic stance. Rather than challenging and pushing the client, the focus of the relationship is on emotional support as the person gets through the immediate crisis, and then a more typical therapeutic stance can be adopted.

One aspect of psychoanalytic treatment that is particularly relevant for all who work with suicidal people is the concept of "countertransference hate." The concept was first introduced in relation to suicidal people in 1973 (Maltsberger & Buie, 1973) and captures the feelings that can arise in engaging in sustained work with a suicidal person. Because suicidal people experience intense and labile emotions and engage in behaviors that are particularly distressing to others, they may cause emotional and behavioral reactions in others. Thus, mental health professionals must continually monitor their own countertransferential reactions to the client, lest their behaviors and attitudes erode the therapeutic alliance. It is worth noting that like psychodynamic therapy with suicidal children and adolescents, psychodynamic therapy with adults has not been empirically studied.

Specific Therapeutic Interventions.   In addition to the approaches outlined above, several specific therapeutic interventions have been advocated in the literature. These are outlined briefly in the following paragraphs. However, it is important to remember that because suicide intervention focuses on the primary causes of the suicidal crisis, rather than on suicide as a specific outcome, all therapeutic modalities that address underlying causes are considered important components of suicide treatment.

Solution-focused therapy is an approach that deemphasizes pathology and instead emphasizes collaborative attempts to find solutions. Originally developed by de Shazer (1988), it questions many of the traditional assumptions of therapy, such as the belief that problems must be fully understood before answers can be determined and the belief that symptoms mask underlying deeper problems that are difficult to understand. The strengths-based approach, is has been argued, makes it particularly useful for working with suicidal clients, although others have noted that the lack of true assessment of underlying risk factors and causes could make it inappropriate for those in suicidal crisis. Those who have advocated the use of solution-focused therapy for suicidal clients note that it should not be used exclusively, and underlying causes must be explored. Nevertheless, they argue, there are some components of solution-focused therapy that could be helpful. These include listening for strengths rather than focusing on pathology, moving from problems to (appropriate) goals, finding exceptions rather than allowing generalizations, exploring how clients cope, and using scaling questions (including assessing safety with scaling questions) (Sharry, Darmody, & Madden, 2002). In an approach to using solution-focused therapy within families with a suicidal member, Softnas-Nall and Francis (1998) took the typical questions that are asked of a suicidal person (e.g., "Are you thinking of killing yourself? Have you attempted in the past? Do you have a plan?") and turned them into strength-based questions (e.g., "When was a time when you felt safe and did not have suicidal thoughts?") or scaling questions (e.g., "On a scale of 1 to 10, with 1 not feeling safe at all and 10 feeling very safe, where are you now? What about when you made the phone call to come in for counseling?"). In these ways, many of the essential components of suicide risk assessment are included, but the strength and solution focus of solution-focused therapy are included. It should be noted that none of the literature on solution-focused therapy for suicide intervention has empirical support.

Dialectical Behavioral Theory (DBT) has been advocated by Marsha Linehan because of the high rates of suicidal and parasuicidal behaviors among people with personality disorders (Linehan, Tutek, Heard, & Armstrong, 1994). DBT includes behavioral, cognitive, and supportive therapies in both an individual and a group format (Linehan, 1993). The focus on the group work is psychoeducation, while the individual interventions help the therapist and client to work through a hierarchy of goals, safety being the primary focus. In both individual and group settings, clients are taught interpersonal effectiveness, emotion regulation, distress tolerance, and mindfulness. Linehan's original model was developed for longer-term (one-year) treatment for people with borderline personality disorder, although it has been adapted to many formats, time frames, and clients.

There is some support for the use of DBT with suicidal people, and research has demonstrated that outpatient clients who received DBT had fewer and less severe suicide attempts, reduced therapy dropout, and few inpatient psychiatric days than those who received standard individual therapy (Linehan, Armstrong, Suarez, Allmon, & Heard, 1991). In addition, women with borderline personality disorder who received DBT also had less anger and better self-rated social adjustment (Linehan et al., 1994). Several components of DBT have been singled out as being particularly important in working with suicidal people. First, the focus on dialectical techniques of balancing acceptance *and* change (rather than traditional therapy focus on acceptance *or* change) appears to be an important mechanism in reducing suicidal behaviors in suicidal people with borderline personality disorder. Second, the inclusion of mindfulness in DBT has been found to help reduce depression and hopelessness among women with borderline personality disorder (McQuillan et al., 2005). Thus, DBT and its components appear to be worthy of further study for the treatment of suicidal people, especially those with borderline personality disorder (Westefeld et al., 2000). Although the empirical base for the effectiveness of DBT for suicidal people is still slim, it is comparable (and in many cases superior) to other systems of psychotherapy (Lester, 2005).

Psychopharmacology is often used with suicidal persons, but there is no body of research on it for suicidal people per se because all interventions are intended to treat the underlying disorder. Thus, pharmacological choices (including whether to medicate and what to use) are based on the type and severity of the underlying disorder. Many individuals who are suicidal, however, will require a referral for consideration for medication, depending on the severity of the disorder. It is for this reason that a medical referral is part of the crisis plan (stage 6: develop an action plan) outlined earlier in the chapter. It is worth noting that many medications can, in and of themselves, become weapons for self-harm, and suicidal people who are being treated with medications must be monitored closely, with mechanisms in place to limit access to potentially lethal doses (Westefeld et al, 2000).

Electroconvulsive Therapy.   In recent years, electroconvulsive therapy (ECT) has been considered a treatment of last resort for severely depressed and suicidal persons. In 2005, a multisite consortium for research in ECT study funded by the National Institute of Mental Health compared the efficacy of ECT and pharmacotherapy versus pharmacotherapy alone for people with severe unipolar depression (Kellner et al., 2005). In this large-scale study (*n* = 444), people ranging from 18 to 85 years in age received at least ten ECT treatments (or more, until the improvement scores reached a plateau) within a one-year period. Only people with unipolar depression were included in the study, and 30% had psychosis (exclusion criteria included schizophrenia, bipolar disorder, neurological illnesses, and substance dependence). Participants were compared on pretreatment, posttreatment, and follow-up depression scales and on expressed suicidal intent. Approximately 80% of those in the study completed the ECT protocol, and dropouts occurred primarily because the physician noted adverse effects (confusion or memory problems in 8%), the patient noted adverse effects (1%), there were interfering medical conditions (2%), or the patient requested to quit or go home or no reason was given (6%).

In general, the remission rate for depression among the 355 people who completed ECT was 85.6% (*n* = 304). Of the 131 people who expressed high suicidal intent before treatment, more than 80% ultimately dropped to a score of 0 on this scale, with more than 50% of those who ultimately responded in this way doing so after one to three treatments. In general, although gains were maintained at follow-up, risk increases after discharge from the hospital, and aftercare must be put into place to consolidate the treatment gains. The authors of this study note that ECT appears to have more efficacy in this use than in its traditional place of last resort, the rapid resolution of expressed suicidal intent perhaps being its biggest strength. Therefore, they argue, ECT should be considered earlier in the algorithm that is used to determine treatment for severe depression. The controversial nature of ECT, the typical reluctance of people to accept ECT before all other options have been exhausted, and, in some states, laws that make ECT a treatment of last resort all contribute to the difficulty in determining the efficacy of ECT with depressed, suicidal persons.

Of course, not all treatment involves therapy. Community support, work and career support, and family networks are all part of the continuum of care. Ongoing treatment options often make use of whatever community supports are available. In the section on levels of risk earlier in this chapter, there were suggestions for engagement of community support systems, such as AA and other support groups. Two other systems are mentioned briefly in the next section: hotlines and crisis intervention centers.

Hotlines and Intervention Centers

Crisis intervention centers and suicide hotlines are staffed 24 hours a day and have professionals or volunteers who have been specifically trained in suicide prevention techniques. Crisis intervention through hotlines and community resources is not the same as suicide prevention, nor does it have ongoing treatment at its core. Its goal is to defuse the current crisis, ensuring that the person survives to get ongoing therapy and care.

Because of the different focus of hotline and crisis centers, the goals of the staff are somewhat different than the goals in other types of suicide intervention. Berger (1984) outlines the staff commitment in the following way:

> The first task confronting the therapist in the phone contact situation is to keep the person talking and then assess the lethality of the situation. The second task is to obtain some idea of the particular state of mind or of the diagnostic picture. The task is much different in dealing with one who is severely depressed than in dealing with a [person who has] schizophren[ia] or an individual in a state of high panic. All of these will commit suicide, but each will respond differently to the kinds of communications that the therapist is likely to deliver. (p. 69)

Suicide hotlines and crisis centers provide an important component of safety for many suicidal people throughout the United States, although data on their effectiveness are mixed. Some research shows that suicide rates are lower in communities with suicide prevention centers than in those without, and there is some evidence that young people, particularly females, are most likely to benefit (Mishara & Daigle, 2001). However, there also is anecdotal support for the finding that young boys are more likely to talk with an anonymous counselor at the other end of a phone line when they are first at risk for suicide than to talk with a counselor in person, particularly if they have been bullied or feel that there is no one they can turn to for support. Although the current state of the research does not yield easy answers, what is clear is that communities that use multidimensional approaches (e.g., hotlines in conjunction with individual and group therapy, clinics, psychiatric consultations, and both inpatient and outpatient treatments) are more effective in their efforts (Westefeld et al., 2000).

The Befrienders Worldwide is an umbrella organization that has more than 31,000 trained volunteers who provide hotline support in 40 countries. Each year, volunteers provide more than five million hours of care to suicide hotlines and crisis centers. Their motto, "Listening saves lives," is the fundamental principle behind suicide hotlines. The Befrienders (now with support from the Samaritans) maintains an international listing of suicide hotlines, available at http://www.suicide-helplines.org/index.html (Befrienders Worldwide, 2005).

Two major national suicide 24 hour free and confidential helplines are available:

National Hopeline Network: 1-800-SUICIDE
National Suicide Prevention Lifeline: 1-800-273-TALK

There are also specialized hotlines for teens (1-800-252-TEEN), for GLBT teens (1-800-4UTREVOR), and for the elderly at Center for Elderly Suicide Prevention (1-800-971-0016), as well as local specialized hotlines in many communities. More helplines and hotlines are listed in Appendix D.

People who are in training to become mental health practitioners often find that experience as a volunteer in a suicide hotline or crisis center can be an invaluable training tool. Most of these community resources provide high-quality training for their volunteers, and the clinical experience that is gained can be useful for future crisis work. And, of course, the community receives the passion and commitment of the practitioner-in-training, making this, in most instances, a win-win-win situation.

Summary

Treatment of suicidal adults, in general, follows a two-tiered model. The first is crisis intervention to get through the immediate suicidal risk; the second is longer-term therapy to resolve the underlying issues that allowed the suicidal risk to escalate. Both are essential, although there is clear evidence that the ongoing, longer-term treatment is less frequently completed. When this is the case and the underlying vulnerability is not resolved, it is quite possible that the suicide risk will reappear over time.

During the crisis management stage of the risk, clinicians will want to assess lethality, establish rapport, identify major problems, deal with feelings, explore alternatives, develop an action plan, and follow-up. From the initial assessment, clients will be identified as being at low, moderate, or high risk, and appropriate treatment will be based on this assessment. Clients also can present in suicide emergency. That is, they are at imminent risk within the next several hours and will complete suicide if given the opportunity. These clients require special handling to prevent suicide. Once the immediate risk of a suicidal crisis has passed, long-term treatment should involve psychotherapy and an assessment for pharmacological interventions.

14

Legal and Ethical Issues in Suicide

Suicide is a complex and often controversial subject, and like other such subjects in modern society, it has both ethical and legal aspects that are important to behavioral health care providers. The phenomenon of suicide often evokes conflict between values concerning the sanctity and preservation of life on the one hand and the democratic ideals of individual freedom and choice on the other. Further, suicide, like many controversial issues that are concerned with life and death (e.g., abortion, the death penalty,) has the potential to provoke intense emotional responses in us all. Combine opposing values with intense emotions, and it is no wonder that suicide has been the fodder of so many social debates and legal battles.

This chapter presents the basic ethical arguments both for an absolute prohibition on suicide and for allowing suicide under some circumstances. These arguments are far from solely academic in nature. They have very real implications for the modern-day issue of physician-assisted suicide. Next, the chapter will turn to the legal realities with which mental health practitioners who work with suicidal clients must cope. This discussion includes the fundamentals of malpractice and negligence as they relate to suicide. To minimize legal risk, suggestions for risk management are included. Finally, some specific issues with regard to the importance of communication and working with managed care in the context of suicide cases will be discussed as a further risk management strategy to help clinicians avoid legal and ethical conflicts.

Ethics, Values, and Suicide

Discussions about the morality of suicide often bring people's most cherished values into conflict with one another (Lester & Leenaars, 1996). Suicide, in fact, continues to be a subject of significant social controversy, with issues such as "the right to die" and "physician-assisted suicide" making news headlines. The material in this section concerning the ethics of suicide is presented for the purpose of increasing the reader's awareness. We have made an attempt to provide all sides of the ethical arguments concerning suicide so that you can decide how you feel and think about these issues. What might be most important for mental health practitioners reading this section is to allow time now to reflect on your own ethical and thus therapeutic stance concerning suicide. Therapists should not wait until they find themselves engrossed in treating a suicidal client to consider how their own values relate to suicide. The clinical decisions that result from those values might be of life and death importance to the client.

Ethical and Moral Arguments against Suicide

The primary ethical argument that supports the prohibition of suicide under all circumstances evokes the principle of the sanctity of life (Battin, 1995). The "sanctity of life" principle is most simply defined as the belief that all life (and particularly human life) is imbued with value. The principle further asserts that the value of human life is fundamentally inherent, intrinsic, and not open for arbitration. If a clinician were to adopt an ethical stance in which the sanctity of life was the central premise, he or she would believe that suicide was never allowable under any circumstances or with any exceptions.

In addition to the "sanctity of life" principle, there have been social arguments for the prohibition of suicide. Many of these social arguments focus on the idea that the suicide of an individual represents a significant "cost" or loss to the society (Battin, 1995; Cholbi, 2004). Individuals who take their own lives deprive the community of their unique talents, labor, and contributions. Therefore, the loss of the individual through suicide is harmful to the social group or community as a whole. The logical result of this argument is that society cannot condone suicide and should take the view that suicide is harmful. A clinician who adopts the social argument ethical stance would see the suicide of an individual not only as affecting the life of the client, but also as having significant implications for the entire social network of potential survivors who are in some way related or connected to that individual.

The arguments that strongly prohibit suicide and illustrate support for the basic value of human life are derived principally from religious traditions and secular philosophy. For example, Christian, Jewish, and Islamic religious traditions argue against the practice of suicide because it is a violation of "natural law" (Battin, 1995). Natural law asserts that life is a gift from God, Allah, or a supreme being and that the human being is only temporarily the keeper of his or her soul. Therefore, destruction of life through suicide is a sin against this higher being or a violation of the natural order (or law). Religious arguments that prohibit suicide view it as an aberration or unnatural act.

In addition to religious arguments, there have been secular philosophical arguments that support the complete prohibition of suicide. The lectures of the philosopher Immanuel Kant are one example. Kant argued that the human being is the only animal capable of constructing moral tenets and laws. He argued that because human beings are capable of being moral, human life has inherent value. Kant viewed self-killing as harmful because it has the effect of diminishing morality and lawfulness, which are arguably the basic building blocks of human society (Cholbi, 2000). Therefore, by destroying a moral agent (a human life), suicide is a form of lawlessness, an antisocial act that society should not condone or make permissible.

Finally, people who fundamentally and in all situations disagree with suicide may view suicide as a symptom of a mental illness (rather than a rational choice). In this view, people who are suicidal are reacting to feelings of hopelessness, despair, depression, substance abuse, and so on. These states are thought to impede the person's ability to reason and make rational decisions, yet they are seen as temporary and treatable conditions. Therefore, suicide prevention is always the priority, regardless of a person's expressed wish to die (Mishna, Antle, & Regehr, 2002).

Ethical and Moral Arguments Permitting Suicide

The primary arguments for allowing suicide are made from both the perspective of protecting the rights of the individual and from viewing the practice of suicide as having potential benefits for a society. The individual rights arguments for permitting suicide are derived primarily from Western democratic ideals of freedom and choice. These arguments present the perspective that there are situations in which the quality of an individual's life is so degraded as to have lost its value. Suicide therefore can be used as a method of ending suffering and protecting the individual's dignity. Many suicide advocates assert that it is a basic human right to be able to choose one's method and time of death. Human beings are the "owners" of their bodies and have a fundamental right to choose to live or die. Thus, the individual's right to choose death is not a power that can be usurped by society or a paternalistic state (Battin, 1995; Clarke, 1999). A clinician who adopted these beliefs as the basis for his or her ethical stance concerning suicide would conclude that individuals are always the final decision makers concerning their choice to live or commit suicide.

Social arguments also have been made in favor of suicide by raising the question: Is suicide an acceptable behavior in certain circumstances? These arguments often argue that there are potential benefits for society in situations in which the good of the many outweigh the value of a single individual's life. The central belief relating to these arguments is that qualifications and special situations exist in which the suicide of an individual might not be unethical or immoral. An example might be the case of a mother or father who sacrifices herself or himself to save the person's children from death. Another example could be an elderly terminally ill person who commits suicide to prevent his or her family from incurring catastrophic medical debts. Examples in wartime abound. These arguments support the idea that there are moral situations in which suicide might be a desirable behavior. A clinician who viewed suicide from this ethical stance might adopt a relativistic approach, concluding that suicide is acceptable in some circumstances but not others, depending on the variables associated with each specific situation.

Finally, mental health clinicians are reminded that cultural, religious, and ethnic diversity are important variables to consider in working with suicidal clients, and practitioners should not assume that clients have the same moral or ethical injunctions prohibiting suicide that they themselves have adopted. For example, in contrast to most of the modern Western religious philosophies, there are some Eastern religious traditions that have prohibitions against suicide but nevertheless allow its practice. Hindu and Buddhist traditions allow for the suicide of an individual if it is performed according to a specific ritual and for the purpose of demonstrating a love of the deity or as part a process of attaining the highest spiritual state (Albright & Hazler, 1995).

Understanding the Complexities of Competing Values

It is important for mental health professionals to consider the moral and ethical arguments both for and against suicide. The issues that are raised by these arguments are not just topics for philosophical discussion, but also relate directly to everyday practice. In our practice as mental health caregivers, we will encounter suicidal clients, be consulted about palliative care decisions, try to positively affect the lives of survivors, and perhaps even influence suicide-related social issues. Our ability to contemplate and clarify our values regarding the moral and ethical issues that surround suicide will provide us with a cognitive frame within which to interpret a future suicide in our personal or professional life. Hopefully, by wrestling with the ethical issues concerning suicide, we will be better able to cope with our responsibilities to patients in the future.

Volker (1994) outlined a model for value analysis that mental health practitioners can use to help with self-understanding around this issue. He noted that clinicians need to come to an understanding of their own personal and professional value system around the following components: responsibility (including who is responsible for what, and in what context, including clients, family members, counselors, and the community), integrity (what are the boundaries that must be maintained and upheld in our lives, the lives of our clients and their families, and the community), commitment (what is the value commitment that the counselor has to the client, the client's family, and the community), freedom of choice (balancing between quality of life and the counselor's value system as it interacts with those of other individuals), empowerment (strengthening the way that clients feel about themselves), and right to grieve (allowing the full expression of situational or developmental stressors and life circumstances). Although this model does not provide easy answers, it does demonstrate the complexity of this struggle for every person who is involved in questions regarding suicide.

Current Issue: Physician-Assisted Suicide

Physician-assisted suicide (PAS) is an issue with both ethical and moral components that is being hotly debated in the United States. Clinicians who are practicing today should be aware of this social debate and determine for themselves where they stand in relation to these important issues, although choices based on personal ethical stances must reside within the available legal imperatives. As with most difficult issues in our society, PAS is being fought over on legal and political battlegrounds (Manetta & Wells, 2001). PAS occurs whenever a licensed medical doctor provides a lethal prescription to a patient, who then self-administers the drug (Manetta & Wells, 2001). The most frequent form of lethal prescriptions used is oral barbiturates, although lethal injections can also be prescribed. Dr. Jack Kevorkian was a central figure in bringing PAS to national awareness through his creation and use of a "suicide machine," which was designed to assist patients with delivery of lethal injections.

BOX 14.1 • *What Would You Do?*

In the following case, mental health practitioners were asked to respond to a hypothetical client who had made a decision to commit suicide.

Joan, a 45-year-old factory worker who is currently a client of yours, has been suffering from severe physical pain related to malignant bone cancer. Despite having received a wide variety of therapies, the cancer is spreading. Joan feels that both you and her physicians have already done all that can be done, and she has no hope that her symptoms will be reduced. Joan is currently experiencing a great deal of pain and is very upset over the fact that her condition is draining the emotional and financial resources of her family and friends. Joan feels that the quality of her life now is very poor and will only get worse. She also fears that she will be an increasingly large burden to her loved ones. With the support of her family and friends, Joan has decided to kill herself.

1. As a professional, how much action would you take to prevent Joan from killing herself?
2. As a friend (in this case, Joan is not a client), how much action would you take to prevent Joan from killing herself?
3. If you were in Joan's circumstances, how viable would you view suicide as an option?

Source: Rogers, J. R., Gueulette, C. M., Abbey-Hines, J., Carney, J. V., & Werth, J. L. (2001) Rational suicide: An empirical investigation of counselor attitudes. *Journal of Counseling & Development,* 79, p. 367. Reprinted with permission. No further reproduction authorized without written permission from the American Counseling Association.

In 1994, Oregon was the first state to pass a law, the Death with Dignity Act, that provides for the legal assistance by physicians in a patient's suicide. The passage of this law, which was reapproved by Oregon voters in 2000, brought on a storm of debate about the practice of PAS on the national scene, which continues to this day.

Supporters of PAS believe that individuals have a basic human right to choose the time and place of their own death in response to incurable pain or suffering (Batavia, 2000). Supporters see PAS as providing a dignified death to individuals who want to spare themselves and their families from extensive mental, physical, and economic burdens. PAS supporters see the ability of individuals to make choices about their own time and method of death as a fundamental human right. Further, for supporters of PAS, the right to commit suicide is not negotiable; the government should not be able to legislate control over the individual's choices concerning suicide.

Opponents of the practice of PAS believe that it is immoral and unethical. Opponents see the practice as a basic violation of the value of human life and argue that there are no cases in which suicide is a valid choice for death. They believe that laws that provide for the practice of PAS should be banned in the United States. One fear of opponents of PAS is that the practice will spread to include not only the cognitively competent terminally ill, but also disadvantaged and vulnerable populations such as elderly people, people with mental illness or developmental disabilities, people with physical disabilities, or infants (Paul, 2000). There is some evidence from other

BOX 14.2 • *A Brief Chronology of the History of Physician-Assisted Suicide in the United States*

1991 and 1992—Assisted-suicide voter referendums are defeated in California and Washington states.

1994—Oregon, through a voter referendum, passes the Oregon Death with Dignity Act, which makes physician-assisted suicide (PAS) legal in that state. Legal injunctions are put into place that do not overturn the law but make the practice of PAS illegal until they are resolved in the courts.

1997—The state of Oregon puts a referendum to voters for the purpose of repealing the Death with Dignity law. The voters do not repeal the law but in fact approve it with a wider margin than occurred in 1994. The Death with Dignity Act is officially in practice in Oregon (Miller, 2000).

1997—The U.S. Supreme Court rules in *Washington* v. *Glucksberg* and *Vacco* v. *Quill* that although assisted suicide is not a protected right under the Fourteenth Amendment to the Constitution, individual states may make laws regarding the practice within their jurisdictions. So each state is left to decide the issue for itself concerning PAS.

2000—Maine voters defeat "aid in dying" referendum legislation.

2001—U.S. Attorney General John Ashcroft issues a directive stating that a doctor could lose his or her federal registration to prescribe controlled substances if it is used to prescribe federally controlled substances for assisted suicide.

2004—The Ninth Circuit Court declares that the Attorney General overstepped his authority in issuing the directive and refuses to rehear the case. Approximately 35–40 Oregon citizens per year have died through PAS since the law went into effect.

2004—The U.S. Department of Justice petitions the U.S. Supreme Court to hear the case.

2005—The Court hears the case in October. The case is entitled *Gonzales* v. *Oregon* (named for the attorney general who replaced Ashcroft) and is case number 04-623.

2006—The U.S. Supreme Court, in an opinion by Justice Kennedy, rules against the Attorney General (6 to 3 decision) and upholds Oregon's Death with Dignity Act.

countries that supports this view. In Holland, where PAS has been in practice for over 20 years, there have been cases in which physicians have assisted in suicides with vulnerable populations (Lester & Leenaars, 1996). PAS opponents further counter the arguments of PAS supporters concerning the need to end extreme suffering through suicide by stating that modern medical pain management approaches are the appropriate response to an individual's pain or suffering.

At present, Oregon's Death with Dignity Act allows medical doctors to assist people with mental illness to commit suicide (Miller, 2000). Physicians can assist a person with a mental health diagnosis with suicide without consulting with a mental health professional. The attending physician only must certify that he or she is of the opinion that the patient is competent to make the decision concerning suicide (Burt, 2000). This is problematic in that many general medical practitioners do not have the appropriate training or expertise to conduct mental health assessments or make psychological diagnoses. One issue, therefore, clearly concerns scope of practice, expertise, and the ability to make decisions about the mental competence of a suicidal individual.

When physicians do have questions about the competency of an individual to make a decision concerning PAS, they may call on a mental health professional for consultation. One study indicated that there are a significant number of mental health professionals who are willing to conduct these types of assessments and even assist with delivery of the lethal substances to the patient (DiPasquale & Gluck, 2001). Thus, the eligibility of clients in these cases to receive PAS services from a physician could become the domain of a mental health clinician to determine. For clinicians who are attempting to determine the competency of PAS clients, there would be considerable complexity and subjectivity in conducting such assessments. How would a clinician differentiate between a genuine wish to die and the symptoms of a depressive disorder or other mental illness? Given the high comorbidity between mental illness (substance abuse, personality disorders, and mood disorders) and suicide, such determinations would be very difficult.

The research on the clinical nature of mental illness, physical illness, and other variables in relation to patients' desire to die is very limited (Rosenfeld, 2000). One study that reflects the volatility of assessing patient's beliefs about PAS was conducted with terminally ill patients and their caregivers. The study indicated that 60% of the patients supported the idea of PAS in a hypothetical case but only 10% had considered the practice for themselves. Perhaps a more important finding from this study was that a few months after the initial assessment, 50% of the patients had changed their minds from their original positions in both directions in considering PAS. Depression was shown to increase the likelihood that a patient would consider PAS (Emmanuel, Fairclough, & Emmanuel, 2000).

Further, although some authors have suggested guidelines for mental health professionals who wish to work with PAS clients (Cohen, 2001; Werth, 1999, 2000), these guidelines have been criticized as being too vague and ill-defined (Burt, 2000; Youngner, 2000). Currently, there are no recognized training programs that a mental health clinician could undertake for the purpose of making a "right to die" competency assessment. In the absence of a standard of practice in this area, mental health clinicians who assisted with PAS determinations would certainly be open to malpractice liability. For the moment, it appears that there are many basic questions that still need to be answered with regard to the involvement of mental health providers in PAS cases. For example, what about the mental health profession's basic ethical principle of "doing no harm"? Would a mental health professional working in a PAS case to determine competency be violating this ethical principle (Kleespies, Hughes, & Gallacher, 2000)? Where do the mental health professions' codes of ethics and standards of practice fall in regard to this issue (Albright & Hazler, 1995)?

Because of this confusion and controversy, mental health clinicians should be very careful in the current practice environment concerning assisting clients with suicide through assessment or any type of direct service. Currently, no standard of care exists for interpreting this type of behavioral health care intervention in a court of law.

Legal Issues and Suicide

Professionals who work in behavioral health care will have suicidal clients in their caseloads, regardless of setting. Unfortunately, many will also be faced with having to cope with the completed suicide of a client. The issues that arise from a client's suicide occur on many different levels, including emotional, professional, and legal. Given today's litigious practice environment, many therapists feel uneasy about treating suicidal clients. Clinicians fear that they will be found somehow incompetent if a client commits suicide and that a malpractice suit will result. The fear of a malpractice suit is a real and tangible fear for many therapists working with high-risk clients. It is, in fact, one of the few occasions when mental health practitioners can be held directly responsible for decisions that have life-and-death consequences (White, 2002). Although many clinicians know that mental health providers are involved in malpractice suits at a much lower rate than in other medical fields, the fact remains that suicide cases are a significant category for malpractice insurance claims. According to the American Psychological Association Insurance Trust, suicide accounts for 5.4% of the claims and 10% of the total malpractice claim costs (Bongar, 2002).

Another factor supporting therapists' uneasiness is that few therapists received much training in crisis management or suicide client management in their graduate programs. Only 35% of graduate programs in clinical psychology offer any formal training in dealing with suicidal clients (White, 2002), and only about half of psychology trainees report having had even minimal training in suicide intervention (Neimeyer, 2000). Although all high school counselors in one randomized study believed that identification of students who are at risk for suicide was part of their job, only one in three high school counselors believed themselves to be trained and capable of doing so. The training that is included in mental health programs appears to be limited primarily to a recitation of risk factors and a cursory discussion of no-harm contracts, leaving mental health practitioners unprepared to engage in the complexities of prevention, intervention, and assessment (Neimeyer, 2000). Anecdotal reports suggest that the average counselor has received less than two hours of formal training on suicide during graduate training. Most mental health practitioners, then, learn how to assess and treat suicidal clients on the job from supervisors who also learned on the job. Many graduate programs also neglect to include training on therapists' legal responsibilities concerning the treatment of suicidal clients, leaving therapists to learn legal intricacies on their own.

Because of the significant potential for malpractice litigation and the general lack of training in this area, it is very important for clinicians to understand the legal ramifications involved in treating and managing suicidal clients. This section will address the basics for understanding the legal issues involved in working with suicidal clients. Included is information on mental health and the law, standards of care, and the basics of malpractice litigation. Finally, and perhaps most important, preventive risk management practices that clinicians should undertake in their practices to help avoid legal involvements will be presented.

Suicide Law in the United States

Many nations have laws relating to suicide (Lester, 2004). However, as of the writing of this book, in the United States, there are no federal laws prohibiting suicide. The state courts, specifically the state appellate courts, are the context within which much of the legal discourse concerning suicide has evolved. It is important to realize, therefore, that each state has its own particular history of suicide case law and thus may have its own unique requirements for clinicians who provide care for suicidal clients. After investigation, there at present does not seem to be any central source for finding summary information about suicide law in each of the states. Therefore, the only recourse for clinicians is to contact their state licensure boards, professional organizations, and state departments of mental health, rehabilitation, or education (depending on practice setting) for information on laws for treating suicidal individuals in their states.

Despite the lack of a national law prohibiting suicide, many states have developed case law that defines malpractice in suicide cases based on the principle of "standard of care."

Most state laws define malpractice as "professional conduct and skill that fall below the *standard of care* established for similar professionals in good standing under similar circumstances" (Swenson, 1993, p. 150). The standard of care is often defined as the professional conduct as practiced by at least a significant minority of the reasonable and prudent practitioners who have special knowledge of and ability in the diagnosis and treatment of clinical conditions (Cohen, 1979; Crawford, 1994; Meyer, Landis, & Hays, 1988, p. 15). Violation of a standard of care is the basis for determining negligence in a malpractice case. Malpractice exists when it can be proved that a client has been harmed directly because a counselor was negligent (failed) in following the standard of care (accepted professional procedure) as it relates to treating a case of a similar type (Granello & Witmer, 1998). In the next section, a brief review of the elements of malpractice is presented before we turn specifically to negligence in suicide cases. This approach is useful to help provide the clinician with a background for understanding the role of negligence in establishing malpractice cases.

Review of Elements of Malpractice Litigation

In malpractice cases, the court tries to determine whether a counselor's behavior falls below or violates the minimum accepted standards of care by drawing on custom, statute, common law, rules of practice of professional groups, and often the testimony of expert witnesses (Bednar, Bednar, Lambert, & Waite, 1991). In relation to mental health, malpractice can be defined as a negligent act by the defendant (in this case the therapist) that causes harm to the plaintiff (perhaps the family of a suicide client) (Simon, 2000). In malpractice cases, the burden of proof rests with the plaintiff. In other words the plaintiff must prove that the defendant committed the negligent act and that because of that act, harm was done to the plaintiff. Let's examine the elements of a malpractice case in some closer detail.

Several elements must be proven to establish malpractice. The first element is *duty*. The counselor must have a duty owed to the client to abide by a particular standard of professional conduct. Many conditions may create a treatment relationship between a counselor and a client and thereby establish a duty owed. An example might be providing an appointment for a client and, of course, accepting any kind of payment for a service rendered. Remember, in the case of a suicidal client, a formal counseling relationship does not need to be established for the clinician to owe a duty to the client. For example, in an emergency room or an outpatient clinic, if a client comes in with a suicidal emergency, the clinician has a responsibility to treat (interim first aid) even if the clinician and the client have not entered into a formal contract (Wheeler, 1989).

The second element that must be present to establish a malpractice claim is *negligence*. It must be proved that the counselor, either by commission or omission of action, has breached the duty owed. A negligent act on the part of a therapist can be either something that the therapist did but should not have done (act of commission) or something that the therapist did not do but should have done (act of omission) (Bongar et al., 1998). Negligent acts may be those that do not meet the minimum standard of care that would be expected by a clinician of reasonable prudence in a similar situation.

At this point, then, we have a duty owed to a client and negligence committed in the fulfillment of that duty. The third element of malpractice is *proximate cause*. It must be established that the client suffered some type of damage as a direct result of the counselor's negligence. If a clinician is negligent but no harm was done to the client, then this does not constitute malpractice. In other words, if the negligent act by the therapist could not be linked by an unbroken chain of events to the damages sustained by the client, then there is no malpractice. If these elements are proved, however, then the plaintiff or client could be awarded financial compensation for the damages sustained (Granello & Witmer, 1998).

Thus, malpractice requires the following three elements:

1. The therapist must have duty to the client (that is, there must be a contract, or implied contract, of professional relationship between the therapist and client).
2. The therapist must have acted in a negligent or improper manner (i.e., acted outside of what is the professional standard of practice).
3. There must be a causal relationship between negligence and damage claimed by client (the therapist's action—or inaction—caused harm to the client).

Standards of Care in Suicide Cases

Perhaps not surprisingly, given the dire consequences of these cases, the standard of care related to the assessment and treatment of suicidal clients is reasonably well developed in comparison to many other areas of clinical practice. This established standard of care has two significant results. First, from a clinical perspective, there are clear guidelines to follow in working with suicidal clients that help to ensure proper care. Second, there is the benefit that clinicians who follow these guidelines are better protected against malpractice suits. A significant body of literature is available to the

BOX 14.3 • *Malpractice Terms Definitions*

Duty: The obligation assumed (as by contract) or imposed by law to conduct oneself in conformance with a certain standard or to act in a particular way; a duty to use due care toward others to protect them from unnecessary risk of harm.

Breach: A violation in the performance of or a failure to perform an obligation created by a promise, duty, or law without excuse or justification.

Negligence: The failure to exercise the degree of care expected of a person of ordinary prudence in like circumstances in protecting others from a foreseeable and unreasonable risk of harm in a particular situation.

Proximate cause: A cause that sets in motion a sequence of events uninterrupted by any superseding causes and that results in damages (as an injury) which would not otherwise have occurred (also called *direct cause*, *legal cause*).

Harm: The losses resulting from injury to person, property, or reputation.

Damages: The money awarded to a party in a civil suit as reparation for the loss or injury for which another is liable.

clinician that thoroughly discusses methods for managing and treating suicidal patients. (See Chapters 11, 12, and 13 in this book.) The seminal work of Dr. Bruce Bongar is one of the best resources concerning the standards of care for suicidal clients and should be acknowledged. His book entitled *The Suicidal Patient: Clinical and Legal Standards of Care* (2002) is an excellent resource for clinicians who want further reading.

Clinicians who treat suicidal clients should become familiar with the literature and derive their therapeutic practices from the established research and empirically supported models when possible. Practicing therapists who operate within the accepted standard of care for their profession are much less likely to have successful malpractice suits brought against them. Unfortunately, as in all professions, not all therapists practice responsibly and within the standard of care. The next section provides an overview of some of the types of negligent acts that therapists have been found guilty of in suicide malpractice cases. It is our hope that sharing this material will help others who work with suicidal clients not only to learn to avoid these specific mistakes, but also to have their general awareness raised. Working with suicidal clients in mental health means taking care to learn the ethical and legal standards; to avoid making mistakes that are the result of inattention to detail, laziness, or other forms of carelessness; and to make efforts to stay abreast of state and national changes to the laws or ethical codes of one's profession.

Examples of Negligence in Suicide Cases

The courts have found for the plaintiff in malpractice cases when it is clear that negligence has occurred on the part of the therapist or the hospital (agency). At present, most of the suicide-related malpractice cases that are reported on in the legal record involve inpatient settings. However, as more and more clients with increased pathology are being seen in outpatient settings, it would be wise for the practitioner to become familiar with these examples of negligence even if he or she is currently practicing only in an outpatient environment. Simply put, the failure to follow what would be considered the standard of clinical care for a particular setting is the foundation of many of these cases. Examples of negligence in suicide cases may include failure to properly assess or diagnose, failure to protect, failure to commit, early or improper release, and client abandonment.

Failure to Properly Assess or Diagnose.

Cindy worked as an intake coordinator in a crisis stabilization unit in a large urban community mental health center. At 3:00 P.M. on a Friday afternoon, an elderly gentleman came in without an appointment. Clearly agitated, he said that he needed an appointment because he felt anxious all the time, he had thoughts that kept running through his head, and he could not sleep. The man said that he had Medicare and that he knew that he needed to see a doctor immediately. Cindy told the man that she could not accommodate his need to see a physician immediately because all of the appointments for that day had been scheduled with the attending psychiatrist. The elderly man insisted that he needed to see a doctor and that his condition was severe. Cindy felt that it was not necessary to create a disruption in the unit's schedule and offered the man the next available appointment with a doctor, on the following Monday afternoon. After debating with her for over 30 minutes, the man seemed to accept the appointment, took an appointment card from Cindy, and left the facility, agreeing to come back on Monday. The man returned home and wrote a long suicide note concerning the inaccessibility of help for his problems. In his note, he portrayed Cindy as the main reason that he was taking his own life. He then shot himself.

What components of this case put Cindy (and her agency) at risk for malpractice? Remember, malpractice has three components: duty, negligence, and harm.

Malpractice in suicide cases based on assessment or diagnosis most often occurs because of the clinician's failure to adequately assess the risk of suicide for a specific client. The standard of care is violated in these cases because it is determined that if normal and customary procedures had been followed, it would have been expected that the client's level of suicidality would have been detected and apparent. It is considered standard and normal for mental health assessments and psychosocial interviews to include questions about suicide risk. All clients should be asked about suicidality as a regular part of admission, intake, or ongoing assessment. Clinicians who do not screen for suicide and or provide any type of suicide assessment are at increased risk for misdiagnosing the presence of suicidal ideation and, therefore, are at increased risk for malpractice. Further, when suicidality is detected or diagnosed, it must be recorded properly in the patient's chart at the time it is assessed. For the courts, failure to adequately document a client's assessed level of suicide risk is the same as not assessing that risk at all. If you did not document your suicide assessment work properly in the client's chart, then there is no proof that the assessment was completed at all, much less completed properly.

In the case of Cindy, there is a strong case for a malpractice suit against her and the agency for several reasons. First, she was working in a clinical environment that was responsible for screening and evaluating the mental health needs of the public. Therefore, she had a duty owed to the man who came in, even if he did not have a scheduled appointment with her. Second, she neglected to provide the minimum standard of care by not screening the man for suicidality and by allowing him to leave the premises without any plan for safety. Rather than spending time arguing with the man about his desire to see a psychiatrist, she should have asked some specific questions to assess his level of suicide risk. In her position as an intake coordinator of a crisis stabilization unit, it would be reasonable to expect that she have the expertise to deliver this standard of care. Finally, it might be shown that her neglect—the failure to offer the man any type of services other than an appointment the following Monday—had the direct result of harm for him, as documented in his suicide note. Thus, in this case, Cindy's failure to properly diagnose the imminent danger of a client put her and her agency at risk for malpractice.

As an interesting side note, this case also reminds us that when we work with populations that are at risk for suicide, we as clinicians are often inconvenienced. Clients threaten suicide on Friday afternoons, when our schedules are full or we have paperwork due, or during on-call hours, when we would rather be at home with friends and family. To work with suicidal clients, we must learn to accept emergency disruptions to our schedules and make allowances for the need to see patients at any time the need arises.

Failure to Protect. Failure to protect or provide adequate protections for a client is a type of negligence that the courts have upheld. It is based on the duty owed to a client. Clinicians have been found guilty of malpractice when treatment plans have not mentioned safety or have been overlooked or when the clinician neglected to implement a plan to help protect the safety of a patient with suicidal tendencies. Again, adequate documentation is essential. In the case of a sudden or unexpected suicide, the courts have traditionally been more lenient with outpatient therapists than with inpatient therapists. The basis for this leniency is the court's understanding of the difficulties in controlling or being present for all patient behaviors in outpatient care. Nevertheless, once suicide risk has been assessed, the person must be protected from harm.

In Chapter 11, we noted that suicide is preventable to the degree that it is foreseeable. The courts have used the key principle of foreseeability to determine negligence in cases in which failure to protect has been charged. Foreseeability can be thought of as the standard of care linked to the quality of the clinician's assessment of a client's potential risk for suicide. A client's suicide would be determined by the court to have been foreseeable if in a similar clinical situation, it would be expected that a reasonable practitioner would have assessed the same client as having significant risk for suicide. The more obvious the client's suicidal intent, the more serious in terms of malpractice is a clinician's failure to properly evaluate (Vandercreek & Knapp, 2001).

Although the courts do not expect doctors and therapists to predict the future, they do expect professionals to take precautions to ensure client safety. In cases of suicidal clients, when the suicide was determined to be foreseeable and when the therapist could have taken preventive interventions to preempt the suicide, the courts have consistently found therapists to be negligent. As was mentioned previously, when clinicians are working with suicidal clients in inpatient settings, the courts have held to a higher standard of care regarding foreseeability. This would appear to be justified, since inpatient facilities are in essence taking custody and responsibility for the safety of the patient who is being served in their facilities. Clients must be adequately observed and put into environments that are free of potentially dangerous objects or opportunities for self-harm (e.g., a client should not be placed on an upper floor with an open window available). Once a client has been determined to be at high risk for suicide, many inpatient facilities will implement suicide watch procedures. This usually means a heightened awareness by the staff of the client's danger to self and increased levels of supervision and observation. Placing clients on suicide watch indicates that there was foreseeability of the client's suicide—hence the response by the facility staff. Therefore, it is very important for inpatient facilities that implement suicide watches to make sure that the procedures for the watch are well specified, carried out properly, and documented. Placing a client on a suicide watch status and then not monitoring the client properly is definite grounds for establishing negligence in a malpractice case.

Failure to Commit.   Failure to commit a client who was assessed to be at serious risk for suicide is a type of negligence for which therapists have been successfully sued for malpractice. Allowing clients who are at serious risk of suicide to wander off or otherwise leave a practitioner's facility without its being reported to the police is inappropriate care.

Once a clinician has assessed a client and has determined him or her to have a serious risk of suicide, follow-through procedures to ensure safety must be implemented. Often, that means arranging admission for the client to a crisis stabilization unit or assessment for placement on an inpatient unit. Mental health practitioners must take it on themselves to do everything in their power to assist the client's safe placement, including arranging for supervised custody and/or transport through police or emergency medical personnel. Direct communication with the unit or hospital admissions staff, doctors, nurses, or other individuals who will be involved with the client is necessary. It is essential to communicate specifically why the client has been determined to be at high risk of suicide and what evidence exists that the client needs the safety of a protected or locked unit at this time. Leaving phone messages or notes for staff is not adequate, as these messages might go unnoticed. The basic rule is: *You are responsible for making sure the client is safely placed.* Again, it is very important to document all interventions and communication and to verify that the client has been properly protected.

Early or Improper Release.   The early or improper discharge of a client from a mental health facility also has been the source of negligence in successful malpractice suits. Many of the errors involving improper discharge of suicidal clients are due to poor communication or failure to assess for suicide risk at the time of discharge.

Inpatient treatment teams must communicate with each other and document in the client's record all events in managing the patient's care. In one famous case involving miscommunication, a psychiatrist released a patient without knowing that the patient had been in restraints earlier in the day. When the client was released, he went home and completed suicide. Communication between the staff on different shifts of a treatment unit is very important, especially when it concerns the care and monitoring of suicidal patients. Documentation of any information and direct verbal communication between staff members regarding any person's suicide status are essential.

Evaluation of suicidality for a client should take place whenever the client is going to increased or decreased levels of care as well as at regularly scheduled intervals in his or her treatment. The level of a client's suicide risk should once again be assessed before the client is discharged from any facility, even if he or she was not originally admitted to the facility for suicidal risk. All clients should be advised as part of their discharge planning about the actions they can take to protect themselves if they feel suicidal. Patients who are being discharged should be furnished in writing with the phone numbers of appropriate crises facilities, therapists, and suicide hotlines. Suicide risk management plans are an essential component of client care.

Client Abandonment.   Abandonment of a client by a therapist has been found to be a source of negligence in suicide malpractice cases. Abandonment of a client can result from two main causes: (1) when the therapist withholds or terminates treatment while a client is still in need of treatment and (2) when a therapist inaccurately determines that treatment is no longer necessary for a client (Bongar, 2002). It is not appropriate to terminate treatment of a client who is in crisis, even if this client can no longer pay for the therapist's services. The mental health provider is responsible for making an appropriate referral or continuing to treat the client until there is no risk of suicide and a normal termination can occur. If a treating therapist can no longer provide care, assistance must be given to find an appropriate referral to another professional. The mental health practitioner must document, allow adequate time for transition, and provide any records at the client's request for the new therapist. It is the treating therapist's responsibility to make sure there is a continuity of care for the client and to provide the client with the support to transition to a new therapist.

Summary of Legal Issues in Suicide

The examples of types of negligent acts that have been used to prove a successful malpractice case against a clinician are not exhaustive but certainly do illustrate the need for clinicians to stay apprised of the legal and ethical standards of care relevant to their scopes of practice. Mental health providers have the responsibility to continually assess their clients for suicide risk, to respond to their clients' needs, and to make sure their clients are receiving the type of care necessary to ensure their safety.

Risk Management

As is often said, the best defense is a strong offense. This maxim applies to protecting oneself with regard to the risk of working with suicidal clients. Prevention, preparation, and care in providing services to at-risk clients can help to minimize the risks that are inherent in treating suicidal clients. Following is a brief discussion of important topics that every therapist should think about when considering working with potentially suicidal clients before a situation occurs that might call into question the practitioner's competence and compliance with the standard of care. This section will provide information about several issues that relate to ensuring that clinicians do their best to prevent the likelihood of being negligent in treating a suicidal client.

Licensure and Scope of Practice

It is imperative that practitioners do not ever work with clients without a license, under a suspended license, or when their license has lapsed. If an individual were to be involved in a malpractice suit while practicing without a license, the legal ramifications would be compounded (Remley, 2004).

Of course, it is not enough just to be licensed; one must also practice within a particular jurisdiction's authorized scope of practice for the type of license that one holds. For example, individuals who are not authorized by their state's licensure to provide psychological testing should not engage in that practice. It is the responsibility of every clinician to know the legal requirements to practice in each and every environment in which the clinician intends to provide services and to make sure that he or she is compliance with those requirements. Most state professional licensure boards can provide a clinician with the specifics on what education and experience are required to practice under a specific license in that state. The scope of practice for any license area outlines the general areas of competency for the profession, gained through appropriate education and experience. An individual's scope of practice, however, is typically narrower than the scope of practice outlined by law. For example, although a legal scope of practice in a particular state might include crisis intervention, if a specific mental health practitioner has not had training or experience in crisis work, then it would be unethical for that person to engage in such work without supervision and/or training. The law broadly defines practice, and the individual determines his or her own limits within the boundaries of the law.

Malpractice Insurance

Suicide malpractice cases account for the highest settlements in behavioral health care (Bongar, 2002). Mental health practitioners should not see clients unless they carry their own malpractice insurance and understand their policy's benefits and coverage. Do not assume that because the agency you work for has malpractice insurance, you are automatically covered by the agency's policy. The malpractice policy might insure the agency but not the individual practitioners for liability. Malpractice suits can be filed against an agency (hospital, practice, educational setting), an individual practitioner, or both.

It is also important to make sure that you understand the benefits of the malpractice insurance you are buying. For example, does the policy provide for an attorney? What is the maximum payout allowed on the policy? Many professional organizations in the mental health fields provide low-cost coverage to their members. If you do not have coverage, you can go to your professional organization's web site and learn about what options the organization has for malpractice insurance. Finally, once you have malpractice insurance, it is important to keep paying your premiums. Do not allow the policy to lapse. A lapsed policy is the same as having no insurance.

Providing Good-Quality Care

The mental health practitioner is always ultimately responsible for the quality of care that she or he provides to clients, no matter what agency, educational, or managed care restrictions are placed on any case. It is not acceptable, for example, for a clinician to omit a thorough suicide assessment of a client because of time pressures or the payment procedures of a client's managed care provider. Providing good-quality care is essential to protecting clients and to protecting oneself from malpractice. Clients who are receiving good-quality care are much less likely to feel abandoned, exploited, or otherwise neglected by the therapist. Clients and families with goodwill are less likely to sue a therapist. In addition, providing good-quality care is ethically correct behavior. Taking care in assessment, diagnosis, treatment plan development, and implementation is the right of every client. People in crisis expect—and deserve—the best we have to offer when they are contracting for services. Taking time to provide good care will ensure minimization of careless mistakes and provide the client's treatment with enhanced efficacy for success.

Quality of care that is in line with accepted standards of care and practice is the measure by which a therapist will be judged in a malpractice case. Mental health practitioners must make sure that their care does not fall below the minimum accepted standard for a practitioner in their setting treating suicidal clients.

Confidentiality and Communication in Suicide

Communication is an essential component for managing suicidal cases in a professional manner. In the case of a suicidal client, the mental health practitioner will need to communicate not only with the client, but also with the client's family and social support system and, frequently, with professional colleagues. The client must clearly understand the limits of confidentiality with regard to danger to self (as well as danger to others and child or elder abuse).

Confidentiality is the counselor's or therapist's duty to keep client information private and not reveal what was said in the context of the therapeutic relationship. The importance of maintaining confidentiality is basic to the therapeutic relationship, and most clinicians agree that it is essential to building trust, the cornerstone of client disclosure. However, the right to confidentiality is not an absolute guarantee, and there are certain situations in which clinicians are both ethically and legally required to break confidentiality. In issues of suicide (danger to self), client safety supercedes a client's right to confidentiality.

Many therapists are familiar with the famous Tarasoff case, which supports breaking of confidentiality when a client is deemed to be dangerous to others. However, Tarasoff has been extended by the courts to apply as a legal basis for breaching confidentiality in cases of potential harm to self (Bongar et al., 1998). The clinician who does an assessment and concludes that a client is at risk might wish to inform the client's significant others, friends, parents, and other social support networks of the client's potential for suicide to gain their support for the client's recovery (Bongar, 2002). Because of the finality of a completed suicide, the courts have supported erring on the side of being overly cautious in terms of enabling and informing potentially protective assistance for a client. This does not mean breaching confidentiality for no apparent reason, but it supports doing so judiciously when it can help to keep clients safe. .

Clients have the right to make informed choices about the therapeutic relationship they are entering into. Informed consent is both a legal and an ethical issue. Legally, mental health practitioners who do not provide the kind of treatment that the client understood to be offered can be sued for breach of contract. Informed consent is an important ethical component of treatment as well. Clients who understand their rights become participants in therapy rather than passively responding. The ethical codes of most of the helping professions include informed consent as an important ethical responsibility.

Informed consent is based on three legal requirements. Clients who enter into a contract (either through a formal written contract or an informal verbal agreement) for counseling must have the following:

- Capacity—the client is able to make rational decisions. When capacity is lacking (either because the client is a minor or because the client lacks the cognitive ability to have capacity), typically a parent or guardian must give consent for the counseling relationship to begin.
- Comprehension—the client must understand the information that is presented by the therapist. That means that information must be presented by the mental health practitioner in a clear and unambiguous manner, using common language (not clinical language or psychological terms). To make sure that the client fully understands what is being agreed to, it is important to check for comprehension, often by asking the client to repeat the main points of the agreement in his or her own words.
- Voluntariness—the client (or person giving consent) must do so freely and without coercion or under duress.

Once it has been established that the individual can give informed consent (has capacity, comprehension, and voluntariness), then the client has the right to know the benefits and risks of all treatment interventions and procedures and to understand that he or she may choose to engage or not engage in those interventions or procedures. The client's right to self-determination with regard to treatment is the basis of the doctrine of informed consent.

However, just as with confidentiality, informed consent is not an absolute in working with suicidal individuals. In managing the case of a suicidal client, the therapist might be forced into pursuing an involuntary hospitalization for the protection of the client. The therapist should make every effort to inform the client that this might happen for the client's protection if the therapist assesses the client as being unable to be safe in an outpatient environment. Communication about the possibility of hospitalization in advance of the event can help to prepare a client and help the client to understand the motives behind the therapist's actions.

As usual, an ounce of preparation is worth a pound of postevent scrambling. Bongar and colleagues (1998) advise discussing with a client who has suicidal issues early in the therapeutic relationship the conditions under which confidentiality will be broken with regard to suicidality. This type of conversation, which prepares the client and delineates the therapist's role in assisting the client to remain safe, can minimize the client's feelings of betrayal by the therapist.

Clinical Assessment

Therapists should always ask all clients about suicidal or homicidal ideation or intention simply as part of clinical screening and good clinical practice. If a client responds affirmatively to these screening questions (or has other risk factors that suggest risk even in the face of a "no" response), then a more thorough clinical assessment of suicide risk should be conducted (see Chapter 11). A clinician might wish to use a formal suicide assessment tool and seek consultation. It is imperative that the results of this assessment and consultation be well documented and serve as the basis for treatment decisions aimed at protecting the client from harm.

Documentation in Suicide Cases

Complete and explicit documentation is essential in cases involving suicidal clients. Clinicians who lose a client to suicide are in a much better position to defend themselves in a potential malpractice case if they have spelled out clearly and thoroughly the assessment and thought process behind their clinical judgments. Clinicians who have neglected their documentation responsibilities put themselves in jeopardy of having their clinical decisions evaluated and speculated on by an expert witness. Further, there is evidence that the very process of engaging in documentation improves client care by reminding clinicians to pay attention to detail (Shea, 2002). In documenting a case involving a suicidal client, make sure to do the following:

- Write with the understanding that your notes, treatment plans, and assessments could be read by administrators, court officials, ethics panels, or licensure boards.
- Immediately begin to document the case on first contact with the client and when knowledge they are suicidal becomes apparent. Write a summary note of client interaction to the current point in time if necessary.
- Document immediately after interacting with the client when events are fresh in your mind. Do not wait or plan to document "later on."
- Make your documentation detailed and factual. Include dates, times, places, specific events, actions, and words. Do not include hypotheses or speculations.
- Keep all originals of your records and documents. If an appropriate request and signed consent are presented, copies of notes or other documentation may be forwarded to other clinicians or appropriate parties on the client's behalf.

Consultation

It is good clinical practice to consult on cases of even moderate suicide risk. Consulting helps clinicians to make sure they are not missing any important assessment or treatment options that could help to protect clients. Because of the stress involved with working with suicidal clients, consultation is particularly important. Shneidman (1981) noted that there is no other time in a professional clinician's life when consultation with a colleague is more important than in dealing with a highly suicidal person, but studies have found that only 27% of clinical psychologists, psychiatrists, and social workers routinely seek consultation in their assessment of suicide (Jobes, Eyman, & Yufit, 1991).

Consultation is important, regardless of the clinician's experience level. From a legal point of view, it demonstrates that the clinician took the case seriously and attempted to consider different treatment options and perspectives. From a therapeutic point of view, it helps to minimize the possibilities of negative influences of countertransference and early decision foreclosure. Finally, it helps to reduce the stress and anxiety of "going it alone" when people's lives are at stake.

Therapists at all levels of experience and training should routinely seek the advice of senior colleagues, those with more experience in managing suicidal clients, and peers. Formal documentation in the medical record in the form of notes by the consultant and the consultee also provides evidence that the therapist was seeking to follow the standard of care in relation to the assessment and treatment of the patient. Formal consultation, well documented, can be a strong defense in demonstrating that at least a significant minority of practitioners were approving of the methods being espoused by the clinician for managing the case.

A Word about Managed Care and Suicide Cases

In today's world, many practitioners working with suicidal clients must also work with the client's managed care provider, which should be informed when a client is in suicidal crisis, especially if a client is at sufficient risk to require hospitalization. Mental health providers who contract with managed care organizations (MCO) need to understand that there might be conflict between the standard of care that is accepted in the therapeutic community and that defined by the MCO. The MCO's standard of care might be based heavily on cost containment and might not represent the standard of care that would be generally accepted by professionals (or the legal system). In other words, the malpractice liability standard has not changed with the changes in health care delivery. Mental health practitioners can find themselves caught between two conflicting requirements: complying with the MCO's cost containment policies to ensure future revenue or ignoring such provisions to avoid malpractice liability. Until recently and still predominantly, MCOs have been able to avoid liability in state malpractice cases. This is because they are regulated by federal law, specifically the Employee Retirement Income Security Act of 1974 (ERISA), which preempts all state laws regulating the management of health care under an MCO. Recently, there have been some cases that have been chipping away at the MCO defense under ERISA, but for now, it is important for treatment providers to understand that they are the ones who will be held ultimately responsible for the care of the patient, not the MCO.

Summary

Suicide continues to be a topic with which the individual and society must grapple. Suicide challenges our ethical values and can have legal ramifications in terms of malpractice for some therapists. It is important to clarify our own values in regard to the issue of suicide before we find ourselves trying to make treatment decisions in a difficult situation with a suicidal client. Further, therapists who choose to work with clients who have the potential risk of suicide must familiarize themselves with the legal requirements related to treatment in their clinical setting with the proper standard of care. This includes, for example, understanding the state requirements of assessment, diagnoses, protection, and documentation of a suicidal client's case. Finally, all therapists must understand that even though it is very important to consult and communicate concerning treatment decisions with colleagues and managed care case workers, the final legal responsibility for the welfare of the client rests with them.

15

Suicide Survivors

In the fourth and final section of this book, we address the aftermath of suicide. When a person completes a suicide, there are many who are left behind to grieve. Although this book is about preventing suicide, the unfortunate reality is that suicides do occur, and we must help the survivors, including the clinicians who tried to make a difference but could not.

- One in every 59 Americans is a survivor of suicide.
- There are over four million suicide survivors in the United States.

A suicide survivor is anyone who is affected by a completed suicide. Suicide survivors, therefore, include spouses, children, parents, immediate family, extended family, friends, neighbors, coworkers, schoolmates, and acquaintances. It is hard to know how many suicide survivors exist. There has never been an extensive epidemiological study conducted on this topic, and there is no hard definition of who would be affected. The self-identification of "suicide survivor" is highly personal. However, about 32,000 people kill themselves each year in the United States, and some officials estimate that, on average, each of those people leave behind six relatives or loved ones as suicide survivors (McIntosh, 1999). Incidentally, we believe—and we know from our own personal and clinical experience—that each suicide has far more widespread effects than that. We have been affected by suicides in our families, our places of employment, our schools, and our neighborhoods, and we are living proof that suicide has effects far beyond the six people in the official government statistics. Nevertheless, keeping the number of survivors at six per completed suicide and doing simple math means that, at minimum, almost 200,000 people a year in the United States are left to deal with the aftermath of a suicide. Take a moment to think about this: 200,000 survivors a year. It is truly staggering.

We must be concerned about the welfare of suicide survivors, not only because so many are created each year, but also because the experience of surviving a suicide death is often very difficult and complicated. Many clinicians and researchers believe that surviving a suicide death is a traumatic psychological phenomenon that produces a unique type of grief reaction in survivors (Bailley et al., 1999; Hawton & Simkin, 2003). Suicide survivor bereavement has been the subject of research and clinical intervention and, as we shall see, can be quite complex.

Coping with Suicide and Its Fallout

Fallout is a term that is used deliberately in the title for this section. *Fallout* means the raining down to earth of the radioactive debris left after a nuclear explosion. A completed suicide in a family or community is like a nuclear explosion, which has both immediate and long-term consequences. Suicide survivors are, of course, immediately and significantly affected by the suicide death. Suicides are frequently unexpected by the survivor, even though there might have been many signs and risk factors. As a result, the survivors experience shock, disbelief, and denial that the suicide has even taken place (Hall & Epp, 2001). Survivors who are witnesses to the suicide or discover the body of a loved one may experience posttraumatic stress reactions (Rubel, 2003). Also, as Rubel (2003) notes, many suicides occur in the home, and suicide survivors might have to clean up blood, bone fragments, or other physical remains of the victim. Van Dongen (1991) reported that 11% of the suicide survivors in his study had recurrent episodes of intrusive imagery, both in their sleep and awake, concerning discovering the victim's body.

In many cases, the victim of the completed suicide is blamed, and there is substantial negative social stigma around the death. Suicide survivors often receive less social support than do survivors of natural deaths; therefore, they might feel more isolated (Calhoun & Allen, 1991). Because of the negative social stigma of a suicide, Berman and Jobes (1997) report that survivors often attempt to conceal the suicide, hastily arrange funerals, and do not disclose the nature of the death to children or other family members and friends. The suicide becomes a family secret, a source of neighbors' gossip, and a syndrome of private shame and public shunning for the survivors (Rubel, 2003).

Beyond the initial blast of the suicide, survivors must also cope with the extended effects—the fallout—of the suicide. It is certainly the case that things will never be the same for the survivors. There is nothing romantic or heroic in a suicide, and survivors are left with intense emotional turmoil and the potentially contaminating suicidal consequences. One unique lasting psychological ramification of a suicide for a survivor is guilt. Numerous studies have shown that suicide survivors have much more guilt and are much more likely to blame themselves for the death than are survivors of deaths from other causes (Silverman, Range, & Overholser, 1994). Suicide survivors are left with many questions and self-blaming statement's such as "What could I have done to stop my loved one from killing themselves?," "Why did I not recognize the signs and get them help" or, "If only I had been a better spouse/child/friend, this would not have happened." The research has shown long-lasting effects of shame and guilt among survivors.

Suicide Survivor Research

A central concern of suicide survivor research is to understand the unique process of grief and bereavement that results from a completed suicide. The study of bereavement is a relatively new field in psychology and counseling, so it should not surprise us that the specific study of bereavement for suicide survivors is also a relatively new endeavor. The first modern "classic" about suicide survivors, *Survivors of Suicide*, was written by A. C. Cain in 1972. Thus, we have been studying this area for only a short time. Consequently, research literature on suicide survivors is small but has been growing.

The most frequently studied question in suicide survivor research concerns the identification of the characteristics of the bereavement process and how those characteristics differ from or are unique to individuals affected by a death from suicide. Suicide survivor research has moved through three distinct phases. The first of these is the "individual accounts" stage. In this stage, most of the literature concerning suicide survivors consisted of individual accounts, often written by the survivors, that described their experiences as a survivor. Although these accounts are not research in the quantitative sense; they are more akin to qualitative narratives. These accounts, often written by spouses or parents, are moving and provide glimpses into the mind of the individual.

The authors of this book are survivors of suicide, and the death of a brother through suicide was the impetus behind this text. The following box is Paul's own account of the loss of his brother.

The second phase of suicide survivor research can be called the *within-group research stage*. In this stage, most of the research examined the characteristics of suicide survivors as a unique group. An example of this type of research would be a study in which the researchers surveyed 159 relatives of victims of suicide death. Results were that 86% felt guilt and 83.6% felt angry. Many of those who were surveyed reported sleep difficulties, concentration loss, feelings of separation and isolation, mental images of the death scene, denial of the cause of death, and difficulty in reconstruction of events leading to the death. Female survivors reported more negative symptoms than did males (Wrobleski & McIntosh, 1987). In another survey study, based on phone interviews with 76 next-of-kin suicide survivors, the top concerns (in order from highest to lowest) voiced by survivors were family relationship problems, stressor-related concerns (e.g., paying bills, physical and psychiatric illness), and bereavement issues related to difficulty expressing grief (Provini, Everett, & Pfeffer, 2000). Further, this study indicated that next-of-kin suicide survivors said that they needed assistance from professional therapists, information about ways to discuss the death with children, and information on how to receive and provide support from other family members.

The legal procedures and media attention that are often associated with suicides have been shown to cause additional problems for suicide survivors (Biddle, 2003). Suicide survivors often must cope with legal issues that survivors of natural deaths might not have. Examples include police activity around the death, the bodies of loved ones being held by coroners for autopsy, official inquests into the causes of death, and difficulty with insurance policies that have antisuicide clauses. These legal issues may become, in and of themselves, a source of intense stress for suicide survivors (Biddle, 2003; Rubel, 2003). Mental health practitioners often focus on the emotional effects of loss. However, one

BOX 15.1 • *Paul's Story*

I am a professional counselor and counselor educator. I have in my practice worked in many clinical settings with individuals with serious mental illnesses. Yes, I have been on treatment teams that have lost clients to suicide. And, yes, these losses have affected me both personally and professionally. I would like to share with you today, however, my personal story concerning suicide. I have not written a cheery story, but a realistic one for me at my stage of dealing with my loss. I hope that if you have lost someone to suicide, you can relate.

My brother's suicide was both expected and sudden. Expected in the sense that he had so many things in common with many of the people who complete suicide. He was a walking risk factor. Sudden because even though he had so many of the characteristics that are supposed to indicate risk for suicide, he had so many other positive attributes (intelligent, handsome, great sense of humor, caring) that it was easy for me and my family to pretend and deny what we knew was always a possibility lurking in the background. Sudden also because the timing and the place were so wrong.

My brother hanged himself in a state mental hospital in Florida. He was in the hospital because of exacerbation of his mental illness. My family and I, of course, thought that at least he was safe there under the watchful eye of mental health professionals. But my parents got a phone call telling them their son was dead. Despite their best efforts, he had not been in a safe place, and now he is dead.

A vacuum now exists in my heart and mind where he used to be. Where is my older brother? An empty place at the dinner table on family holidays aches for his presence. My brother had been diagnosed with a mental illness in his early twenties, having his first psychotic break in the Air Force. He had had many diagnoses and been through so many trials and tribulations, as many people with chronic mental illness must endure, that they are too many to recount here.

He knew he would never marry, never have children, never finish college, subsist dependent on public assistance, and most devastatingly of all, he could not trust his own thinking, his perceptions, or his mood. And the truth is that, no matter how I try and console myself, the fact is simply that his life was miserable and his death just the final capstone.

He was failed by our best private and public behavioral medicine. He had little relief and no chance of a cure. I believe that at age 39, both looking back over and ahead at his life—he just decided that he could not endure another decade of pain. It has been hard as hell for me. It has been seven years now, and I find myself still thinking about him almost every day. I find myself just saying: "What a waste, what a waste of a young man's life."

A variety of mixed feelings and memories are all I have left. Of course I feel guilty. I wish I had been a better brother. I wish I had done more for him. I wish, I wish—he were still here. So I could tell him I love him—just one more time. But that will never be. I become sad sometimes thinking about him. I think about him almost every day. I cannot listen to certain songs on the radio. It is amazing how many little things will remind me of him. I miss him.

Our challenge is to carry on as best as we can. Of course, we must all carry on. What choice do we have? We must pull out our bag of tricks and distractions, and most importantly be willing to heal. We must do this because if we don't, we will be at risk for our own self-destruction.

I have found a few things that seem to help me professionally and personally so I will share them with you.

(continued)

BOX 15.1 • Continued

1. I choose to focus on the positive aspects of his life and my relationship with him. I try to recall funny things he said or did. I try to remember our childhood before he became ill.
2. I talk openly with others who have had the same experience—losing a loved one to suicide, and it sometimes provides solace. I don't know why but it is helpful to know we are not alone in our grief.
3. I have chosen to educate myself about suicide and share that learning with others. I try to read and understand more about suicide. This has helped me. Also, helping others to understand more about suicide has helped me more. Perhaps, I believe that if others' suffering can be eased or deaths prevented then somehow meaning is created out of the meaninglessness of my brother's death.
4. I listen more, and empathize more. I am more keenly aware of my clients' pain and listen to them with more caring.
5. I realize that life is fragile and temporal. I have had a wake-up call, and I don't intend to miss it. I am committed to enjoying my friends. My garden. My family. Everything as much as possible every day. It is very important to realize that when you are blessed with life and loved ones that you must acknowledge that every day.

I have shared a bit of myself here in the hopes that you will see that you are not alone in your loss. Those others who have lost a loved one to suicide understand the intensity of your pain. There is no easy answer or cure, there is only the need to choose life and improve ourselves despite our burdens.

Source: http://www.preventingsuicide.com/professionalsurvivorofsuicideessay.asp.

important factor that these studies reveal is that suicide survivors have not only emotional needs, but also practical needs and concerns. In addition to emotional support, suicide survivors might need assistance with practical problems such as finalizing funeral arrangements, finding competent professional help, paying bills, getting information on how to communicate with children and families on the topic of suicide, and coping with legal issues. This within-group research was a useful start in helping to understand some of the characteristics of suicide survivors and their experiences.

The next phase of suicide research could be called the *between-group stage*, and it is the current focus of study. In this type of research, comparisons are made between suicide survivors and other groups of the bereaved. With these comparisons, researchers and clinicians can gain understanding of how suicide survival differs from other types of bereavement (McIntosh & Kelly, 1992).

Silverman, Range, and Overholser (1994–5) compared suicide survivors with survivors of homicide, accidental death, natural anticipated death, and natural unanticipated death. Several important and interesting results were found concerning suicide survivors in this study:

1. Suicide survivors as a group had more intense grief reactions than any of the other survivor groups.

2. Suicide survivors were more likely to assume responsibility for the loved one's death, believing that they should have somehow prevented it.
3. Suicide survivors scored significantly higher in their self-destructive behavior than any other group.
4. Suicide survivors experienced higher levels of shame and rejection then any other group.
5. Suicide survivors reported more pain in searching for an explanation of the death and more difficulty in making sense out of the death than other groups.

In a more recent study, Bailley and colleagues (1999) compared four other survivor groups and found very similar results. The 1999 results found that suicide survivors, more than any of the other survivor comparison groups, reported the greatest overall grief, the highest feelings of rejection, significantly greater feelings of responsibility for the suicide, greater perceived stigmatizations, and intense feelings of shame and embarrassment following the death.

Although there are clearly between-group differences, several other studies have found some similarities based on classification of death. Some studies have shown considerable similarities between suicide survivors and accidental death survivors. These groups were similar on resignation—not accepting death and experiencing shock significantly more than natural death survivors (McIntosh & Kelly, 1992). In a study of 232 parents (140 separate families), Dyregrov, Nordanger, and Dyregrov (2003) found no difference between bereavement in suicide survivors and bereavement in accidental death survivors. These studies seem to indicate that the mode of death, especially if the death is unexpected, is a significant predictor of the type and severity of the survivor's grief reaction.

Another characteristic of suicide survivor bereavement that has been studied in comparison to other groups is the duration of the grief response. Duration of grief may be longer after suicide than after natural death. Suicide stigma, shame, aggravation, and guilt can overwhelm the bereaved and cause the grief to be longer in duration and place the survivor at increased psychological and physical risk (Dunn & Morrish-Vidners, 1987–8). In one study, Farberow (1992) reported a high rate of physical health problems among subjects. These problems consisted of stomach and sleeping problems, headaches, anxiety, tension, mood changes, fatigue, and others. Psychologically, even ten years after a death, suicide survivors (especially spouses) had more likelihood of having a mental health problem and increased social isolation than general population controls (Saarinen, Hintikka, Lehtonen, Loennqvist, & Viinamaeki, 2002). It would appear from these studies and others that suicide survivor bereavement has its own unique characteristics and complexities that differentiate it from other types of grief reactions.

Special Focus: Child Survivors

Child survivors are a special population that has received very little specific attention in the suicide survivor research literature. Just as the loss of a child to suicide is thought to be particularly difficult for parents, it is also thought that the loss of a parent through suicide is a unique psychological phenomenon that warrants more investigation (Cain, 2002).

In one study, children whose parents died from suicide were compared to those whose parents died from cancer. In this particular study, none of the children had seen the body of the suicide victim, but all of the children in the study had attended the funerals of the parent. The results of the study indicated that the children who were survivors of a parent's suicide had significantly more depressive symptoms, negative mood, interpersonal problems, ineffectiveness, and anhedonia than did the children who were survivors of a parent's death from cancer (Pfeffer, Karus, Siegel, & Jiang, 2000). Other studies also have shown the deleterious effects on the mental health of children caused by parental suicide. Increased risk for major depressive disorder, posttraumatic disorder, and impaired social adjustments have all been linked in children to a parent's suicide (Sethi & Bhargava, 2003). These results indicate how powerfully a parent's suicide affects a child, with both immediately significant and long-lasting effects.

One question that has been asked about child survivors concerns whether or not they should be told of the nature of their parent's death. Cain (2002) reminds us that being told and knowing about the suicide can be two separate things. He cites examples of children who were not explicitly told about their parent's suicide but who knew a great deal about them and, conversely, children who were directly told about their parent's death who refused to believe or could not comprehend the communicated information. Some clinicians and researchers believe that it is best to openly communicate the nature of the parent's death to the child to prevent the child from experiencing anxiety about not knowing or denial on the part of the surviving parent. The question of whether or not to tell children has not been answered by any empirical research, and we cannot say from a research perspective how telling the child would affect grieving or outcomes. Parents and clinicians, it would seem, have to make an informed choice after considering many situational individual factors, such as the age or maturity of the child, the child's ability to comprehend the finality of death, the child's witnessing of events related to the suicide, and the child's relationship with the dead parent. The danger, of course, is that without a full understanding of the death, children could possibly blame themselves for causing this unspeakable horror to occur. Therefore, any decisions to withhold information should be very carefully thought through. However, it does not seem at this point that anyone can give a definitive answer to the question of how best to discuss the circumstances surrounding the death with the child.

An area that is even less understood is the effects of a sibling's suicide. We know that suicide increases risk for other family members, and the effects of the death of a sibling are poorly understood. There is some evidence that within three years following the death, children who experience a sibling's suicide are seven times more likely to develop major depression, posttraumatic stress disorder, or suicidal behavior (Brent, Moritz, Bridge, Perper, & Canobbio, 1996). Any clinician who has ever worked with families after suicide knows all too well the risk these children face. Although we know little about these children, we do know that they need help working through the crisis. There is some very promising research that demonstrates that children who survive a sibling's suicide benefit from therapeutic intervention. In one study, changes in anxiety and depressive symptoms were significantly greater among children who received a group counseling intervention for suicide survivors than in those who did not (Pfeffer,

Jiang, Kakuma, Hawng, & Metsch, 2002). Clearly, more research on assisting children (and families) to cope with the grieving process is essential.

Another area of concern for suicide-surviving children and adolescents is the attempt or completion of a suicide by a peer. Adolescent peer survivors might be at significant risk for psychological disorders and suicidal behaviors. Close friends of suicide attempters or completers are at particular risk, and approximately 25% of friends in one study in Hong Kong required psychiatric treatment, and 15–21% indicated their own suicidal behaviors (Ho, Leung, Hung, Lee, & Tang, 2000). Suicide contagion is always a serious subject, and adequate postvention interventions should be carried out with adolescent survivors. (Please see Chapter 10.)

Although little is known about the effects of suicide on children, there are some resources to help. For example, a book entitled *After a Suicide: A Workbook for Grieving Kids*, produced by the Dougy Center for Grieving Children (www.dougy.org) can be a useful therapeutic tool to help children through the grief process.

A list of web resources for survivors is available in Appendix C.

BOX 15.2 • *Survivors: Making Self-Care a Priority*

Following a suicide, it is very important for survivors to allow themselves to have both the care and support of others as well as engaging in deliberate efforts at self-care. Trying to be "brave" or to deny emotions associated with the suicide death is not admirable or healthy. Using support systems to communicate feelings and thoughts about the suicide (although typically extremely difficult) can eventually help with healing. Here is a list of suggestions which can help suicide survivors in their grieving:

- Talk about the suicide. Do not pretend that it did not happen or use some euphemism to describe it. John hanged himself; he did not "pass into the great beyond."
- Allow yourself to feel the full range of feelings associated with the suicide: shock, anger, sadness, happiness, guilt—all the feelings that come to you. Do not be ashamed if you have strong feelings or feelings that seem inappropriate at first.
- Communicate with supportive others about how you are feeling. Try to listen to how others are feeling as well. Your feelings are normal and need expression. Use a journal or artwork to express yourself.
- Go ahead and tell the story of the suicide as many times as you need to hear yourself say it. It might not make any more logical sense to you than it does telling it the first time, but the story is real, and you can acknowledge the tragic nature of it.
- Reflect on the loss of the loved one. Allow yourself time to grieve. It is okay to be generous to yourself and feel the loss.
- Find a supportive counselor, therapist, or self-help group for coping with the depression, feelings of helplessness, and grief. It is okay to seek help following an event of this magnitude.
- Do not give up habits, activities, or plans that you have made that are normally pleasurable to you. Continue to live your life, finding meaning in your loved ones, activities, and vocation.

Mental Health Assistance for Suicide Survivors

When survivors do seek mental health assistance, they often do so on their own or through encouragement of friends or family. When they come to counseling, they might have a feeling that they "should be doing better by now." The belief that grief ought to be over after a certain period is popular in Western society, and suicide survivors might be getting messages from their social network that something is abnormal about them and their grieving process. As we discussed earlier, the grieving process for suicide survivors is "abnormal" in comparison with other kinds of grief, but the process is "normal" for suicide survivors. For suicide survivors, it appears that certain grief symptoms (e.g., guilt, rejection, shame, stigma) that occur after a suicide death for survivors complicate the bereavement process (Harwood, Hawton, Hope, & Jacoby, 2002). Clinicians need to realize when working with bereaved suicide survivors that they might not recover as quickly as other types of survivors and might have some special issues that complicate therapy. Above all, the experience of these clients will most certainly not fall nicely into the discrete stages of a "normal" grief process.

The most salient aspects of suicide survivor bereavement that have been identified in the literature relate to extreme feelings of guilt and shame. A second theme that emerges is the need to make sense out of the death, to answer questions of "why?". Third is to cope with social stigma and resulting isolation. In addressing these issues, suicide survivors must avoid denial, social withdrawal, self-destructive behavior, failures to communicate, and developing enduring mental and physical health problems. Dunne (1992) stated these issues somewhat differently and listed the following as the dominant psychological themes for suicide survivors in counseling:

- Obsessive search for the why of suicide
- Sense of stigmatizations
- Incomplete or unusual grieving pattern
- An invasion of conscious thought by the idea of suicide
- Sense of helplessness and low self-esteem
- Reduction in size or complexity of social relationships
- Erosion in basic trust of others

Even after identifying useful themes for directing therapy from the literature, clinicians still must remember that clients have many individual differences. Age, gender, cultural background, and life experiences, many of which were covered as risk factors in earlier chapters of this book, all affect the grieving process in general and suicide survivor grieving in particular. However, how these many identities and experiences interact to produce the grieving process is poorly understood. For example, some individuals might not exhibit any grief and, contrary to myth, might not have a delayed grief reaction. At present, there is no long-term study on outcomes of these cases. Others find comfort and meaning in suicide notes left behind, while some find these notes heart-wrenching and more complicating to the process. The relationship of the survivor to the victim and the characteristics of that relationship are important individual modifiers. The perceived closeness by the survivor to the victim might be more important than the actual genetic relationship.

Given the complexity of survivor grief, clinicians might become impatient or discouraged with treating these clients. Fortunately, there are some very real things that mental health professionals can do to help. Farberow (1992) offered the following list of activities that survivors have reported as helpful:

- Talking with friends and family (most helpful)
- Reviewing pictures and mementoes
- Visiting the grave
- Rearranging and storing the belongings
- Individual psychotherapy (50% thought it helpful)
- Group psychotherapy (22% thought it helpful)

Further, it has been suggested that a factor that is of crucial importance to the suicide survivor's recovery is resolving the meaninglessness of the suicide (Rudestam, 1992). Helping clients with the why of the suicide, letting them tell their stories, and helping them to reframe and make some sense out of their loss might be the most helpful thing that a therapist can do. Many survivors use their experiences to reach out and help others. Examples of this "making meaning" range from public legal advocacy such as the passage of the Garrett Lee Smith Memorial Act, the first federal appropriation to colleges and universities for suicide prevention, to private actions such as setting up a remembrance web page or donating to a suicide prevention cause, such as the Jed Foundation or American Suicide Prevention Foundation, or as in our case, to writing a book to help better prepare mental health providers.

Additionally, helping to work through the emotions of guilt, shame, and responsibility associated with the suicide is a task with which professional mental health providers can definitely assist survivors. Clinicians also should remember to monitor the survivor for suicidality, given that survivors are at increased risk themselves. Finally, a therapist can help clients with addressing the survivor's ability to function in their social network, given any stigma they may feel (Jordan, 2001). It is important for survivors not to withdraw and isolate themselves from friends and loved ones following the suicide.

In the United States, there has been a movement to provide support to suicide survivors in the form of groups that are often sponsored by local mental health agencies. Most frequently, these groups are called S.O.S. (Survivors of Suicide) groups, but they may also go by other names. S.O.S. groups are sometimes peer led and sometimes led by a professional and a peer cofacilitator (Faberow, 2001). There has been very little systematic research on these groups, and little is known about their effectiveness (Ruby & McIntosh, 1996). However, one recent study of postvention groups for widowed survivors of suicide revealed some positive outcomes regarding bereavement. The groups met for eight weeks for 1.5-hour sessions that focused on facilitating group discussion and encouraging socialization. The study indicated reduction in overall depression, psychological distress, and grief as well as an improvement in social adjustment (Constantino, Sekula, & Rubinstein, 2001).

A final point concerning clinicians' treatment of survivors is that it is commonly held that clinicians should not treat the survivors of one of their own client's suicides. This belief arises out of concerns that the clinician's own feelings are likely not to be objective and that forming positive therapeutic relationships with the survivors also may be complicated. It is considered best practice for clinicians to refer survivors who are related to one of their own clients to another colleague in the community (Pietila, 2002).

A Proposed Model for Family Interventions Following a Suicide: The Family Debriefing Model

Gerald Juhnke and Marie Shoffner (2005) have proposed an interesting adaptation of the critical incident stress debriefing model that has specifically been used in working with families who have lost a member to suicide. The Family Debriefing Model consists of a five-session structured counseling process that seeks to allow the safe processing of affect within a family, educate the family, and promote coping behaviors among the family members in relation to recovery from the suicide.

Brief Summary: Family Suicide Debriefing Model

Initial Family Debriefing Model Session One (1 to 3 hours).   Provide the seven-step structured process for each family member to discuss the suicide and associated feelings. Assess both individual and family needs. Educate the family members regarding posttraumatic stress disorder symptoms and available mental health community resources (e.g., 24-hour emergency telephone hotlines, support groups for survivors of suicide).

Seven Steps of the Initial Session

1. Introduction: Educate about debriefing process and establish commitment for participation.
   • Family Debriefing Model rule: All family members currently present must stay for the entire session and be willing to commit to each of the four subsequent sessions.
2. Fact Finding: Facilitate family member discussion about nonemotional facts regarding the suicide.
3. Thoughts and Cognitions: Encourage family members to discuss their personal thoughts surrounding the family member's suicide.
4. Reactions to Suicide: Facilitate family members' discussion concerning their affective reactions to the suicide. Allow an opportunity for all family members to share their feelings concerning the loss of their family member.
5. Symptoms: Facilitate emotional containment and identify stress symptoms.
   • Help family members move out of the affective domain back into the cognitive domain.
   • Assess family member's physical, cognitive, or affective symptoms such as trembling hands, inability to concentrate, or depression.

6. Teaching: Educate family members about frequently experienced symptoms (e.g., anger, depression) typical of grief reactions and acute stress disorder.
7. Reentry: Facilitate closure of the first session, discuss any further thoughts or concerns, and make a living pledge (suicide contract) with one another.
   - Provide encouragement concerning the strength and caring of the family system.
   - Distribute a hand-out discussing common symptoms of PTSD and depression. This hand-out also should include a 24-hour helpline number and a place to write down the time and location of the next Family Debriefing Model session.

Family Debriefing Model Sessions Two through Four. Encourage identification of individual and family strengths, resilience, resourcefulness, and support that can help the family to adjust to the suicide. In the later sessions, start the session with a discussion of behaviors previously identified that suggested healing.

Fifth Session. Facilitate summarization regarding the Family Debriefing Model experience and promote a clearly delineated ending point. Ask family members to:

- Report what they have learned about themselves, their family, and the grieving process
- Indicate how their memories of the deceased will not be forgotten
- Restate their living pledge to each other and to promise their willingness to help obtain counseling services if needed
- Identify helping behaviors that have fostered healing and identify means to continue same

This five-session model provides a forum where families can discuss the suicide and its effects on family members, with a therapist as a guide. The major benefit, according to the authors, is the reduction in isolation for family members and the focus on pulling together the family to discuss feelings and methods of coping, thereby strengthening a ravaged family system. Although formal models of critical incident stress debriefing and critical incident stress management are somewhat controversial in terms of their effectiveness and therapy, such as the type outlined might not be required for all survivors, it is still important to provide survivors with access to emotional support and reassurance. Mental health providers can make sure that survivors know that there is help available if they need it, provide information on how to access help, provide education on normal grieving processes, and empower survivors to contribute to generating plans for their own recovery.

Client Suicide: Clinician as Survivor

Mark was a 35-year-old white male who was a successful mechanical engineer. He was from a small town in West Virginia and worked for a consulting firm with major contracts with the chemical industry. He was initially referred to counseling for grief and depression following, in his words, "a very nasty divorce" from his wife of ten years. Mark and his wife had been communicating only through their attorneys. Mark was very bitter and distraught about losing custody of his two sons, ages 8 and 5, to their mother. He believed that the "judge was unfair and automatically was biased to award custody to a woman." Mark was allowed to see his sons every other weekend and have them for an extended time in the summer.

Mark was diagnosed as having major depression and was prescribed an antidepressant medication. After some weeks of outpatient therapy, Mark's therapist was concerned that Mark's depression was becoming more severe and that he was not responding to the medication. The therapist referred Mark to an adult partial hospital program, where he would be in treatment all day, five days a week. Mark took a leave of absence from his work to attend the program. While attending the program, he discussed at length in the group therapy sessions how his life had been destroyed by his divorce and how his children had been taken from him. He stated that without being able to have his children with him all the time, he did not see a reason to continue his life. He complained that his wife was still very bitter and often did not have the children ready to go when he came to pick them up. She had even been late in turning them over to him for his custody time with them. Mark's therapist worked with him daily, using cognitive therapeutic approaches in individual counseling. Mark also saw a psychiatrist daily for medication management. Over the course of the program, he tried several different antidepressant and even antipsychotic medications, yet his depression continued to worsen. Mark was eventually admitted to an inpatient psychiatric unit for safety reasons. After much discussion with his psychiatrist and failing to get a good response from numerous medications, Mark agreed to undergo a course of electroconvulsive therapy (ECT). The staffs at the hospital and at the partial hospital program were all very concerned for Mark, as he did not seem to respond to any of the many modalities of therapy and medications they tried. Mark seemed to have resigned himself to the belief that his life had no meaning without his children being with him all the time. After his inpatient stay and the ECT treatment, Mark was readmitted to the adult partial program and to a respite house that was staffed by a nurse at night. Mark attended the therapy program during the day and stayed overnight in the respite house. He was kept on a suicide watch while at the program, as the staff believed that he continued to be at risk. Over time, however, he appeared to improve and stated that although he did not like being apart from his children so much, at least he could spend time with them on weekends.

After eight weeks of treatment, Mark talked with his counselor and his psychiatrist about going to visit his brother and sister-in-law for a weekend. He stated that he was feeling hopeful and that a family visit would help him to reconnect to his loved ones. Although his psychiatrist and counselor were concerned, they allowed Mark to go home with his brother and sister-in-law for a visit with their children. Mark's brother and other family members were apprised of the treatment team's continued worries about Mark, and they agreed to keep a close watch on him. Mark successfully completed suicided by hanging himself in the bathroom of his brother's home that afternoon.

The terrible tragedy of Mark's suicide is that all best efforts were made by a variety of treatment providers to keep Mark alive. Every resource that was available was tried, but none worked. Mark intended to kill himself, and it is clear that even as he told the treatment providers that he would be safe, he planned to kill himself the moment he was out from under the watchful eye of his protectors.

It is important to address here the fact that you as a mental health provider are, if you work long enough in the field, very likely to become a survivor of a client's suicide. Sometimes, as in the case of Mark, you will encounter people who are not ambivalent about suicide—they truly intend to die, and given any opportunity, they will do so. At other times, suicides will occur because of negligence or because we simply cannot know what exists in the mind of another. Kleespies, Smith, and Becker (1990) studied psychology interns at a Boston Veterans Administration clinic from 1983 to 1988 and found that all 54 interns had a patient complete suicide during their training. Within the field of counseling, McAdams and Foster (2000) found that 24% of counselors had experienced a client's suicide. Within that group, 24% were student counselors or interns at the time. Among psychiatrists, over 61% had experienced one or more completed patient suicides during their residency (Pilkinton, 2003). Clinicians in these studies all reported that their personal and professional lives were highly affected by a client's suicide. In general, a client's suicide affected professional lives by making clinicians more conservative in their decision making, more focused on looking for suicide risk factors, and more likely to seek peer consultation. On a personal level, clinicians reported a loss of self-esteem, intrusive thoughts, intense dreams, strong feelings of anger and guilt, and even considerations of giving up the profession (McAdams & Foster, 2000). Psychiatric residents who experienced a patient's suicide reported great emotional strain but were reluctant to seek help through employee assistance programs, fearing confidentiality issues (Pilkinton, 2003). This last fact is disturbing, as all therapists should be encouraged to work with mentors and peers in coping with the potentially significant professional issues that can arise with the loss of a client through suicide.

Therapists need to address the aftershocks of having a client complete a suicide, which, as we have noted, are significant on both professional and personal levels. Anyone who has ever experienced a client's suicide will know the difficulties firsthand. First, you might feel guilt, thinking that if only you had done X or said Y, then you could have somehow averted the suicide. Next, you might feel doubts about your competence even if you did everything possible to ensure the client's safety. Clinicians often feel shame, anger, betrayal, and fear that others will blame them following a client's suicide. They might even question their desire to continue to work in the mental health field, knowing that death in a real way can result from mental illness (Hendin, Lipschitz, Maltsberger, Haas, & Wynecoop 2000).

Suicide is an issue that gets at the heart of our beliefs and values regarding life and mortality. For any individual, suicide can be a difficult issue to negotiate. For a mental health practitioner or intern, working with a client who is contemplating suicide can be particularly difficult. As professionals, many clinicians feel that the occurrence of suicide is opposite to their goal of helping others. The tension of working with suicidal clients can produce stress and anxiety. The clinician might feel that he or she is in a no-win situation, especially if the client does not respond to treatment. The feelings and questions that can arise require that the counselor have strategies for taking care of himself or herself both while working with a suicidal client and following the attempted or successful suicide by a client (Valente & Saunders, 2002).

There is little information regarding the self-care of the counselor after he or she experiences a client's death due to suicide. Yet self-care is an important topic to consider, since the issue of suicide can generate feelings of incompetence as well as conflict regarding one's own mortality. Following is a brief list of suggestions that a clinician might wish to use when working with a suicidal client and should certainly consider using after a completed suicide by a client:

1. *Process the event with supervisors or professional mentors.* Many mental health professionals have multiple levels of supervision and mentors. Take advantage of the supervision time to discuss the suicidal client with supervisors. Be honest with yourself and your supervisors about the thoughts and feelings that you are having. If possible, discuss both the emotional effects of the suicidal client and any procedural policies for dealing with a client's suicide that are in force where you are counseling. Mental health professionals can help future practitioners by discussing the aspects of the procedure that were helpful as well as those that were not. Supervisors might have had previous experience with suicidal clients. Call on their experience to help you deal with the residual conflicts that you might be feeling. If you do not feel that your supervisor is able to help you process the event, ask your supervisor or a colleague to recommend someone who might be able to help in this area.

2. *Utilize peers and colleagues to help process feelings.* Peers and colleagues can be a great source of social support and can be helpful without breaking confidentiality. Peers can help to put the events into perspective and help to resolve conflicts that can arise from a suicidal client (Bosco, 2000). In much the same way that a counselor might ask clients to call on their social support systems, counselors should use this resource as well.

3. *Seek personal counseling to help resolve the remaining conflict.* Individual counseling can be helpful in instances in which the professional continues to be unable to resolve the personal conflicts that arise. The individual counseling can help the counselor to deal with the increased stress, among other issues. By dealing with the stress in a more proactive manner, the professional can prevent feelings of being burned out or of being jaded by the profession.

4. *Recognize your own personal needs.* Therapists often have a tendency to put others' needs before their own. Working with suicidal clients can be stressful and anxiety provoking, and ignoring the stress and anxiety can result in an accumulation of these feelings. The mental health professional might find himself or herself needing to take time away from the site for his or her own mental health. Be honest with yourself and your supervisor about your needs. This honesty will help you better serve your clients and yourself.

5. *Be cognizant of the personal stress that can result from working with suicidal clients.* It is important that the professional not put pressure on himself or herself to perform at optimal levels in other life areas. By recognizing the stress level and finding ways to eliminate the stress, the counseling professional can help himself or herself to be more well in all life areas.

6. *Recognize the limitations of the profession.* As helping professionals, most clinicians want to help everyone. In reality, there are limitations in the field of counseling and the sophistication of our behavioral knowledge. Take time to realize that as a clinician, you can help only clients who want to be helped. At times, practitioners

might feel that they have done everything right but have not gotten the desired result; the feelings of frustration must be recognized and processed.

It might surprise you to know how many good and competent therapists have lost a client to suicide. Allow yourself to process your feelings and review the case with your colleague. You are a person too, not just a professional machine, so follow the suggestions offered above for self-care. Losing a client to suicide is no small event and should be dealt with deliberately by making a plan for your own grieving and healing process.

Summary

Suicides happen, sometimes because nothing (or too little) is done to prevent them and sometimes in spite of other people's best efforts. Survivors of suicide are at risk of developing mental health problems of their own, including increased risk of suicide. In addition, there is much evidence to support that idea that bereavement from suicide is qualitatively different from other types of grief. Unfortunately, there is no specific treatment that has been supported through research to assist suicide survivors, although a critical incident stress debriefing model, applied to families, has been suggested.

Mental health practitioners who experience a client's suicide also are at increased risk for mental health problems. Because client suicide is a reality that many clinicians will face, it is important to remember to utilize self-care methods, including consultation and counseling, to help process the event.

A Final Note

Although a chapter on suicide survivors is a difficult way to end the book, it is the reality of the world in which we live and the profession in which we work. It is tempting to find a way to "put on a happy face" and end the book on a more positive note. But for 32,000 people each year—and all the people who love and care about them—there is no happy ending. The best that we can do is to try to make a difference each day, every day, in both our personal and professional lives. For most of us, it is why we chose our respective professions in the first place—to make a difference. Recently, we heard Dr. Marsha Linehan say that she decided to become a therapist because she wanted to wanted to work with the most needy people she could find—in her words, to "travel into hell and bring people back" (Linehan, 2005). That is what mental health practitioners do, and we believe that there is no more important or worthwhile endeavor than to bring a person back from the brink of suicide. We started this book with a message of hope. There are people who need us, and with training, compassion, and courage, we can help. We hope that what you have read in this book will help to give you the tools to make a difference and will help to inspire you to make suicide prevention one of your life goals. We wish you the best in your work, and we thank you for your efforts to save lives.

Appendix A

Resource List of Suicide Risk Assessments

Commercially Available Measures of Suicide Risk

For a comprehensive review of the psychometric qualities of these instruments, see *Mental Measurements Yearbooks* or *Tests in Print*, both available through the Buros Institute, University of Nebraska Press (www.unl.edu/buros/).

Beck Scale for Suicidal Ideation.   This is a 19-item self-report scale preceded by five screening items. The scale and its screening items are used to assess a client's thoughts, plans, and intent to commit suicide. The scale can be used to monitor suicidal ideation in people with ongoing risk. Increasing scores reflect greater risk, but any positive response merits investigation. Authors: Beck, A., R., & Steer, R. A. Year of publication: 1991. Age range: 17+ years. Time to complete: 5–10 minutes. Available through the Psychological Corporation.

Inventory of Suicide Orientation.   This is a 30-item self-report brief screening tool designed to help identify adolescents at risk for suicide. An overall suicide risk is obtained, using questions that ask about two primary areas: hopelessness and suicide ideations. Authors: King, J. D., & Kowalchuk, B. Year of publication: 1994. Age range: 13–18 years. Time to complete: 10 minutes. Available through National Computer Systems, Inc.

Suicide Probability Scale.   This brief instrument is designed to help predict the probability of suicidal behavior or self-harm. It may be used for screening, monitoring changes in suicide potential over time, clinical exploration, or research. There is no mention of suicide on the test itself. The four subscales are: hopelessness, suicide ideation, negative self-evaluation, and hostility. Authors: Cull, J. C., & Gill, W. S. Year of publication: 1995. Age range: 14+ years. Time to complete: 5–10 minutes. Available through Western Psychological Services.

Suicidal Ideation Questionnaire.   This instrument is used to assess the frequency of suicidal thoughts in adolescents and may be used to monitor individual youths or as a screening device in large-scale intervention and prevention programs in schools. In particular, this instrument differentiates depression from suicidal ideation, noting that not all depressed adolescents are suicidal and not all suicidal adolescents are depressed. Author: Reynolds, W. M. Year of publication: 1987. Age range: grades 10–12 (grades 7–9, Suicidal Ideation Questionnaire, Jr.). Time to complete: 10 minutes. Available through Psychological Assessment Resources.

Adult Suicidal Ideation Questionnaire.   This is a 25-item self-report instrument used to screen for suicidal ideation in college students and adults. It can be used during intake interviews or as an adjunct during treatment. Clinicians are encouraged to look at critical items on the instrument to be alerted to acute suicidal crisis. Author: Reynolds, W. M. Year of publication: 1987. Age range: adult. Time to complete: 10 minutes. Available through Psychological Assessment Resources.

Published Suicide Risk Assessments (Adults)

For a comprehensive review of the psychometric qualities of these instruments, see: Brown, G. K. (2002). "A review of suicide assessment measures for intervention research with adults and older adults" by the National Institute of Mental Health. Available at: http://www.nimh.nih.gov/research/adultsuicide.pdf. In general, the abbreviated reviews below have been derived from this source.

Firestone Assessment of Self-Destructive Thoughts.   The FAST (Firestone & Firestone, 1998) is an 84-item self-report measure with 11 levels of self destructive thoughts, including Self-Depreciation (eight items), Self-Denial (eight items), Cynical Attitudes (eight items), Isolation (eight items), Self-Contempt (six items), Addictions (eight items), Hopelessness (six items), Giving Up (eight items), Self-Harm (eight items), Suicide Plans (eight items), and Suicide Injunctions (eight items). Respondents rate the frequency of the self-destructive thoughts. Total scores can be developed for four subscales: Self-Defeating, Addictions, Self-Annihilating, and Suicide Intent. The Suicide Intent subscale score has items from the Hopelessness, Giving Up, Self-Harm, Suicide Plans, and Suicide Injunctions levels.

InterSePT Scale for Suicidal Thinking.   The ISST (Lindenmayer et al., 2001) is a 12-item scale to assess current suicidal ideation in people with schizophrenia. Rather than direct questioning of the client, the items are completed by the interviewer after a 20-to 30-minute semistructured, clinician-administered interview that measures the client's current conscious and overtly expressed suicidal thinking.

Lifetime Parasuicide Count.   The LPC (Linehan & Comtois, 1997) is a brief interview developed for use with adults meeting criteria for borderline personality disorder to measure both suicide attempts and nonsuicidal instances of self-harm behavior. Respondents are asked to discuss both the number of parasuicide and suicide attempts as well as whether such behaviors were associated with an intent to die, ambivalence, or no intention of dying.

Positive and Negative Suicide Ideation Inventory. The PANSI (Osman, Gutierrez, Kopper, Barrios, & Chiros, 1998) is a 20-item self-report measure of positive and negative thoughts related to suicide attempts. Respondents rate each item for its presence during the past two weeks. Items measure positive thoughts ("You felt you were in control" or "You felt hopeful" or "You felt life was worth living") and negative thoughts ("You considered killing yourself" or "You felt like a failure" or "You felt lonely."). In addition to its original use with adults, the PANSI has been evaluated for use as a screening device with adolescents in high school (Osman et al., 2003) and adolescent psychiatric inpatients (Osman et al., 2002).

Reasons for Living Inventory (RFL). There are several RFL inventories for different segments of the population. All of these inventories assess the beliefs that protect one from killing oneself if the thought were to occur. There is also an adolescent version, which will be discussed in the section on child and adolescent suicide risk inventories.

Brief Reasons for Living Inventory (BRFL) (Ivanoff, Jang, Smyth, & Linehan, 1994), 12 items.
College Student Reasons for Living Inventory (CSRLI) (Westefeld, Cardin, & Deaton, 1992), 46 items.
Reasons for Living Inventory—Older Adults (RFL-OA) (Edelstein, McKee, & Martin, 1999), 72 items.

Scale for Suicide Ideation—Worst. The SSI-W (Beck, Brown, & Steer, 1997) is a 19-item interviewer-administered rating scale designed to measure the intensity of a person's specific attitudes, behaviors, and plans to commit suicide during the time period when the person was the most suicidal. Unlike most suicide instruments, it does not measure current risk but asks clients to recall the approximate date and circumstances when they felt most suicidal and to answer the questions according to how they felt at that time.

Self-Monitoring Suicide Ideation Scale. The SMSI (Clum & Curtin, 1993) is a three-item scale that is designed to be given on a daily basis to monitor suicidal ideation. The three items measure intensity of ideation ("Today I have had thoughts of making an actual suicide attempt"), duration of ideation ("Today I have thought about making an active suicide attempt"), and control over suicide ideation ("Today I have felt that the control I have over making an active suicide attempt was . . . [four-point scale from "strong" to "absent"]).

Suicide Behaviors Questionnaire. The SBQ (Linehan, 1981) was originally a seven-page structured interview. In 1988, Cole shortened the SBQ to four items: "Have you ever thought about or attempted to kill yourself?" (rated 1–6); "How often have you thought about killing yourself in the past year?" (rated 1–5); "Have you ever told someone that you were going to commit suicide, or that you might do it?" (rated 1–3); and "How likely is it that you will attempt suicide someday?" (rated 1–5).

Suicide Behaviors Questionnaire—Revised. The SBQ-14 (Linehan, 1996) is a revised version of the SBQ. In this version, 34 items assess five behavioral domains (past suicidal ideation, future suicidal ideation, past suicide threats, future suicide attempts, and the likelihood of dying in a future suicide attempt) with nine additional items that assess severity of lifetime suicidal behavior, current suicide plan, availability of method, social deterrents, attitudes toward suicide behavior, and distress tolerance.

Suicide Ideation Scale. The SIS (Rudd, 1989) is a ten-item self-report measure designed to assess the severity or intensity of suicidal ideation, although it does not measure suicidal intent.

Published Suicide Risk Assessments (Children and Adolescents)

For a comprehensive review of the psychometric qualities of these instruments, see: Goldston, D. B. (2000). "Assessment of suicidal behaviors and risk among children and adolescents" by the National Institute of Mental Health. Available at: http://www.nimh.nih.gov/research/measures.pdf. In general, the following abbreviated reviews have been derived from this source.

Adolescent Suicide Interview. The ASI (Lucas, 1997) is a highly structured interview that can be administered by a lay interviewer or a computer. The ASI has four sections: depression, severity of suicidal ideation, severity of suicide attempts, and exposure to suicide. There are some early indications that adolescents might be more willing to disclose suicidal thoughts to a computer than to an adult interviewer. Note: At the time of publication, this instrument is available from: Chris Lucas, MD, Department of Child & Adolescent Psychiatry, Columbia University, New York State Psychiatric Institute, 1051 Riverside Drive, New York, NY 10032.

Challenges and Coping Survey for Lesbian, Gay, and Bisexual Youth. This survey (D'Augelli & Hershberger, 1993) is the only available instrument that focuses specifically on sexual minority youths. The survey includes questions about sexual orientation and behavior, level of openness of orientation, victimization, self-acceptance, suicidal thoughts, and mental health problems.

Child–Adolescent Suicidal Potential Index. The CASPI (Pfeffer, Jiang, & Kakuma, 2000) is a 30-item self-report questionnaire designed to screen for suicidal behavior in children and adolescents. The CASPI has three factors: anxious-impulsive depression, suicidal ideation or acts, and family distress.

Child Suicide Potential Scales.   The CSPS (Pfeffer, Conte, Plutchik, & Jerrett, 1979) was one of the first comprehensive semistructured interviews developed for use with children (6-to 12-year-olds). The interview protocol assesses for demographics and background information, assaultive behavior, suicidal behavior, life events before the evaluation, recent affect and behavior, past affect and behavior, family background, concept of death, current ego functions, ego defenses, and includes a section for recording diagnostic impressions. Although the instrument is quite old, recent studies continue to support its use to collect meaningful suicide risk information.

Columbia Teen Screen.   This (Shaffer et al., 1996b) is an 11-item instrument designed to be a rapid self-report screening questionnaire for assessing suicide risk. The instrument contains four stem items regarding current and past suicidal ideation and attempts as well as stem questions about depression and alcohol and substance abuse. If a respondent answers affirmatively to questions about suicidal ideation, she or he is directed to questions that assess the seriousness of the problem, whether the respondent is receiving help for the problem, and whether the respondent is willing to accept help for the problem.

Evaluation of Suicide Risk Among Adolescents and Imminent Danger Assessment.
The ESRAIDA (Bradley & Rotheram-Borus, 1990) assesses suicidal ideation or behavior through questions such as "Have you thought about hurting yourself or killing yourself in the last week?" and "Have you ever seriously thought about killing yourself? By seriously, I mean every day for a week or more?"

Expendable Child Measure.   This (Woznica & Shapiro, 1998) is a 12-item clinician-rated scale that is predicated on the assumption that suicidal children might perceive that their parents (consciously or unconsciously) wish to be rid of them or for them to die. Sample items include "Patient feels like a burden on parent(s)/family" and "Patient feels unwanted."

Harkavy Asnis Suicide Scale.   The HASS (Harkavy & Asnis, 1989a and 1989b) is an information gathering tool to directly assess current and past suicidal behavior. The first section is used to collect demographic information, current and lifetime suicidal ideation and plans, suicide attempts, and exposure to suicidal behavior. The second section assesses the frequency of current suicide-related and substance-abuse behaviors. The third section assesses past suicide-related and substance-abuse behaviors. The HASS has been used with African American and Hispanic adolescents.

Juvenile Suicide Assessment.   The JSA (Galloucis & Francek, 2002) is a risk assessment instrument for incarcerated juveniles. The JSA assesses a variety of suicide risk factors, including those that are specific to the incarcerated population. Areas of assessment include extent of prior incarcerations; family history of suicide and mental illness; personal history of abuse; history of overt suicidal or serious self-injurious behaviors; recent suicidal or serious self-injurious behavior, ideation, or communications; recent psychosocial stressors and family crises; and various physiological, cognitive, and affective states.

Multi-Attitude Suicide Tendency Scale for Adolescents. The MAST (Orbach et al., 1991) is a 30-item self-report measure that attempts to uncover the basic conflict between life and death. The scale measure four sets of attitudes: attraction toward life, repulsion by life, attraction toward death, and repulsion by death.

Reasons for Living Inventory for Adolescents and Brief Reasons for Living Inventory for Adolescents. The RFL-A (Osman, et al., 1998) and BRFL-A (Osman et al., 1996) were developed to measure the same adaptive or life-maintaining belief system as the adult versions. In general, these instruments measure the beliefs that protect one from killing oneself, if the thought were to occur

Suicidal Behavior Interview. The SBI (Reynolds, 1990) is a ten-item semistructured interview for assessing current suicidal behaviors in adolescents. The SBI has two sections: The first focuses on distress, life events, and social support; the second part focuses on suicidal ideation and attempts.

Suicide Risk Screen and Measure of Adolescent Potential for Suicide. The SRS and MAPS (Eggert, Thompson, & Herting, 1994) are used in combination in a two-stage screening process for identifying youths with a high probability of suicidal behavior. The first stage is a general risk screen about three areas related to suicide risk: current suicidal ideation and behaviors, depression, and alcohol/drug use. The second stage is a computer-assisted face-to-face interview (the MAPS) that lasts approximately two hours and assesses three areas: direct suicide risk factors, related risk factors, and protective factors.

Other Assessment Instruments

Instruments to Measure Practitioner Knowledge

Quiz on Depression and Suicide in Late Life. The QDSLL (Pratt, Wilson, Benthin, & Schmall, 1992) is a 12-item instrument designed to assess the knowledge level of the general public or of mental health providers on depression and suicide in older adults.

Suicide Potential Rating Scale. This scale, also called the Suicide Lethality Scale, (Holmes & Howard, 1980; Litman & Farberow, 1961) is a 13-item self-report questionnaire that assesses general knowledge about suicide. It is administered to physicians, psychologists, social workers, counselors, and the like to measure knowledge about suicide risk.

Instruments That Measure Mood States That Correlate with Suicide

Although there are too many instruments to list, several commercially available instruments that are used to measure mood states can give clinicians a heads-up about potential suicidality. A few of of these are simply listed below, but mental health practitioners who wish to find appropriate screening devices for mood states that correlate with suicide are strongly encouraged to engage in their own investigations to find instruments that are suitable for their particular populations and needs.

Beck Anxiety Inventory.   This is a 21-item scale that measures the severity of anxiety in adults and adolescents. Available through the Psychological Corporation.

Beck Depression Inventory.   This is a 21-item inventory designed to assess clients diagnosed with depression as well as for the detection of depression among the nonclinical population. Available through the Psychological Corporation.

Beck Hopelessness Scale.   This evaluates hopelessness in psychiatric clients and the nonclinical population. It is designed to measure an individual's expectations for the short-term and long-range future. Available through the Psychological Corporation.

Clinical Assessment Scales for the Elderly.   This is designed for clients aged 55+ and measures (among other diagnoses) depression, anxiety, substance abuse, mania, and psychoticism. Available through the Psychological Corporation.

Coping Inventory for Stressful Situations.   This measures coping styles, including task orientation, emotion orientation, and avoidance orientation. Available through Multi-Health Systems.

Coping Resources Inventory.   This measures an individual's resources for coping with stress. Available through Consulting Psychologists Press.

Hamilton Depression Inventory.   This is a self-administered screening tool for depression. Available through Psychological Assessment Resources.

Reynolds Child Depression Scale.   This is for children in grades 3–6 and is used in schools and clinical settings for a quick depression screen. Available through Psychological Assessment Resources.

Reynolds Depression Screening Inventory.   This is a self-report instrument for use with clients ages 18–89 years. It is designed to quickly assess depressive symptoms in an adult population. Available through Psychological Assessment Resources.

Appendix B

Suicide Organizations and Web Sites

The descriptions are taken from the organizations' web sites.

American Association of Suicidology
www.suicidology.org

The goal of the American Association of Suicidology (AAS) is to understand and prevent suicide. Founded in 1968 by Edwin S. Shneidman, Ph.D., AAS promotes research, public awareness programs, public education, and training for professionals and volunteers. In addition, AAS serves as a national clearinghouse for information on suicide. The membership of AAS includes mental health and public health professionals, researchers, suicide prevention and crisis intervention centers, school districts, crisis center volunteers, survivors of suicide, and a variety of laypersons who have an interest in suicide prevention. AAS, a not-for-profit organization, encourages and welcomes both individual and organizational members.

Check under "resources" for a free 16-page downloadable document on guidelines for school-based prevention programs.

Metanoia.org

A site for persons contemplating suicide. Of course, if someone is suicidal, the best thing to do is to turn off the computer and talk with someone. But if the person is unwilling or unable to do so, this site offers support and encouragement. Metanoia means "a change of mind" . . . turning to face a new direction, to turn toward the light. "Because when you face the light, the shadow is behind you." The mission of Metanoia is to break down barriers that keep people from getting the help they need. Through communications, education, and advocacy, we work to make connections that can shed a little light.

Youth Suicide School-Based Prevention Guide
http://theguide.fmhi.usf.edu/

The Youth Suicide Prevention Guide is designed to provide accurate, user-friendly information. The Guide is not a program but a tool that provides a framework for schools to assess their existing or proposed suicide prevention efforts (through a series of checklists) and provides resources and information that school administrators can use to enhance or add to their existing program. [Authors' comment: This is truly an amazing web site for schools that includes prevention, intervention, sample checklists, information for parents, the media, and so on, and it is all *free*!]

American Foundation for Suicide Prevention
http://www.afsp.org/

The American Foundation for Suicide Prevention (AFSP) is the only national not-for-profit organization exclusively dedicated to funding research; developing prevention initiatives; and offering educational programs and conferences for survivors, mental health professionals, *physicians*, and the public.

Suicide Prevention Resource Center
http://www.sprc.org

The Suicide Prevention Resource Center provides prevention, support, training, and resources to assist organizations and individuals to develop suicide prevention programs, interventions, and policies, and to advance the National Strategy for Suicide Prevention.

Suicide Prevention Advocacy Network—USA
http://www.spanusa.org/

SPAN USA accomplishes its mission through SPAN USA affiliates and volunteer organizers of all ages who work to promote and advance suicide prevention. Community Organizers work to raise awareness about suicide in their communities and communicate with their local, state, and federal policy makers to advocate for suicide prevention. Quilt Organizers help send the message that suicide is about individuals and families, not statistics, by creating Lifekeeper Memory Quilts in collaboration with our partner, the Lifekeeper Foundation.

National Mental Health Association (NMHA)
http://www.nmha.org/

The National Mental Health Association (NMHA) is the country's oldest and largest nonprofit organization addressing all aspects of mental health and mental illness. With more than 340 affiliates nationwide, NMHA works to improve the mental health of all Americans, especially the 54 million individuals with mental disorders, through advocacy, education, research, and service.

Preventing Suicide network
www.preventing suicide.com

A resource center for problem-specific information about suicide. Allows for customized searches of the National Library of Medicine.

Suicide and Mental Health Association International
http://www.suicideandmentalhealthassociationinternational.org/
SMHAI is dedicated to suicide and mental health related issues. Our main goal is to prevent suicidal behavior and to relieve its effects on all who may be affected by it. We also promote and advocate education, awareness, and treatment in regard to mental health.

National Association for People of Color Against Suicide (NOPCAS)
http://www.nopcas.com/
NOPCAS was formed to stop the tragic epidemic of suicide in minority communities. The organization is developing innovative strategies to address this urgent national problem. This includes supporting innovative research to identify the unique factors in minority communities that contribute to suicide, community-based strategies to prevent suicide and the associated problems of violence and depression, corporate partnerships to expand opportunity and build alliances in inner cities, and assistance to local government, law enforcement, schools, and mental health officials to make a bigger impact on suicide prevention.

Suicide Awareness/Voices of Education (SA/VE)
http://www.save.org/
SAVE's mission is to prevent suicide through public awareness and education, eliminate stigma, and serve as a resource to those touched by suicide.

The Jason Foundation
http://www.jasonfoundation.com/home.html
The Jason Foundation (JFI) is a nationally recognized provider of educational curriculums and training programs for students, educators/youth workers and parents. JFI's programs build an awareness of the national health problem of youth suicide, educate participants in recognition of "warning signs/signs of concern," provide information on identifying at-risk behavior/elevated risk groups, and direct participants to local resources to deal with possible suicidal ideation.

Association for Death Education and Counseling
http://www.adec.org/
ADEC is one of the oldest interdisciplinary organizations in the field of dying, death, and bereavement. The almost 2,000 members are made up of a wide array of mental and medical health personnel, educators, clergy, funeral directors, and volunteers. ADEC offers numerous educational opportunities through its annual conference, courses and workshops, its certification program, and via its acclaimed newsletter, *The Forum*.

International Association for Suicide Prevention
http://www.med.uio.no/iasp/
IASP is dedicated to preventing suicidal behavior, to alleviate its effects, and to provide a forum for academicians, mental health professionals, crisis workers,

volunteers, and suicide survivors. IASP is a non-governmental organization in official relationship with the World Health Organization concerned with suicide prevention.

Notmykid.org

This web site is sponsored by NIMH. It is a national non-profit organization, devoted to educating individuals and communities about behavioral health issues facing our teens today, believing that through education we can achieve prevention. It also contains links to many informative web sites regarding a variety of behavioral health problems in children and adolescents.

National Institute of Mental Health (NIMH)
www.nimh.nih.gov

The NIMH tracks research related to suicide and suicide prevention. In addition, an NIMH suicide research consortium (http://www.nimh.nih.gov/suicide-research/consortium.cfm) is comprised primarily of NIMH research scientists who conduct and track suicide research.

Centers for Disease Control and Prevention
http://www.cdc.gov/nchs/

This site has information and statistics about suicide.

Yellow Ribbon International Suicide Prevention Program
http://www.yellowribbon.org/

Provides resources for schools, communities, and survivors, and promotes the Yellow Ribbon Suicide Awareness Campaign each autumn.

National Center for Suicide Prevention Training
http://www.ncspt.org/

Provides educational resources to help public officials, service providers, and community-based coalitions to develop effective suicide prevention programs and policies.

Youth Suicide Prevention Program
http://www.yspp.org/

An educational program, housed in the state of Washington, that provides education and training and printable materials for parents and teenagers.

Appendix C

Web Sites for and about Suicide Survivors

Heartbeat: Grief Support Following a Suicide:
http://www.heartbeatsurvivorsaftersuicide.org/
HEARTBEAT is a peer support group offering empathy, encouragement, and direction following the suicide of a loved one.

Sibling Survivors of Suicide
http://www.siblingsurvivors.com/index.htm
A site written and maintained by siblings of suicide survivors, including first-person narratives and resources.

The Gift of Keith
http://thegiftofkeith.org/
Maintained by the family of a man who committed suicide, this site is designed both to comfort and inform survivors and to educate persons who come into contact with survivors.

Therapists as Survivors of Suicide
http://mypage.iusb.edu/~jmcintos/basicinfo.htm
Information for helping professionals who lose a client to suicide.

Tears of a Cop
http://www.tearsofacop.com/index6.html
For suicide and suicide survivors in the police force.

Other sites and links are available through the American Association of Suicidology web site at www.suicidology.org.

Appendix D

Suicide Helplines and Hotlines

The Befrienders Worldwide

http://www.suicide-helplines.org/index.html
The Befrienders Worldwide is an umbrella organization that has more than 31,000 trained volunteers who provide hotline support in 40 countries. Each year, volunteers provide more than 5 million hours of care to suicide hotlines and crisis centers. Their motto, "Listening saves lives," is the fundamental principle behind suicide hotlines. The Befrienders (and now with support from the Samaritans) maintains an international listing of suicide hotlines, available at their web site.

National suicide 24-hour free and confidential helplines:
National Hopeline Network: 1-800-SUICIDE
National Suicide Prevention Lifeline: 1-800-273-TALK
Specialized hotline for teenagers: 1-800-252-TEEN
Specialized hotline for GLBT teens: 1-800-4UTREVOR
Specialized hotline for elderly persons (Center for Elderly Suicide Prevention): 1-800-971-0016

Contact-USA (a network of crisis intervention and telephone helpline centers: http://www.contact-usa.org/

Use the space below to write your local suicide prevention helpline and crisis intervention numbers:

References

Abramson, L. Y., Alloy, L. B., Hogan, M. E., Whitehouse, W. G., Cornette, M., Akhavan, S., & Chiara, A. (1998). Suicidality and cognitive vulnerability to depression among college students: A prospective study. *Journal of Adolescence, 21*, 473–487

Abramson, L. Y., Alloy, L. B., Hogan, M. E., Whitehouse, W. G., Gibb, B. E., Hankin, B. L., & Cornette, M. M. (2000). The hopelessness theory of suicidality. In T. Joiner and M. D. Rudd (Eds.), *Suicide science: Expanding the boundaries* (pp. 17–32). Boston: Kluwer.

Achille, M. A., & Ogloff, J. R. P. (2004). Attitudes toward and desire for assisted suicide among persons with amyotrophic lateral sclerosis. *Omega: Journal of Death and Dying, 48*(1), 1–21.

Adams, D. P., Barton, C., Mitchell, G. L., Moore, A. L., & Einagel, V. (1998). Hearts and minds: Suicide among United States combat troops in Vietnam, 1957–1973. *Social Science & Medicine, 47*(11), 1687–1694.

Adams, W. L., Magruder-Habib, K., Trued, S., & Broome, H. L. (1992). Alcohol abuse among elderly emergency department patients. *Journal of the American Geriatrics Society, 40*, 1236–1240.

Agnew, R. (1998). The approval of suicide: A social-psychological model. *Suicide and Life-Threatening Behavior, 28*(2), 205–225.

Ahrens, B., & Muller-Oerlinghausen, B. (2001). Does lithium exert an independent antisuicidal effect? *Pharmacopsychiatry, 34*, 132–136

Alaska Division of Vital Statistics. (2000). Alaska Suicide Rates. Available at: http://health.hss.state.ak.us/suicideprevention/AlaskaStatistics/AkSR90_98.htm.

Albright, D. E., Hazler, R. J. (1995). A right to die?: Ethical dilemmas of euthanasia. *Counseling & Values, 39*, 177–189.

Allen, W. R., & Farley, R. (1986). The shifting social and economic tides of Black America. *Annual Review of Sociology, 12*, 277–306.

Alvarez, A. (1990). *The savage god: A study of suicide*. New York: W.W. Norton.

Alzheimer's Association. (2002). www.alz.org.

AMA Council on Scientific Affairs. (1987). Results and implications of the AMA-APA Physician Mortality Project. Stage 11. *Journal of the American Medical Association, 257*, 2949–2953.

American Academy of Child & Adolescent Psychiatry. (2005). http://www.aacap.org/.

American Academy of Pediatrics. (2003). *Suicide checklist for parents of teenagers*. Available at: http://www.aap.org/advocacy/childhealthmonth/prevteensuicide.htm.

American Association of Suicidology (1999). Guidelines for school-based suicide prevention programs. Washington, DC: Author.

American Chronic Pain Association. (2002). http://www.theacpa.org.

American Foundation for the Blind. (2002). http://www.afb.org.

American Psychiatric Association. (2000). *Diagnostic and statistical manual of mental disorders* (4th ed, text rev.). Washington, DC: Author.

Amir, M., Neumann, L., Bor, O., Shir, Y., Rubinow, A., & Buskila, D. (2000). Coping styles, anger, social support, and suicide risk of women with fibromyalgia syndrome. *Journal of Musculoskeletal Pain, 8*, 7–20.

Amyotrophic Lateral Sclerosis (ALS) Association. (2005). http://www.alsa.org/.

Anderson, P. L., Tiro, J. A., Price, A. W., Bender, M. A., & Kaslow, N. J. (2002). Additive impact of childhood emotional, physical, and sexual abuse on suicide attempts among low-income African American women. *Suicide and Life-Threatening Behavior, 32*, 131–138.

Angst, J., & Clayton, P. (1986). Premorbid personality of depressive, bipolar, and schizophrenic patients with special references to suicidal issues. *Comparative Psychiatry, 27,* 511–531.

Anthony, S. (1940). *The child's discovery of death: A study in child psychology.* London: Kegan, Paul, Trench, Trubner.

Appel, S. H. (2004). Euthanasia and physician-assisted suicide in ALS: A commentary. *American Journal of Hospice and Palliative Medicine, 21*(6), 405–406.

Appleby, L. (1996). Suicidal behaviour in childbearing women. *International Review of Psychiatry, 8,* 107–115

Apter, A., Bleich, A., Plutchik, R., Mendelsohn, S., & Tyano, S. (1988) Suicidal behavior, depression, conduct disorder in hospitalized adolescents. *Journal of the American Academy of Child and Adolescent Psychiatry, 27,* 696–699.

Apter, A., Horesh, D., Gothelf, D., Graffi, H., & Lepkifker, E. (2001). Relationship between self-disclosure and serious suicidal behavior. *Comprehensive Psychiatry, 42,* 70–75.

Asberg, M., Eriksson, B., Martensson, B., & Traskman-Bendz, L. (1986). Therapeutic effects of serotonin uptake inhibitors in depression. *Journal of Clinical Psychiatry, 47*(Suppl.), 23–35.

Asberg, M., & Forslund, K. (2000). Neurobiological aspects of suicidal behaviour. *International Review of Psychiatry, 12*(1), 62–74.

Association for Adult Victims of Child Abuse. (2003). *Suicide/Harmful behavior checklist.* Available at: http://www.havoca.org/Safety/Safety%20level.htm.

Atchley, R. C. (1991). The influence of aging or frailty on perceptions and expressions of the self: Theoretical and methodological issues. In J. E. Birren, J. E. Lubben, J. C. Rowe, & D. E. Deutchman (Eds.), *The concept and measurement of quality of life in the frail elderly* (pp. 207–225). San Diego: Academic Press.

Australian Institute of Health and Welfare (AIHW). (2000). Morbidity of Vietnam veterans. Suicide in Vietnam veterans' children: Supplementary report no. 1. AIHW cat. no. PHE 25. Canberra: AIHW. Available at: http://www.aihw.gov.au/publications/health/mvv-svvc/ mvv-svvc.pdf.

Baca-Garcia, E., Diaz-Sastre, C., Ceverino, A., Saiz-Ruiz, J., Diaz, F. J., & de Leon, J. (2003). Association between the menses and suicide attempts: A replication study. *Psychosomatic Medicine, 65,* 237–244.

Bagley, C., & Tremblay, P. (1997). Suicidal behaviors in homosexual and bisexual males. *Crisis, 18,* 24–34.

Bailley, S. E., Kral, M. J., & Dunham, K., (1999). Survivors of suicide do grieve differently: Empirical support for a common sense proposition. *Suicide and Life Threatening Behavior, 29,* 256–271.

Bakalim, G. (1969). Causes of death in a series of 4,738 Finnish war amputees. *Artificial Limbs, 27,* 27–36.

Bale, C. (2001). The media as partners in suicide prevention. *Crises, 22,* 141–142.

Barr, H. (1999). *Prisons and jails: Hospitals of last resort.* New York: The Correctional Association of New York and the Urban Justice Center. Available at: http://www.soros.org/ crime/MIReport.htm.

Barrios, L. C., Everett, S. A., Simon, T. R., & Brener, N. D. (2000). Suicide ideation among U.S. college students. *Journal of American College Health, 48,* 229–233.

Battavia, A. I . (2000). The relevance of data on physicians and disability on the right to assisted suicide: Can empirical studies resolve the issue? *Psychology, Public Policy, & Law, 6,* 546–558.

Battin, M. P. (1995). *Ethical issues in suicide.* Englewood Cliffs, NJ: Prentice Hall.

Baumeister, R. F. (1990). Suicide as escape from self. *Psychological Review, 97*(1), 90–113.

BBC Online Network. (1999, October 13). *Mental Health: An Overview.* London: Author. Retrieved November 9, 1999 from the World Wide Web: http://news.bbc.co.uk/hi/english/ health/background_briefings/mental_health/newsid_472000/472797.stm.

Beautrais, A. L. (2000). Risk factors for suicide and attempted suicide among young people. *Australian and New Zealand Journal of Psychiatry, 34*(3), 420–436.

Beautrais, A. L., Joyce, P. R., & Mulder, R. T. (1999). Personality traits and cognitive styles as risk factors for serious suicide attempts among young people. *Suicide and Life-Threatening Behavior, 29*(1), 37–47.

Beck, A. T. (1997). The past and future of cognitive therapy. *Journal of Psychotherapy Practice and Research, 6*(4), 699–702.

Beck, A. T., Brown, G., Berchick, R. J., Stewart, B. L., & Steer, R. A. (1990). Relationship between hopelessness and ultimate suicide: A replication with psychiatric outpatients. *American Journal of Psychiatry, 147,* 190–195.

Beck, A. T., Brown, G. K., & Steer, R. A. (1997). Psychometric characteristics of the Scale for Suicide Ideation with psychiatric outpatients. *Behavior Research and Therapy, 35*(11), 1039–1046.

Beck, T., Brown, G. K., Steer, R. A., Dahlsgaard, K., & Grisham, J. R. (1999). Suicide ideation at its worst point: A predictor of eventual suicide in psychiatric outpatients. *Suicide & Life-Threatening Behavior, 29*, 1–9.

Beckett, A., & Shenson, D. (1993). Suicide risk in patients with human immunodeficiency virus infection and acquired immunodeficiency syndrome. *Harvard Review of Psychiatry, 1*, 27–35.

Bednar, R. L., Bednar, S.C., Lambert, M. J., & Waite, D. R. (1991). *Psychotherapy with high risk clients: Legal and professional standards*. Pacific Grove, CA: Brooks/Cole.

Beedie, A., & Kennedy, P. (2002). Quality of social support predicts hopelessness and depression post spinal cord injury. *Journal of Clinical Psychology in Medical Settings, 9*, 227–234.

Befrienders Worldwide. (2005). Suicide and crisis helplines around the world. Retrieved June 28, 2005 from: http://www.suicide-helplines.org/index.html.

Bellini, M., & Matteucci, V. (2001). Late onset depression and suicide outcome. *Archives of Gerontology and Geriatrics*, (Suppl. 7), 37–42.

Bender, M. L. (2000). Suicide and older African-American women. *Mortality, 5*(2), 158–170.

Bengesser, G. (1998). Pain, suicide, and its prevention. *Nordic Journal of Psychiatry, 52*, 183–184.

Berger, J. M. (1984). Crisis intervention: A drop-in support group for cancer patients and their families. *Social Work in Health Care, 10*(2), 81–92.

Berk, M. S., Henriques, G. R., Warman, D. M., Brown, G. K., & Beck, A. T. (2004). A cognitive therapy intervention for suicide attempters: An overview of the treatment and case examples. *Cognitive and Behavioral Practice, 11*, 265–277.

Berkowitz, B. (April, 2004). *The military's mounting mental health problems*. Alternet. Retrieved December 31, 2005, from: http://www.alternet.org/story/18556/.

Berman, A., & Jobes, D. (1997). *Adolescent suicide assessment and intervention*. Washington, DC: American Psychological Association.

Berman, A. L., & Jobes, D. A. (2001). Treatment of the suicidal adolescent. *Death Studies, 18*, 375–389.

Berman, A. L., & Samuel, L. (1993). Suicide among people with multiple sclerosis. *Journal of Neurologic Rehabilitation, 7*(2), 53–62.

Biddle, L. (2003). Public hazards or private tragedies? An exploratory study of the effect of coroners' procedures on those bereaved by suicide. *Social Science & Medicine, 56*, 1033–1045.

Blaauw, E., Arensman, E., Kraaij, V., Winkel, F. W., & Bout, R. (2002). Traumatic life events and suicide risk among jail inmates: The influence of types of events, time period and significant others. *Journal of Traumatic Stress, 15*, 9–16.

Blaauw, E., Winkel, F. W., & Kerkhof, J. F. M. (2001). Bullying and suicidal behavior in jails. *Criminal Justice and Behavior, 28*, 279–299.

Blaine, B., & Crocker, J. (1995). Religiousness, race, and psychological well-being: Exploring social psychological mediators. *Personality and Social Psychology Bulletin, 21*, 1031–1041.

Blair-West, G. W., Cantor, C. H., Mellsop, G. W., & Eyeson-Annan, M. L., (1999). Lifetime suicide risk in major depression: Sex and age determinants. *Journal of Affective Disorders, 55*, 171–178.

Blanc, A., Lauwers, V., Telmon, N., & Rouge, D. (2001). The effect of incarceration on prisoners' perceptions of their health. *Journal of Community Health: The Publication for Health Promotion and Disease Prevention, 26*(5), 367–381.

Bland, R. C., Newman, S. C., Thompson, A. H., & Dyck, R. J. (1998). Psychiatric disorders in the population and prisoners. *International Journal of Law and Psychiatry, 21*, 273–279.

Blum, R. W., Harmon, B., Harris, L., Bergeison, L., & Resnick, M. D. (1992). American Indian–Alaska Native youth health. *Journal of the American Medical Association, 267*(4), 253–259.

Blumenthal, S. J. (1988). A guide to risk factors, assessment, and treatment of suicidal patients. *Medical Clinics of North America, 72*, 937–971.

Blumenthal, S. J., & Kupfer, D. J. (1990). *Suicide over the life cycle: Risk factors, assessment, and treatment of suicidal patients*. Washington, DC: American Psychiatric Press.

Boardman, A. P., & Healy, D. (2001). Modelling suicide risk in affective disorders. *European Psychiatry, 16*, 400–405.

Bohn, D. K., (2003). Lifetime physical and sexual abuse, substance abuse, depression, and suicide attempts among Native American women. *Issues in Mental Health Nursing, 24*, 333–352.

Bolger, N., Downey, G., Walker, E., & Steininger, P. (1989). The onset of suicidal ideation in childhood and adolescence. *Journal of Youth and Adolescence, 18*, 175–190.

Bongar, B. (1991). *The suicidal patient: Clinical and legal standards of care.* Washington, DC: American Psychological Association.

Bongar, B. (2002). Risk management: Prevention and postvention. In B. Bongar (Ed.), *The suicidal patient: Clinical and legal standards of care* (2nd ed., pp. 213–261). Washington, DC: American Psychological Association.

Bongar, B., Berman, A. L., Maris, R. W., Silverman, M. M., Harris, E. A., & Packman, W. L. (1998). *Risk Management with Suicidal Patients.* New York: Guilford.

Bongar, B., Maris, R. W., Berman, A. L., Litman, R. E., & Silverman, M. M. (1998). Inpatient standards of care and the suicidal patient: Part I. General clinical formulations and legal considerations. In B. Bongar, A. L. Berman, R. W. Maris, M. M. Silverman, & E. A. Harris (Eds.), *Risk management with suicidal patients* (pp. 65–82). New York: Guilford Press.

Borges, G., & Rosovsky, H. (1996). Suicide attempts and alcohol consumption in an emergency room sample. *Journal of Studies on Alcohol, 57*, 543–548.

Bosco, A. F., (2000). Caring for the care-giver: The benefit of a peer supervision group. *Journal of Genetic Counseling, 9*, 425–430.

Bottlender, R., Jager, M., Struab, A., & Moller, H. J. (2000). Suicidality in bipolar compared to unipolar depressed inpatients. *European Archives of Psychiatry Clinical Neuroscience, 250*, 257–261.

Bradley, J., & Rotheram-Borus, M. (1990). *Evaluation of imminent danger for suicide: A training manual.* National Resource Center for Youth Services.

Braham, L. G., Trower, P., & Birchwood, M. (2004). Acting on command hallucinations and dangerous behavior: A critique of the major findings in the last decade. *Clinical Psychology Review, 24*(5), 513–528.

Braun, K. L., Tanji, V. M., & Heck, R. (2001). Support for physician-assisted suicide: Exploring the impact of ethnicity and attitudes toward planning for death. *The Gerontologist, 41*, 51–60.

Breault, K. D. (1986). Suicide in America: A test of Durkheims' theory of family and religious integration, 1993–1980. *The American Journal of Sociology, 92*, 628–656.

Brent, D. A. (1995). Risk factors for adolescent suicide and suicidal behavior: Mental and substance abuse disorders, family environmental factors, and life stress. *Suicide and Life-Threatening Behavior, 25*(Suppl.), 52–63.

Brent, D. A., Kolko, D. J., Wartella, M. E., Boylan, M .B., Moritz, G., Baugher, M., & Zelenak, J. (1993). Adolescent psychiatric inpatients' risk of suicide attempt at 6-month follow-up. *Journal of the Academy of Child and Adolescent Psychiatry, 21*, 95–105.

Brent, D. A., Moritz, G., Bridge, J., Perper, J., & Canobbio, R. (1996). The impact of adolescent suicide on siblings and parents: A longitudinal follow-up. *Suicide and Life-Threatening Behavior, 26*, 253–259.

Brent, D. A., Perper, J. A., & Allman, C. J. (1987). Alcohol, firearms, and suicide among youth. *Journal of the American Medical Association, 257*, 3369–3372.

Bridgeland, W. M., Duane, E. A., & Stewart, C. S. (2001). Victimization and attempted suicide among college students. *College Student Journal, 35*, 63–76.

Brown, G. K. (2002). *A review of suicide assessment measures for intervention research with adults and older adults.* Available at: http://www.nimh.nih.gov/research/adultsuicide.pdf.

Brown, M. N., Lapane, K. L., & Luisi, A. F. (2002). The management of depression in older nursing home residents. *Journal of the American Geriatrics Society, 50*, 69–76.

Bullman, T. A., & Kang, H. K. (1996). The risk of suicide among wounded Vietnam veterans. *American Journal of Public Health, 86*(5), 662–667.

Burr, J. A., Hartman, J. T., & Matteson, D. W. (1999). Black suicide in U.S. metropolitan areas: An examination of the racial inequality and social integration-regulation hypotheses. *Social Forces, 77*, 1049–1081.

Burt, R. A. (2000). Misguided guidelines. *Psychology, Public Policy, & Law, 6*, 382–387.

Cain, A. C. (Ed.). (1972). *Survivors of suicide.* Springfield, IL: Thomas.

Cain, A. C. (2002). Children of suicide: The telling and the knowing. *Psychiatry, 65*, 124–136.

Calhoun, L. G., & Allen, B. G. (1991). Social reactions to the survivors of a suicide in the family: A review of the literature. *Omega, 23*, 95–97.

Callahan, J. (1994). Defining crisis and emergency. *Crisis, 15*, 164–171.

Calvert, P., & Palmer, C. (2003). Application of the cognitive therapy model to initial crisis assessment. *International Journal of Mental Health Nursing, 12*, 30–38.

Cancer Facts and Figures. (2002). http://www.cancer.org./downloads/STT/CancerFacts&Figures 2002TM.pdf.

Candido, C. L., & Romney, D. M. (2002). Depression in paranoid and nonparanoid schizophrenic patients compared with major depressive disorder. *Journal of Affective Disorder, 70*(3), 261–271.

Canetto, S. S., & Lester, D. (1995). Gender and primary prevention of suicide mortality. *Suicide and Life-Threatening Behavior, 25,* 58–69.

Canetto, S. S., & Sakinofsky, I. (1998). The gender paradox in suicide. *Suicide and Life-Threatening Behavior, 28,* 1–23.

Canino, G., & Roberts, R. E. (2001). Suicidal behavior among Latino youth. *Suicide and Life-Threatening Behavior, 31,* 122–131.

Cantor, C. H., Cheng, A. T. A., Lee, C-S., Kerkhof, A. J. F. M., Traskman-Bendz, L., Mann, J. J., Williams, J. M. G., Pollack, L. R., Goldney, R. D., Lonnqvist, J. K., DeHert, M., Peuskens, J., Murphy, G. E., Lineham, M. M., Rizvi, S. L., Welch, S. S., Page, B., Allgulander, C., Bille-Brahe, U., Roy, A., Nielsen, D., Rylander, G., Sarchiapone, M., van Heeringen, K., Hawton, K., & Williams, J. M. G. (2000). Part I: Understanding suicidal behaviour. In K. Hawton & van Heeringen, K (Eds.), *The international handbook of suicide and attempted suicide* (pp. 9–234). New York: John Wiley & Sons.

Caplan, G. (1964). *Principles of preventive psychiatry.* New York: Basic Books.

Capuzzi, D. (1994). *Suicide prevention in the schools: Guidelines for middle and high school settings.* Alexandria, VA: American Counseling Association.

Capuzzi, D. (2002). Legal and ethical challenges in counseling suicidal students. *Professional School Counseling, 6,* 36–45.

Carlson, G. A., Asarnow, J. R., & Orbach, I. (1994). Developmental aspects of suicidal behavior in children and developmentally delayed adolescents. In G. G. Noam & S. Borst (Eds.), *Children, youth, and suicide: Developmental perspectives.* San Francisco: Jossey-Bass.

Carlyon, P., Carlyon, W., & McCarthy, A. R. (1998). Family and community involvement in school health. In E. Marx, S. F., Wooley, and D. Northrup (Eds.), *Health is academic: A guide to coordinated school health programs* (pp. 67–95). Newton, MA: Education Development Center.

Carpenter, K., M., Hasin, D. S., Allison, D. B., & Faith, M. S. (2000). Relationships between obesity and DSM-IV major depressive disorder, suicide ideation, and suicide attempts: Results from a general population study. *American Journal of Public Health, 90,* 251–257.

Cavaiola, A. A., & Lavender, N. (1999). Suicidal behavior in chemically dependent adolescents. *Adolescence, 34*(136), 735–744.

Centers for Disease Control and Prevention. (1992). *Youth suicide prevention programs: A resource guide.* Atlanta: Centers for Disease Control.

Centers for Disease Control and Prevention. (1996). Youth risk behavior surveillance: United States, 1995. *Morbidity and Mortality Weekly Reports, 45,* 41 (Table 10).

Centers for Disease Control and Prevention. (1998). *Ten Leading causes of death: American Indian and Alaskan Native, 1995–1997.* Office of Statistics and Programming, National Center for Injury Prevention and Control.

Centers for Disease Control and Prevention. (2001). *Youth risk behavior surveillance, United States, 2001.* Available at: http://www.cdc.gov/mmwr/preview/ mmwrhtml/ss5104a1. htm.

Centers for Disease Control and Prevention. (2003a). *Postservice mortality of Vietnam veterans: Follow-up of the Vietnam experience study cohort.* Available at: http://www.cdc.gov/nceh/veterans/ default1e.htm.

Centers for Disease Control and Prevention. (2003). *Asian American populations.* Available at: http://www.cdc.gov/omh/Populations/AsianAm/AsianAm.htm.

Centers for Disease Control and Prevention. (2004). National Center for Injury Prevention and Control. Retrieved November 29, 2005 from http://www.cdc.gov/ncipc/wisqars/.

Chamberlain, L. (1995). Chaos and change in a suicidal family. *Counseling and Values, 39,* 117–129.

Chang, E. C. (1998). Cultural differences, perfectionism, and suicidal risk in a college population: Does social problem solving still matter? *Cognitive Therapy and Research, 22,* 237–254.

Chen, Y., & Dilsaver, S. C. (1995). Comorbidity for obsessive-compulsive disorder in bipolar and unipolar disorders. *Psychiatric Research, 59,* 57–64.

Cholbi, M. (2000). Kant and the irrationality of suicide. *History of Philosophy Quarterly, 17*(2), 159–176.

Cholbi, M. (2004). Suicide. In Edward N. Zalta (Ed.), *The Stanford encyclopedia of philosophy (Summer 2004 Edition).* Retrieved June 28, 2005, from: http://plato.stanford.edu/archives/ sum2004/entries/suicide/.

Chotai, J., Renberg, E. S., & Jacobsson, L. (1999). Season of birth associated with the age and method of suicide. *Archives of Suicide Research, 5,* 245–254.

Chung, I. (2000). Suicidal behavior among Asian American college students: A psychosocial study. *Dissertation Abstracts International Section A: Humanities & Social Sciences, 60*(12-A), 4605.

Ciaramella, A., & Poli, P. (2001). Assessment of depression among cancer patients: The role of pain, cancer type and treatment. *Psycho-oncology, 10,* 156–163.

Ciffone, J. (1993). Suicide prevention: A classroom presentation to adolescents. *Social Work, 38,* 197–203.

Clarke, D. M. (1999). Autonomy, rationality, and the wish to die. *Journal of Medical Ethics 25,* 457–462.

Clum, G. A., & Curtin, L. (1993). Validity and reactivity of a system of self-monitoring suicide ideation. *Journal of Psychopathology and Behavioral Assessment, 15*(4), 375–385.

Coalition for Asian American Children and Families. (2001). *Fact Sheet.* Available at: www.cacf.org.

Cochrane-Brink, K. A., Lofchy, J. S., & Sakinofsky, I. (2000). Clinical rating scales in suicide risk assessment. *General Hospital Psychiatry, 22,* 445–451.

Cohen, B. M., & Cooper, M. Z. (1955). *A follow-up study of World War II prisoners of war.* Washington, DC: U.S. Government Printing Office.

Cohen, E. D. (2001). Permitted suicide: Model rules for mental health counseling. *Journal of Mental Health Counseling, 4,* 279–294.

Cohen, R. J. (1979). *Malpractice: A guide for mental health professionals.* New York: Free Press.

Cohler, B. J., & Jenuwine, M. J. (1996). Suicide, life course, and life story. In J. L. Pearson & Y. Conwell (Eds.), *Suicide and aging: International perspectives* (pp. 65–85). New York: Springer.

Cole, D. A. (1988). Hopelessness, social desirability, depression, and parasuicide in two college student samples. *Journal of Consulting and Clinical Psychology, 56,* 131–136.

Colt, G. H. (1992). *The enigma of suicide.* New York: Summit Books.

Conner, K. R., Duberstein, P. R., Conwell, Y., Seidlitz, L., & Caine, E. D. (2001). Psychological vulnerability to completed suicide: A review of empirical studies. *Suicide and Life-Threatening Behavior, 31,* 367–385.

Constantino, R. E., Sekula, L. K., & Rubinstein, E. N. (2001). Group intervention for widowed survivors of suicide. *Suicide and Life-Threatening Behavior, 31*(4), 428–441.

Conwell, Y. (2001). Suicide in later life: A review and recommendations for prevention. *Suicide and Life-Threatening Behavior, 31*(Suppl.), 32–47.

Conwell, Y. (1994). Suicide and terminal illness: Lessons from the HIV pandemic. *Suicide and Life-Threatening Behavior, 31*(Suppl.), 32–47.

Conwell, Y., Duberstein, P. R., & Caine, E. (2002). Risk factors for suicide in later life. *Biological Psychiatry, 52*(3) 193–204.

Coon, D. W., DeVries, H. M., & Gallagher-Thompson, D. (2004). Cognitive behavioral therapy with suicidal older adults. *Behavioral and Cognitive Psychotherapy,* 481–493.

Corbitt, E. M., Malone, K. M., Haas, G. L., & Mann, J. J. (1996). Suicidal behavior in patients with major depression and comorbid personality disorders. *Journal of Affective Disorders, 39*(1), 61–72.

Corrigan, P. W. (1998). The impact of stigma on severe mental illness. *Cognitive and Behavioral Practice, 5,* 201–222.

Corruble, E., Damy, C., & Guelfi, J. D. (1999). Impulsivity: A relevant dimension in depression regarding suicide attempts? *Journal of Affective Disorders, 53,* 211–215.

Cox, B., Direnfeld, D. M., Swinson, R. P., & Norton, G. R. (1994). Suicidal ideation and suicide attempts in panic disorder and social phobia. *American Journal of Psychiatry, 151,* 882–887.

Coyell, W. (1981). Obsessive-compulsive disorder and primary unipolar depression. Comparisons of background, family history, course, and mortality. *Journal of Nervous and Mental Disorders, 169,* 220–224.

Crawford, R. L. (1994). *Avoiding counselor malpractice (Legal Series Vol. 12).* Alexandria, VA: American Counseling Association.

Crosby, A. E., Cheltenham, M. P., & Sacks, J. J. (1999). Incidence of suicidal ideation and behavior in the United States, 1994. *Suicide & Life-Threatening Behavior, 29,* 131–140.

Cuffel, B. J. (1996). Comorbid substance use disorder: Prevalence, patterns of use, and course. In Brake R. E., & Mueser, K. T. (Eds.), *Dual diagnosis of major mental illness and substance disorder: Recent research and clinical implications* (pp. 93–105). Jossey-Bass, San Francisco.

Cull, J. G., & Gill, W. S. (1995). *Suicide Probability Scale Manual.* Western Psychological Services, Los Angeles.

Danto, B. L. (1971). Firearms and their role in homicide and suicide. *Life Threatening Behavior, 1*(1), 10–17.

Dattilio, R. M., & Padesky, C. A. (1990). *Cognitive therapy with couples.* Sarasota, FL: Professional Resource Exchange, Inc.

D'Augelli, A., & Hershberger, S. (1993). Lesbian, gay, and bisexual youth in community settings: Personal challenges and mental health problems. *American Journal of Community Psychology, 21,* 421–448.

Davidson M. W., & Range, L. M. (1999). Are teachers of children and young adolescents responsive to suicide prevention training modules? Yes. *Death Studies, 23,* 61–71.

Davis, P. A. (1983). *Suicidal adolescents.* Springfield, IL: Charles C. Thomas.

Davis, S. E., Williams, I. S., & Hays, L. W. (2002). Psychiatric inpatients' perceptions of written no suicide agreements: An exploratory study. *Suicide and Life-Threatening Behavior, 32*(1), 51–66.

DC Military. (2001). DCMilitary.com.

Dean, P. J., & Range, L. M. (1999). Testing the escape theory of suicide in an outpatient clinical population. *Cognitive Therapy and Research, 23,* 561–572.

Dear, G. E., Slattery, J. L., & Hillan, R. J. (2001). Evaluations of the quality of coping reported by prisoners who have self-harmed and those who have not. *Suicide and Life-Threatening Behavior, 31,* 442–450.

DeLeo, D., Hickey, P., Meneghel, G., & Cantor, C. H. (1999). Blindness, fear of sight loss, and suicide. *American Psychiatric, 40,* 339–344.

de Shazer, S. (1988). *Clues: Investigating solutions in brief therapy.* New York: Norton.

DeVivo, M. J., & Stover, S. L. (1995). Long-term survival and causes of death. In S. L. Stover, J. A. DeLisa, & G. G. Whiteneck (Eds.), *Spinal cord injury: Clinical outcomes from model systems* (pp. 185–212). Gaithersburg, MD: Aspen.

Dicker, R., Morrissey, R. F., Abikoff, H., Alvir, J. M. J., Weissman, K., Grover, J., Koplewicz, H. S. (1997). Hospitalizing the suicidal adolescent: Decision-making criteria of psychiatric residents. *Journal of the American Academy of Child and Adolescent Psychiatry, 36*(6), 769–776.

DiPasquale, T. & Gluck, J. P. (2001). Psychologists, psychiatrists, and physician-assisted suicide: The relationship between underlying beliefs and professional behavior. *Professional Psychology: Research and Practice, 32*(5), 501–506.

Domino, G., Shen, D., & Su, S. (2000). Acceptability of suicide: Attitudes in Taiwan and in the United States. *Omega, 40,* 293–306.

Donahue, M. J., & Benson, P. L. (1995). Religion and the well-being of adolescents. *Journal of Social Issues, 51*(2), 145–160.

Donaldson, D., Spirito, A., & Farnett, E. (2000). The role of perfectionism and depressive cognitions in understanding the hopelessness experienced by adolescent suicide attempters. *Child Psychiatry & Human Development, 31*(2), 99–111.

Doyle, B. B. (1990). Crisis management of the suicidal patient. In S. J. Blumenthal & D. J. Kupfer (Eds.), *Suicide over the life cycle: Risk factors, assessment and treatment of suicidal patients* (pp. 381–423). Washington, DC: American Psychiatric Association.

Drab, K. J. (2001). Ending the pain: Understanding and intervening with suicidal behaviors. Workshop presentation. November 6, 2001. The Horsham Clinic, Ambler, PA.

Duberstein, P. R., Conner, K. R., Conwell, Y., & Cox, C. (2001). Personality correlates of hopelessness in depressed inpatients 50 years of age and older. *Journal of Personality Assessment, 77,* 380–390.

Duncan, M. J., & Hensler, J. G. (2002). Aging alters in a region-specific manner serotonin transporter sites and 5-HT1A receptor-G protein interactions in hamster brain. *Neuropharmacology, 43,* 36–44.

Dunn, R. G., & Morrish-Vidners, D. D. (1987–1988). The psychological and social experience of suicide survivors. Omega: *Journal of Death and Dying, 18*(3), 175–215.

Dunne, E. J., (1992). Psychoeducational intervention strategies for survivors of suicide. *Crises, 13,* 35–41.

Dunnigan, J. F. (2002). *The next war zone: Confronting the global threat of cyberterrorism.* New York: McGraw-Hill.

Durkheim, E. (1951). *Suicide* (Spaulding, J. A., & Simpson, G., Trans). New York: Free Press. (Original work published 1897.)

Dyregrov, K., Nordanger, D., Dyregrov, A. (2003). Predictors of psychosocial distress after suicide, SIDS, and accidents. *Death Studies, 27,* 143–165.

Early, K. E., & Akers, R. L. (1993). "It's a White thing": An exploration of beliefs about suicide in the African-American community. *Deviant Behavior, 14*(4), 277–296.

Echterling, L. G., Presbury, J., & McKee, J. E. (2005). *Crisis intervention: Promoting resilience and resolution in troubled times.* Columbus, OH: Prentice Hall.

Eckersley, R., & Dear, K. (2002). Cultural correlates of youth suicide. *Social Science and Medicine, 55,* 1891–1904.

Edelstein, B., McKee, D., & Martin, R. (1999). Reasons for Living—Older Adults. Unpublished manuscript. Department of Psychology, West Virginia University.

Eggert, L., Thompson, E., & Herting, J. (1994). A measure of adolescent potential for suicide (MAPS): Development and preliminary findings. *Suicide and Life-Threatening Behavior, 24,* 359–381.

Ellis, T. (2001). Psychotherapy with suicidal patients. In D. Lester (Ed.), *Suicide prevention: Resources for the millennium* (pp. 129–152). New York: Brunner-Routledge.

Emmanuel, E. J., Fairclough, D. L., & Emmanuel, L. L. (2000). Attitudes and desires related to euthanasia and physician assisted suicide among terminally ill patients and their caregivers. *JAMA, 284,* 2460–2468.

Erikson, E. H. (1968). *Identity: Youth and crisis.* New York: Norton.

Etzersdorfer, E., & Sonneck, G. (1998). Preventing suicide by influencing mass-media reporting. The Viennese experience 1980–1996. *Archives of Suicide Research, 4*(1), 67–74.

Farberow, N. L. (1975). *Suicide in different cultures.* Baltimore, MD: University Park Press.

Farberow, N. L. (1992). The Los Angeles survivors-after-suicide program: An evaluation. *Crises, 13,* 23–29.

Farberow, N. L. (2001). Helping suicide survivors. In D. Lesters, (Ed.), *Suicide prevention: Resources for the millennium* (pp. 189–212). New York: Brunner-Routledge.

Farberow, N. L., & Shneidman, E. S. (Eds.), (1961). *The cry for help.* New York: McGraw-Hill.

Fawcett, J., & Rosenblate, R. (2000). Suicide within 24 hours after assessment in the emergency department: Look for and manage anxiety. *Psychiatric Annals, 30*(4), 228–231.

Fazel, S., & Danesh, J. (2002). Serious mental disorder in 23,000 prisoners: A systematic review of 62 studies. *The Lancet, 359,* 545–550.

Fenton, W. S., McGlashan, T. H., Victor, B. J., & Blyler, C. R. (1997). Symptoms, subtype, and suicidality in patients with schizophrenia spectrum disorders. *American Journal of Psychiatry, 154*(2), 199–204.

Fergusson, D. M., Horwood, J., & Beautrais, A. L. (1999). Is sexual orientation related to mental health problems and suicidality in young people? *Archives of General Psychiatry, 56,* 876–880.

Fergusson, D. M., & Lynskey, M. T. (1995). Suicide attempts and suicidal ideation in a birth cohort of 16 year-old New Zealanders. *Journal of the American Academy of Child and Adolescent Psychiatry, 34,* 1308–1317.

Fernandez-Pol, B. (1986). Characteristics of 77 Puerto Ricans who attempted suicide. *American Journal of Psychiatry, 143,* 1460–1463.

Feskanich, D., Hastrup, J. L., Marshall, J. R., Colditz, G. A., Stampfer, M. J., Willett, W. C., & Kawachi, I. (2002). Stress and suicide in the Nurses' Health Study. *Journal of Epidemiology and Community Health, 56,* 95–98.

Filiberti, A., Ripamonti, C., Totis, A., Ventrafridda, V., DeConno, F., Contiero, P., & Tamburini, M. (2000). Characteristics of terminal cancer patients who committed suicide during a home palliative care program. *Journal of Pain and Symptom Management, 22,* 544–553.

Finzi, R., Ram, A., Shnit, D., Har-Even, D., Tyano, S., & Weizman, A. (2001). Depressive symptoms and suicidality in physically abused children. *American Journal of Orthopsychiatry, 71*(1), 98–107.

Firestone, R. W., & Firestone, L. A. (1998). Voices in suicide: The relationship between self-destructive thought processes, maladaptive behavior, and self-destructive manifestations. *Death Studies, 22,* 411–433.

Fisher, B. J., Haythornthwaite, J. A., Heinberg, L. J., Clark, M., & Reed, J. (2001). Suicidal intent in patients with chronic pain. *Pain, 89,* 199–206.

Flett, G. L., Madorsky, D., Hewitt, P. L., & Heisel, M. J. (2002). Perfectionism cognitions, rumination, and psychological distress. *Journal of Rational-Emotive and Cognitive-Behavior Therapy, 20,* 33–47.

Flint, E. P., Hays, J. C., Krishnan, K. R. R., Meador, K. G., & Blazer, D. G. (1998). Suicidal behaviors in depressed men with a family history of suicide: Effects of psychosocial factors and age. *Aging & Mental Health, 2,* 286–299.

Flouri, E. & Buchanan, A. (2002). The protective role of parental involvement in adolescent suicide. *Crises, 23,* 17–22.

Foo, L. J. (2002) *Asian American women: Issues, concerns and responsive human and civil rights advocacy.* The Ford Foundation. Available at: http://www.fordfound.org/publications/ recent_articles/.

Foster, P., & Bilsker, D. (2002) Emergency psychiatry and the suicidal patient. *Crises, 23,* 83–85.

Frank, E., & Dingle, A. D. (1999). Self-reported depression and suicide attempts among U.S. women physicians. *American Journal of Psychiatry, 156,* 1887–1894.

Fremouw, W. J., dePerczel, M., & Ellis, T. (1990). *Suicide risk: Assessment and response guidelines*. New York: Pergamon Press.

Fruehwald, S., Loeffler-Stastka, H., Eher, R., Saletu, B., & Baumhackel, U. (2001). Depression and quality of life in multiple sclerosis. *Acta Neurologica Scandinavica, 104,* 257–261.

Galloucis, M., & Francek, H. (2002). The Juvenile Suicide Assessment: An instrument for the assessment and management of suicide risk with incarcerated juveniles. *International Journal of Emergency Mental Health, 4,* 181–200.

Garfinkel, B. D., Froese, A., & Hood, J. (1982). Suicide attempts in children and adolescents. *American Journal of Psychiatry, 139,* 1257–1261.

Genes and Disease. (2002). http://www.ncbi.nlm.nih.gov/disease/Cancer.html.

Giddens, A. (1971). *The sociology of suicide: A selection of readings*. London: Frank Cass & Company.

Gilliland, B. E., & James, R. K. (1997). *Crisis intervention strategies* (3rd ed). Pacific Grove, CA: Brooks Cole.

Gliatto, M. F., & Rai, A. K. (March 15, 1999). Evaluation and treatment of patients with suicidal ideation. *American Family Physician, 59*(6), 1500–1506. Available at: http://www.aafp.org/ afp/990315ap/ 1500.html.

Goggin, K., Sewell, M., Ferrando, S., Evans, S., Fishman, D., & Rabkin, J. (2000). Plans to hasten death among gay men with HIV/AIDS: Relationship to psychological adjustment. *AIDS Care, 12,* 125–136.

Goldston, D. B., Daniel, S. S., Reboussin, D. M., Reboussin, B. A., Frazier, P. H., Kelley, A. E. (1999). Suicide attempts among formerly hospitalized adolescents: A prospective naturalistic study of risk during the first 5 years after discharge. *Journal of the American Academy of Child and Adolescent Psychiatry, 38,* 660–671.

Gordon, R. S. (1983). An operational classification of disease prevention. *Public Health Reports, 98,* 107–109.

Gould, M. S., Marracco, F. A., Kleinman, M., Thomas, J. G., Mostkoff, K., Cote, J., & Davies, M. (2005). Evaluating iatrogenic risk of youth suicide screening programs: A randomized controlled trial. *Journal of the American Medical Association, 293*(13), 1635–1643.

Gould, M., Jamieson, P., & Romer, D. (2003). Media contagion and suicide among the young. *American Behavioral Scientist, 46,* 1269–1284.

Granboulan, V., Zivi, A., & Basquin, M. (1997). Double suicide attempt among adolescents. *Journal of Adolescent Health, 21,* 128–130.

Granello, D. H. (2004). Assisting beginning counselors in becoming more gay affirmative: A workshop approach. *Journal of Humanistic Counseling, Education, and Development, 43*(1), 50–64.

Granello, P. F., & Granello, D. H. (1998). Training counseling students to use outcomes research. *Counselor Education and Supervision, 37*(4), 224–237.

Granello, P. F., & Witmer, J. M. (1998). Standards of care: Potential implications for the counseling profession. *Journal of Counseling & Development, 76*(4), 371–380.

Green, A. H. (1978). Self destructive behavior in battered children. *American Journal of Psychiatry, 135*(5), 579–582.

Greening, L., & Stoppelbein, L. (2002). Religiosity, attributional style, and social support as psychosocial buffers for African American and white adolescents' perceived risk for suicide. *Suicide and Life-Threatening Behavior, 32,* 404–417.

Group for the Advancement of Psychiatry, (1989). *Suicide and ethnicity in the United States*. New York: Brunner/ Mazel.

Gustafsson, L., & Jacobsson, L. (2000). On mental disorder and somatic disease in suicide: A psychological autopsy study of 100 suicides in northern Sweden. *Nordic Journal of Psychiatry, 54,* 383–395.

Gut-Fayand, A., Dervaux, A., Olie, J-P., Loo, H., Poirier, M-F., Krebs, M-O. (2001). Substance abuse and suicidality in schizophrenia: A common risk factor linked to impulsivity. *Psychiatry Research, 102*(1), 65–72.

Gutierrez, P. M., Thakkar, R. R., Kuczen, C. (2000). Exploration of the relationship between physical and/or sexual abuse, attitudes about life and death, and suicidal ideation in young women. *Death Studies, 24,* 675–688.

Guze, S. B., & Robins, E. (1970). Suicide and primary affective disorders. *British Journal of Psychiatry, 117*(539), 437–438.

Hall, B. L., & Epp, H. L., (2001). Can professionals and nonprofessionals work together following a suicide? *Crises, 22,* 74–78.

Hargis, D. L. (1997). Relationships among factors underlying functioning with chronic pain and risk of suicide. *Dissertation Abstracts International, Vol. 57*(8-A), 3403.

Harkavy, F. H., & Asnis, G. (1989a). Assessment of suicidal behavior: A new instrument. *Psychiatric Annals, 19*, 382–387.

Harkavy, F. H., & Asnis, G. (1989b). Correction. *Psychiatric Annals, 19*, 438.

Harrington, R., Kerfoot, M., Dyer, E., McNiven, F., Gill, J., Harrington, V., Woodham, A., & Byford, S. (1998). Randomized trial of a home-based family intervention for children who have deliberately poisoned themselves. *Journal of the American Academy of Child and Adolescent Psychiatry, 37*, 512–518.

Harris, E. C., & Barraclough, B. (1994). Suicide as an outcome for mental disorders. A meta-analysis. *British Journal of Psychiatry, 170*, 205–228.

Harwood, D., Hawton, K., Hope, T., & Jacoby, R. (2001). Psychiatric disorder and personality factors associated with suicide in older people: A descriptive and case-control study. *International Journal of Geriatric Psychiatry, 16*, 155–165.

Harwood, D., Hawton, K., Hope, T., & Jacoby, R., (2002). The grief experiences and need of bereaved relatives and friends of older people dying through suicide: A descriptive and case-control study. *Journal of Affective Disorders, 72*, 185–194.

Harwood, D. G., & Sultzer, D. L. (2002). "Life is not worth living": Hopelessness in Alzheimer's disease. *Journal of Geriatric Psychiatry and Neurology, 15*, 39–43.

Hastings, M. E., Northman, L. M., Tangney, J. P. (1990). Shame, guilt, and suicide. In T. E. Joiner & M. D. Rudd (Eds.), *Suicide science: Expanding the boundaries* (pp. 67–79). Boston: Kluwer Academic Publishers.

Havighurst, R. J. (1972). *Developmental tasks and education*. New York: David McKay Company.

Hawton, K. (2000). Sex and suicide: Gender differences in suicidal behavior. *British Journal of Psychiatry, 177*, 484–485.

Hawton, K., & Simkin, S. (2003). Helping people bereaved by suicide: Their needs may require special attention. *British Medical Journal, 327*, 177–178.

Hawton, K., Simkin, S., Rue, J., Haw, C., Barbour, F., Clements, A., Sakarovitch, C., & Deeks, J. (2002). Suicide in female nurses in England and Wales. *Psychological Medicine, 32*, 239–250.

Hayes, L. M. (1997). From chaos to calm: One jail system's struggle with suicide prevention. *Behavioral Sciences and the Law, 15*, 399–413.

Hazler, R. (1988). Stumbling into unconditional positive regard. *Journal of Counseling and Development, 67*, 130.

Healthy Start. (2000). National Healthy Start Association. Retrieved on December 29, 2005, from: http://www.healthystartassoc.org/.

Hearst, N., Newman, T. B., & Hulley, S. B. (1986). Delayed effects of the military draft on mortality: A randomized natural experiment. *The New England Journal of Medicine, 314*, 620–624.

Heikkinen, M. E., Aro, H. M., & Loennqvist, J. K. (1993). Life events and social support in suicide. *Suicide & Life-Threatening Behavior, 23*, 343–358.

Heikkinen, M. E., Aro, H. M., & Loennqvist, J. K. (1994). Recent life events, social support, and suicide. *Acta Psychiatica Scandinavica, 89*, 65–72.

Heila, H., Isometsa, E. T., Henriksson, M. M., Heikkinen, M. E., Marttunen, M. J., & Lonnqvist, J. K. (1997). Suicide and schizophrenia: A nationwide psychological autopsy study on age- and sex-specific clinical characteristics of 92 suicide victims with schizophrenia. *American Journal of Psychiatry, 154*(9), 1235–1242.

Helms, J. F. (2003). Barriers to help-seeking among 12th graders. *Journal of Educational and Psychological Consultation, 14*(1) 27–40.

Hem, E., Berg, A. M. A., & Ekeberg, O. (2001). Suicide in police: A critical review. *Suicide and Life-Threatening Behavior, 21*, 224–233.

Hemphill, R. F., & Thornley, F. I. (1969). Suicide pacts. *Medical Journal of South Africa, 43*, 1335–1338.

Hendin H., Lipschitz, A., Maltsberger, J. T., Haas, A. P., & Wynecoop, S. (2000). Therapists' reactions to patient's suicides. *American Journal of Psychiatry, 157*, 2022–2027.

Henriques, G., Beck, A. T., & Brown, G. T. (2003). Cognitive therapy for adolescent and young adult suicide attempters. *American Behavioral Scientist, 46*, 1258–1268.

Herek, G. M. (1996). Heterosexism and homophobia. In R. P. Cabaj & T. S. Stein (Ed.), *Textbook of homosexuality and mental health* (pp. 101–113). Washington, DC: American Psychiatric Association.

Hernandez, J. T., Lodico, M., & DiClemente, R. J. (1993). The effects of child abuse and race on risk-taking in male adolescents. *Journal of the National Medical Association, 85*, 593–597.

Herring, R. (1990). Suicide in the middle school: Who said kids will not? *Elementary School Guidance & Counseling, 25*, 129–138.

Hershberger, S. L., Pilkington, N. W., & D'Augelli, A. R. (1997). Predictors of suicide attempts among gay, lesbian, and bisexual youth. *Journal of Adolescent Research, 12*, 477–497.

Higgins, E. T. (1987). Self-discrepancy: A theory relating self and affect. *Psychological Review, 94*(3), 319–340.

Hilliard-Lysen, J., & Riemer, J. W. (1988). Occupational stress and suicide among dentists. *Deviant Behavior, 9*, 333–346.

Hine, T. J., Pitchford, N. J., Kingdom, F. A. A., & Koenekoop, R. (2000). Blindness and high suicide risk? *American Psychiatric, 41*, 370–371.

Hisnanick, J. (1994). Comparative analysis of violent deaths in American Indians and Alaskan natives. *Social Biology, 41*, 96–109.

Ho, T. P., Leung, W-L. P., Hung, S., Lee, C., & Tang, C. (2000). The mental health of the peers of suicide completers and attempters. *Journal of Child Psychology & Psychiatry, 3*, 301–308.

Hockberger, R. S., & Rothstein, R. J. (1988). Assessment of suicide potential by nonpsychiatrists using the SAD PERSONS score. *Journal of Emergency Medicine, 6*, 99–107.

Holland, S., & Griffin, A. (1984). Adolescent and adult drug treatment clients: Patterns and consequences of use. *Journal of Psychoactive Drugs, 16*, 79–88.

Holmes, C. B., & Howard, M. E. (1980). Recognition of suicide lethality factors by physicians, mental health professionals, ministers, and college students. *Journal of Consulting and Clinical Psychology, 48*, 383–387.

Horesh, N., Rolnick, T., Iancut, I., Dannon, P., Lepkifker, E., Apter, A., & Kotler, M. (1997). Anger, impulsivity and suicide risk. *Psychotherapy & Psychosomatics, 66*, 92–96.

Hovey, J. D., & King, C. A. (1997). Suicidality among acculturating Mexican Americans: Current knowledge and directions for research. *Suicide and Life-Threatening Behavior, 27*, 92–97.

Hufford, M. R. (2001). Alcohol and suicidal behavior. *Clinical Psychology Review, 21*, 797–811.

Hughes, D., & Kleespies, P. (2001). Suicide in the medically ill. *Suicide and Life-Threatening Behavior, 31*(Suppl.), 48–59.

Ialongo, N., McCreary, B. K., Pearson, J. L., Koenig, A. L., Wagner, B. M., Schmidt, N. B., Poduska, J., & Kellam, S. G. (2002). Suicidal behavior among urban, African American young adults. *Suicide and Life-Threatening Behavior, 32*, 256–271.

Ikeda, R. M., Kresnow, J., Mercy, J. A., Powell, K. E., Simon, T. R., Potter, L. B., Durant, T. M., & Swahn, M. H. (2001). Medical conditions and nearly-lethal suicide attempts. *Suicide and Life-Threatening Behavior, 32*(Suppl.), 60–67.

Indian Health Service. (2001). *Alcohol & substance abuse: Indian Health Service Clinical Services*. Available at: http://www.ihs.gov/adminmngrresources/budget/old%5Fsite/cj2001/alc%26sub.pdf.

Indian Health Service. (2002). *IHS Injury Prevention Program*. Available at: http://www.ihs.gov/ nonmedical-programs/dehs/documents/orientation_inj_prev_v2.ppt.

Indian Health Service. (2003). *Suicide Prevention Week: May 4–10, 2003*. Available at: http://www. ihs.gov/publicinfo/publicaffairs/pressreleases/press%5Frelease%5F2003/11%2Dsuicide%5Fweek.pdf.

Iribarren, C., Sidney, S., Jacobs, Jr., D. R., & Weisner, C. (2000). Hospitalization for suicide attempt and completed suicide: Epidemiological features in a managed care population. *Social Psychiatry, 35*, 288–296.

Isaacs, M. L. (2003) Data-driven decision making: The engine of accountability. *Professional School Counseling, 6*, 288–295.

Ivanoff, A., Jang, S. J., Smyth, N. F., & Linehan, M. M. (1994). Fewer reasons for staying alive when you are thinking of killing yourself: The Brief Reasons for Living Inventory. *Journal of Psychopathology and Behavioral Assessment, 16*(1), 1–13.

Jacobs, D. G., Brewer, M., Klein-Benheim, M. (1999). Suicide assessment: An overview and recommended protocol. In D. G. Jacobs (Ed.), *The Harvard Medical School guide to suicide assessment and intervention* (pp. 3–39). San Francisco: Jossey-Bass.

Jacobson, G. (1999). The inpatient management of suicidality. In D. G. Jacobs (Ed.), *The Harvard Medical School guide to suicide assessment and intervention* (pp. 383–405). San Francisco: Jossey-Bass.

James, W. (1947). *Pragmatism and other writings*. New York: Penguin.

Jamison, K. R. (1999). *Night falls fast*. New York: Random House.

Jamison, K. R. (2000). *Night falls fast: Understanding suicide*. New York: Vintage.

Janowsky, D. S., Morter, S., & Hong, L. (2002). Relationship of Myers Briggs type indicator personality characteristics to suicidality in affective disorder patients. *Journal of Psychiatric Research, 36,* 33–39.

Jobes, D. A., Berman, A. L., & Josselson, A. R. (1989). Improving the validity and reliability of medical-legal certifications of suicide. *Suicide and Life-Threatening Behavior, 17*(4), 310–325.

Jobes, D. A., Eyman, J. R., & Yufit, R. I. (1991). How clinicians assess suicide risk in adolescents and adults. *Crisis Intervention and Time Limited Treatment, 2*(1), 1–12.

Joe, S., & Kaplan, M. S. (2001). Suicide and African American men. *Suicide and Life-Threatening Behavior, 31*(Suppl.), 106–121.

Johnson, C. (1995). Determinants of adaptation of oldest old black Americans. *Journal of Aging Studies, 9,* 231–244.

Johnson, S., & Maile., L. (1987). *Suicide and the schools: A handbook for prevention, intervention, and rehabilitation*. Springfield, IL: C.C. Thomas.

Joiner, T. (2001). New life in suicide science. In T. Joiner and M. D. Rudd (Eds.), *Suicide science: Expanding the boundaries* (pp. 1–8). Boston: Kluwer.

Jordan, J. R. (2001). Is suicide bereavement different?: A reassessment of the literature. *Suicide and Life Threatening Behavior, 31,* 91–102.

Juhnke, G. (1994). SAD PERSONS Scale review. *Measurement & Evaluation in Counseling & Development, 27,* 325–327.

Juhnke, G. (1996). The Adapted SAD PERSONS: A suicide assessment scale designed for use with children. *Elementary School Guidance & Counseling, 30,* 252–258.

Juhnke, G. A., & Shoffner, M. F. (1999). The family debriefing model: An adapted critical incident stress debriefing for parents and older sibling suicide survivors. *The Family Journal: Counseling and Therapy for Couples and Families, 7,* 342–348.

Kaiser Commission. (1997). *Native Americans and Medicaid: Coverage and financing issues*. Available at: http://www.kff.org/content/archive/2101/polbren.html.

Kalafat, J., & Elias, M. J. (1995). Suicide prevention in an educational context: Broad and narrow foci. *Suicide and Life Threatening Behavior, 25,* 123–133.

Kalafat, J., & Ryerson, D. M. (1999). The implementation and institutionalization of a school-based youth suicide prevention program. *Journal of Primary Prevention, 19,* 157–175.

Kalichman, S. C., Heckman, T., Kochman, A., Sikkema, K., & Bergholte, J. (2000). Depression and thoughts of suicide among middle-aged and older persons living with HIV-AIDS. *Psychiatric Services, 51,* 903–907.

Kaplan, M. S., & Geling, O. (1998). Firearm suicides and homicides in the United States: Regional variations and patterns of gun ownership. *Social Science and Medicine, 46,* 1227–1233.

Kaslow, N. J., Thompson, M. P., Brooks, A. E., & Twomey, H. B. (2000). Ratings of family functioning of suicidal and nonsuicidal African American women. *Journal of Family Psychology, 14,* 585–599.

Kataoka, S. H., Zhang, L., & Wells, K. B. (2002). Unmet need for mental health care among U.S. children: Variation by ethnicity and insurance status. *American Journal of Psychiatry, 159,* 1548–1555.

Katz, P. (1995). The psychotherapeutic treatment of suicidal adolescents. *Adolescent Psychiatry, 20,* 325–341.

Keehn, R. (1980). Follow-up studies of World War II and Korean conflict prisoners. *American Journal of Epidemiology, 111,* 194–211.

Kegan, R. (1994). *In over our heads: The mental demands of modern life*. Cambridge, MA: Harvard University Press.

Kellner, C. H., Fink, M., Knapp, R., Petrieds, G., Husain, M., Rummans, T., Mueller, M., Bernstein, H., Rasmussen, K., O'Connor, K., Smith, G., Rush, A. J., Biggs, M., McClintock, S., Bailine, S., & Malur, C. (2005). Relief of expressed suicidal intent by ECT: A consortium for research in ECT study. *American Journal of Psychiatry, 162,* 977–982.

Kennedy, G. J., & Tanenbaum, S. (2000). Suicide and aging: International perspectives. *Psychiatric Quarterly, 71,* 345–362.

Kennedy, G. J., Kelman, H. R., Thomas, C., Wisniewski., W., Meta, H., & Hinit, P. E. (1989). Hierarchy of characteristics associated with depressive symptoms in an urban elderly sample. *American Journal of Psychiatry, 146,* 220–225.

Kernberg, O. F. (2001). The suicidal risk in severe personality disorders: Differential diagnosis and treatment. *Journal of Personality Disorders, 15*(3), 195–208.

Kessler, R. C., McGonagle, K. A., Zhao, S., Nelson, C. B., Hughes, M., Eshleman, S., Wittchen, H.-U., & Kendler, K. S. (1994). Lifetime and 12-month prevalence of DSM-IIIR psychiatric disorders in the United States: Results from the National Comorbidity Survey. *Archives of General Psychiatry, 51*, 8–19.

Khan, A., Leventhal, R. M., Khan, S., & Brown, W. A. (2002). Suicide risk in patients with anxiety disorders: A meta-analysis of the FDA database. *Journal of Affective Disorders, 68*, 183–190.

Khan, A., Warner, H., & Brown, W. (2000). Symptom reduction and suicide risk in patients treated with placebo in antidepressant clinical trials: An analysis of the food and drug administration database. *Archives of General Psychiatry, 57*, 311–317.

Kimbrough, R. M., Molock, S. D., & Walton, K. (1996). Perception of social support, acculturation, depression, and suicidal ideation among African American college students at predominantly Black and predominantly White universities. *Journal of Negro Education, 65*, 295–307.

King, A., Kovan, R., London, R., & Bongar, B. (1999). Toward a standard of care for treating suicidal outpatients: A survey of social workers' beliefs about appropriate treatment behaviors. *Suicide and Life-Threatening Behavior, 29*(4), 347–352.

King, C. A., Hovey, J. D., Brand, E., Wilson, R., & Ghaziuddin, N. (1997). Suicidal adolescents after hospitalization: Parent and family impacts on treatment follow-through. *Journal of the American Academy of Child and Adolescent Psychiatry, 36*(1), 85–93.

King, J. D., & Kowalchuk, B. (1994). *Manual for the Inventory of Suicide Orientation-30*. Minneapolis, MN: National Computer Systems.

King, K. A., Price, J. H., Telljohann, S., K., & Wahl, J. (1999). How confident do high school counselors feel in recognizing students at risk for suicide? *American Journal of Health Behavior, 23*(6), 457–467.

King, S. R., & Hampton, W. R. (1996). College students' views on suicide. *Journal of American College Health, 44*, 283–288.

Kishi, Y., & Robinson, R. G. (1996). Suicidal plans following spinal cord injury: A six-month study. *Journal of Neuropsychiatry, 8*, 442–445.

Kleespies, P. M., Deleppo, J. D., Gallagher, P. L., & Niles, B. L. (1999). Managing suicidal emergencies: Recommendations for the practitioner. *Professional Psychology: Research and Practice, 30*(5), 454–463.

Kleespies, P. M., & Dettmer, E. L. (2000). An evidence-based approach to evaluating and managing suicidal emergencies, 56(9), 1109–1130.

Kleespies, P. M., Hughes, D. H., & Gallacher, F. P. (2000). Suicide in the medically and terminally ill: Psychological and ethical considerations. *Journal of Clinical Psychology, 56*, 1153–1171.

Kleespies, P. M., Smith, M. R., & Becker, B. R. (1990). Psychology interns as patient suicide survivors: incidence, impact, and recovery. *Professional Psychology: Research & Practice, 21*, 257–263.

Klimes-Dougan, B., Free, K., Ronsaville, D., Stilwell, J., Welsh, C. J., & Radke-Yarrow, M. (1999). Suicidal ideation and attempts: A longitudinal investigation of children of depressed and well mothers. *Journal of the American Academy of Adolescent Psychiatry, 38*, 651–659.

Knop, J., & Fischer, A. (1981). Duodenal ulcer, suicide, psychopathology and alcoholism. *Acta Psychiatrica Scandinavica, 63*, 346–355.

Knott, E. C., & Range, L. M. (1998). Content analysis of previously suicidal college students' experiences. *Death Studies, 22*, 171–180.

Kochenek, K. D., & Smith, B. L. (2004). Deaths: Preliminary data for 2002. National Vital Statistics Report, Vol. 52, No. 13. Hyattsville, MD: National Center for Health Statistics.

Komiti, A., Judd, F., Grech, P., Mijch, A., Hoy, J., Lloyd, J. H., & Street. A. (2001). Suicidal behaviour in people with HIV/AIDS: A review. *Australian and New Zealand Journal of Psychiatry, 35*, 747–757.

Koocher, G. P. (1973). Childhood, death, and cognitive development. *Developmental Psychology, 9*, 369–375.

Kosky, R., Silburn, S., & Zubrick, S. R. (1990). Are children and adolescents who have suicidal thoughts different from those who attempt suicide? *The Journal of Nervous and Mental Disease, 178*, 38–43.

Kovacs, M., Goldstone, D., & Gatsonis, C. (1993). Suicidal behavior and childhood-onset depressive disorders: A longitudinal investigation. *Journal American Academy Child Adolescent Psychiatry, 32*, 8–20.

Kposowa, A. J., Breault, K. D., & Singh, G. K. (1995). White male suicide in the United States: A multivariate individual-level analysis. *Social Forces, 74*, 315–323.

Kreyenbuhl, J. A., Kelly, D. L., & Conley, R. R. (2002). Circumstances of suicide among individuals with schizophrenia. *Schizophrenia Research 58*(2–3), 253–261.

Kroll, J. (2000). Use of no-suicide contracts by psychiatrists in Minnesota. *American Journal of Psychiatry, 157,* 1684–1686.

Kwong, K. (2000). *Depression and suicidal ideation among young Asian Americans.* Coalition for Asian American Children and Families. New York: Author.

Lau, A. S., Jernewall, N. M., Zane, N., & Myers, H. F. (2002). Correlates of suicidal behaviors among Asian American outpatient youths. *Cultural Diversity & Ethnic Minority Psychology, 8,* 199–213.

Lazear, K., Roggenbaum, S., & Blase, K. (2003). *Youth Suicide Prevention School-Based Guide.* Available at: http://theguide.fmhi.usf.edu/pdf/Overview.pdf.

Leenaars, A. A. (1996). Suicide: A multidimensional malaise. *Suicide and Life-Threatening Behavior, 26*(3), 221–236.

Leenaars, A. A. (2001). Suicide prevention in schools: Resources for the millennium. In D. Lester (Ed.), *Suicide Prevention* (pp. 213–235). New York: Brunner-Routledge.

Leenaars, A. A. (2004). *Psychotherapy with suicidal people: A person-centered approach.* Chicester: John Wiley & Sons.

Leenaars, A. A., de Wilde, E. J., Wenckstern, S., & Kral, M. (2001). Suicide notes of adolescents: A life-span comparison. *Canadian Journal of Behavioural Science, 33*(1), 45–57.

Lester, D., & Leenaars, A. A. (1996). The ethics of suicide and suicide prevention. *Death Studies, 20,* 163–184.

Lester, D. (1993a). Challenges in preventing suicide. *Crisis: The Journal of Crisis Intervention and Suicide Prevention, 14*(4), 187–189.

Lester, D. (1993c). *Suicide behind bars: Prediction and prevention.* Philadelphia: Charles Press.

Lester, D. (1993d). Suicide in the military as a function of involvement in war. *Acta Psychiatrica Scandinavica, 88,* 223.

Lester, D. (1994a). Are there unique features of suicide in adults of different ages and developmental stages? *Omega: Journal of Death and Dying, 29*(4), 337–348.

Lester, D. (1994b). Differences in the epidemiology of suicide in Asian Americans by nation of origin. *Omega: Journal of Death & Dying, 29,* 89–93.

Lester, D. (1997). The role of shame in suicide. *Suicide and Life-Threatening Behavior, 27,* 352–361.

Lester, D. (1998). Preventing suicide by restricting access to methods for suicide. *Archives of Suicide Research, 4,* 7–24.

Lester, D. (2000). The social causes of suicide: A look at Durkheim's *Le Suicide* one hundred years later. *Omega, 40*(2), 307–321.

Lester, D. (2004). Guttman scaling national laws on suicide. *Crises, 23,* 89–90.

Lester, D. (2005). Dialectical behavior therapy. In R. I. Yufit & D. Lester (Eds.), *Assessment, treatment and prevention of suicidal behavior* (pp. 279–290). New York: John Wiley & Sons.

Levin, J., Taylor, R., & Chatters, L. (1994). Race and gender differences in religiosity among older adults: Findings from four national surveys. *Journal of Gerontology, 49,* S137–S145.

Lewinsohn, P. M., Rohde, P., & Seeley, J. R. (1993). Psychosocial characteristics of adolescents with a history of suicide attempt. *Journal of the American Academy of Child & Adolescent Psychiatry, 32*(1), 60–68.

Lindeman, S., Heinänen, H., Väisänen, E., & Lönnqvist, J. (1998). Suicide among medical doctors: Psychological autopsy data on seven cases. *Archives of Suicide Research, 4,* 135–141.

Lindenmayer, J. P., Czobor, P., Alphs, R., Anand, R., Islam, Z., & Pestreich, L. (2001). The InterSept Scale for Suicidal Thinking (ISST): A new assessment instrument for suicidal patients with schizophrenia. *Schizophrenia Research, 49*(Suppl. 1–2): 5.

Linehan, M. (1993). *Skills training manual for treating Borderline Personality Disorder.* New York: Guilford.

Linehan, M. M. (1981). Suicidal behaviors questionnaire. Unpublished inventory, University of Washington, Seattle, Washington.

Linehan, M. M. (1996). Suicidal Behaviors Questionnaire (SBQ). Unpublished manuscript, Department of Psychology, University of Washington, Seattle, WA.

Linehan, M. M. (2005). Dialectical Behavior Therapy: Overview and examples with suicidal clients. Presentation at the Evolution of Psychotherapy Conference, December 8, 2005. Anaheim, CA.

Linehan, M., Armstrong, H. Suarez, A., Allmon, D., & Heard, H. (1991) Cognitive-behavioral treatment of chronically parasuicidal borderline patients. *Archives of General Psychiatry, 48,* 1060–1064.

Linehan, M., & Comtois, K. (1997). *Lifetime parasuicide count.* Unpublished instrument, University of Washington, Seattle, WA.

Linehan, M. M., Tutek, D. A., Heard, H. L., & Armstrong, H. E. (1994). Interpersonal outcome of cognitive behavioral treatment for chronically suicidal borderline patients. *American Journal of Psychiatry, 151*(12), 1771–1776.

Lish, J. D., Zimmerman, M., Farber, N. J., Lush, D. T., Kuzma, M A., & Plescia, G. (1996). Suicide screening in a primary care setting at a Veterans Affairs Medical Center. *Psychosomatics, 37,* 413–424.

Litman, R. E. (1995). Suicide prevention in a treatment setting. *Suicide and Life-Threatening Behavior, 25,* 134–142.

Litman, R. E., & Farberow, N. L. (1961). Emergency evaluation of self-destructive behavior. In N. Farberow and E. Schneidman (Eds.), *The cry for help.* New York: McGraw-Hill.

Llorente, M. D., Eisdorfer, C., Loewenstein, D. A., & Zarate, Y. A. (1996). Suicide among Hispanic elderly: Cuban Americans in Dade County, Florida 1990–1993. *Journal of Mental Health & Aging, 2,* 79–87.

Loesch, L. C., & Ritchie, M. H. (2005). *The accountable school counselor.* Austin, TX: Pro-Ed.

Long, D., D., & Miller, B. J. (1991). Suicidal tendency and multiple sclerosis. *Health and Social Work, 16,* 104–109.

Lucas, C. (1997). The Multimedia Adolescent Suicide Interview (MASI). Unpublished instrument. New York: Columbia University, New York State Psychiatric Institute.

Luoma, J. B., Martin, C. E., & Pearson, J. L. (2002). Contact with mental health and primary care providers before suicide: A review of the evidence. *American Journal of Psychiatry, 159,* 909–916.

Lyon, M. E., Benoit, M., O'Donnell, R. M., Getson, P. R., Silber, T., & Walsh, T. (2000). Assessing African American adolescents' risk for suicide attempts: Attachment theory. *Adolescence, 35*(137), 121–134.

Mackenzie, T. B., & Popkin, M. K. (1990). Medical illness and suicide. In S. Blumenthal & D. J. Kupfer (Eds.), *Suicide over the life cycle: Risk factors, assessment, and treatment of suicidal patients* (pp. 205–232). Washington, DC: American Psychiatric Association.

Mackesy-Amiti, M. E., Fendrich, M., Libby, S., Goldenberg, D., & Grossman, J. (1996). Assessment of knowledge gains in proactive training for postvention. *Suicide and Life Threatening Behavior, 26,* 161–174.

Mackinnon, A., Copolov, D. L., & Trauer, T. (2004). Factors associated with compliance and resistance to command hallucinations. *Journal of Nervous and Mental Disease, 191*(5), 357–362.

MacNair, R. M. (2002). Perpetration-induced traumatic stress in combat veterans. Peace and conflict; Journal of peace. *Psychology, 8,* 63–72.

Malbergier, A., & deAndrade, G. (2001). Depressive disorders and suicide attempts in injecting drug users with and without HIV infection. *AIDS Care, 13,* 141–150.

Malley, P. B., & Kush, F. (1994). School-based adolescent suicide prevention and intervention programs: A survey. *School Counselor, 42,* 130–138.

Malone, K. M., Haas, G. L., Sweeney, J. A., & Mann, J. J. (1995). Major depression and the risk of attempted suicide. *Journal of Affective Disorders, 34,* 173–185.

Malone, K., & Mann, J. J. (2003). Serotonin and the suicidal brain. Accessed on January 6, 2003, from: www.afsp.org/about/malone.htm.

Maltsberger, J. T. (1986). *Suicide risk: The formulation of clinical judgment.* New York: New York University Press.

Maltsberger, J. T., & Buie, D. H. (1973). Countertransference hate in the treatment of suicidal patients. *Archives of General Psychiatry, 30,* 625–633.

Manetta, A. A., & Wells, J. G. (2001). Ethical issues in the social worker's role in physician assisted suicide. *Health &Social Work, 26,* 160–164.

Mann, J. J., Waternaux, C., Haas, G. L., & Malone, K. M. (1999). Toward a clinical model of suicidal behavior in psychiatric patients. *American Journal of Psychiatry, 156*(2), 181–189.

Marcus, E. (1996). *Why suicide?* San Francisco: Harper.

Marion, M. S., & Range, L. M. (2003). African American college women's suicide buffers. *Suicide and Life-Threatening Behavior, 33,* 33–43.

Maris, R. W. (1997). Social and familial risk factors in suicidal behavior. *Psychiatric Clinics of North America, 20*(3), 519–550.

Maris, R. W. (2002). Suicide. *The Lancet, 360,* 319–326.

Marrero, D. N. (1998). Suicide attempts among Puerto Ricans of low socioeconomic status. *Dissertation Abstracts International: Section B: The Sciences & Engineering, 58*(7-B), 3929.

Martin, G., & Koo, L. (1997) Celebrity suicide: Did the death of Kurt Cobain affect suicides in Australia? *Archives of Suicide Research 3*(3), 187–198.

Marzuk, P. M., Nock, M. K., Leon, A. C., Porter, L., & Tardiff, K. (2002). Suicide among New York City police officers, 1877–1996. *American Journal of Psychiatry, 159,* 2069–2071.

Maskill C., Hodges, I., McClellan, V., & Collings, S. (2005). *Explaining patterns of suicide: A selective review of studies examining social, economic, cultural and other population-level influences.* Wellington, New Zealand: Ministry of Health.

Mauk, G. W., & Rodgers, P. L. (1994). Building bridges over troubled waters: School-based postvention with adolescent survivors of peer suicide. *Crisis Intervention & Time-Limited Treatment, 1*(2), 103–123.

Mays, D. (2004). Structured assessment methods may improve suicide prevention: Standard patient interview processes can mislead clinicians about acute risk factors. *Psychiatric Annals, 34*(5), 367–372.

McAdams, III, C. R., & Foster, V. A. (2000). Client suicide: Its frequency and impact on counselors. *Journal of Mental Health Counseling, 22,* 107–121.

McDaniel, J. S., Purcell, D., & D'Augelli, A. R. (2001). The relationship between sexual orientation and risk for suicide: Research findings and future directions for research and prevention. *Suicide and Life-Threatening Behavior, 31*(Suppl.): 84–105.

McEvoy, M. L., & McEvoy, A. W. (1994). *Preventing youth suicide: A handbook for educators and human service professionals.* Holmes Beach, FL: Learning Publications.

McIntosh, J. L. (1995). Suicide prevention in the elderly (age 65–99). *Suicide and Life-Threatening Behavior, 25,* 180–192.

McIntosh, J. L. (1999). Research on survivors of suicide. In M. Stimming & M. Stimming (Eds.), *Before their time: Adult experiences of parental suicide* (pp. 157–180). Philadelphia, PA., Temple University Press.

McIntosh, J. L., & Kelly, L. (1992). Survivors' reactions: Suicide vs. other causes. *Crises, 13,* 82–93.

McLean, P., & Taylor, S. (1994). Family therapy for suicidal people. *Death Studies, 18,* 409–426.

McManus, B. L., Kruesi, M. J., Dontes, A. E., Defazio, C. R., Piotrowski, J. T., & Woodward, P. J. (1997). Child and adolescent suicide attempts: An opportunity for emergency departments to provide injury prevention education. *American Journal of Emergency Medicine, 15,* 357–360.

McQuillan, A., Nicastro, R., Guenot, F., Girard, M., Lissner, C., & Ferrero, F. (2005). Intensive Dialectical Behavior Therapy for outpatients with Borderline Personality Disorder who are in crisis. *Psychiatric Services, 56,* 193–197.

Meimeyer, R. A. (2000). Suicide and hastened death: Toward a training agenda for counseling psychology, *Counseling Psychologist, 28*(4), 551–560.

Melear, A. (1973). Children's conceptions of death. *Journal of Genetic Psychology, 123,* 359–360.

Memory, J. M. (1989). Juvenile suicides in secure detention facilities: Correction of published rates. *Death Studies, 13*(5), 455–463.

Menninger, J. A. (2002). Assessment and treatment of alcoholism and substance-related disorders in the elderly. *Bulletin of the Menninger Clinic, 66*(2), 166–183.

Men's Health America. (2002). Special Report. Available at: http://www.menshealthforum. org.uk/newsandevents/USsuicide.html.

Mental Health and Well Being. (2002). Youth suicide in Australia. Available at: http://www. dhac.gov.au/ hsdd/mentalhe/resources/nysps/compare.htm.

Merriam-Webster. (1994). *Merriam-Webster's dictionary of English usage.* Springfield, MA: Author.

Meyer, G. M., Landis, E. R., & Hays, J. R. (1988). *Law for the psychotherapists.* New York: Norton.

Middlebrook, D. L., LeMaster, P. L., Beals, J., Novins, D. K., & Manson, S. M. (2001). Suicide prevention in American Indian and Alaska Native communities: A critical review of programs. *Suicide and Life-Threatening Behavior, 31*(Suppl.), 132–149.

Miles, C. P. (1977). Conditions predisposing to suicide: A review. *Journal of Nervous and Mental Disease, 164*(4), 231–246.

Military and Veterans Health Coordinating Board. (2000). The family's role related to military deployment. Available at: http://www.mvhcb.gov/mvhcb_13h/Plenary2000/Plenary%20Presentations/7-family% 20-%20teitelbaum/tsld001.htm.

Miller, A. L., Rathus, J. H., Linehan, M. M., Wetzler, S., & Leigh, E. (1997). Dialectical behavior therapy adapted for suicidal adolescents. *Journal of Practical Psychiatry and Behavioral Health, 3*, 78–86.

Miller, D. N. (1996). School based prevention of adolescent suicide: Issues, obstacles, and recommendations for practice. *Journal of Emotional & Behavioral Disorders, 4*, 221–231.

Miller, J. S., Segal, D. L., & Coolidge, F. L. (2000). A comparison of suicidal thinking and reasons for living among younger and older adults. *Death Studies, 25*, 257–365.

Miller, K. E., King, C. A., Shain, B. N., & Naylor, M. W. (1992). Suicidal adolescents' perceptions of their family environment. *Suicide and Life-Threatening Behavior, 22*(2), 226–239.

Miller, M., Hemenway, D., & Rimm, E. (2000). Cigarettes and suicide: A prospective study of 50,000 men. *American Journal of Public Health, 90*, 768–773.

Miller, P. J. (2000). Life after death with dignity: The Oregon experience. *Social Work, 45*, 263–271.

Miller, T. C. (November 27, 2005). *A journey that ended in anguish.* L.A. Times. Available at: LATimes.com.

Milsom, A. (2002). Suicide prevention in schools: Court cases and implications for principals. *NASSP Bulletin, 86*, 630.

Mishara, B. L. (1982). College students' experiences with suicide and reactions to suicidal verbalizations: A model for prevention. *Journal of Community Psychology, 10*(2), 142–150.

Mishara, B. L. (1999). Conceptions of death and suicide in children ages 6–12 and their implications for suicide prevention. *Suicide and Life-Threatening Behavior, 29*, 105–118.

Mishara, B., & Daigle, M. (2001). Helplines and crisis intervention services: Challenges for the future. In D. Lester (Ed.), *Suicide prevention: Resources for the millennium* (pp. 153–172). New York: Brunner-Routledge.

Mishna, F., Antle, B., & Regehr, C. (2002). Social work with clients contemplating suicide: Complexity and ambiguity in the clinical, ethical, and legal considerations. *Clinical Social Work Journal, 30*, 265–280.

Mitchell, B., Mitchell, D., & Berk, M. (2000). The role of genetics in suicide and the link with major depression and alcoholism. *International Journal of Psychiatry in Clinical Practice, 4*, 275–280.

Modesto-Lowe, V., & Kranzler, H. R. (1999). Diagnosis and treatment of alcohol-dependent patients with comorbid psychiatric disorders. *Alcohol Research Health, 23*, 144–149.

Moeller, F. G., Barratt, E. S., Dougherty, D. M., Schmitz, J. M., & Swann, A. C. (2001). Psychiatric aspects of impulsivity. *American Journal of Psychiatry, 158*, 1783–1793.

Mohandic, K., & Hatcher, C. (1999). Suicide and violence risk in law enforcement: Practical guidelines for risk assessment, prevention, and intervention. *Behavioral Sciences and the Law, 17*, 357–376.

Montross, L. P., Zisook, S., & Kasckow, J. (2005). Suicide among patients with schizophrenia: A consideration of risk and protective factors. *Annals of Clinical Psychiatry, 17*(3), 173–182.

Morrison, L. L., & Downey, D. L. (2000). Racial differences in self-disclosure of suicidal ideation and reasons for living: Implications for training. *Cultural Diversity and Ethnic Minority Psychology, 6*, 374–386.

Morrissey, R. F., Dicker, R., Abikoff, H., Alvir, J. M. J., DeMarco, A., & Koplewicz, H. S. (1995). Hospitalizing the suicidal adolescent: An empirical investigation of decision-making criteria. *Journal of the American Academy of Child and Adolescent Psychiatry, 34*, 902–911.

Mościcki, E. K. (1989). Epidemiologic surveys as tools for studying suicidal behavior: A review. *Suicide and Life-Threatening Behavior, 19*, 131–146.

Mościcki, E. K. (1995). Epidemiology of suicidal behavior. *Suicide and Life-Threatening Behavior, 25*(1), 22–35.

Mościcki, E. K. (1997). Identification of suicide risk factors using epidemiologic studies. *Psychiatric Clinics of North America, 20*, 499–517.

Mrazek, P. J., & Haggerty, R. J. (Eds.). (1994). *Reducing the risks for mental disorders: Frontiers for preventive intervention research.* Washington, DC: National Academy Press.

Muehrer, P. (1995). Suicide and sexual orientation: A critical summary of recent research and directions for future research. *Suicide and Life-Threatening Behavior, 25*(Suppl.), 72–81.

Mufson, L., Weissman, M. M., Moreau, D., & Garfinkel, R. (1999). Efficacy of interpersonal psychotherapy for depressed adolescents. *Archives of General Psychiatry, 56*, 573–579.

Murphy, S. L. (2000). Deaths: Final data for 1998. *National Vital Statistics Report, 48*(11). Hyattsville, MD: National Center for Health Statistics. DHHS Publication No. (PHS) 2000-1120.

Myslobodsky, M., Lalonde, F. M., & Hicks, L. (2000). Are patients with Parkinson's disease suicidal? *Journal of Geriatric Psychiatry and Neurology, 14*, 120–124.

Nagy, M. (1948). The child's theories concerning death. *Journal of Genetic Psychology, 73*, 3–27.

National Alliance for the Mentally Ill. (2003). Depression in older persons. Retrieved December 27, 2005, from: http://www.nami.org/Template.cfm?Section=By_Illness&template=/ContentManagement/Content Display.cfm&ContentID=7515.

National Alliance for the Mentally Ill. (1996). *Parents survival guide to childhood depression*. King of Prussia, PA: The Center for Applied Psychology.

National Fibromyalgia Association. (2002). http://fmaware.org.

National Household Survey on Drug Abuse. (2002). *Substance use and the risk of suicide among youths*. Rockville, MD: U.S. Department of Health and Human Services.

National Institute of Mental Health. (1999). NIMH Suicide Facts. Available at: http://www. nimh.nih.gov/ publicat/suicidefacts.cfm.

National Institute of Mental Health. (2002). *U.S. suicide rates by age, gender, and racial group*. Available at: http:// www.nimh.nih.gov/research/suichart.cfm.

National Spinal Cord Injury Association. (2002). http://www.spinalcord.org/.

Neeleman, J., Wessely, S., & Lewis, G. (1998). Suicide acceptability in African- and white Americans: The role of religion. *Journal of Nervous and Mental Disease, 186*, 12–16.

Neimeyer, R. A. (2000). Suicide and hastened death: Toward a training agenda for Counseling psychology. *Counseling Psychologist, 28*(4), 551–560.

Nelson, Z. P., & Smith, W. E. (1970). The law enforcement profession: An incident of high suicide. *Omega, 1*, 293–299.

New Freedom Commission on Mental Health. (2003). *Achieving the promise: Transforming mental health care in America, Final Report*. Pub. No. SMA-03-3832. Rockville, MD: U.S. Department of Health and Human Services.

Ng, B. (1996). Characteristics of 61 Mexican American adolescents who attempted suicide. *Hispanic Journal of Behavioral Sciences, 18*, 3–12.

Nicholl, C. R., Lincoln, N. B., Francis, V. M., & Stephan, T. F. (2001). Assessment of emotional problems in people with multiple sclerosis. *Clinical Rehabilitation, 15*, 657–668.

Nisbet, P. A. (1996). Protective factors for suicidal Black females. *Suicide and Life-Threatening Behavior, 26*, 325–340.

No Child Left Behind Act of 2001, 20 U.S.C. § 6301 (2003).

Normand, C., & Mishara, B. L. (1992). The development of the concept of suicide in children. *Omega: International Journal of Death and Dying, 25*(3), 183–203.

Novins, D. K., Beals, J., Roberts, R. E., & Manson, S. M. (1999). Factors associated with suicide ideation among American Indian adolescents: Does culture matter? *Suicide and Life-Threatening Behavior, 29*, 332–346.

O'Donnell, I., Farmer, R., Catalan, J. (1996). Explaining suicide: The views of survivors of serious suicide attempts. *British Journal of Psychiatry, 168*, 780–786.

Oquendo, M. A., Ellis, S. P., Greenwald, S., Malone, K. M, Weissman, M. M., & Mann, J. J. (2001). Ethnic and sex differences in suicide rates relative to major depression in the United States. *American Journal of Psychiatry, 158*, 1652–1658.

Oquendo, M. A., Malone, K. M., Ellis, S. P., Sackeim, H. A., & Mann, J. J. (1999). Inadequacy of antidepressant treatment for patients with major depression who are at risk for suicidal behavior. *American Journal of Psychiatry, 156*, 190–194.

Oquendo, M. A., Waternaux, C., Brodsky, B., Parsons, B., Haas, G. L., Malone, K. M., & Mann J. J. (2000). Suicidal behavior in bipolar mood disorder: Clinical characteristics of attempter and nonattempters. *Journal of Affective Disorders, 59*, 107–117.

Orbach, I. (1984). Personality characteristics, life circumstances, and dynamics of suicidal children. *Death Education, 8*, 37–52.

Orbach, I. (1997). A taxonomy of factors related to suicidal behaviors. *Clinical Psychology: Science and Practice, 4*, 208–224.

Orbach, I., & Glaubman, H. (1979). The concept of death and suicidal behavior in young children: Three case studies. *Journal of the American Academy of Child Psychiatry, 18*, 668–678.

Orbach, I., Milstein, I., Har-Even, D., Apter, A., Tiano, S., & Elizur, A. (1991). A Multi-Attitude Suicide Tendency Scale for adolescents. *Psychological Assessment, 3*, 398–404.

Osman, A., Barrios, F. X., Gutierrez, P. M., Wrangham, J. J., Kopper, B. A., Truelove, R. S., & Linden, S. C. (2002). The Positive and Negative Suicide Ideation (PANSI) Inventory: Psychometric evaluation with adolescent psychiatric inpatient samples. *Journal of Personality Assessment, 79*, 512–530.

Osman, A., Downs, W., Kopper, B., Barrios, F., Baker, M., Osman, J., Besett, T., & Linehan, M. (1998). The Reasons for Living Inventory for Adolescents (RFL-A): Development and psychometric properties. *Journal of Clinical Psychology, 54*, 1063–1078.

Osman, A., Gutierrez, P. M., Kopper, B. A., Barrios, F. X., & Chiros, C. E. (1998). The Positive and Negative Suicide Ideation Inventory: Development and validation. *Psychological Reports, 82*, 783–793.

Osman, A., Gutierrez, P. M., Kopper, B. A., Barrios, F. X., Linden, S. C., & Truelove, R. S. (2003). A preliminary validation of the Positive and Negative Suicide Ideation (PANSI) Inventory with normal adolescent samples. *Journal of Clinical Psychology, 59*, 493–512.

Osman, A., Kopper, B., Barrios, F., Osman, J., Besett, T., & Linehan, M. (1996). The Brief Reasons for Living Inventory for Adolescents (BRFL-A). *Journal of Abnormal Child Psychology, 24*, 433–443.

Pastore, D. R., Fisher, M., & Friedman, S. B. (1996). Violence and mental health problems among urban high school students. *Journal of Adolescent Health, 18*, 320–324.

Patten, S. B., & Metz, L. M. (2002). Hopelessness ratings in relapsing-remitting and secondary progressive multiple sclerosis. *International Journal of Psychiatry in Medicine, 32*, 155–165.

Patterson, W. M., Dohn, H. H., Bird, J., Patterson, G. A. (1983). Evaluation of suicidal patients: The SAD PERSON Scale. *Psychosomatics, 24*(4), 343–349.

Patton, J. H., Standford, M. S., & Barratt, E. S. (1995). Factor structure of the Barratt Impulsiveness Scale. *Journal of Clinical Psychology, 51*, 768–774.

Paul, M. T. (2000). Responses to life after death with dignity: The Oregon experience. *Social Work, 45*, 467–468.

Peck, R. C. (1956). Psychological developments in the second half of life. In J. E. Anderson (Ed.), *Psychological aspects of aging* (pp. 44–49). Washington, DC: American Psychological Association.

Persson, M-L. I., Runeson, B. S., & Wasserman, D. (1999). Diagnoses, psychosocial stressors and adaptive functioning in attempted suicide. *Annals of Clinical Psychiatry, 11*(3), 119–128.

Petronis, R. K., Samuels, J. F., Mościcki, E. K., & Anthony, J. C. (1990). An epidemiologic investigation of potential risk factors for suicide attempts. *Social Psychiatry and Psychiatric Epidemiology, 25*, 193–199.

Pfeffer, C. R. (1984). Death preoccupation and survival behavior in children. In H. Wass & C. A. Corr (Eds.), *Childhood and death* (pp. 261–278). Washington, DC: Hemisphere.

Pfeffer, C., Conte, H., Plutchik, R., & Jerrett, I. (1979). Suicidal behavior in latency age children: An empirical study. *Journal of the American Academy of Child Psychiatry, 18*, 69–692.

Pfeffer, C., Jiang, H., & Kakuma, T. (2000). Child-Adolescent Suicidal Potential Index (CASPI): A screen for risk for early onset suicidal behavior. *Psychological Assessment, 12*, 304–318.

Pfeffer, C. R., Jiang, H., Kakuma, T., Hwang, J., & Metsch, M. (2002). Group intervention for children bereaved by the suicide of a relative. *Child & Adolescent Psychiatry, 41*, 505–513.

Pfeffer, C. R., Karus, D., Siegel, K., & Jiang, H. (2000). Child survivors of parental death from cancer or suicide, depressive and behavioral outcomes. *Psycho-oncology, 9*, 1–10.

Pfeffer, C. R., Klerman, G. L., Hurt, S. W., & Kakuma, T. (1993). Suicidal children grow up: Rates and psychosocial risk factors for suicide attempts during follow-up. *Journal of the American Academy of Child & Adolescent Psychiatry, 32*(1), 106–113.

Pfeffer, C. R., Solomon, G., Plutchik, R., Mizruchi, M. S., & Weiner, A. (1982). Suicidal behavior in latency-age psychiatric inpatients: A replication and cross-validation. *Journal of the American Academy of Child Psychiatry, 21*, 564–569.

Pfeffer, C. R., Zuckerman, S., Plutchik, R., & Mizruchi, M. S. (1984). Suicidal behavior in normal school children: A comparison with child psychiatric inpatients. *Journal of the American Academy of Child Psychiatry, 23*, 416–423.

Pietila, M. (2002). Support groups: A psychological or social device for suicide bereavement? *British Journal of Guidance & Counseling, 30*, 401–414.

Pilkinton, P. (2003). Encountering suicide: The experience of psychiatric residents. *Academic Psychiatry, 27*, 93–99.

Pirkis, J., Burgess, P., & Jolley, D. (2002). Suicide among psychiatric patients: A case-control study. *Australian and New Zealand Journal of Psychiatry, 36*(1) 86–91.

Placidi, G. P., Oquendo, M. A., Malone, K. M., Brodsky, B., Ellis, S. P., & Mann, J. J. (2000). Anxiety in major depression: relationship to suicide attempts. *American Journal of Psychiatry, 157*, 1614–1618.

Potash, J. B., Kane, H. S., Chiu, Y., Simpson, S. G., MacKinnon, D. F., McInnis, M. G., McMahon, F. J., & DePaulo, J. R. (2000). Attempted suicide and alcoholism in bipolar disorder, clinical and familial relationships. *American Journal of Psychiatry, 157*, 2048–2050.

Potkin, S. G., Anand, R., Alphs, L., & Fleming, K. (2003). Neurocognitive performance does not correlate with suicidality in schizophrenic and schizoaffective patients at risk for suicide. *Schizophrenia Research, 59*(1), 59–66.

Potter, L. B., Kresnow, M-J., Powell, K. E., Simon, T. R., Mercy, A. J., Lee, R. K., Frankowski, R. F., Swann, A. C., Bayer, T., & O'Carroll, P. W. (2001). The influence of geographic mobility on nearly lethal suicide attempts. *Suicide & Life-Threatening Behavior, 32*(Suppl.), 42–48.

Powell, K. E., Dresnow, M., Mercy, J. A., Potter, L. B., Swann, A. C., Frankowski, R. F., Lee, R. K., & Bayer, T. L. (2001). Alcohol consumption and nearly lethal suicide attempts. *Suicide and Life Threatening Behavior, 32*, 30–41.

Pratt, C. C., Wilson, W., Benthin, A., & Schmall, V. (1992). Alcohol problems and depression in later life: Development of two knowledge quizzes. *The Gerontologist, 32*(2), 175–183.

Pritchard, C., & Baldwin, D. S. (2002). Elderly suicide rates in Asian and English-speaking countries. *Acta Psychiatrica Scandinavica, 105*, 271–275.

Provini, C., Everett, J. R., & Pfeffer, C.R., (2000). Adults mourning suicide: Self-reported concerns about bereavement, needs for assistance, and help-seeking behavior. *Death Studies, 24*, 1–19.

Qin, P., Agerbo, E., Mortensen, P. B. (2002). Suicide risk in relation to family history of suicide and psychiatric disorders: A nested case-control study based on longitudinal registers. *Lancet, 360*, 1126–1130.

Rabkin, J. G., Remien, R., Katoff, L., & Williams, J. (1993). Suicidality in AIDS long-term survivors: What is the evidence? *AIDS Care, 5*, 401–411.

Raimbault, G. (1975). *L'enfant et la mort. Des enfants maladies parletn de lar mort: Problèmes de la clinique du deuil.* Toulouse: Privat.

Ramberg, I-L., & Wasserman, D. (2000). Prevalence of reported suicidal behaviour in the general population and mental health-care staff. *Psychological Medicine, 30*, 1189–1196.

Range, L. M., Leach, M. M., McIntrye, D., Posey-Deters, P. B., Marion, M. S., Kovac, S. H., Baños, J. H., & Vigil, J. (1999). Multicultural perspectives on suicide. *Aggression and Violent Behavior, 4*, 413–430.

Range, L. M., MacIntyre, D. I., Rutherford, D., Billie, S., Payne, B., Knott, E., Brown, M., & Foster, C. L. (1997). Suicide in special populations and circumstances: A review. *Aggression and Violent Behavior, 2*(1) 53–63.

Rao, R., Dening, T., Brayne, C., & Huppert, F. A. (1997). Suicidal thinking in community residents over eighty. *International Journal of Geriatric Psychiatry, 12*, 337–343.

Raskin, N. J., & Rogers, C. R. (1989). Person-centered therapy. In R. J. Corsini & Wedding, D. (Eds.), *Current psychotherapies* (4th ed., pp. 155–194). Itasca, IL: F. E. Peacock.

Rathus, J. H., & Miller, A. L. (2002). Dialectical Behavior Therapy adapted for suicidal adolescents. *Suicide and Life-Threatening Behavior, 32*(2), 146–157.

Reich, J. (1998). The relationship of suicide attempts, borderline personality traits, and major depressive disorder in a veteran outpatient population. *Journal of Affective Disorders, 49*(2), 151–156.

Reid, S. (1998). Suicide in schizophrenia: A review of the literature. *Journal of Mental Health, 7*(4), 345–353.

Remley, T. P. (2004). Suicide and the Law. In David Capuzzi (Ed.), *Suicide across the lifespan: Implications for counselors.* Alexandria, VA: American Counseling Association.

Reynolds, W. (1990). Development of a semistructured clinical interview for suicidal behavior in adolescents. *Psychological Assessment, 2*, 382–393.

Rigby, K., & Slee, P. (1999). Suicidal ideation among adolescent school children, involvement in bully-victim problems, and perceived social support. *Suicide and Life-Threatening Behavior, 29*, 119–130.

Rihmer, Z., & Kiss, K. (2002). Bipolar disorders and suicidal behaviour. *Bipolar Disorders, 4*, 21–25.

Riskind, J. H., Long, D. G., Williams, N. L., & White, J. C. (2000). Desperate acts for desperate times: Looming vulnerability and suicide. In T. E. Joiner & M. D. Rudd (Eds.), *Suicide science: Expanding the boundaries* (pp. 105–115). Boston: Kluwer Academic Publishers.

Rittenmeyer, S. D. (1999). Student suicide and Illinois' small schools: Breaking the silence. *Rural Research Report, Illinois Institute for Rural Affairs, 10*, 1–8.

Rittner, B., & Smyth, N. J. (1999). Time-limited cognitive-behavioral group interventions with suicidal adolescents. *Social Work with Groups, 22*, 55–75.

Roberts, A. R. (1991). *Contemporary perspectives on crisis intervention and prevention*. Englewood Cliffs, NJ: Prentice Hall.

Robertson, J. D. (1988). *Psychiatric malpractice: Liability of mental health professionals*. New York: Wiley.

Robins, W. T-B., Bäckman, L., Lundin, A., Haegermark, A., Winblad, B., & Anvret, M. (2000). High suicidal ideation in persons testing for Huntington's disease. *Acta Neurologica Scandinavica, 102*, 150–161.

Rogers, C., & Stevens, B. (1967). *Person to person*. New York: People to People Press.

Rogers, J. R. (2001). Theoretical grounding: The "missing link" in suicide research. *Journal of Counseling and Development, 79*, 16–25.

Rogers, J. R., Gueulette, C. M., Abbey-Hines, J., Carney, J. V., & Werth, Jr. J. L. (2001). Rational suicide: An empirical investigation of counselor attitudes. *Journal of Counseling & Development, 79*, 365–372.

Rogers, J. R., Lewis, M. M., & Subich, L. M. (2002). Validity of the Suicide Assessment Checklist in an emergency crisis center. *Journal of Counseling and Development, 80*, 493–502.

Rohde, P., Mace, D. E., & Seeley, J. R. (1997). The association of psychiatric disorders with suicide attempts in a juvenile delinquent sample. *Criminal Behaviour and Mental Health, 7*(3), 187–200.

Romanov, K., Hatakka, M., Keskinen, E., Laaksonen, H., Kaprio, J., Rose, R. J., & Koskenuvo, M. (1994). Self-reported hostility and suicidal acts, accidents, and accidental deaths: A prospective study of 21,443 adults aged 25–59. *Psychosomatic Medicine, 56*, 328–336.

Rosenfeld, B. (2000). Methodological issues in assisted suicide and euthanasia research. *Psychology, Public Policy, and Law, 6*(2), 559–574.

Rothberg, J. M., Fagan, J., & Shaw, J. (1990). Suicide in United States Army personnel, 1985–1986. *Military Medicine, 155*, 452–456.

Rotheram-Borus, M. J., Walker, J. U., & Ferns, W. (1996). Suicidal behavior among middle-class adolescents who seek crisis services. *Journal of Clinical Psychology, 35*, 654–663.

Roy, A. (1993). Risk factors for suicide among adult alcoholics. *Alcohol Health & Research World, 17*, 133.

Roy, A. (2000). Relation of family history of suicide to suicide attempts in alcoholics. *American Journal of Psychiatry, 157*, 2050–2051.

Rubel, B. (2003). The grief response: Experienced by the saviors of suicide. Available at: Grief Work Center Inc., http://www.griefworkcenter.com/newpage3.htm.

Rubio, A., Vestner, A. L., Steward, J. M., Forbes, N. T., Conwell, Y., & Cox, C. (2001). Suicide and Alzheimer's pathology in the elderly: A case-control study. *Society of Biological Psychiatry, 49*, 137–145.

Ruby, C. T., & McIntosh, J. L., (1996). Suicide survivors groups: Results of a survey. *Suicide and Life Threatening Behavior, 26*, 351–358.

Rucci, P., Frank, E., Kostelnik, B., Fagiolini, A., Mallinger, A. G., Swartz, H. A., Thase, M. E., Siegel, L., Wilson, D., & Kupfer, D. J. (2002). Suicide attempts in patients with bipolar I disorder during acute and maintenance phases of intensive treatment with pharmacotherapy and adjunctive psychotherapy. *American Journal of Psychiatry, 159*, 1160–1164.

Rudd, M. D. (1989). The prevalence of suicidal ideation among college students. *Suicide & Life-Threatening Behavior, 19*, 173–183.

Rudd, M. D. (2004). Cognitive therapy for suicidality: An integrative, comprehensive, and practical approach to conceptualization. *Journal of Contemporary Psychotherapy, 34*, 59–72.

Rudd, M. D., Joiner, T. E., Jobes, D. A., & King, C. A. (1999). The outpatient treatment of suicidality: An integration of science and recognition of its limitations. *Professional Psychology: Research and Practice, 30*, 437–446.

Rudd, M. D., Rajab, M. H., Orman, D. T., Stulman, D. A., Joiner, T., & Dixon, W. (1996). Effectiveness of an outpatient intervention targeting suicidal young adults: Preliminary results. *Journal of Consulting and Clinical Psychology, 64*, 179–190.

Ruddell, P., & Curwen, B. (2002). Understanding suicidal ideation and assessing for risk. *British Journal of Guidance and Counselling, 30*(4), 363–372.

Rudestam, K. E. (1992). Research contributions to understanding the suicide survivor. *Crises, 13*, 41–46.

Rutz, W. (2001). Preventing suicide and premature death by education and treatment. *Journal of Affective Disorders, 62*, 123–129.

Saarinen, P. I., Hintikka, J., Lehtonen J., Loennqvist, J. K., & Viinamaeki, H. (2002). Mental health and social isolation among survivors ten years after a suicide in the family: A case control study. *Archives of Suicide Research, 6*, 221–226.

Sabbath, J. C. (1969). The suicidal adolescent: The expendable child. *Journal of the American Academy of Child Psychiatry, 8*(2), 272–285.

Sachs-Ericsson, N. (2000). Gender, social roles, and suicidal ideation and attempts in a general population sample. In T. E. Joiner & M. D. Rudd (Eds.), *Suicide science: Expanding the boundaries* (pp. 201–220). Boston: Kluwer Academic Publishers.

Safren, S. A., & Heimberg, R. G. (1999). Depression, hopelessness, suicidality and related factors in sexual minority and heterosexual youth. *Journal of Consulting and Clinical Psychology, 67*, 859–866.

Sanchez, L. E., & Lan, T. L. (2001). Suicide in mood disorders. *Depression and Anxiety, 14*, 177–182.

Santy, P. A. (1982). Observations on double suicide: Review of the literature and two case reports. *American Journal of Psychotherapy, 36*, 23–31.

Sareen, J., Cox, B. J., Afifi, T. O., de Graaf, R., Asmundson, G. J. G., Have, M. T., & Stein, M. B. (2005). Anxiety disorders and risk for suicidal ideation and suicide attempts: A population-based longitudinal study of adults. *Archives of General Psychiatry, 62*, 11, 1249–1257.

Satcher, D. (1999). Mental health: A report of the Surgeon General. Retrieved December 28, 2005, from: http://www.surgeongeneral.gov/library/mentalhealth/home.html.

Saunders, J. M., & Valente, S. M. (1987). Suicide risk among gay men and lesbians: A review. *Death Studies, 11*(1), 1–23.

Schaar, I., & Ojehagen, A. (2001). Severely mentally ill substance abusers: An 18-month follow-up study. *Social Psychiatry and Psychiatric Epidemiology, 36*(2), 70–78.

Schmidt, N., Woolaway-Bickel, K., & Bates, M. (2001). Evaluating panic-specific factors in the relationship between suicide and panic disorder. *Behaviour Research and Therapy, 39*, 635–649.

Schneider, B., & Philipp, M., Muller, M. J. (2001). Psychopathological predictors of suicide in patients with major depression during a 5-year follow up. *European Psychiatry, 16*, 283–288.

Schneider, S. G., Taylor, S. E., Hammen, C., Kemeny, M. E., & Dudley, J. (1991). Factors influencing suicide intent in gay and bisexual suicide ideators: Differing models for men with and without human immunodeficiency virus. *Journal of Personality and Social Psychology, 61*, 776–788.

Schutz, B. M. (1982). *Legal liability in psychotherapy.* San Francisco: Jossey-Bass.

Schwab, J. J., Warheit, G. J., & Holzer, C. E. (1972). Suicidal ideation and behavior in a general population. *Diseases of the Nervous System, 33*, 745–748.

Schwartz, R. C., & Cohen, B. N. (2001). Psychosocial correlates of suicidal intent among patients with schizophrenia. *Comprehensive Psychiatry, 42*(2), 118–123.

Scocco, P., & DeLeo, D. (2002). One-year prevalence of death thoughts, suicide ideation and behaviours in an elderly population. *International Journal of Geriatric Psychiatry, 17*, 842–846.

Scott, T. F., Allen, D., Price, T. R. P., McConnell, H., & Lang, D. (1996). Characterization of major depression symptoms in multiple sclerosis patients. *Journal of Neuropsychiatry & Clinical Neurosciences, 8*, 318–323.

Seidlitz, L., Conwell, Y., Duberstein, P., Cox, C., & Denning, D. (2001). Emotion traits in older suicide attempters and non-attempters. *Journal of Affective Disorders, 66*, 123–131.

Seligmann, J., Holt, D., Chinni, D., & Roberts, E. (1994). Cops who kill themselves. *Newsweek*, September 26, p. 58.

Sethi, S., & Bhargava, S. C. (2003). Child and adolescent survivors of suicide. *Crises, 24*, 4–6.

Shaffer, D., Fisher, P., Hicks, R. H., Parides, M., & Gould, M. (1995). Sexual orientation in adolescents who commit suicide. *Suicide and Life-Threatening Behavior, 25*(Suppl.), 64–70.

Shaffer, D., Gould, M. S., Fisher, P., Trautman, P., Moreau, D., Kleinman, M., & Flory, M. (1996a). Psychiatric diagnosis in child and adolescent suicide. *Archives of General Psychiatry, 53*, 339–348.

Shaffer, D., & Pfeffer, C. R. (Eds.) (2001). Practice parameter for the assessment and treatment of children and adolescents with suicidal behavior. *Journal of the American Academy of Child and Adolescent Psychiatry, 40*(7), 24S–51S.

Shaffer, D., Wilcox, H., Lucas, C., Hicks, R., Busner, C., & Parides, M. (1996b) The development of a screening instrument for teens at risk for suicide. Poster presented at the meeting of the Academy of Child and Adolescent Psychiatry, New York.

Shafii, M., & Shafii, S. L. (2003). School violence, depression, and suicide. *Journal of Applied Psychoanalytic Studies, 5*, 155–169.

Sharry, J., Darmody, M., & Madden, B. (2002). A solution-focused approach to working with clients who are suicidal. *British Journal of Guidance and Counselling, 30*, 383–399.

Shea, S. (2002). *The practical art of suicide assessment. A guide for mental health professionals and substance abuse counselors.* Hoboken, NJ: John Wiley & Sons.

Shiang, J., Barron, S., Xiao, S. Y., Blinn, R., & Tam, W.-C. C. (1998). Suicide and gender in the People's Republic of China, Taiwan, Hong Kong, and Chinese in the U.S. *Transcultural Psychiatry, 35*, 235–251.

Shiang, J., Blinn, R., Bongar, B., & Stephens, B. (1997). Suicide in San Francisco, CA: A comparison of Caucasian and Asian groups, 1987–1994. *Suicide and Life-Threatening Behavior, 27*(1), 80–91.

Shneidman, E. S. (1981). Psychotherapy with suicidal patients. *Suicide and Life-Threatening Behavior, 11*, 341–359.

Shneidman, E. S. (1985). *Definition of suicide.* New York: Wiley.

Shneidman, E. S. (1987). A psychological approach to suicide. In G. R. VandenBos & B. K. Bryant (Eds.), *Cataclysms, crises, and catastrophes: Psychology in action* (pp. 147–183). Washington, DC: American Psychological Association.

Shneidman, E. S. (1996). *The suicidal mind.* New York: Oxford University Press.

Shneidman, E. S. (2005). How I read. *Suicide and Life-Threatening Behavior, 35*(2), 117–120.

Sidley, G. L., Calam, R., Wells, A., Hughes, T., & Whitaker, K. (1999). The prediction of parasuicide repetition in a high-risk group. *British Journal of Clinical Psychology, 38*(4), 375–386.

Silverman, E., Range, L., & Overholser, J. (1994). Bereavement from suicide as a compared to other forms of bereavement. *Omega, 30*, 41–51.

Silverman, M. M., & Felner, R. D. (1995). The place of suicide prevention in the spectrum of intervention: Definitions of critical terms and constructs. *Suicide and Life-Threatening Behavior, 25*, 70–81.

Silverman, M. M., & Maris, R. W. (Eds.). (1995). *Suicide prevention: Toward the year 2000.* New York: Guilford Press.

Silverman, M. M., Meyer, P. M., Sloane, F., Raffel, M., & Pratt, D. (1997). The Big Ten Suicide Study: A 10-year study of suicide on Midwestern university campuses. *Suicide and Life-Threatening Behavior, 27*, 285–303.

Simon, R. I. (1988). *Concise guide to clinical psychiatry and the law.* Washington, DC: American Psychiatric Press.

Simon, R. I. (1991). The suicide-prevention pact: Clinical and legal considerations. In R. I. Simon (Ed.), *American Psychiatric Press review of clinical psychiatry and the law, II* (pp. 441–451). Washington, DC: American Psychiatric Press.

Simon, R. I. (2000). Taking the "sue" out of suicide: A forensic psychiatrist's perspective. *Psychiatric Annals, 30*, 399–407.

Simon, R. I. (2002). Suicide risk assessment: What is the standard of care? *The Journal of the American Academy of Psychiatry and the Law, 30*, 340–344.

Simon, T. R., Swann, A. C., Powell, K. E., Potter, L. B., Kresnow, M., & O'Carroll, P. W. (2001). Characteristics of impulsive suicide attempts and attempters. *Suicide and Life-Threatening Behavior, 32*(Suppl.), 49–59.

Simpson, S., & Stacy, M. (2004). Avoiding the malpractice snare: Documenting suicide risk assessment. *Journal of Psychiatric Practice, 10*(3), 185–189.

Slaby, A. E. (1998). Outpatient management of suicidal patients. In B. Bongar, A. Berman, R. Maris, M. Silverman, E. Harris, & W. Packman (Eds.), *Risk management with suicidal patients* (pp. 34–64). New York: Guilford Press.

Soderberg, S. (2001). Personality disorders in parasuicide. *Nordic Journal of Psychiatry, 55*(3), 163–167.

Softas-Nall, B. C., & Francis, P. C. (1998). A solution-focused approach to suicide assessment and intervention with families. *The Family Journal: Counseling and Therapy for Couples and Families, 6*, 64–66.

Soloff, P. H., Lynch, K. G., & Kelly, T. M. (2002). Childhood abuse as a risk factor for suicidal behavior in borderline personality disorder. *Journal of Personality Disorders, 16*(3), 201–214.

Soloff, P. H., Lynch, K. G., Kelly, T. M., Malone, K. M., & Mann, J. J. (2000). Characteristics of suicide attempts of patients with major depressive episode and borderline personality disorder: A comparative study. *American Journal of Psychiatry, 157*(4), 601–608.

Sommers-Flanagan, J., & Sommers-Flanagan, R. (1995). Intake interviewing with suicidal patients: A systematic approach. *Professional Psychology: Research and Practice, 26*(1), 41–47.

Sommers-Flanagan, R., & Sommers-Flanagan, J. (1999). *Clinical interviewing* (2nd ed). New York: Wiley.

Speaker, K. M., & Petersen, G. J. (2000). School violence and adolescent suicide: Strategies for effective intervention. *Educational Review, 51*(1), 65–73.

Stack, S. (1996). Suicide risk among dentists: A multivariate analysis. *Deviant Behavior, 17,* 107–117.

Stack, S. (2001a). Occupation and suicide. *Social Science Quarterly, 82,* 384–396.

Stenager, E. N., Koch-Henriksen, N., & Stenager, E. (1996). Risk factors in multiple sclerosis. *Psychotherapy & Psychosomatics, 65,* 86–90.

Stenager, E. N., & Stenager, E. (1992). Suicide and patients with neurologic diseases. *Archives of Neurology, 49,* 1296–1303.

Stewart, S. E., Manion, I. G., & Davidson, S. (2002). Emergency management of the adolescent suicide attempter: A review of the literature. *Journal of Adolescent Health, 30,* 312–325.

Stewart, S. W., Manion, I. G., Davidson, S., & Cloutier, P. (2001). Suicidal children and adolescents with first emergency room presentations: Predictors of six-month outcome. *Journal of the American Academy of Child and Adolescent Psychiatry, 40,* 580–587.

Stillion, J. M., & McDowell, E. E. (1996). *Suicide across the lifespan: Premature exits* (2nd ed). Washington, DC: Taylor & Francis.

Stillion, J. M., & McDowell, E. E. (1991). Examining suicide from a life span perspective. *Death Studies, 15*(4), 327–354.

Stillion, J. M., & Stillion, B. D. (1999). Attitudes toward suicide: Past, present, and future. *Omega, 38*(2), 77–97.

Stockmeier, C. A., Shapiro, L. A., Dilley, G. E., Kolli, T. N., Friedman, L., & Rajkowska, G. (1998). Increase in serotonin-1A autoreceptors in the midbrain of suicide victims with major depression: Postmortem evidence for decreases in serotonin activity. *Journal of Neuroscience, 18*(18), 7394–7401.

Strauss, J., Birmaher, B., Bridge, J., Axelson, D., Chiappetta, L., Brent, D., & Ryan, N. (2000). Anxiety disorders in suicidal youth. *Canadian Journal of Psychiatry, 45*(8), 739–745.

Stravynski, A., & Boyer, R. (2001). Loneliness in relation to suicide ideation and parasuicide: A population-wide study. *Suicide & Life-Threatening Behavior, 31,* 32–40.

Svetaz, M. V., Ireland, M., & Blum, R. (2000). Adolescents with learning disabilities: Risk and protective factors associated with emotional well-being: Findings from the National Longitudinal Study of Adolescent Health. *Journal of Adolescent Health, 27*(5), 340–348.

Swahn, M. H., & Potter, L. B. (2001). Factors associated with the medical severity of suicide attempts in youths and young adults. *Suicide & Life-Threatening Behavior, 32*(Suppl.), 21–29.

Swenson, L. C. (1993). *Psychology and law for the helping professions.* Pacific Grove, CA: Brooks/Cole.

Taiminen, T., Huttunen, J., Heila, H., Henriksson, M., Isometsa, E., Kahkonen, J., Tuominen, K., Lonnqvist, J., Addington, D., & Helenius, H. (2001). The Schizophrenia Suicide Risk Scale (SSRS): Development and initial validation. *Schizophrenia Research, 47*(2–3), 199–213.

Tartaro, C., & Lester, D. (2005). An application of Durkheim's theory of suicide to prison suicide rates in the United States. *Death Studies, 29,* 413–422.

Texas Association of Hostage Negotiators. (2003). Suicide lethality checklist. Available at: www.tahn.org.

Thompson, R. A. (1995). Being prepared for suicide or sudden death in schools: Strategies to restore equilibrium. *Journal of Mental Health Counseling, 17*(3), 264–277.

Traskman, L., Asberg, M., Bertilsson, L., & Sjostrand, L. (1981). Monoamine metabolites in CSF and suicidal behavior. *Archives of General Psychiatry, 38*(6), 631–636.

Trovato, F. A. (1992). Durkheimian analysis of youth suicide: Canada 1971 and 1981. *Suicide and Life-Threatening Behavior, 22,* 413–427.

Turner, S. M., & Hersen, M. (1994). The interviewing process. In M. Hersen & S. M. Turner (Eds.), *Diagnostic interviewing* (2nd ed., pp. 3–24). New York: Plenum Press.

Tyrer, P. (1999). Stress diathesis and pharmacological dependence. *Journal of Psychopharmacology, 13*(3), 294–295.

Ullman, D. G., Egan, D., & Fiedler, N. (1981). The many faces of hyperactivity: Similarities and differences in diagnostic policies. *Journal of Consulting and Clinical Psychology, 49,* 694–704.

Ullman, S. E., & Brecklin, L. R. (2002). Sexual assault history and suicidal behavior in a national sample of women. *Suicide and Life-Threatening Behavior, 32,* 117–130.

Ungemack, J. A., & Guarnaccia, P. J. (1998). Suicidal ideation and suicide attempts among Mexican Americans, Puerto Ricans, and Cuban Americans. *Transcultural Psychiatry, 35*, 307–327.

U.S Census Bureau. (2000). *Census 2000 Briefs and Special Reports*. Available at: http://www. census.gov/ population/www/cen2000/briefs.html.

U.S. Department of Defense. (1998). *Survey of health related behaviors among military personnel*. Available at: http://www.tricare.osd.mil/analysis/surveys/98survey/survey.html.

U.S. Department of Defense. (1999). *Healthwatch: DOD Pursues Mental Health Initiatives*. Available at: http://www.dcmilitary.com/navy/seaservices/archives/aug6/ss_c8699.html.

U.S. Department of Health and Human Services. (1998). *Trends in the Well-Being of America's Children and Youth: 1998*. Washington, DC: Author.

U.S. Department of Health and Human Services. (1999). *Call to action to prevent suicide*. Available at: http://www.surgeongeneral.gov/library/calltoaction/default.htm.

U.S. National Strategy for suicide prevention: Goals and objectives for action. (2001). Publ. No. 02NLM:HV 6548.A1. Rockville, MD: U.S. Dept. of Health and Human Services.

U.S. Department of Health & Human Services. (2002a). *Asian American/Pacific Islander mental health fact sheet*. Available at: www.cdc.gov/omh/AMH/factsheets/mental.htm.

U.S. Department of Health and Human Services (2002b). *Air Force suicide prevention program: A population-based, community approach*. Available at: http://www.osophs.dhhs.gov/ophs/BestPractice/usaf.htm.

U.S. Department of Justice. (2002). Office of Justice Program. Bureau of Justice Statistics. Available at: http://www.ojp.usdoj.gov/bjs/correct.htm.

U.S. Public Health Service. (1999). *The Surgeon General's call to action to prevent suicide*. Washington, DC: Author.

United Nations. (1998). *1996 demographic yearbook*. New York: Author.

Valente, S. M., & Saunders, J. M. (2002). Nurses' grief reactions to a patient's suicide. *Perspectives in Psychiatric Care, 38*, 5–14.

Van den Boom, F. (1995). AIDS, euthanasia, and grief. *AIDS Care, 7*, S175–S185.

Vandercreek, L., & Knapp, S. (2001). Tarasoff and beyond: Legal and clinical considerations in the treatment of life-endangering patients. Sarasota, FL: Professional Resource Press.

van der Weide, J., Marijke, C., Onwuteaka-Philipsen, B. D., & van der Wal, G. (2005). Granted, undecided, withdrawn, and refused requests for euthanasia and physician-assisted suicide. *Archives of Internal Medicine, 165*, 1698–1704.

Van Dongen, C. J. (1991). Experiences of family members after a suicide. *The Journal of Family Practice, 33*, 375–379.

Van Dras, D. D., & Siegler, I. C. (1997). Stability in extraversion and aspects of social support at midlife. *Journal of Personality and Social Psychology, 72*, 233–241.

Van Hooff, A. (2004). Paetus, it does not hurt: Altruistic suicide in the Greco-Roman world. *Archives of Suicide Research, 8*(1), 43–56.

van Praag, H. M. (2000). Serotonin disturbances and suicide risk: Is aggression or anxiety the interjacent link? *Crisis, 21*(4), 160–162.

Van Winkle, N. W., & May, P. A. (1993). An update on American Indian suicide in New Mexico, 1980–1987. *Human Organization, 45*, 296–309.

Vega, W. A., Gil, A., Zimmerman, R. S., & Warheit, W. J. (1993). Risk factors for suicidal behavior among Hispanic, African American, and non-Hispanic White boys in early adolescents. *Ethnicity and Disease, 3*, 229–241.

Violanti, J. M. (1996). *Police suicide: Epidemic in blue*. Springfield, IL: C. C. Thomas.

Volker, T. (1994). Value analysis: A model of personal and professional ethics in marriage and family counseling. *Counseling & Values, 38*, 193–204.

Waern, M., Rubenowitz, E., Runeson, B., Skoog, I., Wilhelmson, K., & Alleback, P. (2002). Burden of illness and suicide in elderly people: Case-control study. *British Medical Journal, 324*, 1355–1357.

Wallace, D. M. (2001). The origin of suicide prevention in the United States. In Lester, David, (Ed.), *Suicide prevention: Resources for the millennium* (pp. 239–254). New York: Brunner-Routledge.

Walter, H. J., Vaughn, R. D., Armstrong, B., Krakoff, R. Y., Maldonado, L. M., Tiezzi, L., & McCarthy, J. F. (1995). Sexual, assaultive, and suicidal behavior among urban minority junior high school students. *Journal of the American Academy of Child and Adolescent Psychiatry, 68*, 383–388.

Washington County Department of Public Health & Environment. (2001). *Adolescent depression and suicide opinion survey*. Washington, DC: Author.

Waters, A. B. (1999). Domestic dangers: Approaches to women's suicide in contemporary Maharashtra, India. *Violence Against Women, 5*, 525–547.

Weissman, M. M., Markowitz, K. C., & Klerman, G. L. (2000). *Comprehensive guide to interpersonal psychotherapy*. New York: Basic Books.

Weissman, M. M., Wolk, S., Goldstein, R. B., Moreau, D., Adams, P., Greenwald, S., Klier C. M., Ryan, N. D., Dahl, R. E., & Wickramaratne, P. (1999). Depressed adolescents grown up. *JAMA, 12*, 1701–1713.

Welch, S. S., & Linehan, M. M. (2002). High-risk situations associated with parasuicide and drug use in borderline personality disorder. *Journal of Personality Disorders, 16*(6), 561–569.

Weller, E. B., Young, K. M., Rohrbaugh, A. H., & Weller, R. A. (2001). Overview and assessment of the suicidal child. *Depression and Anxiety, 14*, 157–163.

Werth, J. L. (1999). When is a mental health professional competent to assess a person's decision to hasten death? *Ethics & Behavior, 9*, 141–157.

Werth, J. L. (2000). Requests for physician assisted death: Guidelines for assessing mental capacity and impaired judgment. *Psychology, Public Policy, & Law, 6*, 348–372.

Werth, J. L. Jr., & Holdwick, D. J. Jr. (2000). A primer on rational suicide and other forms of hastened death. *The Counseling Psychologist, 28*, 511–539.

Westefeld, J. S., Cardin, D., & Deaton, W. L. (1992). Development of the College Student Reasons for Living Inventory. *Suicide and Life-Threatening Behavior, 22*(4), 442–452.

Westefeld, J. S., Lillian M. R., Rogers, J. R., Maples, M. R., Bromley, J. L., & Alcorn, J. (2000). Suicide: An overview. *The Counseling Psychologist, 28*, 445–510.

Wetzler, S., Asnis, G. M., Hyman, R. B., Virtue, C., Zimmerman, J., & Rathus, J. H. (1996). Characteristics of suicidality among adolescents. *Suicide and Life-Threatening Behavior, 26*(1), 37–45.

Weyrauch, K. F., Roy-Byrne, P., Katon, W., & Wilson, L. (2001). Stressful life events and impulsiveness in failed suicide. *Suicide and Life-Threatening Behavior, 31*(3), 311–319.

Wheeler, S. (1989). ED telephone triage: Lessons learned from unusual calls. *Journal of Emergency Nursing, 15*, 481–487.

White, T. W. (2002). Improving the reliability of expert testimony in suicide litigation. *The Journal of Psychiatry & Law, 30*, 331–353.

Whitlock. F. A. (1986). The psychiatric complications of Parkinson's disease. *Australian and New Zealand Journal of Psychiatry, 20*(2), 114–121.

Wikipedia contributors. (2005). Cultural views of suicide. *Wikipedia, The Free Encyclopedia*. Retrieved December 31, 2005, from: http://en.wikipedia.org/w/index.php?title= Cultural views of suicide&oldid=31491944.

Williams, R., & Morgan, H. G. (1994). *Suicide prevention: The challenge confronted*. London: NHS Health Advisory Service.

Willis, L. A., Coombs, D. W., Cockerham, W. C., & Frison, S. L. (2002). Ready to die: A postmodern interpretation of the increase of African-American adolescent male suicide. *Social Science & Medicine, 55*, 907–920.

Winfree, L. T. (1988). Rethinking American jail death rates: A comparison of national mortality and jail mortality. *Review of Policy Research, 7*(3), 641–659.

Wise, A. J., & Spengler, P. M. (1997). Suicide in children younger than age fourteen: Clinical judgment and assessment issues. *Journal of Mental Health Counseling, 19*(4), 318–335.

Witty, T. E., Heppner, P. P., Bernard, C. B., & Thoreson, R. W. (2001). Problem-solving appraisal and psychological adjustment of persons with chronic low-back pain. *Journal of Clinical Psychology in Medical Settings, 8*, 149–160.

Wooddell, V., & Kaplan, K. J. (1998). An expanded typology of suicide, assisted suicide, and euthanasia. *Omega, 36*(3), 219–226.

Woods, T. E., Antoni, M. H., Ironson, G. H., & Kling, D. W. (1999). Religiosity is associated with affective status in symptomatic HIV-infected African-American women. *Journal of Health Psychology, 4*(3), 317–326.

World Health Organization. (2006). New York: WHO and HIV/AIDS. www.who.int/hiv/en/.

Woznica, J., & Shapiro, J. (1998). An analysis of adolescent suicide attempts: A validation of the expendable child measure. In Allan Z. Schwartzberg (Ed.), *The adolescent in turmoil* (pp. 82–90). Praeger Publications.

Wrobleski, A., & McIntosh, J. L., (1987). Problems of suicide survivors: A survey report. *Israeli Journal of Psychiatry & Related Sciences, 241*, 137–142.

Yalom, I. D. (1975). *The theory and practice of group psychotherapy.* New York: Basic Books.

Yoder, K. A. (2001). Suicidal ideation among American Indian youth. *Dissertation Abstracts International, Section A: Humanities & Social Sciences, 62*(6-A), 2247.

Young, M. E. (2004). *Learning the art of helping* (3rd ed.). Columbus, OH: Prentice Hall.

Young, S. (2001). Poverty, despair cloud future of Indian children. Available at: ArgusLeader.Com.

Young, S., Twomey, H., & Kaslow, N. J. (2000). Suicidal behavior in African American women with a history of childhood maltreatment. In T. Joiner & M. D. Rudd (Eds.), *Suicide science: Expanding the boundaries* (pp. 221–240). Boston: Kluwer.

Youngner, S. J. (2000). Bureaucratizing suicide. *Psychology, Public Policy, & Law, 6*, 402–407.

Yu-Chin, R., & Arcuni, O. J. (1990). Short-term hospitalization for suicidal patients within a crisis intervention service. *General Hospital Psychiatry, 12*(3), 153–158.

Zayas, L. H., Kaplan, C., Turner, S., Romano, K., & Gonzalez-Ramos, G. (2000). Understanding suicide attempts by adolescent Hispanic females. *Social Work, 45*, 53–63.

Index